A Fast Walk through American History

1492-1992

by

Mary Liebman

DORRANCE PUBLISHING CO., INC.
PITTSBURGH, PENNSYLVANIA 15222

ISBN #0-8059-4290-4
Printed in the United States of America

First Printing

For information or to order additional books, please write:
Dorrance Publishing Co., Inc.
643 Smithfield Street
Pittsburgh, Pennsylvania 15222
U.S.A.

Dedication

For Charles, Tom, Beth, Becky, Charlie, Dinah, Walker, Liz, Paul, Gerry, Katherine, and Peter

Dr. Paul Arthur Schilpp, a distinguished philosophy teacher at Northwestern University, made sure none of us would ever forget: "All facts are selected facts. All facts are interpreted facts." It's probably the most important thing we learned in college.

Acknowledgments

Thanks to Connie Black; the research staff at the McHenry Public Library; most of all to Shelley Rudeen, for her thorough and tireless efforts and encouragement during the past months; Bruce Felknor, who made me feel like a fellow professional while correcting and improving my text; and, with love, Lynn Goldberg, who took all those messy pages and made them look like a real manuscript.

Contents

Author's Note to the Reader

I hope you will write in this book. The left hand margins leave plenty of space for your own notes. For example, write your birthday where it belongs, and the birthdays of your parents and grandparents. In what year did your forbears immigrate to America, and when did they move on? Where did they go? In what wars did they serve? Add your family history to this book, because you are now a part of the whole story.

Feel free, too, to make your own additions and corrections, to argue with the author, for that's what history is — a long argument among those who love it. Speak up!

FOR OPENERS

American history usually starts with Columbus, but if he hadn't bumped into one of the Bahama Islands in 1492, other Europeans would certainly have found the Americas a few years later. Overland trade routes to the Far East developed after Marco Polo returned from China (1275), and when war and Turkish conquests closed those routes, European traders began looking for a sea route to China. Exploratory voyages along the coast of Africa had been going on for more than fifty years. Columbus was convinced that the world was round, and he intended to reach the Far East by sailing west. He didn't know that two continents were in the way.

Of course, the new world that he discovered wasn't new to the Native Americans who lived there. The Arawak-speaking people he found were simple farmers and, by most accounts, a gentle and peaceful people. They had come from the mainland of South America to settle this island in the not too distant past. The climate was ideal, the surrounding blue waters teemed with fish, and agriculture was very productive without much effort. They had time for ceremonies and games. They painted their bodies and wore ornaments hammered from gold nuggets they picked up in island streams. Columbus called them Indians because he thought he had reached the East Indies. Elsewhere in the islands, the Spanish encountered hostile Caribs and Siboney—estimates of the island populations range from a quarter of a million to six million—but whether fierce like the Caribs or friendly like the Arawak, it didn't really matter. Within twenty years all the native people were dead, killed by white men's diseases or white men's weapons.

When Spanish explorers invaded the mainland (Cortez in Mexico, 1519; Pizzaro in Peru, 1532), they found empires that were older and bigger than any kingdom in Europe, advanced civilizations with wealth far greater than any Europeans had yet brought from Asia. That marvelous and tragic history is not part of this book.

Europeans were ready for new conquests. The Black Death, an outbreak of bubonic plague that wiped out half of Europe's population, had subsided; the Hundred Years' War was settled; the Last Crusade was abandoned; the Renaissance had begun. Printing had been invented, and the rifle. A new century was dawning, and a new chapter of human adventure was about to open.

So let's begin at the end of the fifteenth century, with the three brave captains who made the earliest voyages.

1492

Christopher Columbus (1451-1506), was born in Genoa, Italy, and went to sea as a boy. Settled in Portugal, his studies and experience persuaded him that the world was round, and he wanted to prove it by a western expedition. The King of Portugal turned him down, but King Ferdinand and Queen Isabella of Spain paid for his ships. After sailing for three months, he reached the Bahamas at what is now usually identified as Watlings Island and claimed his discoveries for Spain.

The king and queen quickly asked Pope Alexander VI to validate their claim. In 1493, the Pope drew a line "from pole to pole," 100 leagues west of the Portuguese Azores Islands. East of that line, everything would belong to Portugal; Spain would possess whatever lay west of the line. Columbus left Spain again with seventeen ships and fifteen hundred men, of whom twelve hundred were armed soldiers. He also carried domestic animals and plants for propagation in the new colonies. On his third voyage (1498), he discovered the mainland of South America at the Orinoco River. But after reports of trouble in the colonies, an investigator was sent from the court. Columbus traveled back to Spain in chains. He was later released but stripped of his honors. A fourth voyage (1502) yielded little of interest to Ferdinand and Isabella. Columbus could not regain his position and at fifty-five died, in poverty, still thinking he had found a sea route to Asia.

1497

Amerigo Vespucci (1451-1512) did he explore our coast from the Gulf of Mexico to Chesapeake Bay in 1497? Historians now doubt it, though he knew Columbus and helped outfit Columbus' ships. Later he was the navigator for voyages that explored the coast of South America from 1499 until 1502. He, too, thought it was Asia but finally realized and reported to the Spanish court that this was a New World. So in 1507 Martin Waldseemuller, a German mapmaker, gave

2

Amerigo's name to the new land on his first maps, and it has been "America" ever since.

1498   Giovanni Caboto (1450-1488) was also born in Genoa but later moved to England where he was known as John Cabot. King Henry VII agreed to finance his western exploration. In 1498 he reached Cape Breton Island in Nova Scotia; the next year he returned to explore the coasts of Greenland, Baffin Island, and Newfoundland, which were claimed for England.

THE SIXTEENTH CENTURY

We will summarize this century in four pages, limited to discoveries in that part of North America that became the United States. Twenty years after Columbus, Spain had settlements in the Caribbean, and adventurers were eager for new western conquests and fortunes. Profitable sugar plantations were established in Puerto Rico and Cuba, and slaves were brought from Africa to work them, but where were the mountains of gold and other wonders of which Europeans dreamed?

1513	Juan Ponce de Leon had sailed with Columbus on the second voyage and was made governor of Puerto Rico. But he had heard of a Fountain of Youth on another island and, being sixty years old, set out to find it. Instead he found Florida, and sailed along the eastern and western coasts. In 1521 he made efforts to settle, but he was driven off by native inhabitants, was wounded, and died in Cuba.
1519	In the same year that Cortez conquered Mexico, Alonzo de Pineda found the mouth of the Mississippi River.

In 1519 Martin Luther, a German, broke with his Catholic Church and the Pope to begin the Protestant Reformation. The religious wars that followed tore northern Europe apart for many years, while Catholic Spain continued to explore in the new world.

1524	Giovanni de Verrazano sailed north along the Atlantic coast from Carolina to Nova Scotia, exploring what is now the New York harbor and up to Narragansett Bay.
1528	Panfilo de Narvaez was shipwrecked on the Florida coast with 600 men and died near the mouth of the Mississippi, trying to get to Mexico. Another member of the expedition, Cabeza de Vaca, survived to wander through Texas and the southwest for eight desperate years. He and three companions were found in northern Mexico in 1536. Their stories led to further expeditions.

1539	Marcos de Niza, a missionary, explored in Arizona and New Mexico.
1540-42	Fray Marcos traveled with Francisco de Coronado, discovering the Colorado River and the Grand Canyon, the California peninsula, the Rio Grande River, traveling across the Texas panhandle and Oklahoma into Kansas.
1540-42	At about the same time, Hernando de Soto took the fortune he had made with Pizarro in Peru and set out to conquer Florida. Pushing north and west, determined to find more gold, he crossed the Mississippi River and died there in 1542. His body was sunk in the river.
1539	Meanwhile, other expeditions explored the Pacific coast. Francisco de Ulloa sailed along the coast of the lower peninsula of California. In 1542, Juan Cabrillo found San Diego Bay, Catalina Island, and the Santa Barbara Channel.
1562	Religious wars raged in France. The Huguenots were French Protestants, driven out by persecutions, led by Jean Ribault to South Carolina, and then by Rene de Laudinniere to the mouth of the Saint John's River in Florida.
1563	Their island settlement was wiped out by Menendez de Aviles, who built a fort at Saint Augustine and consolidated Spanish power in Florida.
1570	In his youth, Francis Drake had sailed to the Gulf of Mexico with his uncle. Queen Elizabeth of England commissioned him a privateer, with license to plunder Spanish ships wherever he found them and Spanish settlements wherever they could be attacked. After three years of raiding in the West Indies, he crossed the Isthmus of Panama, the first Englishman to see the Pacific. In 1577 he was the first Englishman to navigate the perilous passage

around Cape Horn that Ferdinand Magellan had discovered fifty years earlier, and sailed up the west coast of South America to California. He called it New Albion and claimed it for the Queen. He went on to circle the globe, defeat the Spanish armada, and win knighthood and honors in England. But he was soon back in the Spanish Indies, leading twenty-five ships against Spanish colonies, almost destroying Saint Augustine in 1586.

1584

Sir Walter Raleigh, another favorite of Queen Elizabeth, was licensed to gain American lands for her. He sent Arthur Barlow and Phillip Amadas, who explored the coast of Florida to what is now North Carolina. They claimed it all for England and named it "Virginia" in honor of the Virgin Queen, recommending a settlement on Roanoke Island.

1585

Raleigh sent settlers to the island, but abandoned it a year later. He was no more successful with other Virginia colonies.

1598

Espanola, New Mexico, is now a small town north of Santa Fe. When Juan de Oñate established his tiny settlement there, he intended it to be the capital of—well, of a country whose extent he couldn't even guess. But there it was built, and there it is: America's first capital.

THE SEVENTEENTH CENTURY

Many European countries watched and feared the rise of Spanish power, envying the wealth its New World colonies produced. In 1606, King James I of England granted two charters to commercial traders who hoped to get rich in America. The London Company (sometimes called the South Virginia Company) and the Plymouth Company (sometimes called the North Virginia Company) were authorized to explore and colonize. At that time, "Virginia" meant everything from Maine down to Cape Hatteras, Florida, and west to the Mississippi. Since nobody knew anything about American geography, they assumed that "Great Water" to be the western edge of the continent.

In the following year, both companies sent out ships with hopeful colonists. The Plymouth Company landed a party on the coast of Maine, but they abandoned the site and sailed home a year later, saying their hopes "had been frozen to death." (Samuel de Champlain had mapped the coast three years earlier, and a party of French settlers had reached the same decision.)

1607

Ships of the London Company, after a bad trip, sailed into Chesapeake Bay. Men landed to explore but were driven off by Indians. At their next landing, near what is now Newport News (named for their blundering captain), they were welcomed and feasted by the Kecoughtan Indians and given their first taste of local tobacco. They liked it. Weeks later they found the mouth of a river they called the James, where the Paspahegh Indians were curious and friendly. At last, on May 13, they founded a settlement about fifty miles upstream, in a dismal swamp that lacked even drinkable water. They had exhausted their provisions on the voyage and missed the planting season, but the gentry among them weren't farmers anyway. Servants were put to work building rude shelters, and when the ships sailed back to England in June, they left about 100 colonists behind, totally unprepared for the hardships they would face.

Despite the efforts of Captain John Smith and others, most died of hunger and disease. Thirty-eight were saved when the Powhattan Indians fed them, then new settlers

7

arrived. All the Virginia colonists were under contract to the London Company for seven years. During that time there would be no private trade, private property, or private enterprise. English investors expected the settlers to find gold, or a new route to China, or something else of value. Instead they found indescribable suffering. The winter of 1609-1610 came to be known as The Starving Time. When the next ships appeared nine months later, only sixty of the 300 colonists were left, many having drunk the blood and eaten the bodies of their comrades.

Jamestown was saved by tobacco, which John Rolfe began to cultivate in 1612, crossing Virginia tobacco with the milder Jamaican leaf. He learned about growing tobacco from the Indians, and in 1614 he married Chief Powhattan's daughter, the lively and lovely Pocahontas. He renamed her Rebecca and took her to London, where the climate killed her in 1619. But as we'll see, tobacco paid.

1609
While Samuel de Champlain explored what is now upstate New York, the English navigator Henry Hudson sailed a Dutch expedition into New York harbor and 150 miles up the river that now bears his name. He got as far as Albany before deciding it wasn't a passage to China.

1610
Meanwhile, the Spanish pushed further into the American southwest. Santa Fe was settled as the capital of their new province, New Mexico.

The religious reformation set off by Martin Luther in 1510 swept through Europe in a century and a half of conflict. Henry VIII left the Catholic Church and established the Church of England, Catholic in almost every way except that it was obedient to Henry instead of to Rome. John Knox established the Presbyterian Church in Scotland. Other leaders and rulers used religious issues to achieve their own objectives. A deadly mix of politics and prayer climaxed in 1618 with the Thirty Years' War. European Protestants and Catholics fought until they were exhausted. Persecuted people looked toward the New World, which offered safety, religious freedom, and economic opportunity.

1619   For a hundred years Portuguese traders had been sellingblack men for transport to Spanish colonies in the West Indies, where hard labor in mines and sugar fields was killing off the native population. The African slaves were sometimes prisoners captured in tribal wars or simply victims sold by their own rulers to traders in return for European goods. Ships from many countries brought slaves to the New World, but it was a Dutch ship carrying blacks from Guinea that arrived at Jamestown in 1619 and sold part of its human cargo to tobacco planters. ("Negro" is simply the Spanish word for "black".)

John Rolfe and others had experimented with planting and curing Indian tobacco, and in 1616 the Virginia colony shipped 2,300 pounds to England. As more Indian land was taken and more settlers arrived, production quickly increased. Nineteen thousand pounds were exported in 1617, and exports tripled by 1620. This was profitable for the company, but most of the laborers were poor people who came from England and Ireland as indentured workers. They signed contracts which bound them to work without pay for seven years, in return for their passage and their keep when they arrived. Planters bought their contracts from company agents; some planters were fair and decent to their help, but many were not.

The work force grew as criminals from England were sentenced to serve time in Virginia. Children between the ages of eight and sixteen, begging on the streets of London, were picked up and shipped across the ocean. Indians were forced to pay tribute or work on plantations, but many of them could escape to their own forests and people. Poor whites were not so lucky. They were worked to the limits of their endurance, cheated and mistreated, beaten and branded, and their indenture contracts were extended as punishment for misconduct.

The first Africans brought to America were also indentured, sold on contract to work for a period of years, after which they would be sent back to their homelands. But though few blacks were imported for the next several decades, even fewer got back to Africa. By midcentury, there were only about 300 Africans among the colony's 15,000 inhabitants, and most of these were slaves. One way or another, their servitude was extended to last their lifetimes. (In an early court case, a free black planter sued to have a runaway black servant returned to him, claiming to have "ye Negro for his life," and the court upheld his claim.) After all, planters had figured out that they could keep a couple of dozen blacks for little more than it cost to keep a white worker, and by 1669, by law, slaves were property. The London Company sold women, too. With more than thirty men for every woman in the colony, there was already market for "choyce Maids." Agents of the company recruited, or kidnapped, or simply plucked from English prisons, hundreds of women—choice and not so choice—and shipped them to Jamestown. Only free men (that is, no indentured worker) could buy a wife. The price was 150 pounds of the best tobacco (more than $1,000), and until she was sold the woman had to work for her keep. No wonder many sickened and went "crasey" when they found themselves landed in the swamps of Virginia. They were hungry and ragged, surrounded by forests full of increasingly hostile Indians, waiting for marriage to a desperate stranger.

1619   The first representative assembly in America met at the church in Jamestown to establish local self-government. Chief Powhattan died. He had been a wary but interested observer of the first colony, befriending it in the early, desperate days, and willing to establish trade relations as the colony grew. But now his half-brother, Opechancano, became chief of the Powhattan confederacy, a leader who took a dark view of the white man's intentions.

1620   After failing to colonize in Maine, the Plymouth Company found new interest among people who wanted to leave the Church of England and establish their own churches, calling themselves Separatists. Many had fled to Holland to escape persecution. Now they were offered a chance to find religious freedom and a new life in America. As in Virginia, English investors would finance a settlement and colonists would work it for seven years, after which profits would be divided. Captain John Smith, of Jamestown fame, had explored the New England coast four years earlier and offered to lead them, but the colonists said it was cheaper to buy his map. Thirty-seven Separatists sailed from

Leyden, picked up sixty-seven more recruits in Plymouth, and sailed on the Mayflower to found New Plymouth in Massachusetts. The Compact they signed in the Mayflower cabin before landing became the basis for local government.

1621

The Wampanoag Indians and other local tribes were good farmers, cultivating bountiful crops of corn and a wide variety of vegetables and fruit. But their earlier contacts with Europeans had brought deadly epidemics of smallpox and other white man's diseases, against which they had no immunity. Many thousands died, leaving abandoned fields and villages. Disease and a severe winter also took its toll on the colonists. Massasoit, the Wampanoag chief, and Squanto, a Pawtuxet leader, helped them survive. Squanto had been captured some years earlier and taken to Malaga, Spain, where he was sold first to Spanish friars and then to an Englishman. He learned to speak English in London. After two years he was released, returning to North America by way of Newfoundland. Eventually he boarded a ship bound for home and arrived to find that all his people had died of smallpox. Almost alone, he stayed on until he learned of the Pilgrim landing. He went to investigate; the colony was starving. Because he knew their language, Squanto could and did teach the colonists Indian farming and fishing methods, but only half of them were left to plant the Indian fields and reap a harvest. They celebrated the first Thanksgiving Day with Indian friends. However, the settlement produced no profits for the English investors, and within ten years the contract with the company was ended; survival now depended on private enterprise, and colonists ran local affairs in their own town meetings.

1622

Indians in Virginia at last tried to drive out the foreigners who had invaded their homeland. Led by Chief Opechancano, they attacked

Jamestown and killed more than 300 settlers, nearly a third of the colony. War went on for fourteen years, followed by a decade of "peace," then broke out again, until the English forced the Indians to make a truce. The captain who met with them in a Powhattan village negotiated a treaty and proposed a toast to its success. Two hundred Native Americans drank his poisoned wine and died. His soldiers killed the rest. Finally Opechancano, 100 years old, was captured and taken to Jamestown, where one of his guards shot him dead.

1623   English investors, wanting to develop trade and fisheries, sent a few settlers to New Hampshire. Others followed, hoping to obtain furs from Iroquois hunters, but the Iroquois were hostile, and growth of the colony was slow.

1626   The Dutch had forts near Albany and claimed the territory as New Netherland. In 1626 Peter Minuit bought Manhattan Island from the Indians and established New Amsterdam as the capital of the colony.

1630   The Puritans in England (so-called because they wanted to "purify" the Church of England), whose demands on King James I had been moderate, were still restricted in what they could preach or print. They persisted in their non-conformity, growing stronger. King Charles I responded with more severe repression, and a "Great Migration" to America began. The Crown had chartered the Massachusetts Bay Company, but Puritans soon took control, and within ten years, 300 ships arrived with 20,000 settlers. These were not the convicts, kidnapped children, or poor Irish laborers who were forced to settle in Virginia. The Puritans were country property owners and middle-class businessmen who intended to run their own affairs their own way. They also intended to worship their own way, but religious freedom for Puritans did not mean freedom for others who worshiped differently. There was no more religious liberty in Puritan "New England" than there had been in old England.

1632

George Calvert, the first Lord Baltimore, was given Newfoundland by the king, but he didn't like the cold, so the king gave him Maryland, where the family established a long rule and a haven for persecuted Catholics. There was little trouble with the Indians, and in a moderate climate, the well-run colony avoided the mistakes of earlier settlements. There was no starvation or disease, and the Toleration Act made Maryland a model for religious freedom.

1633

The Dutch settled in Connecticut on the site of what is now Hartford, and in the next year, members of the Plymouth colony settled in the Connecticut River Valley. Colonists dissatisfied with the Puritan authorities in Massachusetts also relocated in Connecticut, where there was no religious requirement for citizenship. The Fundamental Orders of Connecticut, written in 1639, was the first constitution in America.

1634

The French explorer, Jean Nicolet, brought to America by Champlain, was the first white man to see Lake Michigan and Wisconsin.

Even with tobacco and cheap labor, the swampy Jamestown settlement couldn't make a profit for the Virginia Company. The company had spent investor's money hand over fist (some charged that funds were stolen by company agents) and settlers died like flies (some called the colony a slaughterhouse). After investigation, the king revoked the charter and took over the government of the colony. The company continued to operate its commercial affairs until it went bankrupt. As Captain John Smith wrote in his account, the company was "broke."

1636	Harvard College was founded at Cambridge, Massachusetts, the first college in the New World.

Roger Williams, loud in his pleas for religious tolerance, was banished from the Massachusetts Bay Colony. He founded Rhode Island. He preached to the Indians in their own language, insisting that they be paid for their land. Ann Hutchinson, another outspoken critic of the Puritan clergy, was banished in 1637, after which she established her own Rhode Island settlement.

1637	The Pequots were a numerous and prosperous people until the Massachusetts colony took their land in the Pequot wars. Hundreds of Pequots were massacred, and among the prisoners seized was a visiting boy from the Algonkian tribe. He became a servant in an English home and learned their language.

John Eliot, a Puritan minister in Roxbury, wanted an interpreter who could translate his Christian message to the Massachusetts tribes. Because local Indians under stood the Algonkian dialect, he took the boy as his traveling companion and began to establish Praying Towns for his converts, the "Red Pilgrims." In time, there were twenty-one Praying Towns. The Indians took up his mission with considerable enthusiasm, for the Christian God obviously had powers they did not possess; His people were thriving while the native people perished. Converts achieved special status among the Indians, and enjoyed other benefits—more education, trading opportunities, and a measure of security for their families.

But the cruel war went on, getting more savage as the Pequots found allies among the Narragansetts and Niantics. In the summer of 1637, colonists attacked a native village at Mystic, Connecticut, killing nearly 700 Pequot men, women, and children; many were burned to death when whites torched their stockade. The survivors were pursued and 200 captured. Most of the captives were enslaved when the war ended the following year and the tribe was wiped out. Looking for a less bloody solution to the "Indian problem," a reservation was established for the Quinnipacs near New Haven, Connecticut, in 1638. And John Eliot went on preaching.

1638

The Dutch had tried to found colonies in Delaware, but failed until the Dutch West India Company attracted Swedish investors and Peter Minuit led settlers to establish Fort Christina on land he bought from the Indians, the site of present-day Wilmington. They called their settlement New Sweden, and Swedes and Finns in the party knew how to build log cabins. A great improvement over the huts and dugouts of Jamestown, log cabins would spring up on the American frontier for the next 200 years. When New Sweden quarreled with New Netherland, small wars followed.

Religious violence continued to tear Europe apart, and war came to England in 1642. When King Charles I ignored Puritan calls for church reform, the Puritan Parliament led a rebellion and fought the king's party for nine years. In the end they won, cutting off the king's head and replacing him with Oliver Cromwell. Their Commonwealth lasted just three years, until Cromwell declared himself their Lord Protector (some would say dictator). When he died in 1658, his son quietly gave the country back to Charles II.

Of course, events in Europe and England influenced events in the colonies. Depending on what religious group had the upper hand in any country at any time, dissenters fled to America to practice their own brand of Christianity. But it took three months for a letter to cross the Atlantic, so isolated American settlements got their news late. In any case, most colonists were too busy with day-to-day struggles to worry much about what happened anyplace else.

1647

Massachusetts passed a law requiring every town with fifty families or more to hire a teacher for instruction in writing and reading.

1648

Margaret Brent was born in England at the turn of the century. The family was large, rich, powerful, and Catholic. They lost most of their property and privileges when they refused to accept the Church of England, but some Brents found safety and freedom when they joined the colony that Lord Baltimore had founded in Maryland. Margaret became rich and powerful in the New World, eventually owning thousands of acres in Maryland and Virginia and taking a leading role in government and business. When Lord Baltimore was dying, he named Margaret as his executor. In 1648, to represent his rights and her own, Margaret asked for two votes in the Maryland assembly. Her request was denied because she was a woman, but she went on to own and manage huge landholdings, develop new settlements, act as a lawyer and judge, raise and maintain a small army, and wield as much power as any man in the colony. She never married and was formally identified as Margaret Brent, Gentleman, but she was never allowed to vote.

1654   Sephardic Jews from Spain, Portugal, and elsewhere arrived in New Amsterdam, founding a synagogue for their community of twenty-three members. Persecuted in Europe, they were admitted to full membership in the Dutch colony in 1657.

After a century of religious wars, the population of Europe was growing again, and its people had a growing list of needs and wants. Most were lucky if they had shelter and enough to eat, but more and more Europeans wanted a few luxuries—tea, and sugar for their tea, spices for their food, and shirts dyed blue with indigo juice. No country in Europe (or, for that matter, the world) could grow or make everything that people wanted. Trade among people and between countries was as old as history, but now it was big business, and the business of governments. In order to buy what they wanted, countries had to sell their own products. Since they all wanted to sell more than they bought, governments tried to limit and control how many foreign products could be imported.

We have seen that business promoters financed the first English colonies. They advertised for settlers (and told a lot of lies about what settlers would find in the New World); they paid for the ships that carried hopeful colonists across the ocean, and supplied the settlements with tools, seeds, livestock and so on. The settlers themselves were often poor people with little chance for a better life in

England, willing to take a chance in the American wilderness. Investors expected the colonies to supply products like sugar, tobacco, and furs, which England could sell to other countries, and settlers would have to buy what they needed from the English companies, shipped over the ocean in English ships.

While Spain was fully involved with exploiting its empires in Mexico and South America, the Dutch had risen as a commercial power. Holland was a small country with not much to sell, but the Dutch had always been fishermen, supplying European markets with herring. Now these herring fleets were expanded; the ships were bigger and faster; and Dutch crews carried cargoes of all kinds of goods around the world. The years of civil war in England were good years for the Dutch, and for many colonists. While half the English navy, loyal to the king, was sinking other English ships under Puritan command, thousands of Dutch ships carried on trade between Europe and American ports. When English workmen left their jobs to fight each other, Dutch goods found ready markets in the colonies.

Earlier Navigation Acts had tried to exclude the Dutch from English commerce. The Act passed in 1660 and 1663, not only required all colonial trade be carried on English ships, but required that goods produced in Europe for the colonies had to be shipped through English ports and taxed in England. This led to conflict with Americans. Why could they not sell their tobacco wherever they got the best price for it? Why did they have to buy expensive pots and pans and nails and cloth and other "enumerated articles" from England? During the years of civil war and Cromwell's rule, England was too distracted to enforce the Navigation Acts, so colonists carried on illegal but profitable trade wherever they could buy or sell. American merchants and shipbuilders made a lot of money. When Charles II regained the throne, he needed to reassert control over colonial industry and commerce.

1663	John Eliot, "the Apostle to the Indians," with the help of his now grown Algonkian interpreter, translated the Bible into the Indian language. In fact, "Um-Biblum God" was the first Bible of any kind published in North America, and in the same year, he published "Um-Bookum Psalms."
1664	The Dutch had done well in New Amsterdam, expanding their territory and capturing Swedish settlements on the Delaware River. Charles II wouldn't put up with Dutch expansion, or Dutch domination of colonial commerce. The second trade war between England

and Holland ended in a Dutch defeat, and New Amsterdam surrendered to the British. King Charles gave all the Dutch holdings to his brother James, the Duke of York, and New Amsterdam became New York. James, in turn, gave part of the colony to his friends Lord Berkely and Sir George Carteret, who named their lands New Jersey.

1672

During the third Anglo-Dutch war, the Dutch fleet recaptured New York, but the peace treaty of 1674 claimed it for England, and that was the end of the Dutch grip on colonial trade.

1673

The year after English settlers founded Jamestown, the great French explorer Samuel de Champlain established a western outpost at Quebec, on the Saint Lawrence River. From there, French explorers and missionaries moved on. Like Spanish explorers coming up from Mexico, they heard Indian reports of the Big River, which they hoped would lead to the Pacific coast and a passage to Asia. Louis Jolliet, sent out to look for copper in the Lake Superior region, was joined by Father Jacques Marquette, a Jesuit missionary. Together they followed Indian routes down the Fox River to the Wisconsin, discovering the Mississippi in June. They floated south to the mouth of the Arkansas River before they turned back, returning by way of the Illinois River and Lake Michigan. French exploration strengthened their hold on the valuable fur trade. Indians decided that the English wanted their land, the Spanish wanted their souls, but the French were, for the most part, satisfied with furs.

1675

Massasoit was chief of the Wampanoag Indians between Cape Cod and Narragansett Bay. When the Pilgrims landed in Massachusetts, he negotiated a peace that lasted fifty-four years, and remained an interested friend of the colony until his death. But no Indian treaty could withstand the settler's hunger for land. Fifty-two thousand colonists had invaded Indian hunting grounds, and forced on the Indian—that "great naked dirty beast"—a series of humiliations and restrictions that Massasoit's son could not tolerate. Metacomet (the English called him King Philip) organized a federation of tribes that extended from Maine to Connecticut and attacked frontier settlements with surprise raids. King Philip's War was short and bloody. Perhaps five hundred colonists were killed or captured, and twice as many Indians, before Metacomet was seized and executed, and an uneasy truce ended the war in southern New England. Fighting continued in the northern settlements until 1678.

1676

Because maps were sketchy and communications bad, the governor of New York was selling property in New Jersey. New lines had to be drawn. Sir George Carteret kept East Jersey, and West Jersey was given to the first Quaker colony in America. The following year, 230 Quakers arrived to found what became Burlington.

Nathaniel Bacon was a rich young man when he studied law in England, but he wanted more. He was continually involved in disputes with his rich father-in-law, as well as fraudulent dealings to get hold of a neighbor's land, until the family offered him two plantations if he would move to Virginia. Times were hard in Virginia because the Anglo-Dutch wars had ruined the tobacco trade, and Indian wars threatened small farms on the frontier. Bacon's connections soon got him a seat on the Governor's Council, where he took the side of poor farmers against the governor and aristocratic planters who ran the colony. He raised his own frontier army, fought the governor's troops, burned Jamestown, and for a while, controlled most of Virginia, requiring colonists to take a personal oath of loyalty to him. Bacon's Rebellion ended abruptly when he died of fever in the same year. His army turned into a leaderless mob, quickly suppressed when the governor returned and hanged as many of the rebels as he could find.

We haven't given much attention to what was happening in the southwest part of the country since the expeditions of Coronado and DeSoto. Like the English, the Spanish tried to subdue the native people and build settlements. They found little gold along the Rio Grande (or anywhere else in the region) but they kept looking. In their wake came disease and missionaries. Indian medicine men hated the missionaries, but, in fact, those men of God often pleaded the Indian case against the brutality of governors like Don Juan de Oñate, who had been given the province of New Mexico. Early in the century, the Indians moved out of the town of Tewa so that Oñate and his settlers could move in—400 men, some with their families and Mexican servants, and with plenty of cattle, sheep, goats, and so on. But after a dispute with his neighbors, Oñate attacked their pueblo and killed more than 800 Ancona people; some estimates run as high as a thousand   dead. All the men who survived had a foot cut off. Oñate was replaced in 1606, but by that time, most of the settlers had gone back to Mexico.

1680

The missionaries frequently protested the harsh treatment of Indians given into their charge. After all, Pope Julius II had ruled that Indians were human beings, descended from Adam and Eve, possessing souls. Nevertheless, a Tewa medicine man named Popé (yes, really) refused to convert and organized the first wide spread revolt among the pueblo people in 1680. There had been other revolts, but Popé sent runners throughout the region until he had raised an army of 500 warriors to face the Spanish garrison of fifty at Santa Fe.

Though the Spanish soldiers had cannon behind the palace walls, Popé's force fought for four days before retreating into the surrounding hills. Four hundred Spanish residents were killed; the rest decided to abandon Santa Fe and started the long march back to El Paso, joined along the way by perhaps 2,500 other Spanish settlers. This was the biggest and most successful fight against the European invasion in the history of North America. Eastern Indian leaders who tried to hold back the colonial tide are better remembered, but Popé and the pueblo dwellers resisted white power for more than a decade. He made himself the dictator of the territory, determined to stamp out every trace of Spanish culture and religion. But in the end it was a losing fight. The Spanish reconquered Santa Fe in 1692.

1681

The Swedes and Finns who settled along the Delaware river had been overpowered by the Dutch, who were, in turn, defeated by the English. But many Swedes and Finns were still in their log cabins when the Quaker, William Penn, got a grant of land from Charles II and laid out his "city of brotherly love" between the Delaware and the Schuylkill. His fair treatment of Delaware Indian neighbors led to decades of peace, growth, and prosperity. English, Welsh, and Dutch Quakers were followed by others seeking religious freedom and economic opportunity; Germantown welcomed Pietists, Mennonites, Amish, Baptist Dunkers, and Lutherans. The Penn family governed until the American Revolution.

1684

King Charles II was still trying to regulate colonial trade. His revenue collector in Massachusetts drew up a list of twenty-nine charges against Puritan merchants, of which twenty-three were violations of the Navigation Acts. When Boston refused to comply, the colony's charter was annulled.

1685

James II followed his brother as king, determined to bring not only stubborn Boston, but all of New England, under his absolute rule. One administration for seven colonies would

21

make it easier and cheaper to regulate American affairs, so he abolished the charters and legislatures of those colonies and created the Dominion of New England, under a single governor. Puritans were infuriated by having the Church of England pushed down their throats; threats to land titles, new taxes, and enforcement of the Navigation Acts infuriated Puritans and everybody else.

1688   Four members of the Mennonite congregation in Germantown, Pennsylvania, spoke out against slavery, protesting that it was wrong to bring "men thither to rob or sell them against their will."

1688   James II also made many enemies in England before his subjects forced him out in favor of his son-in-law, William of Orange. News of the "Glorious Revolution" set off a small revolution in Boston, and the Dominion of New England fell apart. Connecticut, Rhode Island, and Plymouth went back to their original governments. Massachusetts was granted a new charter in 1691. The new charter made it clear that England would retain a monopoly on commerce, and the independence of the colony was curtailed.

1689   The Dutch were defeated in New York, but now the power of France threatened England and its American colonies. From their Canadian bases, the French claimed all of North America, and their Newfoundland fishing industry competed with New England's most basic trade. Their grand plan included an empire in middle America, and the possibility of capturing Mexico from Spain. Pierre Lemoyne d'Iberville was one of six sons of a Canadian colonist enobled by Louis XIV. His oldest brother served as commandant general of Canada, and other brothers fought in major Canadian campaigns. Pierre, a naval officer, founded a settlement at Biloxi, near the mouth of the Mississippi River, where LaSalle had died five years earlier.

1690   England had to confront French power. King William's War reached America when the French attacked in skirmishes along the Maine-New Hampshire border, at Fort Loyal, and at Schenectady, New York. Troops commanded by Jacques Lemoyne de Sainte Helene destroyed that city. The war went on, fought by colonial armies and their Indian allies on both sides, until France and England made peace in 1697.

1691   In Salem, Massachusetts, young girls shivered through winter evenings listening to the spook stories of servants. Carried away by their imaginations and their love of attention, they began to accuse poor old village women of witchcraft. Their hysteria grew and spread until nineteen people were hanged and one man was pressed to death, bravely protesting his innocence with his last gasp. Under torture, fifty-five other people confessed. When respectable people were accused, the madness cooled and executions ceased. Samuel Sewell, one of the examining judges, soon realized his terrible error, admitting his "blame and shame" in an open meeting five years later. For the rest of his life, he prayed for forgiveness.

1696   England continued its efforts to control American commerce. Newer and tougher Navigation Acts were passed; a new Board of Trade and Plantations was set up to bring the colonies under the royal thumb.

THE EIGHTEENTH CENTURY

On their first contacts, Native Americans and European settlers felt a mix of emotions, but their excitement, curiosity, and apprehension hardened into fear and hatred on both sides.

The Indian population of North America was unknown. Present day estimates run between fifteen million and four times that number, scattered over the whole continent before Columbus. By 1700, there were probably no more than two Indians per square mile along the wooded eastern coast, living in villages and loosely organized into Nations. In Virginia, Powhatan led about 14,000 people in thirty tribes. The famous Five Nations (Seneca, Onandaga, Cayuga, Mohawk, and Oneida) lived in what we now call New York State and belonged to the larger family of the Iroquois. Some tribes, like the Massachusett, reduced by fighting and epidemics, lost their tribal identity and were Christianized by the mid-1600s.

There was war among the tribes, as there was war between the countries from which the settlers came. As England, France, Holland, and Spain competed for huge chunks of the New World, each tried to enlist Indian allies. Alliances constantly shifted with the fortunes of war and the commercial interests of all concerned.

The Iroquois were at first subdued, but not beaten, by French troops from Canada. Then the Indians sided with England, but failing to get help in their own struggles, they soon tried to mend relationships with the French. For their part, the French wanted to expand their fur trade. With their eyes on the important Mississippi Valley, they had to cross Iroquois country, and so they were eager to negotiate.

In New York, England now controlled the fur trade developed by early Dutch settlers. Traders bought furs from the Indians for trinkets, tools, and weapons; they sold the furs in Europe for 100 percent profit. War is never good for traders, so the French and English made peace with the Indians, and with each other, in 1701. Neutrality was established, with the Indians as middlemen, holding the balance of power in the territory. No such truce prevailed in New England, where the French continued to harass border settlements. There were also rumors of a threat to Boston.

Queen Anne's War was the next chapter in seventy-five years of war. In Europe, these wars had other names (the War of the Spanish Succession, or the Austrian Succession, or the War of Jenkins' Ear) and cost thousands of lives. In the colonies, they were called by the name of England's ruling monarch, and were hardly more than skirmishes at isolated locations in the vast American wilderness.

| 1704 | Deerfield, a village on the banks of the Connecticut River, had suffered many Indian attacks, surviving a bloody massacre in 1675. During Queen Anne's War, the sleeping town was surprised by French and Indian troops. Fifty-three villagers were killed, and 111 were captured and forced to march back to Canada. For this and other incidents, angry New Englanders blamed the New York traders who sold the Indians guns that killed settlers on the frontier. There were calls for the conquest of Canada; the French must be driven from American soil. Eventually, the war in the colonies reached a stand-off, leaving the French in Canada, the Spanish in Florida (and, of course, in California, about which eastern colonists knew little or nothing), and growing numbers of English settlers in-between. The big war, in Europe, went on for another ten years. |

| 1712 | The first slave revolt took place in New York. There were slaves in almost all the colonies, captured or bought from African chiefs, and sold in America for between $100 and $150. Many died during the terrible sea voyage, and almost half died during their first year in slavery. But it was a profitable business, and prices kept rising. About 3,500 Africans were imported each year, and they made up nearly 10 percent of the colonial population. Most slaves were sold to southern farmers. Northern farms and small industries had less need for the large labor force wanted on the tobacco and rice plantations of the south. |

The revolt in New York was quickly put down. Twenty-one blacks were executed and six committed suicide.

| 1732 | James Oglethorpe was a young member of the British parliament, serving on a board to investigate English prisons. He found poor people, guilty only of debt, kept with thieves and murderers in brutal confinement. Moved by pity and disgust, Oglethorpe got a royal charter to |

found a colony, where these miserable people could start a new life on small farms. Since England needed another southern colony as a buffer against expansion from Spanish Florida, he was given the land he called Georgia, to honor George II. He arrived in September with thirty-five families, and founded the town of Savannah, which he ran with military discipline.

Oglethorpe's laws excluded slaves and Catholics, but encouraged settlement by Swiss and German Protestants; there would be no rum, but plenty of Bibles, and Indians were to be treated as friends. Within ten years there were about 3,000 colonists, most of them very unhappy about Oglethorpe's strict rules. Many left the colony and took their chances in the wilderness. At last, a governor was sent from England, and Georgia became a colony—number thirteen—run like other English colonies, with an elected assembly and a council appointed by the king. Landowners began developing large plantations. By 1750, both rum and slaves were legal.

1735

While life on the frontier was still risky and hard, large cities were growing in America, with shops, schools, churches, and for the first time, newspapers. The *Boston Newsletter* was started in 1704; next came the *Pennsylvania Gazette*, 1728, in which young Benjamin Franklin had an interest.

John Peter Zenger was editor of the *New York Weekly Journal* (1732). Like many papers that followed it, the Journal was a mix of news, advertising, scandal, and politics. German-born Zenger was so outrageous in what he printed about public officials that the governor stopped the presses and jailed Zenger for ten months. The paper's owner hired a famous lawyer, who won the case by proving that Zenger had printed the truth. This was a new, American interpretation of English law, and weakened the censorship powers of judges appointed by the king. Newspapers used their new freedom to print the complaints of the colonists, and feed their discontent with British rule.

Exhausted by the last war, European powers paused to rebuild their armies, change their alliances, and increase their trade. Trading companies now dominated the economic life of nations. The French Mississippi Company was in charge of the French mint and collected the country's taxes; the British South Seas Company managed England's national debt. Investors with stock in those companies clamored for territorial expansion and bigger profits.

The steady sources of profit for the trading companies were fishing and furs. The biggest fort in North America was the French stronghold on Cape Breton Island, from which French ships controlled northern waters, costing New England and British investors millions in income from fisheries. In competition for the fur trade, both countries were moving into the west, into Pennsylvania, Ohio, and the Great Lakes country. The French built forts as trading posts and gained Indian allies. A million and a half English colonists were being outmatched by 90,000 Frenchmen.

Spain, too, constantly threatened English trade in the Caribbean claiming territory in the South. From their Florida bases they incited slave revolts and Indian attacks on Georgia and South Carolina. But while rich men in London worried about their American investments, colonists worried about Indians, harvests, and their souls.

1740   The colonies were swept up in the "Great Awakening," one of the religious revivals that occur from time to time in our history. Led first by Jonathan Edwards, Gilbert Tennant, and George Whitefield, Puritan preachers of every creed terrified their congregations with sermons that threatened the wrath of an angry God. It was strong stuff! Money was the root of all evil; lust for worldly pleasure was a sin; the pits of hell waited for all who worshiped at the golden altars of the proud and powerful. Thousands of people flocked to open-air meetings, where the fear brought men, women, and children, black and white, to their knees in penitent prayer. Their message was printed in tracts, read in every home.

Eventually this hysterical fervor cooled, and the Puritan grip on colonial worship was weakened. Poor people, with new faith in the grace of God, doubted not only the authority of the established church but also the divine rights of the King.

King George's War was the American name for the war that broke out in Europe when Frederick the Great of Prussia invaded Austria (1740), and England (already at war with Spain) supported the Austrians. When France allied herself with Spain, England declared war on France.

As in earlier wars, this had little effect on the colonies. But the governor of Massachusetts, pushed by rich men with large landholdings and big fisheries, was able to whip up the Protestant passions of the Great Awakening and recruit troops for an expedition against Catholic French Canada. It cost many lives and a lot of money (paper money was printed in Massachusetts for the first time) and accomplished nothing.

1753

The question had to be settled. Who would own and rule North America? The French were established in Canada and Louisiana; they needed short and safe routes for trade between those colonies and for further exploration of the unknown and unclaimed interior of the country.

As English settlers moved west from Pennsylvania and Virginia into Ohio country, the Iroquois Indians were forced to make a treaty, giving the rights to hundreds of thousands of acres to Virginia investors. In 1753 a young Virginian named George Washington was sent to inform the French about the treaty. He told them that their new forts on Lake Erie and along the Allegheny River trespassed on English territory. The French replied with the French equivalent of "So what?" and continued down the river to build Fort Duquesne, on the site of present day Pittsburgh.

Washington returned to Virginia, where he was given a major's commission in the English army and 150 men to drive the French out of Ohio. Then he made the long trek back to Fort Duquesne, ordered his men to fire, took a few prisoners, and started the French and Indian war. It decided the future of

America and changed the world.

The population of Canada was small and its government was corrupt, but French soldiers were brave and tough. They were reinforced by Indian allies, whose relationships with the French were long-standing; Indians trusted French fur traders because they seemed satisfied with profitable commerce, while the English appetite for land was never satisfied. Chippewas, Ottawas, Potawatomis, Winnebagos, Hurons, and Miamis—western Indians came east to help the French. Both sides took many scalps in the bloody combat that at first went badly for England.

English General Braddock marched to Fort Duquesne with 1,400 men and was soundly whipped by the much smaller force of French troops. His aide-de-camp, George Washington, escaped with 500 survivors, and perhaps some private thoughts about British military prowess. (Another survivor was young Daniel Boone.)

But England won in Nova Scotia and deported more than 5,000 French settlers to colonies south of New Hampshire. One group reached Bayou Teche in Louisiana, and in that French community they preserved their distinctive Acadian ("Cajun") culture until the present day.

1756

English strategy concentrated on cutting off French forces in the Ohio valley from Quebec and the armies of the north. French General Montcalm pulled back into Canada as the tide turned; French forts fell under assaults by English redcoats, and the western Indians went home. At last both armies were cooped up in Canada, waiting through the long winter for reinforcements that never arrived. In the climactic battle of the war, Montcalm faced English General Wolfe, and Montreal surrendered; both generals were killed in the fighting.

1763

France lost the war and everything it claimed

in North America. Victorious Britain got all of Canada, as well as the rich lands west of Ohio to the Mississippi. She took Florida from the Spanish, in exchange for Cuba and the Philippines. To compensate for the loss of Florida, France had to give Spain New Orleans and Louisiana, which to Spain meant everything west of the Mississippi, a vast territory that nobody had yet mapped.

No native Americans signed the peace treaty. In backing the French, they had bet on the wrong horse, but the western tribes were sure that the French would rise again. In any case, their French connections were based on trade; they had never been ruled by Canada and did not now accept the idea of British rule. Pontiac, the Ottawa chief, began to put together a loose federation that included not only the tribes that had fought for France, but the Illinois, the Kickapoos, and the Menominees, as well as the Iroquois, the Delawares, and other eastern tribes. He organized the biggest Indian uprising in colonial history, attacking twelve forts on the Great Lakes and capturing eight; he kept Detroit under siege for six months. In the end his rebellion failed, but a proclamation came from London creating the first Indian Country.

England had a new king. George III issued a proclamation declaring that everything between the Appalachian Mountains and the Mississippi River would henceforth be reserved for "the Indians under Our protection." There would be no more surveys or settlements, and white men who had already taken up land in the area had to get out. The colonists were furious because this new Indian Country was almost two-thirds of what they had won in the French and Indian War. Everything west of the mountains to the Mississippi! The Great Lakes region, north into Canada for limitless miles! If all that was to be Indian "hunting grounds," why had they fought for it?

The proclamation was, in fact, only a

way for Britain to buy time and figure out what to do with its new empire. Pontiac and his warriors had to be quieted, while in London the Lords Commissioners for Trade and Plantations could make an orderly plan for future action. They were very far away from where the action would take place.

England now owned the fur trade. Indians might be savage, but you could do business with those savages. French-speaking voyageurs would buy blankets, cloth, iron and hardware items, weapons, and other trade goods, all manufactured in England and packed into neat bales that weighed exactly ninety pounds. The voyageurs loaded these goods into birchbark canoes, now manufactured by business-like Indians, and paddled them down the rivers of America. It was dangerous work; the hardy travelers steered their fragile craft through whitewater rapids and carried their packs over long portages to trade for beaver skins. Furs were then collected by larger canoes which could carry as much as 4,000 pounds and sent down the Mississippi to St. Louis or New Orleans, from where they were shipped to England and on to European markets. And all this effort was exerted in the service of fashion! Beaver hats were all the style for rich men. The trade paid the Indians and voyageurs very little, but was enormously profitable for the crown. To maintain the trade, American settlers had to be kept out of Indian Country—at least until styles changed.

Benjamin Franklin was sent to England again by the colonies as their agent; he had served there earlier representing the Philadelphia Assembly in a tax dispute. He now protested the restrictions which the King's proclamation imposed on westward-looking settlers. But nobody in England paid any attention; the King and his lords were too busy making grand plans for British Canada. For example, they passed an act permitting their new French-speaking citizens to keep their local French law and Catholic religion. This was almost the last straw for Protestant Massachusetts.

1764

The colonists, as loyal subjects of King George III, cheered the British triumph in the French and Indian War—after all, they played a big part in the victory. Their cheering stopped when they were asked to help pay for it.

Facing huge war debts, Parliament passed a law called the Sugar Act, so that new taxes would be paid on sugar, coffee, wine, and other products which the colonists had to buy from England. In the following year, Parliament passed the Stamp Act, which taxed almost every kind of printed material the colonists needed, from legal documents and newspapers to playing cards. Riots broke out in America; angry colonists stopped buying the taxed products, and then refused to buy other English-made goods. When the boycott began to hurt English merchants, the law was repealed.

But Parliament was slow to learn, and still badly in need of money. In 1767 it passed the Townshend Acts, to tax glass, paper, paint, lead, and tea, and created a new board of commissioners to enforce the law and collect the taxes. And this time, when the colonists tried to protest, England sent troops.

1770

Boston was now a city of about 16,000 people, a major center of colonial trade and political turmoil. The arrival of 4,000 redcoats infuriated the residents. Though men from Massachusetts had fought beside British soldiers in the past, they now resented the troops who not only patrolled the streets of Boston and guarded the offices of tax collectors, but invaded the private life of the city. To save the King's money, soldiers had to be given beds and meals in private homes; many were expected to find work in the city, competing with Boston laborers for much needed jobs. Ugly incidents raised the level of anger on both sides. In March, waterfront toughs started to pester a sentry in front of the State House, throwing icy snowballs, then rocks. A group of soldiers responded, but panicked as the mob grew bigger and louder. When the soldiers raised their muskets and fired, five townspeople were killed and several wounded. The first to die was a black sailor, a former slave, named Crispus Attucks.

Though the British soldiers were quickly withdrawn from the city and stationed in a harbor fort, political organizers in Boston fanned the flames of revolt by spreading word of the "Boston Massacre." Paul Revere engraved a picture of the shootings which was spread through the community with Sam Adams' propaganda pamphlets. But Sam's cousin, John Adams, defended the British soldiers in a murder trial that brought him to prominence in the colony. With his eloquent plea for justice, most of the soldiers were acquitted; only two were branded and dismissed from the army.

Parliament repealed the Townshend Acts, except for the tax on tea.

1773

During the uneasy months that followed, people in Boston and throughout the colonies began to sort themselves into two groups. On one hand were wealthy landowners and merchants with strong ties to the English ruling class. These men were fiercely loyal to George III, though the thirty-five-year-old king had begun to move in and out of the madness that would trouble him all his life. On the other hand were men who had begun to call themselves Patriots, men like Sam Adams.

Though he had graduated from Harvard College as a lawyer, Sam Adams hated the upper classes, blaming them for the bank failure that ruined his father. He hated British rule because it supported an aristocracy, both in the mother country and in the colonies. He sided with the working class and small tradesmen who were exploited and taxed by the crown. Neglecting his own business, Sam Adams wrote for the newspapers, signing his articles with different names so readers would think that his opinions were the opinions of a growing political party. He served in the colonial Assembly, and at Boston Town Meetings, a fiery speaker who urged members to organize Committees of Correspondence with other towns, adding their grievances to Boston's complaints.

Anti-British feelings built up until, on a winter night, Sam Adams could lead 150 men disguised as Mohawk Indians to board three

English merchant ships in Boston Harbor. Using hatchets, they broke up cases of tea— and only tea—and dumped them into the water. Soon the harbor was thick with tea; it washed back over the decks of the ships, and over the docks where a large crowd watched. After three hours, the Patriots shouted their last war-whoops and left the ships, applauded by their audience. The Boston Tea Party was followed by tea parties in other cities. Between Loyalists and Patriots, the line was being drawn.

1774

Parliament quickly passed a series of "Intolerable Acts" (as these new laws were called in the colonies), the first of which demanded that Boston pay for the tea that had been destroyed. A new governor was sent from London, along with new troops. The King clamped down on Boston, wiping out almost all the rights guaranteed by the Massachusetts Charter. Americans everywhere, from north to south, watched, and knew that what was happening in Boston could happen to them.

Virginia asked for a conference in Philadelphia, midway between the northern and southern colonies. At this first Continental Congress, fifty-six delegates from every colony except Georgia met in Carpenter's Hall. For the next two months, they tried to decide how much authority the King and Parliament had over American colonies, and what the colonies should do about the "Intolerable Acts."

Their debate went back to English common law, which for hundreds of years had asserted that Englishmen had certain natural rights, rights that neither the King nor Parliament could ignore. Though living in America, the colonists claimed the same rights, but they didn't have any voice in their government; no American sat in Parliament to help make the laws that governed him. While most of the men who met in Philadelphia still thought themselves part of the British empire, they would not accept the idea that Parliament could tax them, or make laws that decided their rights, without their consent.

All during September and October men like John Dickinson of Pennsylvania, John Jay of New York, Sam and John Adams from Massachusetts, Richard Henry Lee and Patrick Henry from Virginia, with delegates from the other colonies, debated the issues that united or divided them. In the end they adopted a declaration which would be sent to Parliament; they formed a Continental Association to boycott English goods; and they agreed to hold another meeting if the King did not listen to their demands.

1775

The new British governor knew rebellion when he smelled it. He had to find the hidden guns and ammunition which Patriots might decide to use, and he had to arrest their leaders. Sam Adams and John Hancock should be sent to England and tried for treason. In April, the governor learned that weapons were being stockpiled in the small towns of Lexington and Concord. He sent 700 redcoats to seize the rebel arsenal.

Paul Revere had organized a system of signals from a Boston church. As the troops marched out, the signal came. Revere and Billy Dawes rode hard for Lexington, where they spread the word and picked up young Sam Prescott. Revere and Dawes were stopped by a British patrol; Prescott rode on to warn the Minutemen of Concord.

When the British soldiers reached Lexington, seventy-seven armed men were waiting for them on the village green. As the troops marched past, a nervous citizen fired. The redcoats returned fire, and eight Americans died.

At Concord, the soldiers found a small store of weapons and destroyed them. On the march back to Boston, they were shot at by farmers and townsmen hidden behind every house, barn, stone fence, and tree. The King's army was trained to fight in formation; the tactics of these colonial militiamen were unfair. After a short battle, the redcoats were reinforced by another 1,500 British troops, and this considerable force retreated, under sniper fire all the way. During the retreat, seventy-five died and 174 were wounded.

A month later, Connecticut and Massachusetts sent militia, led by Ethan Allen and Benedict Arnold, to attack British forts at Ticonderoga and Crown Point in upper New York State. They captured badly-needed heavy artillery and other war supplies. But still fearful of invasion from the north, the Continental Congress called for a Canadian campaign. Troops from Ticonderoga marched toward Quebec, where they would meet an American army sent from Boston and establish a fourteenth state. Instead, the campaign turned into a nightmare. Starvation, disease, Canadian blizzards and British resistance defeated the colonial forces. Nine months later, the exhausted survivors limped back to Ticonderoga.

Still, while they held that base, small American boats were able to control shipping on Lake Champlain. They prevented supplies from Canada reaching the Hudson River and the British armies stationed in New York. Finally, a British naval force appeared on Lake Champlain, gunships and schooners whose cannon made short work of the tiny American "navy."

In June, the Continental Congress realized that it had to raise a continental army. Thirty thousand men were assembling around Boston. During the coming war, Massachusetts would send almost as many men as were recruited in Connecticut, Pennsylvania, and New York combined. These New England men wanted a New England general. But to insure the full commitment of southern colonies, John Adams argued for a southern commander. The Congress chose a member of the Virginia delegation, a forty-three-year-old planter named George Washington who had made his military reputation while serving as a British officer during the French and Indian War.

Washington wrote a letter to his wife at Mt. Vernon, leaving Philadelphia for Boston on June 23, unaware that a week earlier Americans had already fought the bloodiest battle of the war. Twelve hundred Yankee militiamen were holding Breed's Hill when they faced the first charge by a powerful British force. They stood off the first assault, and the second, but when the redcoats charged again, the Americans had to retreat; they were out of ammunition. They had killed more than 1,000 British soldiers, themselves losing about half that many, in the fighting that has come down in history as the Battle of Bunker Hill.

In July, still trying to avoid a final break with the crown, some members of the Continental Congress sent a petition to George III, pleading with him to stop the worst abuses of his colonial government and avoid a war. The King rejected their petition.

News of the fighting reached George Washington on the road to Boston. He set up his headquarters in Cambridge, occupying the house of the president of Harvard College while enlisted men were housed in college dormitories, or wherever shelter could be found. His army was now about 15,000 men, for these local militia came and went. Their terms of enlistment were short—they were often called grasshopper soldiers—and while they would fight fiercely if their own towns and homes were threatened, they had no enthusiasm for fighting elsewhere in the not-yet-united states. They showed up in their work clothes, or scraps of local uniforms; a general who saw action at Breed's Hill fought in shirt sleeves and an old hat, "as if he was still in the cornfield." As one of his first acts, Washington ordered 10,000 hunting shirts. Later his army would wear uniforms of brown homespun, which they paid for themselves. Some men brought their own muskets, but most had no weapons, and the country lacked factories to produce weapons. Ben Franklin suggested bows and arrows, or spears that could be turned out by any blacksmith. There was no money to buy rifles, or cannon, or ammunition, or to supply any of the army's needs: food, transport, medical supplies. And Washington had no navy at all.

He faced the greatest naval power on earth, and the British army had veteran soldiers and experienced officers, with money to buy what they needed. It was a small army by modern standards, only about 30,000 men in all, of whom 9,000 were serving in the American colonies and the rest in other parts of the empire. But Britain could enlarge its army quickly by conscripting bums and vagrants, and sentencing criminals to army duty. In America, it would also have the service and support of Loyalists and Indian allies (though a group of Oneida chieftains spoke to New England leaders assuring them of neutrality: "Possess your minds in peace. We cannot intermeddle in this dispute between two brothers. The quarrel seems to us unnatural ... Should the Great King of England apply to us for our aid, we shall deny him. If the Colonies apply, we will refuse...").

Above all, the British could afford to hire mercenaries, the soldiers that German rulers hired out to other governments for stiff prices. Since most of these troops came from the German state of Hesse-Kassel, the Americans called them all Hessians. Eventually almost 30,000 mercenaries fought for Britain in the course of the war.

But the Americans would fight on their own ground and had trained under British officers in earlier colonial wars. For generations they had been fighting off surprise Indian attacks, learning the tactics of frontier warfare, hit-and-run warfare, quite unlike the formation fighting that British troops were used to. Though Washington's army was outnumbered almost two-to-one, and though Britain spent almost ten times as much as the states could spend in the war effort, the King had problems. There was the obvious need to transport and supply his army from the other side of the Atlantic Ocean, but even more important, the war was run from London, by men who knew almost nothing about the country their armies would fight in, or the men they would fight against. Instructions to officers in America took weeks to cross the water and were often muddled and late.

British troops held the cities—Boston, New York, Philadelphia, Charleston, and Savannah—while British ships harassed smaller coastal towns because Washington had no way to protect them. But the colonies had fishing fleets and merchant ships and thousands of experienced sailors. The merchant ships were usually armed against pirates and had often fought in earlier wars as "privateers," seizing enemy vessels. Now Washington authorized arming fishing boats in New England waters, and the Congress began to commission privateers for service between southern ports and the Caribbean. As at Lake Champlain, this makeshift navy was able to interfere with supply vessels and, by British count, captured 733 British ships with their tons of cargo. They became a major source of guns and ammunition for the American armies.

Washington settled down to a siege of Boston, hoping that the redcoats could be starved out. His men surrounded the city and prevented any smuggling of food to its 17,000 citizens and 13,500 soldiers, who began to feel very hungry. Huge shipments of food were sent from England, but much of it was lost at sea, and the little that arrived was rotten. Winter came on.

1776

The Americans accomplished an almost incredible feat when they managed to drag captured British cannon from upstate New York, Ticonderoga, on Lake Champlain, through the frozen New England woods to

Washington's fortifications. Now they began shelling the city. In March, the British commander decided to evacuate Boston, loading his troops and frightened Tories into seventy-eight ships and sailing to Nantucket Island.

It was Washington's first victory as commander in chief. Coming after the victories at Lexington and Concord, the capture of British forts in New York, and a strong showing at Breed's Hill, his army began to feel quite cocky. Even more encouraging was the news that France and Spain had agreed to supply arms for the colonists. He began to think about a summer campaign against the British in New York.

Meanwhile, an anonymous pamphlet was circulating in the colonies. It was called Common Sense, but the language was uncommonly tough. Its author tore into the idea of kings who ruled by divine right. Kings, it said, were nothing but "crowned ruffians." Eventually half a million copies of Common Sense were printed, and the author, Tom Paine, was a superb propagandist for independence. He helped Americans make up their mind.

Richard Henry Lee of Virginia offered a resolution to the Continental Congress: The colonies should declare their independence and join together in an American federation. This last step was postponed until a committee could draft a statement, setting forth the reasons for their defiance of their King. They asked Thomas Jefferson, John Adams, and Ben Franklin to write it. Adams and Franklin deferred to Jefferson.

On July 2, the Congress passed Lee's resolution, and on July 4, they adopted Jefferson's Declaration of Independence with only three dissenting votes. Later, when the document was properly copied out and all the minor revisions included, John Hancock put his bold signature at the bottom, and fifty-five delegates lined up to add their names.

Jefferson began by addressing history and mankind, saying

that certain truths are "self-evident"—that all men are created equal, that they have certain God-given rights, and that they establish governments to protect their "safety and happiness." He then carefully listed all the specific acts of George III which interfered with the happiness of the American people and threatened their safety. The King had abused his power and broken his contract with the people he ruled; therefore, they would no longer be ruled by him. The colonies would be "FREE AND INDEPENDENT STATES."

In signing this Declaration, each man pledged his life, his fortune, and his "sacred honor." It was no empty pledge. Every signer knew in his heart that he was putting himself and his family at terrible risk. What read as a brave and rational decision on one side of the ocean would be read as treason on the other side. "We must hang together," said Hancock.

"Yes," said Benjamin Franklin, "we must all hang together, or most assuredly we shall all hang separately."

Jefferson now resigned from the Continental Congress and went home to Virginia, where he sat in the legislature that was trying to form a state government and write a state constitution. In the following months, most states produced constitutions that expressed an American determination to get rid of nobility and aristocracy and a state church, to have free elections and short terms of office, to have a system of justice based on jury trials, a free press, and a government in which most of the power was held by the legislature rather than by a governor.

Of course, the right to vote for a governor, or a legislature, or to serve in any office or on any jury, was limited to free white men who could meet certain property requirements. No women voted, no indentured workers, no slaves, no Indians—the extension of these "fundamental rights" to all Americans lay many years in the future.

And still to be settled was the question of a central government for the states, now loosely joined in a federation that was little more than a "firm league of friendship." While the Continental Congress in Philadelphia was trying to decide how much central government the federation needed or wanted, George Washington was struggling with the problems of winning a war; the outcome of the war would decide whether any American government could survive.

The Continental Congress finally voted $20 million to support an army. Instead of local militia serving short enlistments (the brave grasshopper soldiers), each state would send troops to serve under George Washington. Soldiers were paid about $6.75 a month; lieutenants $13.50; generals $166.

Quotas were set for towns, and bounties offered to recruits. Slaves who fought would be freed—Virginia offered $100 and 300 acres of land to any slave who would volunteer. But it would take months to supply an army, and meanwhile, the British could easily outman and outgun these raw American recruits.

Because half the population and resources of the states were located north of Chesapeake Bay, the military lords who were running the war from London decided to move the British base of operations from Boston to New York. From there they would establish a line down the Hudson River Valley and join a British army marching from Canada, cutting off New England from the rest of the country. The King sent reinforcements, the largest expeditionary force of the century—500 ships and 34,000 troops. When Washington tried to fortify New York City, the redcoats drove him out, out of Manhattan and Long Island, pursuing him through New Jersey until he could get half of his battered army across the Delaware River into Pennsylvania.

It was in the Long Island fighting that the British captured Lieutenant Nathan Hale, a Connecticut school teacher, who had volunteered to serve as a spy. The maps and notes he was carrying made a trial unnecessary. He was hung the next morning. An inspiring legend reported his last words: "I only regret that I have but one life to lose for my country."

Would Philadelphia be the next city to fall? The Continental Congress fled to Baltimore, voting "full power" for the war effort to General Washington. Full power! He was already collecting old clothes for his soldiers, and borrowing money to buy flour for their bread! Tom Paine wrote another stirring pamphlet, but morale in the army was low as Christmas approached.

Nevertheless, with those troops, Washington decided to re-cross the Delaware and attack the British troops at Trenton, New Jersey. The ice-choked river was about 1,000 feet wide. With thirty to forty men in a boat and five men at the oars, it took him nine hours to get 2,500 soldiers and eighteen cannon to the other side. It was Christmas night; the Hessian troops and their Officers were sleeping off their celebration when Washington's men overran their camp; they retreated under heavy fire. The Americans took 900 Hessian prisoners, who were paraded through the streets of Philadelphia on New Year's Day.

1777

Now Washington moved boldly to re-take New Jersey. The enlistment time of many of his men had expired; he offered them $10 apiece to serve just six more weeks. They fought their way back to a position where they could prevent the British army coming from Canada from joining the British force in New York.

The citizens of Philadelphia felt safe again and Congress returned. In June it adopted a flag, the Stars and Stripes. American morale was much improved; recruitments picked up. In the spring, the main threat was from a small-pox epidemic. Though it was still a risky idea, Washington had the whole army vaccinated. He also gave a safe conduct to Tory sympathizers who wanted to stay behind the British lines.

But by July the British army was on the move. Leaving part of his force to hold New York, the British general began to send troops to Philadelphia by sea. Washington's army, still in hunting shirts and homespun, followed by land. When the fighting began, there was a fierce battle at Brandywine Creek outside the city. But the Americans could not hope to win against 17,000 well-equipped redcoats, and the Continental Congress fled again as the British occupied the city.

It was a costly victory, for when the Canadian army finally reached Albany (remember, in this wilderness war it sometimes took an army three weeks to march twenty miles), they found thousands of New England farmers waiting for them. The British attacked but suffered heavy losses, and they were badly outnumbered when they tried a second assault. In October, the whole Canadian army was surrounded and forced to surrender at Saratoga. The Americans permitted about 5,000 troops to sail home to England, on condition that they would never again return to fight in America.

This was the turning point in the Revolution, because it meant the end of British plans to divide the northern states from the south. Even more important, the American success in upper New York, and Ben Franklin's diplomatic charm in Paris, persuaded France to come into the war on America's side.

But none of this helped Washington, who took his men into winter quarters at Valley Forge. Many members of the Congress, and many of his own officers, now thought he should be replaced as commander in chief, but he was worrying about his troops freezing in the Pennsylvania hills. There was not enough food to feed them; they slept in unheated shacks and cabins; they had no overcoats or blankets. Their shoes were worn out. They wrapped their feet in rags, but their legs and feet froze, turned black, and had to be amputated. The camp was full of disease, and then swept by a "putrid fever." There were no medicines or hospitals. It was the worst winter of the war, and Washington never forgot the men who suffered and died there. Somehow, he held an army together, sending out raiders to seize cattle and stored crops from Pennsylvania farmers who would not sell their produce for worthless American money. By March, he was pleading with the governors of every state to send food, clothing, wagons, supplies of any kind.

1778

Unexpected help arrived in the appearance of a splendidly uniformed German volunteer, with a letter from Ben Franklin. He claimed to be "Baron Friedrich Wilhelm Ludolph Gerhard Augustin von Steuben," the King of Prussia's right-hand man, an experienced officer and drillmaster. In fact, he was the son of a Lutheran minister and had invented his title and military rank. Steuben was one of many Europeans who offered their services and lives to the American cause. The nineteen-year-old Marquis de Lafayette came from France, fought, and was wounded at Brandywine. Polish-born Thaddeus Kosciusko was another volunteer, an engineer who helped strengthen the fortifications at Ticonderoga (but nothing could prevent its recapture by the British). Later he was in charge of fortifications at West Point.

Casimir Pulaski was another Polish nobleman who arrived with a letter from Franklin. He served as a volunteer before earning a Congressional commission. He organized cavalry troops who were ordered south, where Pulaski died in the siege of Savannah.

But the winter of '78 was Von Steuben's season. Always short of capable officers, and desperately concerned with other problems, Washington accepted the Baron's story, and Steuben was soon putting any man who could march through drills and rifle practice. His phony medals clanked; he swore at them in foreign languages; order and morale were greatly improved! By spring, the Americans could celebrate the announcement of a new French alliance with a grand parade. The band played while Washington reviewed the regiments of his ragged but proud army, ready to fight again.

Far away, on the Fourth of July, 175 Virginia volunteers led by George Rogers Clark attacked the British fort at Kaskaskia, on the Mississippi River. They had floated 1200 miles down the Monongahela and the Ohio, and marched sixty miles, but it took them just fifteen minutes to surprise and overpower the British garrison. They went on to take the Illinois town of Cahokia, across the river from the Spanish outpost at St. Louis (remember that everything west of the Mississippi still belonged to Spain). Then they marched for two weeks to fight at Fort Vincennes, the oldest settlement in what is now Indiana. Its French-speaking inhabitants surrendered and cheerfully pledged allegiance to the Republic of Virginia.

Clark was a young Virginia surveyor and Indian fighter, a neighbor of Thomas Jefferson. He slowly developed his own strategy for winning the war on the western frontier, and persuaded Governor Patrick Henry to authorize the expedition, though the state had no money to pay for it. The governor agreed because it would extend Virginia's claims to vast western lands.

Those lands, of course, were Indian country. When England won the territory from France in the French and Indian War, King George III had proclaimed that everything between the Appalachian Mountains and the Mississippi would be reserved for Indians under his "protection." In fact, French fur traders did business as usual, and American settlers kept moving in.

There was continuous savage warfare on the frontier. Throughout the territory, and down into Kentucky and Tennessee, the tribes fought against white men or each other, changing sides, fighting for land, honor, revenge, or pay. The Shawnees, Delawares, Piankeshaws, Miamis, Illini, Sauk, Fox, Potawatomies, Menominees, Ottawas, Chippewas, Hurons, Sioux from the North, Cherokees from the south—at one time or another, warriors from every frontier tribe followed the warpath. Sometimes they were led by regular British officers; sometimes they were joined by renegade Americans like the Girty brothers, who made their own warpath. Simon Girty took hundreds of scalps as he burned, tortured, mutilated, and murdered across Ohio and Indiana, for British pay and his own pleasure.

Lieutenant Governor Henry Hamilton, the British commandant at Detroit, was known and hated as the "Hair Buyer" because he incited the Indians against settlers and paid well for American scalps. Now he moved to retake Fort Vincennes, and his troops went into winter quarters there. The French inhabitants cheerfully renewed their allegiance to King George.

Clark was already 250 miles away, but he mustered his small force and marched back through February floods. His men waded up to their necks in icy water, holding their rifles over their heads. Out of food and almost out of ammunition, Clark boldly attacked. With little more than the racket of his drummer boys and the accuracy of his riflemen, he tricked Hamilton into surrender and took the "Hair Buyer" prisoner. As Indian scalping-parties returned to the fort, they were massacred and their bodies thrown in the river. Clark did not lose a single man in the fighting at Vincennes, winning the whole territory for the American cause. It was the greatest conquest of the Revolution, but neither Clark nor his men ever received a penny for their service.

And it would be many years before anything like peace came to the frontier. Clark would fight again, and even after the Treaty of Paris that ended the Revolution, the Indian wars went on. Paris was a long way from that "dark and bloody ground."

1779   From his West Point headquarters, Washington commanded an army that had shrunk to fewer than 4,000 men fit for combat. There was never enough food, ammunition, transport, or supplies of any kind. The redcoats, too, suffered; blunders and fraud in their high command reduced their rations. Soon they resorted to looting the countryside. Then they joined Tory sympathizers as roving outlaw bands that terrorized farmers and townspeople alike. They kidnapped citizens who could afford to pay a ransom, plundered and burned villages.

Where the armies went, women followed. Martha Washington and other officers' ladies spent as much time in camp with their husbands as the campaign allowed. Many British wives did the same thing. But not all the women in camp were wives. Many poorer women crossed the ocean and stayed with the troops as cooks and laundry women, as well as providing other comforts. Colonists said that the British women were worse than the men when it came to looting occupied territory. American women played many roles. As in British camps, there were plenty of good-time girls, as well as women who did useful work. And some women actually fought.

Margaret Corbin was a Pennsylvania woman, cooking for her husband's regiment at the battle of Fort Washington. When her cannoneer husband was shot, she stepped in and took over his cannon until she was wounded. Mary Hays McCauley carried water for the bloody and thirsty soldiers at the battle of Fort Monmouth. They called her "Molly Pitcher," the name they gave to all women who brought water. Deborah Sampson disguised herself and enlisted in the fourth Massachusetts in 1782. Under the name of "Robert Shurtleff," she served until she was discovered in 1783. These women are known; the courage and strength of many others has been forgotten.

Fighting went on in the north, where French ships and troops had made their first appearance. French naval strength would be decisive in the coming months, both in American waters and in the Caribbean. French ships on the other side of the Atlantic kept British ships bottled up. French shipyards built the small fleet commanded by John Paul Jones. In a famous night battle off the coast of England, he refused to surrender. "I have not yet begun to fight," he said, and then defeated the heavily armed British warships.

1780

The main British force was moving south, counting on support by southern Loyalists. They took Savannah, Georgia, then captured Charleston, South Carolina, and swept into

North Carolina. They were defeated at King's Mountain by American troops, "over-mountain" men, who had taken little part in the war until their own home country was invaded. Their savage frontier tactics and deadly rifle fire resulted in the killing or wounding of 400 Loyalists and the taking more than 600 Loyalist prisoners, on some of whom the mountain men inflicted brutal frontier justice.

Meanwhile, Washington had discovered a plot to betray West Point. That important Hudson River fort was not only his headquarters, but an essential defense against another invasion from Canada. General Benedict Arnold, an American hero in early fighting, was furious at being passed over for promotion. After managing to be named commander at West Point, he plotted to enable a surprise British attack from the river, whereupon he would surrender the entire fort, with its artillery and 3,000 American soldiers. But when his British contact was captured, Washington learned of his treason, and the plot failed. Arnold escaped, and, though he didn't collect the full payoff for West Point, Arnold was made a British officer and led troops in the last battles of the war. Later he was paid enough to live comfortably in England.

1781

The British won in Georgia and the Carolinas, and overran Virginia, but suffered heavy losses in months of fighting. Their general pulled back to a position on the Yorktown peninsula, not far from the site of the first settlement at Jamestown, in 1607. After almost 175 years, the English adventure in America was ending where it began. Colonial history had come full circle.

Washington saw his chance. The French fleet in Chesapeake Bay prevented enemy ships from supplying the base, and on land 6,000 British troops were surrounded by more than 16,000 American and French soldiers. After a short siege, the British General Cornwallis surrendered on October 19. The

49

war for American Independence was over.

1782

The American army went into winter quarters at Newburgh, Virginia, while negotiations for a peace treaty got underway. They had won a long war and changed the course of history, but they still didn't have enough food, enough shoes, or enough blankets, and their commander spent the next months pleading with the Continental Congress for supplies to meet their needs. But the Congress was flat broke. It had borrowed $2.5 million since the war began; the states had borrowed another $200 million; and now there was no money to feed the army, and no money to pay them. Only Washington's personal strength and influence kept the soldiers' complaints from flaring into mutiny.

Many Americans saw difficult times ahead. They were glad to be rid of George III, but now the states were wrangling with the Congress and each other, drifting out of control. They needed a new king, an American King. When one of his officers proposed the idea of a crown to George Washington he answered in no uncertain terms, "Be assured, sir, ...you could not have found a person to whom your schemes are more disagreeable."

1783

When a peace treaty was finally signed in Paris, Washington spoke an emotional farewell to his comrades before the army was disbanded. No medals, no parades, no pay—only paper promises that the Continental Congress had no way of keeping. The men straggled home on foot; Washington rode back to Mount Vernon carrying Christmas presents for his family, and there he stayed for the next three years while America tried to figure out what to do next.

1785

The Continental Congress was still doing business under the old Articles of Confederation when it adopted the Northwest Ordinance. All the land America had won in the long war, everything not included in the original thirteen states, was now owned and administered by the federal government. Congress called for a survey and divided the territory into one-mile-square sections of 640 acres; thirty-six sections constituted a "township." Sections were offered for sale at $1 an acre. As yet there were few takers, but Congress looked forward to the growth of new states—what would some day be Ohio, Indiana, Illinois, Michigan, Wisconsin, and much of Minnesota. When the population reached 60,000 free males, a state could apply for admission to the Union, with the same powers and rights as any of the original thirteen. And after 1800, slavery in the Northwest Territory would be banned.

Of course, nobody consulted the native Americans who lived there. The land where they had hunted and fished, raised their children and buried their dead, could now be claimed by new Americans.

1786
Massachusetts, cradle of the Revolution, had already written its own constitution and bill of rights. For one thing, its constitution said that all men were born free and equal, and its court took that statement literally. Slavery was abolished in the state. But the constitution still barred most men, free but poor, from holding state office or even voting. They had fought a war for representation, yet didn't get it.

1787
Massachusetts' veterans were poor. Patriotic military service left them with debts they couldn't meet; their farms were being sold to pay taxes. They rose up in another rebellion and followed Daniel Shays in a march on Springfield, Massachusetts, where they tried to seize the arsenal. That attempt failed, but for the next six months, they harassed public officials and kept judges out of their courtrooms. When they marched to Boston, they were met by the state militia. The same officers who had led these men in battle now shot them down and pursued them; Shays escaped, but others

were caught and hanged.

Similar riots from Vermont to South Carolina scared political leaders in every state. Those who had opposed a strong central government as a threat to liberty, now realized that weak government invited dangerous disorder. They were ready to talk about uniting in a new kind of federal system.

Delegates from the states were meeting in Philadelphia in an effort to repair the Articles of Confederation. There were many familiar faces; some men had signed the Declaration of Independence, many had served together in the Continental Congress or in the army; there were old friends and old antagonists. They had deep differences, but they had shared a cause and now they shared a country of almost 600 million acres, from Maine across the Great Lakes to the Mississippi, and south to Spanish territory in Louisiana and Florida. They soon realized that the flaws of the Articles were beyond mere amendments. They would have to decide on a whole new charter, stating how their vast new country should be governed, and who would govern it.

In most countries, for centuries, governments had grown by bits and pieces, haphazardly, with power going to the person who could grab and hold it. In Philadelphia, for the first time in history, everything would be thought through and written down, the rules for government to live by. The delegates began by stating their purpose in a brief Preamble:

> "... to form a more perfect Union, establish justice,
> insure domestic tranquility, provide for the common
> defense, promote the general welfare, and secure the
> blessings of liberty..."

Then they proceeded to Article I of their new Constitution. They intended to divide the powers of government into three branches, so that responsibility would be defined and shared. The first and most important responsibility was the power to make laws affecting citizens in all the states. For that purpose they created a House of Representatives, to which members would be elected, and a Senate, to which members would be appointed by state legislatures. (As you read, remember that we are talking about the original Constitution, written by forty men we frequently call the Framers. There would be changes later; amendments would be added as America changed.)

Article II created the office of president, a chief executive to administer the laws agreed upon by the House and the Senate.

Article III created a Supreme Court, to settle disputes between the federal government and the states, or between the states, or between citizens and federal or state governments.

In these and four other Articles (it's a short document; only about 4,000 words), the Framers described the duties of federal officers, and tried to provide for all the basic needs of a new country. The United States of America needed an army and a navy; they needed money, actual coins that would have the same value in every state; they needed a postal service, because letters and newspapers were the only means of communicating; they needed a procedure for admitting new citizens into the country, and new states into the Union as the country grew; they needed to collect taxes for all the services the country required and would require in the future.

But the Constitution was only concerned with national government. All other questions were left to the states and whatever local governments the citizens of those states wanted to establish. For example, the new national government would build and maintain roads for a mail service, but communities had to build whatever local roads they needed for their own use.

It took the Grand Convention four months to hammer out all the details of a Constitution, four summer months of hot weather and hot argument. When the delegates finished their work and signed the document, it was submitted to the states for ratification. When nine states accepted and ratified the Constitution, it would become the law for all the states. That took more time and more argument, for many states—still afraid of the power a new federal government could exercise—insisted on adding a Bill of Rights which would further limit that power.

To support the case for ratification, Alexander Hamilton and James Madison wrote a series of articles. With added contributions from John Jay, these papers were published in 1787-1788 as "The Federalist," and are still a classic treatise on the constitutional system. But Richard Henry Lee wrote "The Letters of the Federal Farmer," which warned against ratification before a Bill of Rights was added.

So while the states debated and voted on ratification, a delegate from Virginia went to work on twelve amendments to the original document. George Mason had refused to sign the Constitution because it said nothing about the individual rights of American citizens. He prepared a Bill of Rights to be added as soon as the new Congress took office, amendments relating to the freedom of religion, the right to free speech and a free press, the right to bear arms, the right to trial by jury, and so on. Some of these rights we now take for granted, and others are still the subject of loud dispute.

In any case, the process of ratification went forward, and elections for the new Congress began, each state making its own election rules. In those days, American citizens did not vote directly for a president. As further safeguard against the sudden rise of a dema-gogue, a dictator who could mislead and misrule the country, the Constitution provided a system by which states would choose a group of "electors," and those men would vote for two candidates; the man with the largest number of votes would be president, and the runner up would become vice president.

1788

By June, ten states had ratified the Constitution; state legislatures had appointed their Senators; citizens had begun voting for members of the House of Representatives, and electors had been chosen. Until a census could be taken, the Constitution said that Virginia would have ten seats in the House of Representatives; Massachusettsand Pennsylvania would each have eight; New York and Maryland, six; Connecticut, North Carolina and South Carolina, five; New Jersey, four; Georgia and New Hampshire, three; Delaware and Rhode Island, one. Each man would represent 30,000 citizens. In the Senate, each state had two seats. Large and small states would have equal representation.

1789

George Washington

By spring, the voting was finally over and the new government began to arrive in New York. Legislators came by coach or on horseback, delayed by weather and bad roads, finding what lodging they could in a city jammed with spectators. Private money had been raised to remodel meeting space for Congress and to decorate the streets. Finally enough Senators were assembled for a quorum and the meeting was called to order for purposes of reading the electors' ballots. The presiding officer solemnly announced that "it appeared that George Washington Esquire was elected president." Nobody was surprised, but everybody cheered. From among several candidates, John Adams was elected vice-president. Everybody cheered him, too.

Then riders were sent to inform both men. Adams got the news first and left for the inauguration ceremony, accompanied by forty carriages and sixty horses. It took the rider a week to reach Mount Vernon, and two days later Washington set out. His coach was stopped every few miles by adoring crowds. Every city through which he passed had prepared an ovation—parades, speechmaking, banquets. When he reached New York, the city went wild in celebration, bells rang, bands played, fireworks lit up the sky.

On the last day in April, Washington and Adams took their oaths of office before the Congress in Federal Hall, and then the new president made his inaugural address. He wore a brown suit with eagles on the buttons and white silk stockings. His hands shook as he awkwardly read his speech, but all present realized that they were witnessing the birth of a nation. The celebration went on long into the night.

The president and the Congress immediately went to work. What should the president be called: His Highness? His High Mightiness? His Excellency? Finally they settled on simply, "Mr. President."

A Supreme Court was appointed, and John Jay was named as Chief Justice of the United States. Congress quickly created the Departments of State, Treasury, and War, and the president named his cabinet: Thomas Jefferson would be his Secretary of State, Henry Knox, his dependable old wartime comrade, would be Secretary of War. For legal advice, the President chose Edmund Randolph to be Attorney General. The most urgent questions of the day, however, involved money, and as Secretary of the Treasury, he appointed thirty-two-year-old Alexander Hamilton, his wartime aide-de-camp.

America was saddled with enormous war debts. Hamilton said that the government should pay its creditors every penny they were owed. A lot of money had been loaned by ordinary people, by farmers and small producers who had supplied the army and taken notes (promises to pay) from the Continental Congress; soldiers had taken notes in return for their long years of service. But after the war, many people were badly in need of money, so they sold those notes for whatever they could get, often very little. The notes were now held by the country's richest men—e.g., merchants, bankers, speculators. Nevertheless, Hamilton insisted, they had to be paid in full.

And the states had raised militia regiments, and paid with notes. Hamilton now proposed that the federal government should take over the states' war debts. This argument almost tore the new country apart. Some states had spent heavily for the war, some much less. Southern states objected violently to taxing their citizens to pay the obligations of Massachusetts. Hamilton brought them into line by promising them the new capital city; it would be located in the south. And he sweetened the deal for Pennsylvania by promising to locate the temporary capital in Philadelphia.

As part of his complicated financial schemes, Hamilton wanted a national bank. It would be owned partly by the government, but 80 percent of its stock would be sold to private investors. Thomas Jefferson protested, but Washington supported his Secretary of the Treasury.

Another long debate concerned George Mason's Bill of Rights, the twelve amendments to the Constitution that were promised during the campaign for its ratification. President Washington opposed the idea, and in his inaugural address he advised the Congress to give the amendments special attention. From France, where he was serving as United States Minister, Thomas Jefferson shrugged off the idea of such a Bill as not very important, one way or the other. James Madison, who had written much of the Constitution, was also opposed, but he won his seat in Congress because he told Virginia voters that he would support a Bill of Rights (it was modeled on similar Virginia legislation), so now he kept that political promise. He made extensive revisions in the amendments and advocated their passage, although the debate wore him out. It had become, he said, "a nauseous project."

Of the twelve amendments submitted to Congress in 1789, only ten survived and were sent to the states for ratification. Again there was debate, but after two years they were approved by the necessary three-quarters of the states, becoming what we now revere as the Bill of Rights. Connecticut, Massachusetts, and Georgia did not ratify the Bill of Rights until 1939. One of the amendments rejected in 1789 related to Congressional pay, and was finally added to the Constitution in 1992 as the twenty-seventh Amendment. So we should remember that the Founding Fathers foresaw the need for changes in the Constitution and provided for it. Even our cherished Bill of Rights was not graven in stone. It was argued then, and will be argued again, but argument shouldn't scare us. Instead, we should respect the wisdom of our forebears, who guaranteed us the basic right to change our minds.

Until this point, America did not have political parties. The Constitution said nothing about how candidates for office would be put forward. Now two parties began to emerge. On one side was the brilliant young Hamilton and his friends, rich city men—men with money to invest in a national bank. On the other side was Thomas Jefferson, who envisioned a country of farmers and workmen, as free as possible from any government meddling. Even before Washington's first term was over, the lines between Hamilton and Jefferson were being drawn.

And poor Vice-President John Adams was caught somewhere in between, unable to take part in the political debates, but a plump little target for everybody who was dissatisfied with the new government. "My country," he said, "has in its wisdom contrived for me the most insignificant office that ever the invention of man conceived..."

1790

The first national census counted 3,929,625 Americans, of whom 1,556,572 were women. Indians were not counted because, at least in theory, they had their own country west of the Appalachian Mountains. There were 59,557 free blacks and 697,624 slaves. For purposes of representation in Congress, each state would count a slave as $3/5$ of a person. Of course, women, Indians, and slaves could not vote, and each state set its own voting requirements for men.

Free of British trade regulations, the foreign trade of the United States expanded rapidly. In August, Captain Robert Gray sailed the ship Columbia back to Boston after a three-year voyage, the first United States vessel to circle the globe. Its cargo of tea and silks from China made huge profits for the New York trading company that owned the ship; the poorly fed and poorly paid sailors got little more than three years of hard, dangerous work and the fun of telling their families about exotic foreign cities. But the Columbia established America's claim to the Oregon Territory, and soon the China trade carried not only the produce and product of the eastern states, but also furs and lumber from the northwest to Asian markets.

The government now moved to the temporary capital at Philadelphia. In the first term of the first President and Congress, there were more "firsts" than we can include here. Congress not only had to build the structure of a new government and figure out how to pay for it, but it had to deal with the outside world. There were, for example, boundary disputes among the states and also with Britain: Exactly where was the boundary between Maine and British Canada? And what about the Mississippi, the boundary between the states and the Spanish west? What were American navigation rights? And most important, what were the present relations between America and France?

At the same time that Washington was being sworn in as President, revolution flamed up in France, a country with which America had a treaty of alliance. Lafayette, who had led American troops during our revolution, returned to lead his own people; when the Bastille fell in Paris, Lafayette sent the key to that grim prison to his idol and former General, President Washington. America's example was spreading the dream of political liberty to Europe, and many Americans strongly supported the uprising in France. Thomas Jefferson, who had served at the French court during our struggles for independence, had high hopes for a revolutionary government there.

Meanwhile, in Pawtucket, Rhode Island, a twenty-two-year-old English immigrant named Samuel Slater was making another kind of revolution. The spinning machines he built in Moses Brown's old barn were finally in operation spinning cotton. It was an event of far more importance to Americans than any of the uproar in Paris.

Ever since Roman times, England was famous for woolen cloth. For centuries it was the main source of national wealth. Farmers also grew flax, a weedy plant that was woven into linen, but in cool, rainy England, nobody could grow cotton. Cotton cloth was almost unknown, sometimes imported, but too expensive for any but the very rich. Woolens were the "strength and revenue and blood" of the kingdom.

This huge industry depended on the labor of women, working at their spinning wheels in every English home. Colonial women, too, spent hours at their wheels. In Massachusetts, bounties were paid for spinning and weaving, with penalties for families that didn't meet their quota.

To spin yarns from any raw material required weeks of hard, sweaty work. Tough flax plants, pulled up by the roots, had to be dried, retted, pounded with heavy sticks, and scraped, hackled-Twenty separate operations were needed to make linen thread. As for wool: after sheep were sheared, the greasy fleece had to be sorted and picked over. The wool was washed (with homemade soap, in many tubs of water hauled from the well), and perhaps dyed with the juice of leaves and bark. Next came carding and combing, on heated wool combs; the more carding and combing, the finer the wool could be spun. One expert was said to have spun so fine that she could get forty-eight miles of thread from a pound of wool.

Cotton lent itself to smoother thread and lighter cloth, but it had to be imported. American cotton required a day just to pick out the seeds, one at a time, by hand. Little was used except on plantations with slave labor.

Prepared fibers were wound on a spindle turned by a spinning wheel. Women stood for hours, taking a few steps backward to feed the spindle, walking forward to push the wheel, sometimes stopping to do other household chores, returning to the wheel in their "free" time. In an ordinary day of spinning a woman might walk ten miles, backwards and forwards, to tend the wheel; a fast spinner, giving all her attention to the job, might walk twenty miles a day. Small children were taught to spin. Grandmother sat in a corner and carded more wool or flax or cotton for the spinner. The room was full of dust and lint. Whether a woman used the large walking wheel or a smaller wheel operated by a foot pedal, the yarns she produced were tied together and wound on reels, then used to set up a hand loom. Every home had spinning wheels and most had looms. On Southern plantations there were loom-rooms, where black women wove all the cloth needed to make jeans for slaves and fine shirts for their masters, as well as cloth for bedsheets and tablecloths and every other household use. Men became professional weavers, buying yarns from housewives to weave in their own shops, or going from town to town, carrying their looms on their backs.

You can see why English inventors began to look for better ways to turn raw materials into cloth. The breakthrough came when Richard Arkwright invented the spinning jenny (1769). It turned many spindles at one time with water power, producing a strong, smooth thread. This was quickly followed by Edmund Cartwright's power loom (1785-1787). These technologies gave England world supremacy in the textile industry. New developments were closely guarded by English manufacturers. They had no intention of sharing their secrets with anybody else. The Royal Navy searched passengers and cargo on departing ships so that no machines could be smuggled out of England. Skilled workmen were forbidden to leave the country.

One of those workmen was Samuel Slater, who was employed in a cotton mill when he was fourteen, and made manager of a new mill by the time he was twenty-one. But Sam was an ambitious boy, and his prospects looked brighter in America. He disguised himself as a farm laborer and ran away, sailing off to the United States without even telling his mother. He soon heard of a new enterprise in Pawtucket, Rhode Island. There, Moses Brown, a canny old Quaker, was trying to manufacture cotton thread, using a team of horses to drive a spinning jenny. Brown came from a large family with many interests, from candlemaking to grinding "choklit." He had failed with silkworms, but if America could grow cotton, he saw possibilities in cotton products. Therefore, he was delighted to get a letter from Sam Slater, offering to build the best spinning equipment then available in England, "If I do not make as good yarns as they do...I will have nothing for my services but will throw the whole of what I have attempted over the bridge."

Sam had no designs or patterns but relied on his memory to reproduce the complicated machines. Moses Brown took him on as a partner, to be paid a dollar a day and half the profits of the enterprise, if there were any profits. He worked almost a year of sixteen-hour days, building spinning wheels from oak parts, finding sources for iron shafts, carding rollers, gears, belts; and at last he had three machines ready to go. In December, 1790, Sam connected his jenny to a small waterwheel in the Blackstone River—wading into the frozen river to break the water-wheel out of the ice. The shafts and gears and belts began to turn, spinning the first cotton yarn ever produced by an American manufacturer, in the first American factory.

He went on to a long, and very profitable, career. His wife, Hannah, examined the cotton they imported from South America and thought it might make good sewing thread. She twisted a few yards on her own spinning wheel. The cotton thread she invented rapidly replaced linen thread, and they built a whole new industry around her idea. Eventually they had mills and factories in several towns, turning out yarns and threads for sewing, knitting, and weaving almost every kind of fabric. And that's how Sam Slater brought the Industrial Revolution to America.

In the same year, Congress passed the first patent law. The Constitution gave Congress the power "to promote the Progress of Science and useful Arts by securing for limited Times to Authors and

Inventors the exclusive Right to their Writings and Discoveries." Soon many Sam Slaters and Moses Browns would be inventing and improving machinery to replace hand labor. Their ingenuity would shape the future of the country.

1791

In March, Vermont joined the Union.

Alexander Hamilton had won his fight for a national bank, and on July 4 the stock in the bank went on sale in New York. A horde of investors and speculators trampled each other in their enthusiasm for the venture. The price of shares skyrocketed. Crooked manipulators had a field day until a month later, when America experienced its first stock market crash. Hamilton used government money to stop the panic, and by fall the Bank of the United States was operating under sound management.

Hamilton was soon involved in another investment scheme, a Society for Establishing Useful Manufacturers. He saw the need to industrialize the country, to make it less dependent on products from Europe and more competitive in world trade. He proposed to create a manufacturing center in New Jersey, and again stock was sold in a company that would make everything from blankets to beer. Again, there was a fever of speculation among northern investors; southern planters, whose wealth was mainly in land, had little cash to invest. Eventually the plan collapsed.

Of more interest to Washington and Jefferson were plans for a new national capital, to be developed on ten square miles along the Potomac River. A French planner and engineer was hired to design it. Pierre L'Enfant had come to America with Lafayette and served as a captain in the Revolutionary War. He laid out a magnificent city of public buildings and broad boulevards, but he came into conflict with Jefferson (himself an architect of distinction) and American engineers. When the costs of the project became outrageous, the temperamental Frenchman was fired but construction went forward in the District of

Columbia.

Since the first months of the Union, the national government had tried to deal fairly with the Indians, but it was inevitable that frontier settlers would continually invade Indian lands. There was more or less continual warfare in the western territories. Congress passed laws; treaties were negotiated; but the settlers had no interest in treaties—their motto was, "shoot first." At last, in response to border massacres led by the Wabash Indians, Congress sent a small army of inexperienced, poorly supplied, and mutinous troops to restore order. They were soundly defeated and suffered heavy losses. Expeditions that followed were no more successful; British and Spanish agents continued to incite and arm western tribes.

Jefferson thought it would be cheaper to bribe the Indian leaders than to fight them; Washington and Knox urged Congress to pass stronger laws against the greed and cruelty of white settlers. But in October, 1791 another American army marched through the wilderness to subdue warriors of the Miami tribe. They were annihilated in the bloodiest fighting the border had yet known. The Indians were not ready to surrender to the United States.

In December, George Mason's Bill of Rights was ratified, and ten amendments were added to the original Constitution.

1792

Alexander Hamilton, still wrestling with problems of government finance, asked for a tax on whiskey. At a time when it was difficult and costly to transport wagonloads of grain to market, farmers and backwoods settlers distilled their corn into hard liquor and sold it by the barrel. When Congress passed the whiskey tax, western producers rioted and chased the tax man off their land. Hamilton wanted to call out the army; Washington preferred to let local militia deal with the matter. He issued a stern proclamation telling the rioters to restore order. They obeyed, reluctantly and temporarily.

Kentucky joined the Union in May. For almost thirty years, Daniel Boone had explored its mountains and forests, a restless man, always moving west. His Quaker family moved from Pennsylvania Dutch country to the Carolinas; young Daniel moved on, over the Cumberlands. In 1760 he carved his name on a tree where he "cilled a bar," and moved on, putting his mark on trees and rocks. Though he had seen military service in the British army, fighting under George Washington in the French and Indian war, Boone took no part in the War for Independence. He was already independent, working as a teamster, surveyor, hunter, Indian fighter, and land agent. He guided hundreds of pioneers who followed his Wilderness Road into "Kentucke." In 1775, while Bostonians were facing British troops at Breed's Hill, Boone was building a fort at the new settlement of Boonesboro. His own land claims in Kentucky didn't stand up, so he moved on into Virginia, where he held various public offices. Finally, in Missouri territory, he got a land grant from Congress, and settled down. He was eighty years old. Six years later he died and became an American legend.

Rather than use his tremendous personal influence to shape the policies of the new government, President Washington acted mainly as a patient referee, letting the Congress and his Cabinet debate and arrive at decisions without his interference. States fought for the special interests of their citizens; Hamilton and Jefferson quarreled violently about the importance of manufacturing and commerce versus the rights of small farmers and tradesmen; Washington represented the whole country and held the Union together.

Now it was an election year, and he wanted to retire and go home to Mount Vernon. He asked James Madison to write his farewell address, but Madison joined Hamilton and Jefferson in begging him to serve another term. Washington wearily agreed. Rival political factions concentrated on winning electoral votes for their Vice-Presidential candidates. John Adams, suspected of "monarchical" tendencies, squeaked through in a close election and returned to his insignificant office; both Hamilton and Jefferson would continue to serve in Washington's cabinet.

The second Congress voted salaries for the President and Vice-President. Washington would receive $25,000 a year; Adams, $5,000 a year. Americans were already complaining about Congressional salaries—$5 or $6 a day, paid only for actual attendance.

And in this year, the first federal mint was established in Philadelphia to supply a uniform coinage for the United States.

In colonial times, many kinds of money were in circulation, although not much of it. Most trade was conducted by barter. As we've seen, a wife could be bought for tobacco in early Virginia; a house in Connecticut was sold for a herd of goats; shoes were traded for eggs; the minister was paid with firewood. This system worked in small communities, but it wouldn't work for trade among the states.

Before the Revolution, most of the hard money used in the colonies was Spanish and Portuguese, often supplied by pirates— Portuguese gold joannes (called joes and half-joes by Americans) and Spanish-Mexican silver dollars, often cut into eight pie-shaped pieces (we still say "two-bits" for a quarter, "four-bits" for half a dollar). Colonies began to issue their own paper money, which Britain made repeated efforts to control. The crown tried to discourage trade between the colonies, because a colony was supposed to supply raw materials, buying whatever manufactured goods it needed from British trading companies, with gold and silver or British paper money.

After the Declaration of Independence, still more kinds of money complicated daily life. States printed money. As coined money disappeared during the war, states printed paper nickels and dimes. Private banks printed money. The Continental Congress printed more than $240 million to pay its soldiers and buy supplies for the army. Each bill promised to pay the bearer $10 or $30 or $50, or whatever its denominated value, in "Spanish milled dollars," gold or silver. But even the most patriotic Americans realized that Congress didn't have that much gold or silver, and soon the money was worthless.

To standardize the money a new country needed for its business, Alexander Hamilton established the first mint. Experience with paper money had been disastrous, so it produced only gold and silver coins. The Constitution prohibited any state from issuing money. But people got tired of doing business with heavy bags of metal, so eventually the federal government had to print paper money again. Free of colonial controls, American trade brought in enough gold and silver to back it up. But the value of any money is only what the people who use it believe it to be.

In January, 1793, the revolutionary French beheaded King Louis XVI. All over Europe, kings trembled. France was now at war with Austria, Prussia, Holland, Spain, and England, but Americans were strong in their support of the revolutionary cause. News of early French victories set off joyous celebrations in eastern cities. In Boston, Sam Adams organized wild parties with parades, bonfires, dancing in the streets and plenty of drinking; in Philadelphia, Jefferson overflowed with emotion and eloquence.

The American ambassador in France had a different view of the revolution. He sent back frightening reports as Lafayette, an early revolutionary leader, was replaced by more violent men and bloodthirsty Paris mobs. Lafayette was driven from the country, a fugitive. In October, Marie Antoinette followed her husband to the guillotine.

Though America had old treaties with the French, Washington and his cabinet were determined to maintain neutrality in the war. A presidential proclamation warned Americans to stay out of it, to avoid "all acts and proceedings whatsoever" that might involve them or their country in hostilities. His countrymen agreed not to sell arms or ammunition to any of the combatants, but they intended to make money out of the war. They would continue to trade freely, despite efforts by foreign navies to stop American ships.

When America recognized an envoy from the revolutionary French government, it turned out to be a bad idea.

1793

The envoy, Citizen Charles Genet, arrived in Charleston and got a rousing welcome. He immediately made a deal with the governor of South Carolina to arm and supply four French ships, recruiting Americans to serve as officers. These ships began to attack British vessels in the West Indies, capturing rich prizes and sending them to American ports. When Genet reached Philadelphia, French sympathizers hailed his boldness.

Of course, the British protested this outrageous breach of American neutrality, and retaliated by an attack on American ships. Genet began to recruit a private army to fight the Spanish in Florida. Jefferson had defended Genet, but at last the Frenchman's insolent behavior toward the President was too much for even the most partisan friends of France. Full of swagger and bluster, Genet swore he would go over Washington's head and appeal to the American people, but when Washington finally decided to deport him, the French agitator changed his tune. Rather than risk execution by returning to France, he humbly asked for permission to stay in the United States as a private citizen. Washington granted his petition; Genet married the daughter of the governor of New York and settled down on a Hudson Valley farm.

While the government was distracted by foreign affairs, a worse enemy struck Philadelphia. The yellow fever, a deadly plague for which there was no treatment, spread rapidly to other cities. As the death toll mounted, public officials fled the city; Hamilton contracted the disease and barely survived. Black servants who were left behind had some strange resistance to the disease; they stayed to nurse the sick and bury the dead. After three months, the epidemic was over. Outbreaks continued for many years, until doctors discovered that yellow fever was carried by mosquitoes.

And perhaps the most important event of the year went almost unnoticed when Eli Whitney invented his cotton gin. He was a Yale graduate, hired as a tutor for the children of Mrs. Nathaniel Greene. He listened to the drawingroom conversation on her Georgia estate, and the talk was all of cotton. The seeds of Georgia cotton clung so tightly to the boll that a slave could clean no more than a pound a day. Mrs. Greene suggested a machine for the purpose, and in ten days Whitney built one— a simple cylinder with teeth to comb the cotton and a fan to blow it out. It was so simple that Mrs. Greene's friends, invited to watch its operation, immediately copied it. Though Whitney never made much money from the cotton gin, it transformed southern agriculture. Ten years later, cotton production had increased to eighty million pounds, supplying northern manufacturers like Sam Slater. Worthless land became valuable, settlers moved to clear more land in the west, and the price of a slave doubled.

At the end of the year, Thomas Jefferson resigned from the cabinet. He was twenty-six when he entered the Virginia legislature, and now he was fifty. The feud with Hamilton had soured the last years; the Genet affair had been an embarrassment. After a quarter-century of public service, he returned to Virginia to wait until new opportunities developed.

Although there were no political parties when our country held its first elections, parties began to take shape four years later, and by 1794 they were well defined. Of course, Washington needed no party; he was elected twice without opposition. But some of the men who served in his administration began to be known as Federalists—Adams, Hamilton, John Jay, (who wrote some of The Federalist arguing for ratification of the Constitution), and John Marshall (a former member of the Virginia legislature now sitting in the House of Representatives). These men believed in strong central government, and they wanted the country to develop its manufacturing and commercial base. They drew support from prosperous men in northern cities. The violence of the French revolution made those people very nervous.

On the other side were Jefferson and Madison and all those who stood for states' rights and agricultural interests. They were still devoted to the French revolutionary cause, and they called themselves Republicans. Men like Albert Gallatin in western Pennsylvania and Aaron Burr in New York began to organize in opposition to the Federalists. They would soon be identified as Democratic-Republicans. But whatever their political convictions, don't forget that these men were also driven by personal ambition, and their choice of a party was often decided by which party offered a quicker path to power.

1794   President Washington had his hands full trying to keep America out of the war between

France and Britain. His Proclamation of Neutrality did not prevent Britain from seizing American merchant ships and forcing American sailors to serve in the British navy. In June, he sent John Jay, now Chief Justice of the United States, to negotiate a treaty of peace and commerce. James Monroe was sent to Paris, to reassure the French.

At the same time, Washington had to face rebellion at home. Western farmers in Pennsylvania, the Carolinas, and Virginia exploded when Congress raised the tax on whiskey and made serious efforts to collect it. They organized and armed their own militia; they faced and whipped the small contingents of regular troops available to keep order. And when they caught a tax man, he was tarred and feathered.

And all along the border, Indian tribes resisted the steady invasion of their lands by white settlers. British agents from the north, and Spanish from the south, promised aid to the Indians and incited continuous bloody warfare. Henry Knox had fought beside Washington through every major campaign of the American Revolution, and now he served as his commander's Secretary of War. His was a lone voice pleading for justice and humane treatment of Native Americans. Most people cheered when Anthony Wayne, another famous general, was sent to Ohio to crush the Indians once and for all.

When Knox resigned from the cabinet, Hamilton took over the duties of the War Office. He had been urging the president to send federal troops to Pittsburgh, a hotbed of the Whiskey Rebellion, and against his better judgment, Washington agreed. In fact, state and federal officers had already met with the rebels, and after weeks of bargaining, the distillers had come to terms and signed an oath of obedience to the United States. But it took more weeks for the news to reach the government in Philadelphia. By that time 13,000 troops were already on the march.

It woke proud memories for Washington to review this army of young men, eager for action—a larger force than most he had commanded during the Revolution. Reluctantly, he went back to his presidential duties while Hamilton stayed with the troops for the long, back-breaking haul over the mountains. But if Hamilton and the army hoped to win military glory, they were disappointed. By the time they reached Pittsburgh, most of the rebels had dispersed. A few hundred were rounded up; some brought to trial. Only two were convicted of anything, and later given pardons. Still, an important point had been made. When the federal government imposed a tax, that tax had to be paid.

The military honors went to General "Mad Anthony" Wayne in a decisive western Indian fight. Michikinikwa was a Miami chief, but it's easier for us to write his Indian name, Little Turtle. He led almost 2,000 warriors, camped around a British fort near Detroit, in Indian country. It was a loose federation of tribes Delawares, Ojibways, Ottawas, Pottawatomis, Miamis, Shawnees—and they had already beaten two American expeditions. Wayne had a bigger force, better trained and better equipped. Some efforts were made to negotiate a treaty, but Little Turtle and other chiefs wanted the lands they were promised by earlier British treaties. They still hoped for and expected British help, but except for a few Canadian militia, they didn't get it. Little Turtle saw that his warriors could not hold out against the American force, and so counseled peace. The tribes chose another leader. They were defeated by Wayne at the Battle of Fallen Timbers, near present day Toledo. Wayne went on to destroy the federated tribes and subdue the territory. A year later, Little Turtle was among the chiefs who signed the Greenville Treaty, making the first formal cession of Indian lands to the United States. Ohio was opened up for white settlement.

Both Spain and Britain saw this expansion as a threat to their

North American holdings, and they were right. Spain "owned" all the unexplored land west of the Mississippi, as well as the Florida peninsula and a strip along the Gulf coast that connected the peninsula with New Orleans. That city controlled Mississippi navigation, essential to the fur trade and the movement of westering Americans.

Though Spanish explorers had dominated the sixteenth century, and conquests in Mexico and Peru had lavishly repaid their efforts, Spain rested for the next two hundred years. In 1769, ships were sent up the California coast and established a mission at San Diego, followed the next year by a mission at Monterey. Further voyages explored as far north as Alaska, where British and Russian vessels were also poking around. Spain claimed Alaska two years before the American colonists fought at Bunker Hill.

In July, 1776, Silvestre de Escalante, a Franciscan missionary, set out from Santa Fe with nine men to explore northwest of New Mexico. He hoped to find a route to Monterey, but he had no idea of the distance involved. For six months they marched (or climbed, or limped, or crawled) an incredible 1,500 miles, almost to the Great Salt Lake in Utah. By then they were lost. Facing the prospect of winter in the mountains, Escalante turned south again, reaching the Grand Canyon, looking for a ford where they could cross the Colorado River. By the end of the year, they made their way back to Albuquerque and up the Rio Grande to their starting point. They still didn't know—nobody knew—the extent or geography of the west.

1795

Of more immediate importance to President Washington was the northern boundary dispute. From Canadian posts along the Great Lakes, Britain and its Indian allies continued to threaten American settlers and block American trade. This issue was finally settled by the treaty John Jay brought back from London: British troops would be evacuated within two years, and the actual border between the United States and Canada would be drawn by a joint commission. But the rest of Jay's treaty was a political disaster.

Britain and Spain were at war with revolutionary France. Washington was determined to keep America out of a European conflict. Of course, in proclaiming American neutrality, he was well aware of his country's debt to its French allies; in the final victory at Yorktown, the number of French troops had exceeded the size of his own army. He had an obligation to France that he was unlikely to forget, as well as treaties he could not ignore.But Washington could not afford an open break with Britain because the old enemy was now America's best customer. In the first years of independence, American exports had grown by 250 percent, and most of those exports went to British markets. Furthermore, most of those exported goods were produced by northern men of business, the Federalists who supported his administration.

Although Jay's treaty imposed humiliating conditions and restrictions on American trade, Federalists decided it was the best they could get. Republicans reacted with a firestorm of protest, and rejected every line. Small farmers, mechanics, and shopkeepers, all of whom supported France in its revolutionary struggle, saw the treaty as a betrayal of that great cause and took to the streets. Angry mobs surrounded the President's residence in Philadelphia; there were cries for his impeachment. In Boston, Charleston, and Richmond, crude posters were pasted up, circulars passed from hand to hand. A cartoon showed Washington under the guillotine. When Hamilton tried to speak to a huge crowd in New York, he was pelted with rocks and left the platform with a bloody head.

While this frenzy spread up and down the Atlantic states, America scored a diplomatic victory in Madrid. A new treaty with Spain won free access to the Mississippi River and free shipping through the port of New Orleans; a southern border was fixed between Georgia and the Floridas; both countries agreed to restrain their Indian allies, bringing a measure of peace to the territory. But this treaty was overlooked while the Jay treaty fed the country's anger and political appetite.

1796

Also overlooked was the rapid growth and general prosperity of the United States. Before retiring from the Cabinet in 1795, Hamilton had given the Senate an encouraging report on the nation's financial situation and prospects for retiring the national debt. He added that citizens were always concerned about national debt, which "if not excessive, will be to us a national blessing." In any case, citizens opposed taxes to pay it off.

Ten years earlier, federal land was auctioned at a starting price of $1 an acre for sections of 640 acres. Much western territory had been bought up by speculators when war-poor eastern farmers didn't have $640 in ready cash to buy a 640-acre section. Now quarter sections were offered for $2 an acre. Ninety percent of the population made a living from agriculture, so the bidding was lively. After Anthony Wayne's Greenville Treaty with the Indians, 30,000 settlers a year were pushing across the Allegheny Mountains to take up the rich farmlands of the Ohio valley. In June, Tennessee was admitted to the Union.

America was supporting education on a scale the world had never seen. For the last 150 years, public and private schools had provided elementary and secondary education in many communities. The Land Grant Act of 1785 had set aside one section in each township to support public schools. Noah Webster's speller and reader were bestsellers. There were pauper schools in Maryland, and Quaker schools for black children in Pennsylvania. Jefferson wanted a system free to all children everywhere. Ten states offered college education, and now Washington proposed his personal endowment for a national university where young men from every part of the country could learn together in the new capital city.

For a million dollars, America bought peace in the Mediterranean. Barbary pirates had infested those waters for centuries, but now the United States paid an Algerian ruler to permit the passage of American ships. This bribe was not a source of national pride, but it freed American sailors held as captive slaves and enlarged Mediterranean commerce. And it was cheaper than a war.

Independence also brought the growth of a vigorous free press. Approaching an election year, American journalism was not only vigorous but violent. The Jay Treaty had been ratified by the Senate, but now debate began in the House. Federalist and Republican newspapers energetically took sides and added to the national uproar.

The Treaty eventually became law, but not before George Washington, the father of his country and formerly the idol of his countrymen, had been the target of bitter Republican abuse, accused by the papers of every crime a president could commit, a traitor and a tyrant, who should be "hurled from his throne." Old comrades in his Cabinet had all departed, Knox, Jefferson, Hamilton—they were replaced by lesser men, some competent, some conspiratorial. If he had ever considered a third term (and many Federalists were still urging him to run), he now refused to accept nomination.

The presidency was open for the first time to party politics. The Federalists chose John Adams as their candidate and wanted Thomas Pinckney, who had negotiated the successful treaty with Spain, as Vice-President. The Republicans named Thomas Jefferson and Aaron Burr, the powerful boss of politics in New York. In September, Washington delivered his Farewell Address, eloquent advice to his beloved America, scarcely heard in the furor of campaigning.

Under the electoral system, ballots could be cast for any of these men for either office, and Hamilton urged Federalist electors to give equal support to Adams and Pinckney. He privately hoped that Pinckney would be President, but he was determined to defeat Jefferson. His strategy backfired. By a margin of only three votes, Adams was elected President, and Jefferson became Vice-President. It was the only time in history that a President and Vice-President were chosen from opposite parties.

As Washington prepared to leave office, the Republican press cheered his departure. Benjamin Franklin Bache (yes, the grandson of the great Founder) was the editor who wrote, "If ever a nation was debauched by a man, the American Nation has been debauched by Washington. If ever a nation has suffered from the improper influence of a man, the American Nation has suffered from the improper influence of Washington. If ever a nation was deceived by a man, the American Nation was deceived by Washington ... This day ought to be a JUBILEE ..." Bache's famous grandfather had died six years earlier, and didn't have to read this abuse of his old friend.

But George and Martha Washington packed up—not forgetting the dog and the parrot—and after a great public dinner in their honor they left Philadelphia for Mount Vernon, never to return.

1797

John Adams

John Adams was an American patriot of superior intelligence and total integrity. Unfortunately, he didn't have much personal enthusiasm for democracy. He regarded the presidency as a sort of non-hereditary monarchy; as president, he was an elected king. He worried terribly about the cost of the office: $2,700 to rent a house in Philadelphia (the White House in the new Capital was still under construction); untold expense to furnish it; wages for secretaries and servants; and $2,500 for a new carriage and horses! It pained his purse and his New England conscience, but he did his best to meet his royal obligations. Behind his back, even the staunchest members of his Federalist party referred to President Adams as "His Rotundity."

The country was still arguing about the Jay Treaty. France was now governed by the Directory, a committee named to clean up after the French Revolution. The Directory read the treaty between England and America as an insult, and a violation of French-American agreements. When Adams sent a new ambassador to Paris, the Directory rejected him and ordered the seizure of more than 300 American merchant ships.

Still hoping to maintain neutrality and peace, President Adams appointed a three-man delegation to resolve the dangerous situation. The Americans were astounded when French negotiators (identified only as Messieurs X, Y, and Z) reduced the discussion to cold cash. They demanded a loan of $12 million to the Directory government, and a bribe of $250,000 to Charles Maurice Talleyrand, the French foreign minister. Adams reported this outrage to Congress, and its Federalist majority rose up in righteous indignation.

1798

Across the country, Americans were defiant. "Millions for defense, and not one cent for tribute!" became the rallying cry. The navy launched three new frigates—the United States, the Constellation, and the Constitution (later known proudly as Old Ironsides)—and soon found itself fighting an undeclared war at sea.

Vice-President Thomas Jefferson and his Republican party blamed the Federalists for this strife. The Jay Treaty, they said, had betrayed and provoked the French; the possibility of open war with our former revolutionary allies was unthinkable. Nevertheless, America continued to prepare for full-scale hostilities. George Washington was confirmed as Commander-in-Chief of the army, should he be needed again for a land war. Alexander Hamilton wanted the job and did everything in his power to get it. His schemes divided the Federalist party and weakened President Adams.

When Republican attacks on their policy became too violent, the Federalists moved to gag their critics. In quick succession, Congress passed four controversial laws. The first three dealt with aliens living in the United

States—French refugees and, of even more concern, wild Irish immigrants who were anti-British and joined the Republican furor. The Alien Acts gave the president the right to imprison or expel any foreigner suspected of secret plotting against the government. The Sedition Act provided fines and prison sentences for anybody who wrote or distributed "false, scandalous, or malicious" material about the government. This was political hardball. Benjamin Franklin Bache was arrested, and a loud-mouthed Republican Congressman from Vermont got a $1,000 fine and four months in jail. Political debate, in the press and in corner saloons, cooled down.

But other fevers persisted. Yellow fever struck again in coastal cities. In New York and Philadelphia, citizens dropped while doctors debated remedies. War fever, on the other hand, made some people rich.

Young Eli Whitney went broke in the cotton gin business, but now he saw another opportunity, and wrote a cocky letter to the secretary of the treasury. If the government was buying guns, he wanted an order for "Ten or Fifteen Thousand Stand of Arms." No matter that he had never manufactured that quantity of anything, let alone guns; he got the order and a $5,000 advance. He developed molds, milling machines, and other machine tools to produce interchangeable parts. He could, therefore, assemble muskets more efficiently than the most skilled gunsmiths. In his New Haven factory, Eli Whitney perfected methods of mass production that were quickly and widely adopted, and new patent laws protected him. He had created the cotton empire of the south, and now he helped build the industrial power of New England, the two Americas that would confront each other a half century later.

At the end of the year, Thomas Jefferson resigned the office of Vice-President and returned to his beloved Monticello. With James Madison, Jefferson worked on a series of resolutions that would also foreshadow future confrontations. They were determined to defeat the Alien and Sedition Acts by asserting the principle of states' rights against the abuse of federal authority. Jefferson worked through the legislature in Kentucky; Madison's resolution was introduced in Virginia. Both insisted on the fundamental right of "nullification"—within its own borders, any state could declare a federal law null and void, and ignore it. Both resolutions passed, but Jefferson was bitterly disappointed when those states were denounced by the rest of the Union. He began talking about secession, and only Madison's wise counsel calmed him down.

President Adams left Philadelphia to care for his sick wife at home in Massachusetts. Alexander Hamilton, still dreaming of battlefield glory, was quite willing to take charge of the government as well as the army. He encouraged the military buildup, hoping to lead a force that could not only whip France and, if necessary, the English, but oust Spain from Florida and Louisiana. He even thought "we ought to take a squint at South America." But America's warlike temper waned as taxes for defense spending went up. In the end, it was not an American statesman who settled the standoff with France, but Napoleon Bonaparte, who took power in Paris when the Directory collapsed.

Another era ended in the United States. In December, George Washington fell ill, and his doctors could offer no treatment except to bleed him to death. On the day after Christmas, huge silent crowds followed a funeral procession through the streets of Philadelphia, but the coffin was empty. Washington had been buried in Georgetown, in his native Virginia soil. The head of the family was gone.

THE NINETEENTH CENTURY

In 1800, the federal government moved from the comforts of Philadelphia to the raw new city of Washington, the capital envisioned almost ten years earlier.

The Constitution provided for a federal District, not to exceed ten square miles, to become "the Seat of the Government of the United States"; the Constitution did not specify a location. Many cities vied for this honor, and the financial benefits it was expected to produce. But in the end, it was President Washington who chose a stretch of property along the Potomac River, most of it in the State of Maryland, the rest in Virginia. He appointed three commissioners and a surveyor to establish exact boundaries for the new District. Then he hired a young French engineer, Major Pierre Charles L'Enfant, to plan an urban site, the actual city where government offices would be constructed. It is to L'Enfant that we owe the grand concept, the boulevard connecting the Executive Mansion and the Capitol building[1], around which the other imposing federal buildings would converge. But when L'Enfant quarreled with commissioners, Washington had to fire him—a hard decision, since the young Frenchman was a veteran of the Revolutionary War.

Then Washington turned to his next task: persuading private landowners within the soon-to-be District of Columbia to sell at a price the government could afford. Eventually, ten square miles were purchased for $25 an acre. The private owners kept half the lots, and the rest of the real estate belonged to the government. Congress hoped that the sale of property for homes and shops would finance construction of splendid government offices and broad boulevards. As it turned out, there wasn't much demand for swampy lots along the Potomac River. Maryland and Virginia advanced $190,000 to get the project started.

The land was surveyed again by Benjamin Banneker, a black mathematician and astronomer, publisher of a popular almanac. Architects were invited to submit designs for the Capitol building, where the Senate and the House of Representatives would meet.1 Dr. William Thornton, an amateur architect, won the competition, and President Washington laid the cornerstone in 1793. In 1800, it was far from finished. The Executive Mansion, which people would soon call the White House, was designed by James Hoban, a recently arrived Irishman. It was also unfinished when President Adams and his wife moved in. Abigail Adams hung out the family wash in its empty rooms.

The rest of the village, home to 2,464 free citizens and 623 slaves, was a sea of mud. Workmen came and went; carpenters,

[1] The City is our CapitAL; the building is our CapitOL

78

masons, wagoneers, ditch diggers, all sweated and swore in the hot, humid weather. And 137 members of Congress arrived to take up the nation's business.

1800

But first there was politics, because this was an election year. John Adams confidently expected to be re-elected, but his Federalist party was divided by the long wrangle about foreign affairs. Adams worked to keep the country out of war, while Alexander Hamilton saw the chance of war as an opportunity for American expansion.

The Constitution provided for election of a President and Vice-President. Electors from each state would cast two ballots: The man with the most electoral votes (regardless of the popular vote) would be President, with the runner up as Vice-President. The Democratic-Republican party nominated Thomas Jefferson and Aaron Burr, and they won. John Adams and the Federalists were defeated.

But it wasn't over yet, because both Jefferson and Burr got the same number of electoral votes. According to the Constitution, the House of Representatives would have to decide which man would be President.

1801

Thomas Jefferson

In February in the new Capitol building, the voting began. A vote was taken every hour, and at midnight, after nineteen ballots, there was still no winner. Representatives began to fall asleep in their seats, but voting went on until 8 A.M., when the House adjourned. At noon they began again.

Hamilton and Jefferson were on opposite sides of the political fence and had debated hotly for many years. But Hamilton respected Jefferson. He hated and feared Aaron Burr, a New York lawyer and a man very like Hamilton himself. They both had a taste for pretty women and political scheming; they were both brilliant, brave, and ambitious; they both craved fame and power. Now Hamilton used all his influence to change votes and keep

Burr out of the White House.

After three days, on the thirty-sixth ballot, Thomas Jefferson was named President of the United States, with Aaron Burr as his Vice-President. (And after that experience, everybody knew that the system had to be changed. Congress went to work on an amendment to the Constitution, which was ratified in 1804 requiring electors to vote separately for the top offices.

As he neared the end of his term, John Adams also sat late into the night, signing appointments for new federal judges, including John Marshall to be Chief Justice of the Supreme Court. Then John Adams left town. He didn't stay for Jefferson's inauguration. In fact, he didn't speak to Thomas Jefferson again for twelve years. He turned his back on the Capital and went home to retirement in Massachusetts.

The new President quickly took charge of an administration that reflected his commitment to states' rights and the rights of ordinary citizens. Jefferson changed tax laws; he encouraged agriculture and the settlement of new land; he cut the cost of government and tried to pay off the national debt. Internationally, he sent ships and Marines to North Africa to put an end to attacks on American shipping by Barbary pirates. This led to a small war with Tripoli, now almost forgotten except in the Marine Hymn.

1803

The great achievement of Jefferson's first term was the Louisiana Purchase.

Big chunks of North America had changed hands during 200 years of European wars. Vast lands which no Europeans had ever seen, much less explored and mapped, were passed around the table when peace treaties were signed. Now Spain lost American territory to Napoleon, and Jefferson saw a threat to American interests. He first sent an envoy to Paris with an offer to buy New Orleans. When that failed, he hinted at a new American alliance with England, to oppose Napoleon's plans for further conquests. The last thing Napoleon wanted was an Anglo-American alliance, and the first thing he wanted, always, was money for his armies and his next campaign. He suddenly agreed to sell not only New Orleans, but the whole Louisiana Territory.

Neither Jefferson nor Napoleon, nor anybody else, knew the exact extent of that unmapped wilderness, but east to west it stretched from the Mississippi to the Rocky Mountains, and south from Canada to the Gulf of Mexico. James Monroe and Robert Livingston, the American negotiators in Paris, signed the agreement without any further consultation with their government. It cost about $15 million to double the size of the country. From that territory would someday be created the states of Louisiana, Mississippi, Missouri, Arkansas, Iowa, North Dakota, South Dakota, Nebraska—and most of Kansas, Colorado, Wyoming, Montana, and Minnesota.

Jefferson organized an exploration. It would be led by his private secretary, Meriwether Lewis, a Virginian who fought in the Revolution. As co-captain, Lewis recruited William Clark, the younger brother of George Rogers Clark and a veteran Indian fighter. Jefferson gave them lengthy instructions. They were to explore the Missouri River and its tributaries, looking for a direct water route to the Pacific. They would also count and study the Indian population, and record information about the soils, plants, animals, minerals, climate—and volcanoes, if any.

In December, 1803, they left St. Louis with a party of forty men, including fourteen United States soldiers, two French guides, and Clark's sturdy black servant, York. They paddled up the Mississippi in three boats loaded with weapons, supplies, and goods to trade with the Indians. At the mouth of the Missouri, they were stopped by Spanish officials who had not yet heard about the Louisiana

Purchase, and there they spent the winter.

1804

By the following winter Lewis and Clark reached the middle of what is now North Dakota, where they built Fort Mandan. They were joined by Toussaint Charbonneau, a French trapper, his young Shoshone wife, Sacagawea, and her child. They hoped the young woman would act as their interpreter. Then they pushed on.

They crossed the Rocky Mountains, the Bitterroot Range, the Cascades. They learned that there was no water route to the Pacific. Where there were no rivers, they rode horses; after they ate the horses, they walked. Finally they followed the Columbia River until they reached the ocean. Then they turned back and crossed the mountains and prairies again. They met thousands of native Americans, speaking hundreds of languages unknown even to Sacagawea. There was only one hostile encounter, and the expedition lost only one man, to illness. They brought back careful records full of scientific information. They returned to St. Louis in September, 1806, having been gone two and a half years and having traveled 8,000 miles. It was the grandest adventure in American history.

The saddest event in Jefferson's first term took place in New Jersey. Aaron Burr, too, found the Vice-Presidency an "insignificant office." At home in New York, he had real political power. In Washington he was given little work, responsibility, or respect. He brooded over the election, how Alexander Hamilton kept him out of the White House. When Jefferson did not ask him to run again, Burr decided to seek the governorship of New York. Once more Hamilton worked hard to defeat him, and once again Burr lost. Even after the campaign, Hamilton kept up his political attacks. Overcome with rage and bitterness, Burr challenged Hamilton to a duel.

On a midsummer day they met in a field outside of Weehawken, New Jersey.

Hamilton fired into the air; Burr took careful aim and pulled the trigger; Hamilton was fatally wounded. While the country mourned the death of the brilliant young Hamilton, Burr laid low. The man who was almost president became a fugitive. But when the scandal passed, Burr returned to politics, plots, and crazy schemes at home and abroad.

Meanwhile, the State of Ohio was admitted to the Union (1803), and Thomas Jefferson was re-elected. New England Federalists campaigned furiously against him—that Louisiana Territory wilderness "probably might have been acquired much more cheaply"—but Jefferson won by a huge majority of electoral votes.

1806

Congress authorized a National Road, using much of the old Cumberland Trail, extending 800 miles from Baltimore, Maryland, into what would later become the state of Illinois. Construction didn't begin until 1811, and the road wouldn't reach Vandalia, Illinois for almost forty years. But it was a good road, and you can still follow it on United States Route 40.

1807

Most roads were built by private companies, and travelers paid to use them. But they could-n't handle the increasing freight traffic as America grew. River boats were the cheapest way to transport people and goods, so canals were built to connect rivers. And American inventors tried to improve on British efforts to construct steam engines and steam-powered boats.

Robert Fulton was born in Pennsylvania but went to England to study painting. He soon became interested in mechanical design. He built some small machines and won some patents before he began to think about water transport. In Paris, he developed a submarine, which didn't inter-est Napoleon but got the attention of Robert Livingston, who still represented the

American government in France. Livingston commissioned a steamboat, which Fulton demonstrated in trial runs on the Seine. Then Fulton returned to America and built the Clermont, a steam-powered paddleboat that made the Hudson River run between New York and Albany, 150 miles, in thirty-two hours. With Livingston as a partner, Fulton got a twenty-one-year monopoly on steamboats in New York, and another contract for the lower Mississippi. The "fast" new boats led to a tremendous increase in river traffic. As freight rates and passenger tickets became cheaper, New York and New Orleans became world ports. The Clermont was not the first steamboat, but it was the first that paid its owners a profit, and that, after all, was the point.

Jefferson was also concerned with commerce, but his problem was the ongoing war between England and France. Napoleon had conquered Europe, put most of his relatives on European thrones, and crowned himself Emperor of the French. But England still ruled the seas, and they declared a blockade that kept American goods out of European markets.

Both sides harassed American shipping, seized cargoes, and captured American sailors, who were forced to serve on their vessels. In 1807, a British man-of-war fired on an American frigate, killing three seamen and wounding eighteen others. After that outrage, Congress passed the Embargo Act, banning all trade with the combatants and closing American ports to foreign ships. Of course, the act was ignored by smugglers, but most trade was cut off, and thousands of Americans in cities along the eastern coast were thrown out of work. Nevertheless, Jefferson managed to keep the embargo in force for fifteen months, maintaining American neutrality as long as possible.

1808

On January 1, a new law took effect, banning the importation of slaves into the United

James Madison

States. There were now more than a million slaves in America, and during the next half century, a quarter of a million Africans would be imported illegally while the slave population more than tripled.

Though Jefferson's friends urged him to run again, he would not break with Washington's two-term example. He hand-picked James Madison, his neighbor, friend, and lifelong political ally as the next presidential candidate of the Democratic-Republican party. Madison was easily elected, and Jefferson went home to Monticello, freed from "the shackles of power."

1811

The great Shawnee chief, Tecumseh, was in his late twenties when he refused to sign the treaty that ended Little Turtle's war. No person or tribe, he argued, could give away land that belonged to all native Americans. He spent the next fifteen years traveling, urging Indians to set aside tribal differences and disputes and stand together against the white man's greed. He was joined by his brother, Tenskwatawa, The Prophet. They founded the town of Tippecanoe, near where that river joins the Wabash in Indiana territory, a place where all Indians could meet peaceably, and organize.

Tecumseh was away on another visit to southern tribes when William Henry Harrison, governor of the territory, arrived with a thousand militiamen. The Prophet assured his warriors that spiritual powers would protect them, and they attacked under cover of night and rain. The casualties were about equal on both sides, but Harrison declared victory and burned the Indian village to the ground.

1812

Louisiana joined the Union.

In June, Americans declared war on Great Britain, the War of 1812. President James Madison tried to follow Jefferson's foreign policy and stay out of the European conflict, but war fever was rising in the United States. Young Republican-Democrats, newly elected to Congress, pushed the president toward a decision. They were called the War Hawks: Henry Clay and Richard Johnson of Kentucky; John Calhoun of South Carolina; Felix Grundy of Tennessee; Peter Porter of New York. They wanted expansion along the western frontier, where British forts guarded the fur trade against American settlement. They clamored for a war which would annex Canada. They were ready to push Spain into the ocean and claim Spanish Florida.

In November, James Madison was re-elected with the overwhelming support of southern and new western states, though Federalists protested the "Virginia Dynasty."

1813

Early American victories by our infant navy cheered the War Hawks, who continued to shout for "Canada, Canada, Canada!" But three attempts to invade that country failed. Tecumseh became a brigadier general in the British army, and led some of the forces that captured Detroit.

Commodore Oliver Hazard Perry commanded the fleet of ten ships that defeated the British in the battle of Lake Erie. General William Henry Harrison was preparing another invasion of Canada when he got Perry's famous message, "We have met the enemy and they are ours." Not to be outdone, Harrison beat British and Indian troops in Ontario, at the Battle of the Thames. In that fighting, Tecumseh was killed by Richard Johnson, one of the War Hawks who actually fought in the war.

1814

In August, fifty British ships entered the Potomac and 4,000 British soldiers marched on Washington, D.C. It was defended only by untrained militia, who put up a brief resistance and then ran away. President Madison and his wife escaped before the British occupied the city and burned the White House and other official buildings (as Americans had burned provincial government buildings in Canada).

Then the British marched to Baltimore and Fort McHenry. Francis Scott Key was a young American lawyer, detained on a British ship during the fierce bombardment of the fort. He watched as the Americans stood off the invaders and kept their flag flying. When he was released the next day he went back to his hotel and wrote a poem describing the battle. In 1931, "The Star-Spangled Banner" became our national anthem.

The war reached a stalemate. On Christmas Eve, America and England signed a peace treaty.

1815

Even while the diplomats were meeting in Europe, another meeting was going on in Hartford, Connecticut. Federalist businessmen had strongly opposed Mr. Jefferson's embargo and Mr. Madison's war. Now, delegates assembled from Connecticut, Massachusetts, New Hampshire, Rhode Island, and Vermont, and there was talk of leaving the Union. Secession. They calmed down enough to write a set of Resolutions, protesting taxes, insisting on new rules for the admission of new states, opposing interference with trade and commerce, and limiting the government's right to declare war. They also wanted to prohibit the election of successive presidents from the same state—no more Virginia Dynasties!

At the same time, Andrew Jackson was winning a smashing victory at the Battle of New Orleans. In just half an hour, the British had more than 2,000 dead and wounded, while Jackson lost just sixteen men. Report of this triumph reached the Capital, and was followed by news of the peace treaty. So the Hartford Resolutions arrived amid a frenzy of national pride and celebration. Mr. Madison won his war, and nobody was interested in Federalist politics or secession talk.

1816

Madison's choice for the presidency was his fellow Virginian and old friend, James Monroe. Even within his own party, there was

James Monroe

discontent with the Virginia Dynasty, but Monroe had served as Senator, minister to France, governor of Virginia, and Secretary of state under Madison. He became the candidate of the Democratic-Republicans and was elected.

The only excitement was provided by Henry Clay, the ardent War Hawk, now Speaker of the House of Representatives. He expected to be named as Monroe's Secretary of State, an office regarded as the stepping-stone to the White House. When Monroe passed him over for John Quincy Adams, Clay was so mad that he refused to let the inauguration be held, as usual, in the House. So for the first time, a President was inaugurated in the open air, before a crowd of enthusiastic citizens.

Indiana was admitted to the Union.

The final defeat of Napoleon brought an end to the wars between France and England, ending the foreign policy disputes that dominated American politics for twenty years. Americans could turn their own attention to their own growing and prosperous country.

1817   Mississippi was admitted to the Union.

1818   Illinois was admitted to the Union.

1819   Alabama was admitted to the Union.

Spanish claims on the North American continent had extended from Florida to New Orleans, north to St. Louis, and west by way of Santa Fe to San Francisco. Pieces of New Spain had been traded to or taken by France and England, and taken back, half a dozen times. As Secretary of State, John Quincy Adams bought Florida for $5 million, signing a treaty that established the boundary between New Spain and the Louisiana Purchase territory all the way to the Pacific Ocean.

1820   There were now twenty-two American states. In half of them, slavery was permitted, and in the other half, slavery was banned. When Missouri applied for admission to the Union as a slave state, it set off months of bitter Congressional debate. Did Congress have the right to prohibit slavery in a new state? Or did new states have the same rights granted to existing states, the right to choose?

Henry Clay negotiated a compromise. The eastern part of Massachusetts had decided to break away, and asked for admission as the new state of Maine. The deadlock in Congress was decided by admitting Missouri as a slave state and Maine as a free state, thus preserving the balance in the Union. But in the Louisiana Purchase territory, west of the Mississippi River, there would be no more slavery north of Missouri. Thus, for the moment, the Missouri Compromise avoided the basic question: did any human being, anywhere, have the right to own another human being?

Three quarters of the people living in the southern states never owned slaves. But most of them defended the institution of slavery and were stubborn in their insistence on states' rights. Southerners who saw the crime of slavery began to leave. Quakers from the Carolinas moved north, into free territory. James Madison's former secretary took his slaves with him into Illinois, set them free, and gave each black family a 160-acre farm. A Kentucky owner went to Indiana, giving $50 to blacks who chose to stay behind and taking the rest with him to start new lives.

There were now more than 300,000 free blacks in America, but many people who opposed slavery still could not see a way to integrate blacks into the white population. Britain had established a base at Freetown, on the west African coast, to be a haven for Africans rescued from slave traders, and a new home for freed or free-born blacks who chose to settle there. In 1820, eighty-six American black men and women decided to make the trip. So the American Colonization Society began to raise money for a similar project. The

Society had a long list of distinguished members, and many were no doubt well-intentioned people. Two years later they founded the African colony of Liberia, with a capital "city" named Monrovia, in honor of the president. But not many African-Americans were eager to return to a continent and a life they no longer remembered. For better or worse, free black people would try to make their way in the United States. Two million blacks were still held in hopeless slavery.

Meanwhile, in what came to be known as an "Era of Good Feelings," James Monroe was re-elected. The Federalist party didn't even bother to run a candidate against him, and he received all but one electoral vote.

1823

Inspired by the revolutions in America and France, and by great leaders like Simon Bolivar, some Spanish colonies in South America made their own revolutions. They declared themselves to be free and independent countries, and they were recognized by the United States. Soon President Monroe heard of European plans to reclaim lost colonies, and of a Russian scheme to move down the Pacific coast from Alaska, into the Oregon territory.

He issued a strong statement. America would not permit "any portion of this hemisphere" to be seized again by any foreign government. America would not interfere with existing colonial arrangements, but independence was independence, and America would defend it. This Monroe Doctrine was, and continued to be, the most important foreign policy statement ever made by an American president.

1824

The federal government got most of its revenue from taxes on foreign goods shipped into the country. The issue of these tariffs, what products got taxed and how much, was of great regional importance and angry Congressional debate. Tariffs helped some businesses, like new textile factories, but hurt others, like shipbuilding. The American Revolution had been ignited by similar British taxes. Once again Henry Clay stepped in to negotiate. He proposed The American System, under which the government would impose high tariffs to protect infant American industries, but government would spend that revenue on internal improvements for the country. Roads and canals and so on would benefit every state and promote national development. Did the Constitution permit the federal government to manage commerce in such a way? Clay was able to convince the Congress, and once more a sectional argument was compromised—temporarily.

There were political repercussions. The Democratic-Republican party had dominated elections for more than twenty-five years, and a powerful group in Congress, the party caucus, chose its candidates. Now the Federalist party was finished, and the Democratic-Republicans split into rival factions, reflecting different interests. They offered the voters four candidates.

General Andrew Jackson, hero of the Battle of New Orleans, got the largest number of popular votes, followed by John Quincy Adams and Henry Clay. William Crawford, the caucus candidate, ran last. This is the first election for which the popular vote count is known, but none of the candidates had a majority of electoral votes. So once more an election had to be decided in the House of Representatives, where each state had one vote. Henry Clay used his great powers to elect Adams. When Adams named Clay as his Secretary of State, there were loud charges of corruption, a political deal. Jackson voters were infuriated, and General Jackson was coldly determined to whip Adams and Clay when he got another chance.

1825

As the oldest son of John Adams, John Quincy was probably the best prepared man ever to

John Quincy Adams

reach the White House. He was eleven years old in 1776, so he grew up with the country, traveled with his father on foreign missions, saw the presidency from the inside during his father's administration, and went on to his own career as a Senator, diplomat, and Secretary of State. Like Clay, he strongly favored government spending for national development. He called for a national university and federal support for scientific research. He extended the National Road, and wanted money for more roads, canals, and national investment. Like his father, John Quincy was logical, energetic, and politically courageous, but he could never charm the public, or the Congress.

State money built the Erie Canal. Governor DeWitt Clinton pushed his New York legislators to complete a water route between Albany, on the Hudson River, and Buffalo, on Lake Erie. He raised $7 million with state lotteries and taxes on steamboat travel. It was the largest engineering project ever undertaken by any government, anywhere. The canal trip took five days to cover 363 miles, but it was the fastest way to ship cargo, and lowered shipping costs by 90 percent. It made New York City the biggest port on the east coast. Suddenly every state saw the importance of internal improvements.

1826

On the Fourth of July, the President's father, John Adams, aged ninety-one, died in Massachusetts, and Thomas Jefferson, aged eighty-three, passed away in Virginia. They had an early friendship, broken by years of enmity, renewed in a long correspondence. Their letters shared memories and exchanged opinions about the progress of the country they founded. And maybe on the fiftieth anniversary of the Republic, their old hearts simply burst with pride in that accomplishment.

1828

So the era of the Cocked Hats was over. New

Andrew Jackson

winds from the west blew through the country. The old Democratic-Republican party divided into two hostile camps, with Adams and Clay leading a new National Republican party, and the Jackson people beginning to call themselves Democrats. Their campaign started even before Adams took office, and it was a dirty campaign. The pro-Jackson people ridiculed the President; the pro-Adams organizers denounced Jackson as a bloodthirsty savage.

Andrew Jackson was the son of Irish immigrants, born poor in South Carolina. At thirteen, he fought in the Revolution and survived to educate himself and study law. He moved to Tennessee and made money speculating in land, acquiring slaves and a large estate. He gained a military reputation fighting Indians and went into politics. He had dueling scars. In short, he was a frontiersman, with all the strengths and faults of that world, and voters loved Old Hickory, the hero of New Orleans.

The political system, too, was changing. In former times, each state made its own rules for choosing members of the Electoral College; in most, Electors were named by state legislatures. Now, in all but two states, the names of Electors appeared on the ballot with the names of the candidates, and therefore represented the popular vote. This reduced the chance that a man could lose in the general election but win by the votes of Electors, as Adams had done four years earlier.

Jackson was swept into office, and his inauguration turned into a mob scene. Thousands of people, young and old, rich and poor, stampeded through the White House, grinding mud into the carpets, breaking furniture and windows and china, eating and drinking everything in sight. Women fainted and men fought on the White House lawn, but everybody stayed to consume the punch that was brought out in buckets. Democracy had arrived.

One of President Jackson's first acts was to find government jobs for political allies. They stood by the old saying, "to the victors belong the spoils," and brought "the spoils system" into the American political vocabulary. It reflected Jackson's loyalty to friends, his suspicion of opponents, and his determination to run the country. John Calhoun, the Vice-President, was a friend. They both had roots in South Carolina and shared many southern prejudices and values. But a quarrel developed (begun by, of all things, a social squabble about Cabinet wives), and got worse when South Carolina once more brought up the issue of nullification.

1830

Henry Clay had pushed through the highest tariffs in the nation's history, and South Carolina declared the right to nullify the tax. They wouldn't pay it, and they wouldn't let federal officials collect it. The question of states' rights had been raised many times before, in many parts of the country. It was a fundamental question which the Constitution did not answer: What was the relationship between the states and the federal government? Where did the ultimate power lie? Now the issue was debated in some of the greatest speeches ever delivered on the floor of the Senate.

There was no doubt where President Jackson stood. He was an unwavering defender of the Union, and all the powers of the central government. He was ready to lead 35,000 troops into South Carolina, and to hang Vice President Calhoun. Calhoun chose to resign and return to the Senate, where he became a powerful voice for states' rights and the South. Henry Clay, the Great Pacificator (we might say, deal-maker) worked out a compromise on the tariff, and South Carolina withdrew its ordinance of nullification.

1831

His name was Turner because he was born a slave on the Turner plantation. Later, Nat

Turner was sold to Joseph Travis, and in his twenties he began to have visions. He saw black and white angels struggling in a red sky. Divine voices spoke to him and inspired his preaching in the slave cabins. Without any formal education, Nat could read and write a bit, and his powerful religious convictions made him a natural leader. There was only one way for slaves to win the freedom that Nat Turner saw in his visions.

In August, 1831, a few desperate blacks followed him in rebellion. They murdered the master and his family, and raged through the Virginia countryside, growing in numbers until about eighty blacks had joined the uprising. In days of frenzy, they killed fifty-seven white men, women, and children. It was the bloodiest revolt in the history of American slavery, but it was put down within a week. The militia captured most of Turner's band, and Nat was finally taken in October and hung in November.

The predictable response in the South was panic. There had been other slave plots, but nothing to compare with Nat Turner's Rebellion. Innocent blacks suffered white revenge; white northerners were attacked on the streets; abolitionist newspapers were banned and debate on slavery was gagged, even in the country's Capital. Slave laws in the South were made harsher, but the federal government could not yet deal with the issue.

1832

Though Andrew Jackson upheld the national government, he would not tolerate government that gave rich men too much power over the lives of ordinary citizens. The Bank of the United States was a private corporation that held a monopoly on government funds and made huge profits on its transactions at home and abroad. Nicholas Biddle of Philadelphia, president of the bank, boasted that he had been for years "in the daily exercise of more personal authority than any president." In 1832, he applied for a new federal charter, which would extend the bank's monopoly for another fifteen years.

Congress granted the charter, and Jackson vetoed it. Nicholas Biddle and his rich friends—including many politicians on the bank's payroll—began to spend thousands of dollars to defeat Jackson at the next election. Jackson wrote to Martin Van Buren, his new choice for the vice-presidency, "The bank, Mr. Van Buren, is trying to kill me, but I will kill it." And he did.

Jackson took his case to the country and was re-elected by an even greater majority. Then he began withdrawing government money from the bank, depositing it in state banks where he thought it would help his people, "the humble members of society—the farmers, mechanics, laborers —."

Who were these people, and where were they?

The census of 1830 counted 12,860,702 Americans living in a country of 1,787,880 square miles. The country had more than doubled its size in the fifty years since Independence.

As the frontier moved across the midwest toward the Mississippi, most frontier families lived very much as the first settlers had lived. The land was heavily wooded. After a farmer staked his claim, the trees had to be chopped down and stumps burned or pulled out by teams of mules or oxen, before he could get a plow into the ground. Woodlands gave way to prairies, even harder to break and cultivate. The settler's plow was made of wood, like everything else he owned—his cabin, wagon, tools, buckets, bowls, plates. The only metal objects he owned were axe blades and cooking kettles, perhaps a few precious handmade nails, and his gun. His wife spun and wove cloth for their clothing, sheets, blankets. If their cabin was near a creek or river, they hauled water; otherwise they dug a well, and collected rain water in a cistern. On rare trips to town, they bought sugar, salt, flour, boots, harness, a new axe blade. Sometimes a peddler came down the trail with longed-for city goods and news.

But in the next decade, all that would change, due to the astonishing ingenuity of American inventors. Jethro Wood had invented a cast iron plow, now John Lane made a steel plow, and a blacksmith named John Deere improved it. Steel plows cut through virgin soils much more easily than wood, or wood and iron, and could be pulled by horses, instead of oxen. Deere set up his works in Moline, Illinois, and was soon making hundreds, then thousands of plows a year. Obed Hussey and Cyrus McCormick patented their reapers. Hiram and John Pilt developed a thresher. And in quick order came harrows, planters, seed drills, all vastly reducing farm labor and increasing productivity. Now American farmers had crops to sell, hauled by horse and wagon, or shipped by river or canal to more distant markets.

The Baltimore and Ohio (B&O) railroad was organized, laying down thirteen miles of track between Baltimore and Endicott's Mills. Cars pulled by teams of horses carried freight and passengers, until Peter Cooper built a steam locomotive called the "Tom Thumb." In 1830 he demonstrated its ability to negotiate hills and curves, and saved the B&O from financial disaster. But the first locomotive in regular service was the "Best Friend of Charleston," which pulled four cars at average speeds of twenty miles per hour between Charleston and Hamburg, South Carolina. When the line was completed in 1833, it consisted of 136 miles of track, the longest railroad in the world. Within ten years, there were 400 railroad companies, with more track than all of Europe.

These new developments created a tremendous demand for iron. British law had prevented the colonies from building iron mills to produce anything but pig iron, the basic material that results from melting iron ore in a blast furnace. The industry made progress after Independence, growing rapidly when hard coal from Pennsylvania began to replace wood fuels in mill furnaces. Steel, the material produced when a small amount of carbon is added to iron, was available only in small quantities and would be expensive for another twenty years.

But Americans applied for 585 patents in 1830, tinkering with an endless list of new ideas and devices. New machinery for making paper made America the world's largest producer and led to a great increase in publishing. In 1830 there were 863 newspapers in circulation, and soon no frontier village was too small for its own weekly paper. Joseph Henry sent an electric current through a wire and rang a bell. Samuel F. B. Morse, a talented painter, began to think about a telegraph.

New machinery for making nails allowed Augustine Taylor to design the "balloon frame" house, which revolutionized American housing. Frontier people had brought their cabins to a high degree of comfort. Where stone was available, they built stone houses. In cities there were many brick buildings. There was never any shortage of wood, and the country had water-powered sawmills for generations, but early mills could only produce a few hundred board feet of lumber in a day. Now steam power drove better blades, and millions of feet of lumber came from Maine, New York, Virginia, and the Carolinas, and increasingly from the upper midwest. But nails held a frame house together. Lightweight boards were braced and nailed to construct walls and support the roof, instead of the thick posts and beams of old houses and barns. The boxy frame house, with or without its familiar front porch, became standard construction for farm and town alike.

This was the Industrial Revolution which transformed American life in the first half of the nineteenth century, new machinery for farmers, new products and conveniences for the home, new technologies coming together in a huge country with seemingly inexhaustible natural resources.

On a trip to England, Francis Cabot Lowell visited English textile mills, and like Sam Slater, he kept the machinery designs in his head until he got back home. There he organized the Boston Manufacturing Company, which brought together all the operations of clothmaking under one roof, from baled cotton to finished goods. It was Lowell who persuaded Henry Clay to impose a high tariff on imported goods, which protected mill owners although it hurt many other American industries.

Visitors marveled at his spinning and weaving production, and even more marvelous was the town of Lowell itself. Many mill owners like Sam Slater hired children, but Lowell employed young women. Country girls were happy to work twelve hours a day, six and a half days a week, for which they were paid $6 to $10. It was better than staying home on the farm, or going out as a "hired girl" in somebody else's house. It was their best opportunity for economic independence.

The pretty, lively Lowell girls lived in company boarding houses (two girls to a room) which provided three good meals a day and a landlady who gave them motherly supervision. For this housing, the company deducted $6 a month from their paychecks, and something more for laundry, church, newspapers and magazines. Even after sending a little money home and spending a bit on new finery from the company store, most girls were able to open an account in the company bank, and save for a future wedding day.

In Pawtucket, Rhode Island, Sam Slater paid children much less, perhaps $1.25 a week for fourteen hour days. The Rhode Island system tried to hire whole families, so that men and older boys did heavier work and nimble young children tended the spinning machines. More than half the mill workers were under fourteen years old, but families were glad to get factory jobs which paid five or six times as much cash income as they could earn on the farm. Still, it took getting used to. It was one thing to work long hours, seven days a week on your own farm, or in your own home or blacksmith shop, but it was something else to live by a factory whistle and the company's rules.

Early mill owners were proud of this family relationship with their workers. After all, many factory towns provided housing, shops, churches, schools: Sam Slater kept school for the children in his mills, though they had to give up half a Sunday, their only free day, to go to classes. The Lowell girls had to go to church, and their pay was docked if they failed to attend. But the labor force was changing, and the relationship changed. More than half a million immigrants arrived between 1830 and 1840, most settling in eastern cities, eager for work. These newcomers were willing to take factory jobs for a dollar a day, and women were paid half as much.

Sam Slater's mill was the first factory in America, and it was the scene of the country's first strike. When he and other mill owners announced a longer work day and a 25 percent pay cut, the workers walked out. They paraded through the streets, and were joined by other citizens of Pawtucket, demonstrating before the home of their employers. When the owners responded by shutting down the mills, the protest got uglier; somebody tried to set fire to one of the wooden factory buildings. Fortunately, the strike was soon settled, both sides reaching agreement on wages and hours. But both sides began to organize. The Pawtucket strike was followed by labor unrest in other cities through New England, New Jersey, Pennsylvania, and finally even the model town of Lowell was hit.

In 1834, more than 800 Lowell girls struck against an announced pay cut. Two years later, almost 2,000 women walked out when company boarding houses raised the cost of their lodging and food. These were not immigrants, but Yankee women who called on the example of their patriotic ancestors when they asserted their rights. An eleven-year-old girl stood up on a pump and gave a speech, after which she led her comrades into the streets. Win or lose, these women showed remarkable courage and solidarity, and their talk of UNION threw a scare into the men they worked for. In the end, the mill owners had more resources. They could afford to close the mills and wait it out. More important, they had influence in local courts, and unions were ruled illegal.

Where did justice lie? Many industrialists of the time, men like Moses Brown, John Deere, Cyrus McCormick, and Peter Cooper, became millionaires. Most of them were self-made men, risen from the farm or shop, who by their inventiveness and energy gave employment to people who needed work. They made the work lighter, the products better, and life infinitely easier for all Americans. Moreover, they gave generously to important causes and institutions, supported hospitals and libraries, founded great universities. They must have felt dismayed at the ingratitude of working people. Why shouldn't a healthy child work fourteen hours a day? Less work was a "waste of life." And how could the labor of a child, a little slip of a girl, be worth more than 15 cents an hour?

1836   Arkansas was admitted to the Union.

Texas was a northern province of Mexico, but more Americans lived there than Mexicans. Most were immigrants from the south, and many were slaveowners. That country's president, Antonio Lopez de Santa Anna, banned slavery and laid heavy taxes on the Americans. They decided to rebel and secede, proclaiming the Republic of Texas. Mexico sent an army to hold onto the province. In February, General Santa Anna and more than 3,000 troops began a siege of The Alamo, an old Spanish mission in the heart of San Antonio. One hundred eighty-three Americans were holed up there, including William B. Travis, Jim Bowie, and Davy Crockett. Experienced fighting men, they held out for thirteen days. When they were finally overwhelmed, all the men—most of them wounded—were killed. The Mexicans spared women, children, and blacks. The bodies of the dead men were thrown on a pile and burned. Six weeks later, the Texans had their revenge at the Battle of San Jacinto, driving the Mexican army back across the Rio Grande. Santa Anna was captured, but later released. Sam Houston, the victor at San Jacinto, became the first president of the Republic of Texas.

Everybody expected Texas to join the Union, another increase in the seemingly inexhaustible resources of the American West. The sale of western public land had already paid off the national debt, covered all the operating expenses of the federal government, and created a Treasury surplus of $37 million. When Jackson reported the problem to Congress, Republican John Calhoun insisted that the money be divided among the states as loans. With that bonanza, the states immediately began building roads and canals and railways, setting off boom times like the country had never seen before.

Martin Van Buren was a successful lawyer and a brilliant politician. He built a powerful political organization in New York and moved up through state and national offices until he decided to join Andrew Jackson and the Democrats. Now Jackson bulldozed the party into naming Van Buren as its presidential candidate, but it was hard to accept his running-mate. Colonel R.W. Johnson, of Kentucky, was one of the young War Hawks in 1812, who gained fame when he killed Chief Tecumseh in that fighting. Southern Democrats were reluctant to support a man who lived openly with a black woman and their two daughters.

Jackson's long fight with the Bank of the United States caused a lot of confusion and serious problems for American business. Now his enemies, rich men, bankers, manufacturers, merchants, southern states' rights men, assorted anti-Catholic, anti-Mason, and anti-Jackson factions, joined in a new political party, the Whigs. They organized the first convention in our history, and established many of the forms that later conventions made familiar—delegate credentials, a rules committee, a party platform, and so on. The party was rich in political talent. Its leader was the brilliant Henry Clay, whose "American system" of national development was the heart of the Whig platform. He was joined by Daniel Webster, Horace Greeley, Thaddeus Stevens, General William Henry Harrison, and others. In spite of this dazzling list of presidential possibilities—or perhaps because of it—the party couldn't get together on a candidate. Different states were allowed to put forward their favorite sons, which resulted in four Whig candidates, none of whom could beat Jackson's candidate. Martin Van Buren went to the White House to preside over a long national depression.

1837

Martin Van Buren

Following Jackson's policies, President Van Buren established an independent treasury system to replace the Bank, but he refused to use land sale revenues to prop up the economy. He insisted that public land purchases had to be paid for in gold or silver, instead of bank notes—the paper money of the time. The boom immediately collapsed, banks failed, states repudiated their bonds, and a long depression began. Soon thousands of farms were foreclosed and factories shut down, putting millions of people out of work. The depression caused widespread suffering.

Michigan was admitted to the Union.

In 1825, when John Calhoun was serving as Secretary of War for President Monroe, he defined a new "Indian Country" west of Missouri, covering what is now Oklahoma and much more. Most northeastern Indians had already been pushed across the Mississippi. Their hunting grounds were cheaply bought or stolen by treaties with the conquering white man, but this western territory would be reserved for Indians.

Midwest Indians held out until the Black Hawk War. Black Hawk was a Sauk chief who supported Tecumseh's cause: no tribe "owned" land, and none could sell or cede land without the agreement of all Indians. After a series of skirmishes, Black Hawk's small army of 600 faced a large contingent of federal troops and state militia at the junction of the Mississippi and the Rock River, on the Illinois border. Among the forces mustered there were Colonel Zachary Taylor, Lieutenant Jefferson Davis, and Captain Abraham Lincoln.

In the first fighting, a small force of Black Hawk's warriors thoroughly defeated 275 militiamen. He led his army upriver into Wisconsin. American soldiers followed while General Winfield Scott called for reinforcements. The Indians were exhausted and hungry, but Black Hawk tried to lead them across the Mississippi where it joined the Bad Axe River on the Wisconsin side. They were met by an American steamboat with cannon. Black Hawk escaped northward with some of his men, but 1,300 American troops massacred the rest, killing warriors, women, and children as they tried to launch canoes or swim across the river to safety. Some who reached the west bank of the Mississippi were killed by hostile Sioux. In 1832, Black Hawk surrendered, was paraded through eastern cities like a wild animal, then released to a reservation.

Meanwhile, American troops in the southeast were carrying out the Indian Removal Act, signed by President Jackson in 1830. The southeastern tribes were often called the Five Civilized Nations—Cherokee,

Chickasaw, Choctaw, Creek, and Seminole. They were farmers rather than hunters. The Cherokees in Georgia had established a government patterned after the government of the United States, with their own laws and courts and an elected chief. They had a written language, their own books, and newspapers. Some cultivated cotton on plantations with black slaves.

First the Choctaws were pushed out, herded like cattle in groups of 500 to 1,000, with soldiers riding herd. Then the Creeks and Chickasaws, uncertain whether they should fight or move to promised land in the Indian Country, were mercilessly evicted. Then the Seminoles, after brave resistance, were crushed and relocated. And finally the Cherokees were driven from their farms by Georgia militia, families trying to carry what they had managed to salvage, the old, the sick, mothers nursing infants, prodded along an 800-mile march. There was never enough food or water or time to rest. Thousands died of disease. They were easy prey for angry western Indians, and for white outlaws who stripped them of the little they possessed.

This forced migration of 1838-1839 became known as the Trail of Tears. The name has come to stand for all the atrocities inflicted on native Americans in those years. More suffering and betrayal lay ahead.

1840

The business depression lasted for five years, and doomed Martin Van Buren's hopes for re-election. The Whigs got their party together and hit on a very modern political idea. Instead of trying to set forth a policy, a clear statement of political philosophy, they would just try to find a winning candidate. They chose William Henry Harrison, hero of the Battle of Tippecanoe, with John Tyler as his running-mate. The Whig campaign was a circus, the first to use modern techniques of advertising, campaign songs, and sloganeering— "Tippecanoe and Tyler, too!" Sixty-eight year-old Harrison won a landslide victory, gave the longest inaugural speech on record, and served the shortest term. After a month in office he died, and John Tyler became the first Vice-President to reach the White House.

But "His Accidency," as they called him, was not a staunch Whig. When Henry Clay twice pushed bills for a national bank through Congress, Tyler twice vetoed the measure. Almost the whole Whig Cabinet resigned. As a southerner, he was a strong states' rights man. He made a treaty with the Republic of Texas which would annex Texas to the Union as a slave state. Northern Whigs fought him.

1841

William Henry Harrison

John Tyler

Horace Greeley was a Whig and, in the opinion of many people, a crackpot. In 1841, at the age of thirty, he founded the *New York Tribune*, which would be for many years the most influential newspaper in the country. He spoke to and for the common man, but mainly he spoke for himself. Greeley favored Henry Clay's high tariffs to protect American industry, and he supported unions to protect American workers. He opposed slavery and votes for women. He was a teetotaler, a spiritualist, and a constant booster for national expansion. "Go West, young man," he said, "and grow up with the country!" Which was just what every red-blooded young man wanted to do.

Government land in the Louisiana Territory could now be bought in lots of 80 acres, for $1.25 an acre. In advance of government surveyors, squatters went west and staked claims, then refused to leave when the land was offered for sale. President Tyler signed the Pre-emption Act of 1841, which recognized squatter's rights and allowed them to buy a quarter section, 160 acres, at the $1.25 price. Many people favored a homestead law, which would give free land to farmers willing to settle and cultivate it. But red-blooded young men dreamed of more than free farms. They were drawn west by the promise of adventure.

One such was Lieutenant John C. Fremont of the Army Topographical Corps, who received a Congressional charter to explore the Oregon Trail. It was an old fur-trader's route northwest across the mountains, a 2,000 mile trip that started in Missouri and took six months by wagon. With a party of soldiers and experienced guides like Kit Carson, Fremont had a strenuous and glorious time, scouting passes through the Rockies and mapping the Trail as far as Wyoming. Returning to Washington, he and his wife wrote a best-selling book about the expedition.

But Fremont was not the first. Ten years earlier, a pregnant woman had made the trip, guided only by prayer. Narcissa Whitman traveled with her husband, Dr. Marcus Whitman, Mr. and Mrs. Henry Spaulding, and W. H. Gray. They were missionaries, sent west to convert and teach the Indians. The Oregon Territory then stretched from Russian Alaska down to California, still a part of Mexico. But Whitman heard rumors that the British Hudson's Bay Company planned to take it over. The few American settlers in Oregon were alarmed, and Dr. Whitman set out to warn the President.

He left their small mission in 1842, too late in the year, alone on horseback. He got lost in mountain blizzards. In Colorado he reached the frozen Grand River, and followed it on a 1,500 mile detour south, to Mexican Santa Fe. Then he headed east for another 2,000 miles, finally reaching Washington. His heroic exertions to protect American interests in Oregon did not interest Daniel Webster, the Secretary of State, but President Tyler promised help for American settlements.

Whitman went to New York and talked to Horace Greeley, who responded immediately and with his usual zeal. His articles and editorials in the *Tribune*, and Fremont's book, fired the public interest, adding patriotic purpose to the dream of great adventure. One thousand emigrants left Independence, Missouri, in 1843, and Marcus Whitman rode back west with the largest wagon train the Oregon Trail had yet seen.

1844

James K. Polk

Expansionism was the temper of the times, but for their own various reasons, prominent Whigs like Clay, Webster, and Calhoun opposed the annexation of Texas. As to control of Oregon, Daniel Webster said something like "Who needs it?" So the Democrats nominated James K. Polk, the first "dark horse" candidate, a southerner who favored both. The Whig candidate was Henry Clay, who had his eye on the White House for a long time. Polk and the Democrats won a narrow victory, because Americans had come to believe that Divine Providence intended them to own and civilize the continent, from sea to shining sea. They soon found a phrase for it: Expansion was America's Manifest Destiny.

Samuel F. B. Morse sent the first telegraph message from Washington to Baltimore. It asked, "What hath God wrought?"

1845

Florida was admitted to the Union.

Texas was annexed to the Union.

1846

Iowa was admitted to the Union.

Mexico had never recognized the Republic of Texas and planned to recapture its former province. In payment of a debt to Britain, Mexico would give up California, adding that territory to lands Britain wanted on the west coast. An American envoy was sent to Mexico City with an offer to settle Texas issues, and to buy New Mexico and California. He was turned away, and the new head of the Mexican government prepared for war while negotiating with foreign nations.

General Zachary Taylor was sent to the Rio Grande border. When some Mexican soldiers attacked an American patrol, Polk quickly asked Congress for a declaration of war and got it. A new treaty with Britain, setting a boundary between Canada and the United States, ended any threat to Oregon, so Polk could concentrate on Texas. As fast as the War Department could mobilize, three armies were dispatched.

General Taylor occupied the city of Monterey, and defeated a larger force, again commanded by General Santa Anna, at the Battle of Buena Vista. Another American army moved through New Mexico to occupy California. John Fremont rushed ahead with 100 soldiers, from Kansas by way of Santa Fe, and claimed California before the army arrived. Later he fell afoul of his commander, was charged with mutiny and court-martialed. President Polk set the conviction aside, but Fremont resigned from the army.

General Winfield Scott landed a third army from the Gulf of Mexico near Vera Cruz, the most heavily fortified city on the continent. After a long bombardment, the stronghold fell, and Scott marched on toward Mexico City. Peace negotiations began, and General Santa Anna asked for an armistice. After three months of talk, the negotiations failed.

Chapultepec is a rocky crag overlooking Mexico City, and there the Mexican army made its last defense of the country. Peasant troops and young boys from the military academy could not withstand a heavy American shelling of the old palace that crowned the hill. Scott's superior force and big guns captured the city, where civilian casualties were heavy.

1847

Marcus and Narcissa Whitman had built a mission at Waiilatpu, in what is now the state of Washington. The work among the Cayuse Indians was hard, and not very successful. The Board of Missions back east decided to abandon the effort. But after Whitman's long trip and the promise of government help, they changed their minds. In 1847, an epidemic of measles hit the Indians at Waiilatpu. Though Dr. Whitman and his wife nursed the sick and dying in their small church, the Cayuse were terrified, convinced that the whites were poisoning them. The Whitmans and twelve others were savagely murdered on November 29.

1848

The Mexican War ended with the Treaty of Guadalupe Hidalgo. The United States took more than 500,000 square miles of Mexican territory, half the country, the future states of California, Nevada, Utah, most of Arizona and New Mexico, parts of Colorado and Wyoming, and, of course, Texas, with a border at the Rio Grande and the Gila rivers. Many men in government thought we should have seized all of Mexico while we were at it.

In exchange, the United States gave Mexico $15 million and paid Texas settlers $3.2 million for claims against Mexico. The war cost 13,000 American lives, mostly through disease in the camps. It was valuable military experience for men like P. T. Beauregard, Ulysses S. Grant, Thomas Jonathan (later "Stonewall") Jackson, Robert E. Lee, James Longstreet, George McClellan, and William Tecumseh Sherman. These men would fight again, in opposing armies. General Zachary Taylor and Brigadier General Franklin Pierce would reach the White House, and Colonel Jefferson Davis would head the Confederate States of America.

Horace Greeley opposed the Mexican War, but the *Tribune* sent reporters, as did most newspapers. Democrat papers glorified the war and the American victory. But in Washington, the northern Whigs had kept up a barrage of opposition, calling the war a totally unjust attack on a weak neighbor, and accusing Polk of criminal aggression. Abraham Lincoln, a young Whig congressman from Illinois, got up in the House and demanded that the president identify the exact spot where Mexicans had first engaged an American patrol. If those sites were on Mexican soil, what right had America to declare war? David Wilmot of Pennsylvania was a Democrat, but he joined the "Conscience

Whigs" in opposing slavery. He managed to slip a Proviso through the House, banning slavery in any new territory acquired by war. "Cotton Whigs" in the Senate killed the measure, but the Wilmot Proviso would be hotly debated in the future.

Meanwhile, in the winter of 1847-1848, about 2,000 Mormons reached the Salt Lake Valley in far-off Utah. The Church of Jesus Christ of Latter Day Saints was founded in 1830, by the Prophet Joseph Smith. He said that he had been led by the Angel Moroni to discover a set of golden plates, on which were inscribed the text of a holy book, written by an Indian historian in the year 400. With the help of magical spectacles, he was able to read the plates and dictate a translation, which he published as the Book of Mormon, a supplement to the Bible. Believers made thousands of converts, but angered their neighbors. The Mormons were hounded out of New York, to Ohio and Missouri, and at last to the town of Commerce, Illinois.

He renamed the town, and planned the city of Nauvoo, where his followers built a temple. With Smith as mayor, the city prospered until he began the practice of polygamy. Mormon men not only could have, but should have as many wives as possible. Neighbors were outraged, and a local paper printed harsh words about the Saints. Smith and his brother burned the paper's shop. They were arrested and jailed in Carthage, Illinois, and murdered by a lynch mob.

Brigham Young assumed leadership of the Church and abandoned Nauvoo for the long, hard trek west. The first group of 148 pioneers reached Utah in 1847, and the faithful kept arriving, joined by new converts from England and Scandinavia. They colonized hundreds of settlements throughout the west and built their Tabernacle in Salt Lake City. Brigham Young hoped to found the new state of Deseret. Instead, the government recognized his administrative ability and made him the first territorial governor of Utah. He gave his church a lifetime of service, leaving behind a thriving community and a large family. He had more than twenty wives and fifty-six children.

1848   Wisconsin joined the Union.

President Polk was a bone-deep Democrat and a strong executive. He knew exactly what he wanted to accomplish during his term, and he pursued his Jacksonian principles, lowering the tariff and re-establishing the independent treasury system. Most of all, he wanted to settle the Oregon dispute with Britain and acquire California. Having achieved those objectives, he did not seek re-election. His party was split by the slavery issue, and he had no use for extremists on either side of the question. A large anti-slavery faction in New York broke away to form the Free Soil party, nominating former President Martin Van Buren. The regular Democrats nominated Senator Lewis Cass of Michigan.

The Whig party was also split. Its most brilliant men, Henry Clay and Daniel Webster, were unacceptable to the "Cotton Whigs," so the party turned again to a war hero, General Zachary Taylor, with Congressman Millard Fillmore of New York as his running mate. Taylor had no government experience, had never even voted in his forty-year army career. But he made a name for himself in the Indian wars and won a great victory at the Mexican battle of Buena Vista. He appealed to both Whigs and Democrats across the country, and in a three-way contest, "Old Rough and Ready" won a narrow but decisive political victory.

Thirty states voted, and an Act of 1845 established the Tuesday after the first Monday in November as the national election day. But not for 100 years did all states vote on that day.

The big news was coming from the west. John Sutter, a German immigrant, had arrived in America ten years before the war and settled in California when it was still Mexican territory. He started a small colony at Sacramento, became a Mexican citizen, and received a land grant from the Mexican governor. He worked hard to develop his ranch, then took on a partner to help build a sawmill. On a January day in 1848, Jim Marshall came in from the excavation site with a rag full of glittering dust. And there it was, at last, what every adventurer in the New World had hoped to find—gold!

It took months for the news to cross the continent, but by fall eastern papers were printing accounts of the discovery. In December, retiring President Polk confirmed those reports in his message to Congress. His war had won the west for the United States, not only land and a secure grip on the Pacific Coast, but the prospect of wealth beyond imagining. The country's Manifest Destiny had been fulfilled.

1849

Zachary Taylor

Thousands of red-blooded men left home. They traveled from every state, by wagon or by ship around the tip of South America and up to San Francisco. They brought little more than picks and shovels, and pans to sift gold nuggets from California gravel. They were joined by red-blooded Mexicans, Hawaiians, Australians, and Russians who crossed the Pacific to make their fortunes. Soon there were tens of thousands. They swarmed over Sutter's ranch and through the surrounding territory, staking their claims and asserting their squatter's rights—with guns, if necessary.

The village of San Francisco became a wild boom town, full of hard-drinking prospectors, gamblers, swindlers, army deserters and sailors who jumped ship. The federal authorities lost control. There was no law and no order. While Congress considered admission of California into the Union, Californians took action. They wrote their own constitution, elected a governor and a legislature, and petitioned for statehood. John Sutter was ruined. His land and livestock were stolen, everything he built up in his years of pioneer struggle was destroyed. Jim Marshall went crazy. They both died poor.

1850

The future of California brought the question of slavery to the fore. When New Mexico and Utah followed California's example and adopted their state constitutions, Congress could no longer avoid it. Would the new states be slave or free? President Zachary Taylor proposed admission of California as a free state (as clearly set forth in its new constitution), and admission of New Mexico and Utah with no further reference to the issue.

In the long and angry debate that followed, there was not much talk about the fate of black people. The speeches were about the Wilmot Proviso, which would have banned slavery in all the territory won by the Mexican War. The Proviso had passed in the House of Representatives but failed in the Senate. Now it was argued again, along with popular sovereignty, states' rights, Constitutional protection of property, and preservation of the Union, but very little discussion about human pain and degradation, the daily suffering of black men and women. The threat of disunion was very real, if new states upset the brittle balance of the 1830 Missouri Compromise. Southerners watched the growth of the north in size and population. They knew they could be outvoted in the House, but fought to keep their power and influence in the Senate, where each state had two votes, and the Missouri Compromise pledged that half the states would be slave and half free.

Senator Henry Clay of Kentucky, a leader in Congress for thirty-seven years and three times candidate for president, author of the 1830 Compromise, once more stepped in as the Great Pacificator. He offered a more complicated compromise. It would admit California as a free state, but postpone any decision on New Mexico and Utah. They would continue as territories under federal law, like the rest of the land won in the War. Texas would be paid to give up all claims on parts of New Mexico, and a new boundary would be drawn between them. The slave trade would be stopped in the District of Columbia, but slavery would not be abolished in the District without consent of the state of Maryland. Fugitive slave laws would be strengthened and enforced. Congress would not otherwise interfere with slave trade between the states.

This offer, too, was rejected by John Calhoun, the Senator from South Carolina, for so many years the mind, soul, and voice of the South. Clay and Calhoun had been young together, the eager War Hawks of 1812. Now they were old men in their last fight, and Calhoun's voice was failing. His defiant answer to Clay was read by Senator James Mason of Virginia: If Congress would not give the South an equal share of the new territories won in the Mexican War, a war that the South had helped to win, then North and South should separate in peace. And if peaceful separation was not possible—"tell us so, and we will know what to do."

Daniel Webster rose to speak for the Union, as he had twenty years earlier. He had opposed the annexation of Texas, but he supported Clay. Peaceful separation of North and South was not possible, unthinkable. The Union must be preserved, at any cost. In July, President Zachary Taylor suddenly died. The debate which had raged for nine months was interrupted by his passing and the inauguration of Millard Fillmore as the thirteenth President.

Millard Fillmore

Fillmore quickly signed the compromise bills. California came into the Union as a free state. James Mason was asked to draft a stronger fugitive slave law, permitting federal officers to arrest runaways who escaped to free states and return them to slave owners. He was the grandson of George Mason, who wrote the Constitution's Bill of Rights, but blacks still had no rights in America. The new law meant that free blacks in the north could be seized. They had no way to prove their status as free men, or defend themselves against transport back to a slave state, where almost any white man could claim ownership. The law enraged northern abolitionists and gained wider audiences for men like William Lloyd Garrison and Frederick Douglass.

Garrison had been publishing his Boston paper, *The Liberator*, for twenty years, demanding immediate and total freedom for all slaves. He was threatened, beaten, and hung in effigy; some of his followers were murdered. But Garrison could not be silenced. Douglass was a black man who bought his freedom and became the most important black leader of his time. He traveled widely, spoke to huge crowds at meetings of the Massachusetts Anti-Slavery Society and other groups, and edited his own paper.

Both men wrote for many causes. Garrison was a profound Christian who dreamed of a better world, governed by higher moral law. He preached temperance and pacifism, rights of women and working people. He scorned politics and relied on the American conscience to end slavery, what he called the country's "bargain with hell." Douglass worked with Garrison for a long time, sharing those social concerns. But in the end, he was a more logical and practical man. He saw that slavery had to be a political issue.

1852

Mrs. Harriet Beecher Stowe was not an abolitionist agitator. She was forty years old, daughter, sister, and wife of churchmen, and mother of seven children. Born in Connecticut, she lived much of her life in the frontier town of Cincinnati. Her only personal experience with slavery consisted of a short visit to a Kentucky plantation. But the Fugitive Slave Act was to Harriet a "nightmare abomination." When she and her husband moved back to New England, she started to write the stories that became *Uncle Tom's Cabin*. Three hundred thousand copies were sold within the year. It was translated into many foreign languages, and eventually found millions of readers around the world. For the first time, many Americans began to comprehend the human tragedy of slavery. Her book was about people, not property laws.

She was remarkably fair to southern whites, showing Southern graces as well as greed, kindness as well as cruelty. Her villain was a Northerner, moved South to exploit the system. It was the system that Harriet hated, the institution of slavery that killed blacks and corrupted whites. When critics denied her charges, she wrote another book offering careful proof of the suffering she described. Politicians read the book but ignored its message. Certainly they did not foresee its stunning impact on public opinion.

Cotton growers tightened their grip on the Democratic party. The South could not afford to have a conscience about slavery. Cotton was a labor intensive crop, and a husky field hand cost $1,000. Slave breeding and slave trading were big business. And cotton wore out the land. Europeans were always surprised to observe that plantation owners did not practice crop rotation, or even use animal manure to fertilize their fields. But land was plentiful and still relatively cheap in the new territories; growers spent the land, and needed more.

Cotton was also important to the economy of the North. Mill owners depended on affordable cotton produced by slave labor. Northern bankers were heavily invested in cotton mills and cotton plantations. Northern middlemen took 40 cents out of every cotton dollar for freight charges, insurance, commissions, and interest on loans to growers. Northern shipyards built special vessels for the slave trade, designed to pack as many human beings as possible into the dark, stinking hold. What matter how many died, if the ship owner could sell the survivors for a fat profit?

Northern politicians supported the Southern cause and the Democratic party because they needed financial contributions and votes. Anti-slavery voters called them doughfaces, too weak to take a moral position on slavery if that morality would cost them an election. But the Whigs were no braver. Millard Fillmore did everything in his power to hold on to the Cotton Whigs, and he sent Admiral Matthew Perry to Japan with four gunboats and an invitation to expand American trade.

This mission was calculated to interest northern commercial men. It did not interest the Japanese, or help him win re-nomination.

In this election year, the Whigs rejected Fillmore and passed over their great leader, Daniel Webster, who was aging and fuddled by drink. Their convention nominated another military hero, General Winfield Scott, the Virginian who commanded American forces in the Mexican War.

The Democratic convention needed forty-nine ballots to agree on Franklin Pierce of New Hampshire. He had been a member of Congress for nine years before he served in the war as a brigadier general under Scott, and he was the youngest man yet to seek the presidency. Disgusted voters in both parties broke away to organize small parties and name their own candidates, but "Handsome Frank" and the Democrats won by a comfortable majority.

1853

Franklin Pierce

The new President wanted no more arguments about slavery. The subject was closed, settled by the Compromise of 1850, and the country could move on with plans for internal development and improvements.

America had about 9,000 miles of railroads, more than all of Europe, but many lines were unconnected, offering limited service. Woodburning locomotives hauled freight cars between Chicago and the east, providing faster and cheaper transport over more direct routes than rivers and turnpikes. Now Pierce wanted a railroad to the Pacific coast. His envoy to Mexico, Charles Gadsden, negotiated the purchase of 29,000 square miles south of the Gila River, for $10 million. Construction would be easier, and the project had the approval of his secretary of state, Jefferson Davis.

Stephen Douglas, the Senator from Illinois, wanted a central route through Chicago (where he happened to have a financial interest in the matter). It would require moving the Indians out and reorganizing the old Territory of Nebraska. Nobody cared about the Indians, but once more the balance between slave and free states was threatened, because the territory had been part of the Louisiana Purchase, where slavery was banned by the Northwest Ordinance.

1854

In January, Douglas presented his Kansas-Nebraska bill, which divided Nebraska into two new territories. Settlers would have popular sovereignty—they could choose slavery or free soil by local referendum. Douglas thought that Nebraska would vote for free soil and Kansas for slavery, preserving the balance of the Missouri Compromise. The debate was short and furious, but the bill passed and the doughface president signed it.

In February, a young lawyer in Ripon, Wisconsin, wrote a letter to Horace Greeley. Forget the old parties, he said. The country needed new leadership from a new party. Horace Greeley was still editing the powerful *New York Tribune*.. He was weary, almost worn out by years of political activism, but willing to help. The small meeting in the Ripon schoolhouse included Conscience Whigs, Independent Democrats, and other anti-slavery men. It was followed by another meeting in Jackson, Michigan, which marked the beginning of the new party, the Republicans. With Greeley's publicity, similar committees sprang up around the country. In March, thirty Congressmen assembled in Washington, D.C., and formally adopted the party name.

1855

Early in the year, Kansas settlers tried to hold their first popular sovereignty election. It turned into mob violence when 5,000 ruffians crossed the border from Missouri, armed with knives and guns, to guarantee a pro-slavery vote. They kept free soil voters away from polling places and terrorized the community, casting their own ballots to elect a pro-slavery state government.

There was a quick response in the North. Churches took up collections to buy rifles, and sent colonies of abolitionists to the territory. These tough newcomers were in no mood for compromise. They wrote their own constitution and elected their own, anti-slavery, government, with its capital in Topeka. The country watched in horror as civil war broke out in "Bleeding Kansas."

Oratory broke out in Congress. Massachusetts Senator Charles Sumner made a fiery speech, attacking the South and Democrats like Senator Butler of South Carolina. Butler's nephew, Congressman Preston Brooks, invaded the Senate chamber and all but tried to murder Sumner, beating the old man until he was badly injured, almost blind in one eye. A judge in pro-slavery Washington let Brooks off with a small fine.

In May, Missouri thugs again came across the Kansas border and burned the Free Soil town of Lawrence. Three days later, John Brown struck in a small settlement along the Pottawatomie Creek. Brown was from West Virginia, a lifelong abolitionist, taught by his father to love God and hate slavery. Both father and son were part of the Underground Railroad, the chain of safe and secret locations by which escaping slaves traveled North. Brown failed in many businesses, moving around the country and joining abolitionist work in many states. For a while he lived in the black town of North Elba, New York, then moved on.

When his five sons went to Kansas to take up land and help the Free Soil cause, John Brown followed. The looting and burning of Lawrence roused his fury and incited him to fanatic vengeance. With his boys and two neighbors, he dragged five pro-slavery settlers out of their cabins and slaughtered them. He continued to raid along the border and into Missouri, stealing horses, wagons, and slaves, and killing a slave owner. These might have been forgotten incidents in the Kansas war that claimed 300 lives, but half-crazed John Brown had bigger plans. He fled to Massachusetts to get help in establishing a new, free, mountain state in the south. He went to Canada to organize a revolutionary army with himself as commander in chief, plotting to overthrow Southern governments.

President Franklin Pierce could not deal with any of this western turmoil. He occupied himself with foreign affairs, sending Admiral Perry back to Japan, this time with seven bigger ships. The Japanese were surprisingly agreeable, ready to sign a trade agreement. Pierce talked of buying Hawaii, and of a naval base in Santo Domingo. He arranged a fishing treaty with Canada. But when it came to domestic policy, he left decisions to Jefferson Davis, the Secretary of State.

1856

It was an election year, and the Democrats could not hope to win with Pierce. Stephen Douglas, the "Little Giant" from Illinois, was opposed by a growing number of anti-slavery party members. So they chose, as their presidential candidate, James Buchanan, a Pennsylvanian, much of whose experience was in foreign service. He had spent the last three years as minister to Great Britain, remote from the Kansas-Nebraska strife.

Former President Fillmore, a Whig, was nominated by the American Party, usually called the Know-Nothings. They came out of an earlier secret society. When asked about the political opinions, members were sworn to say, "I know nothing." In fact they had strong opinions, rooted in bigotry and prejudice, tending toward lunatic suspicion of anybody they didn't like.

The party had been growing for many years. In 1844, they rioted against Catholics in Philadelphia, burning Irish neighborhoods and two churches, killing twenty-four people. In 1849, they formed the Order of the Star-Spangled Banner in New York, anti-Catholic and anti-foreigner, protesting the tremendous wave of Irish and German immigration. An early organizer was E. Z. C. Judson, who wrote dime novels under the pen name of Ned Buntline. His own life was like a cheap thriller: a bad episode in the navy, alcoholism, the murder of his girlfriend's husband, dishonorable discharge from the army, before he took up politics. The party attracted many such disturbed and disreputable characters, but also men like Samuel Morse, inventor of the telegraph; the publisher, James Harper; and the prominent church leader, Lyman Beecher, brother of Harriet Beecher Stowe. The Know-Nothings opposed Catholics, voted only for born-in-the-United States of America candidates, and wanted a twenty-one-year residency requirement for immigrants seeking citizenship. Millard Fillmore had never been interested in the party's policies or secret rigamarole, but when they offered him their nomination, he accepted.

The new Republican party found its candidate in John Fremont, the dashing explorer who mapped the Oregon Trail, helped win California, served as one of its first Senators, and was recently involved in plans for the western railroad. Fremont was a spokesman for expansion and Free Soil, and he had a beautiful wife. Before his western adventures, he had eloped with the daughter of Thomas Hart Benton, a Democratic power in Congress since the days of Andrew Jackson. John and Jessie made a glamorous, romantic couple, and she was always shown beside him on party posters, where the slogan was "Free Soil, Free Speech, Free Men, Fremont!"

The Know-Nothings printed scandal about his illegitimate birth (true) and rumors that he was a devout Catholic (false). The Democrats poured money into the campaign, calling the Republicans nigger-lovers, radical abolitionists, and socialists who wanted to share the wealth and the women. When election day arrived the Democrats won, the Know-Nothings ran last. John Fremont and the Republicans got 42 percent of the vote, an impressive showing in their first time on the ballot. Abraham Lincoln of Illinois, a Conscience Whig, had hesitated to join the new party, but when the campaign began, he made more than fifty speeches for Fremont and began to play a bigger part in Republican leadership.

James Buchanan

Sixty-five-year-old James Buchanan moved into the White House. He was a rich, fastidious bachelor, well-received in Washington social circles, without the slightest idea of how to cope with the coming crisis. He thought that slavery was wrong, but what could be done about it?

Many men in public office hoped the Supreme Court would decide, and in March the Court handed down a verdict in the Dred Scott case. Scott was a black man, born to slave parents on a Virginia plantation. He had a series of owners, including an army doctor who took Scott and his wife from the slave state of Missouri into the free state of Illinois, and later to a post in the free Territory of Wisconsin. After the doctor died, Scott was returned to St. Louis. By then his owner was a New York man named Sanford. An agent for Sanford hired the fifty-year-old black man out for odd jobs, at $5 a month.

Anti-slavery lawyers convinced Scott that he could sue his owner, on the grounds that his years in free territory made him a free man and a citizen of Missouri. When the state court ruled against him, the case went to the federal circuit court, where he lost again. Finally his lawyers appealed to the Supreme Court. The famous case was *Dred Scott v. Sandford* (the owner's name was misspelled).

The Court's decision was based on the Constitution, and Chief Justice Roger Taney wrote the verdict: Dred Scott was not a citizen, because no blacks were citizens when the Constitution was adopted. Though free blacks had lived in several states ever since Independence, exercising many of the same rights as their neighbors, they were not citizens of the United States "within the meaning of the Constitution." The Northwest Ordinance, the Missouri Compromise, the Kansas-Nebraska Act—none of those laws were constitutional. There was no such thing as a free territory, "free soil," where slavery was banned. No black man was free because he lived in a free state. Blacks were not men as the Constitution used the word "man." Slaves were property, "merchandise," to be bought and sold, within and among the states, like any other property.

Six Justices agreed with Taney's long opinion. Two dissented, and Justice Curtis cited a lot of constitutional arguments in support of the free soil cause. But Dred Scott lost the case. "The black man," wrote Chief Justice Taney, "has no rights which the white man is bound to respect."

He no longer had much value as a slave. Mr. Sanford set him free, and Dred Scott worked as a hotel porter in St. Louis until he died of tuberculosis a year later.

1858   Minnesota was admitted to the Union.

"Bleeding Kansas" and the Dred Scott decision were the issues in the summer debates between the Republican Abraham Lincoln and the Democrat Stephen Douglas, both running for the Illinois seat in the Senate. The debates began with Lincoln's historic "House Divided" speech in Springfield. "A house divided against itself cannot stand. I believe this government cannot endure permanently half slave and half free..."

Douglas accused Lincoln of kindling a war, but even he defied the Supreme Court. As author of the Kansas-Nebraska Act, he insisted on popular sovereignty: "...the right of the people to make a Slave Territory or a Free Territory is perfect and complete." Douglas was returned to the Senate, and Republicans began talking about Abraham Lincoln as a possible president.

1859   For two years John Brown traveled between

124

Kansas and eastern cities, recruiting and planning his attack on the South. Many people fell in with his mad schemes. He got support from Frederick Douglass, and from a group of rich and influential abolitionists, the "Secret Six," who supplied him with guns and money. In his last Missouri raid, a planter was killed and slaves taken. The slaves were sent to Canada, and John Brown headed back across Iowa, Illinois, Michigan, and Ohio, while President Buchanan offered a $250 reward for his capture.

He rented a farm in Maryland, and from that base chose his first objective, a federal arsenal in the small town of Harper's Ferry, Virginia. On October 16, 1859, his revolutionary army of eighteen men surprised the sleeping town, took sixty white hostages, and began freeing the slaves. Several people were killed. By morning the militia had arrived, with the United States Horse Marines, under the command of Robert E. Lee. Brown, his men, and the freed slaves were trapped inside the armory but exchanged fire until a Marine broke down the door and beat the old man bloody. Of his army, ten men were dead, including two of his sons. A third son and five others escaped. The rest were captured, tried, and executed. John Brown was hung in Charleston, West Virginia, on December 2.

1860
Oregon became a state.

The Democratic nominating convention met in Charleston, South Carolina, in April. Northern delegates wanted Senator Stephen Douglas, but his stand on popular sovereignty had angered the South. To delay any vote on a presidential candidate, they demanded a platform first, the policy statement on which their candidate would run. Cotton state delegates demanded a platform which made Congress responsible for protection of slavery in the Territories, a demand which northerners recognized as political suicide. What the platform committee finally offered was totally unacceptable to the South. Many Southern delegates walked out, but the convention continued to vote on the platform. After fifty-seven ballots, they adjourned, resolving to meet again in June.

The Republicans met in Chicago. Several well-known, experienced, and ambitious men wanted the nomination. Their backers spent hectic days wheeling and dealing, trading votes, enjoying the great American political game. Senator William H. Seward of New York was one of the country's leading abolitionists, but the new party looked for a more centrist candidate to win its first national election. Abraham Lincoln stayed in Springfield while his managers worked hard to convince other delegates that Lincoln could carry crucial states in the November election.

Lincoln sent a message, "I authorize no bargains, and will be bound by none." But they continued to deal, offering Cabinet offices and other jobs in return for delegate support. When the voting began, the hall had been packed with Lincoln men, ready to yell and cheer for Honest Abe. The vote was very close. On the last ballot, Lincoln still needed $1 \frac{1}{2}$ votes to win the nomination, and the convention broke into jubilant uproar when Ohio changed five votes and gave him the count. One by one, state delegations switched their votes until the nomination was unanimous.

The divided Democrats met again in Baltimore, but they were still unable to reach any agreement. Stephen Douglas was still the choice of northern and western Democrats. Bitter Southern delegates walked out, to convene in Charleston and nominate John Breckinridge of Kentucky.

In October, Governor W.H. Gist of South Carolina wrote to the governors of other cotton states, asking if they would join in a secession movement if they lost the election. He got affirmative replies, but he waited until a telegram arrived with the expected bad news. The Democratic split had assured the election of Abraham Lincoln.

On December 20, South Carolina became the first State to secede from the Union: "...the Union...between South Carolina and other states under the name of the United States of America is hereby dissolved." On December 27, South Carolina militia marched on the tiny federal fortress at Castle Pinckney. It was surrendered by the only American officer still on duty. The commander, Major Robert Anderson, had already withdrawn his troops to heavily armed Fort Sumter, on an island in Charleston Bay.

1861

Abraham Lincoln

President Buchanan denied South Carolina's right to secede. He asked for a new Constitutional Convention, which would decide the issue of American slavery once and for all. A sullen Congress refused to consider any of the steps he offered to save the Union, but voted to admit Kansas.

Mississippi, Florida, Alabama, Georgia, and Louisiana seceded in January, Texas on the first of February. In some of those states, the decision of their legislature was followed by a popular vote on secession, and though a sizable minority of voters wanted to stay in the Union, the secessionists won by large majorities. Forty-two delegates from the first six Confederate states met in Montgomery, Alabama, on February 4, joined later by Texas. By the ninth they had written a provisional constitution and elected a provisional President and Vice-President, Jefferson Davis of Mississippi and Alexander Stephens of Georgia, respectively.

On March 4, Abraham Lincoln was inaugurated and delivered his first presidential address. "My fellow countrymen," he said, "the momentous issue of civil war is in your hands. We must not be enemies."

But they were. On April 12, the Confederate cannon in Charleston began firing on Fort Sumter, where Major Anderson commanded sixty-five soldiers, ten officers, and one New York City policeman. They had little ammunition and less food, because President Lincoln could not re-supply the fort, surrounded by Confederate heavy guns and 8,800 troops under the command of General P.G. T. Beauregard. After thirty-four hours of shelling, Sumter was a smoking ruin. Major Anderson surrendered and was evacuated by federal ships. The Civil War had begun, and President Lincoln called for 75,000 volunteers to serve in the Union Army.

Virginia, the birthplace of presidents, seceded on April 17. But when the legislature voted, representatives from the western third of the state voted no. They were far from the capital at Richmond; they owned few slaves. They felt under-represented and over-taxed, and had talked of separation for many years. Now a convention was held at Wheeling, and secession was nullified. The arrival of Union troops bolstered their determination, and they began the two-year process of applying for statehood.

North Carolina and Arkansas seceded in May, Tennessee in June.

Kansas became a state.

In area, the Confederacy of eleven states was bigger than the eighteen Northern states they faced. (California and Oregon, separated from the rest of the Union by the vast western Territories, were too distant to take any part in the war. The border states between North and South—Maryland, Kentucky, and Missouri—were still undecided.) But the population of the Northern states was almost twice that of the Confederacy, 18 million people, compared to 9 million in the South, of whom more than 3.5 million were black slaves. The North had far more money, more railroads, more industry, and more food and livestock. The South raised cotton and tobacco, and would depend heavily on exports to finance the war.

Neither side was prepared militarily for what lay ahead. The general in chief of the Union Army was seventy-five-year-old Winfield Scott, a veteran of the War of 1812 (fifty years earlier) and the Mexican War. He was authorized to offer command to Robert E. Lee, a graduate of West Point and one of Scott's staff officers during the Mexican expedition. Lee's loyalties were tragically divided. He opposed slavery and did not think the South had a Constitutional right to secede.

But his first allegiance was to Virginia, his native state. After twenty-five years of service to the Union, he resigned his commission and left for Richmond.

That city was now the capital of the Confederacy—110 miles from Washington, D.C. Lee was welcomed by President Jefferson Davis, also a graduate of West Point, a veteran of the Mexican War, and formerly Secretary of War under President Pierce. So many Union officers were volunteering to fight under the Confederate flag that Davis had a wide choice of commanders. Except for those killed in action, most of his generals would serve brilliantly until the end of the war. But he was hampered by the fact that each Confederate state wanted to run its own affairs. They did not see the need for a unified command and an overall war strategy. General Lee was given command of the Army and Navy of Virginia.

President Lincoln lacked the benefit of Davis's experience. In naming his generals, he had to accept advice, and it was too often political advice as members of his administration pushed their favorites. Eager young men poured into recruiting stations, ready to sign up for ninety-day enlistments, but there was a shortage of junior officers to organize and train them. Regular army officers were serving in the Territories, and there, for many months, they remained. But in the one respect that mattered most, the North had a tremendous advantage: it had guns and ammunition, and factories to build more. The Confederacy would have to buy arms from Europe, to be paid for by the sale of cotton—if its ships could break through the Union naval blockade that immediately appeared off the Southern coast.

Along the border, there were confrontations and skirmishes. Kentucky tried to maintain its neutrality. In Missouri, citizens who favored neutrality fought with Southern sympathizers. In Maryland, Secessionists defied their governor and attacked Massachusetts men as they marched through the streets of Baltimore. Four men died, the first casualties of the war, before the city was brought under Union control.

Jefferson Davis hoped to fight a defensive war. He had no intention of invading the North, and wanted only to resist until Northerners got tired of fighting. A few thousand men were sent to guard the Virginia frontier, along the Potomac; more were camped at Manassas Junction, a small railroad town southeast of Washington. Another army stood by in the Shenandoah Valley.

But the North had to invade and defeat the Confederacy, a huge country that stretched from the Atlantic to the Mississippi, and beyond. Old Winfield Scott would have let the Confederates wait until his ninety-day volunteers could be trained into real soldiers, but public opinion in the North clamored for action. Newspaper headlines cried, "On to Richmond!"

So Scott ordered an attack on Manassas. On July 21, General Irwin McDowell led his regiments across a little stream called Bull Run, to face his West Point classmate, General P. G. T. Beauregard, in the first major battle of the war. And McDowell's assault should have succeeded. He had a much larger army, and the Southern boys were no more ready for combat than their nervous young enemies. They would have been over-whelmed if General Thomas J. Jackson had not stood "like a stone wall," rallying his Virginia brigade until reinforcements arrived.

Although it was a very hot day, hun-dreds of spectators had followed McDowell's march from Washington. Congressmen, Cabinet members, any citizen who wanted to pack his wife and a picnic hamper into a car-riage, joined the parade. Now they gathered on the banks of Bull Run to watch the show. To their consternation, what they witnessed was the total defeat of McDowell's army, and when Union troops tried to make an orderly with-drawal, spectators blocked the way.

The retreat became a panic. Under heavy Confederate fire, the Yankees threw down their weapons and fled the battlefield. The only road was choked with army supply trains and ambulances, carriage horses and cavalry, terrified civilians and even more terri-fied soldiers. Parasols, guns, sandwiches, and bloody blue uniform jackets were trampled in the dust as everybody ran, not stopping until the last exhausted straggler was safe behind the trenches of Washington.

This pandemonium is known as the First Battle of Bull Run, or First Manassas. (Northern history usually calls battles by the name of a nearby river; Southern accounts use the name of the nearest town.)

In the middle of it all was Clara Barton, a Massachusetts schoolteacher before she moved to Washington and took a job in the Patent Office. At the age of forty, on her own initiative, she gathered supplies and went to the battlefield to nurse the wounded. Her tenderness in caring for men in pain was matched by her abilities as a leader and organizer. Clara went on to nurse in other wars, and in 1881 she founded the American Red Cross, which she headed for almost a quarter of a century.

Miss Barton was only one of many women, north and south, black and white, who would serve during the conflict and in the years that followed. In particular, two black women had amazing stories that began long before the war. Stubby little Harriet Tubman was probably fifty-six in 1861. She had left her master and her family and run away from slavery in Maryland long before, but she took up the liberation of slaves as her life work. She made about twenty trips back South to help her husband, parents, brothers, and sisters escape, and then helped perhaps three hundred other blacks travel on the Underground Railroad to freedom.

It was not, of course, a railroad. It was only a loose network of sympathizers, mainly black, but many white abolitionists, who would give a runaway a meal and shelter for a night, and direct him or her on to the next possible resting point. Pistol-packing Harriet Tubman was a dependable but tough leader. She tolerated no discouragement or change of heart, but insisted that runaways keep going until they reached safety. When war broke out, she worked as a nurse, and then as a spy and scout for the Second Carolina Volunteers. The toothless old black woman moved easily through the countryside and picked up invaluable information for Colonel James Montgomery, their commander. After the war she cared for poor elderly blacks in her own home, and in 1896, still active and determined, she helped organize the National Association of Colored Women.

Sojourner Truth was older than Harriet and began her work earlier. In New York her slave name was Isabella and while working for her Dutch master in New York state she bore several children to her slave husband, many of whom were sold away from her. She escaped when she was about forty to live with a Quaker family, but very soon found her own voice and mission in evangelical religion. Six feet tall, she turned out to be a powerful orator. She took the name "Sojourner Truth" and during the 1840s she traveled through New England and the Midwest preaching against slavery. She spoke out, too, on the subject of equal rights and the vote for women. During the war she was working out of Battle Creek, Michigan, walking the countryside to collect food and clothing for black regiments, sixty-four years old but tireless, strong in the Lord. She met Lincoln and stayed on in Washington to help and teach its newly freed black citizens. She knew that blacks needed more than emancipation; they also needed economic opportunity. Perhaps, she thought, the government could establish a Black State somewhere in the West. She died at eighty-six, still a believer, still a feminist, still a beacon for American blacks.

Before the war, women had worked for many humanitarian causes, and now hundreds volunteered for the big work of the U.S. Sanitary Commission. Mary Ann Bickerdyke was a forty-four-year-old widow who volunteered to deliver medical relief funds to a military hospital. Shocking hospital conditions kept her there for nine months as nurse, cook, and laundress. The men called her "Mother Bickerdyke" as she moved on to other hospitals, hospital ships, and battlefields—sometimes the only woman nursing hundreds of Union wounded. After the war, Congress awarded her a pension of $25 a month.

But at least one woman decided to fight. As "Albert Cashier," young Jennie Hodgers, born in Ireland, managed to join the 95th Infantry and served for three years, seeing action in forty battles and skirmishes. She continued to live as a man after the war, but when she was hit by an auto in 1910, she entered the State Soldiers' and Sailors' Home at Quincy, Illinois, where her gender was finally discovered. They made her wear a dress until she died. But she was buried in her uniform, with full military honors, in 1915.

Counting casualties on both sides, nearly 5,000 men died at Bull Run—not many, by the measure of later fighting. But it taught President Lincoln and Congress that this would not be a ninety-day war. Congress passed the first income tax law to pay for it, and terms of enlistment were increased to two years.

Gloom deepened when the Union was beaten in the west. General John Fremont, the dashing explorer, conqueror of California, former Senator and candidate for president, was whipped in Missouri. He retaliated by putting the state under martial law and freeing its slaves. When Lincoln countermanded his orders, Fremont refused to comply. He was removed from command and sent to serve in Virginia.

Another 1,900 Yankees fell in October, a few miles from Washington at Ball's Bluff, and more in minor engagements along the border. But no fights were minor to mothers who lost their sons, or to an angry Federal government.

1862

President Lincoln replaced General Scott with young George B. McClellan, who went to work with admirable zeal. "I can do it all," he said. But he was slow to respond when Lincoln issued General War Order Number One, calling for a Union offensive. McClellan's strategy proposed encirclement of the South by land and sea, for which he would need an army of 273,000 men, with engineers, heavy artillery, transport, supply trains, and all that a modern army required, as well as a modern navy with armored gunboats.

Every navy in the world had always fought in wooden boats, under sail. But John Ericsson, a Swedish inventor, was working on ironclad ships, and two were already afloat in

American waters. The Confederate ship, *Virginia*, was built for the Union in the shipyard at Norfolk, and originally christened the *Merrimack*. It was captured and burned when Virginia seceded, then rebuilt and plated with four-inch iron plates. Still untested in March, it took on ships of the Northern blockade fleet on Chesapeake Bay. It rammed and sank two Federal ships and ran a third aground before night fell.

But in the morning, a new opponent came into view, the comparatively tiny U.S. *Monitor*. It had only two guns in a revolving turret, but they were bigger guns, and her plating and maneu verability were superior to the *Merrimack/Virginia*. After six hours of fighting, both ships withdrew, but they had revolutioized naval warfare.

Meanwhile, an officer named Ulysses S. Grant was opening a Union offensive in the Mississippi Valley. Grant was a West Point graduate who served in the Mexican War, but then resigned his commission. He failed in ten years as a small farmer and business man. At the outbreak of the Civil War, he re-enlisted and commanded forces in Cairo, Illinois. He now mounted an expedition to cut communication and rail transport between eastern and western Confederate armies. He took Fort Henry, on the Tennessee River, and Fort Donelson, where 14,000 troops surrendered.

Since these were the first victories the North could celebrate, Grant was promoted and sent to join an attack on Southern forces in Mississippi. Their great general, Albert Sydney Johnston, did not wait to be attacked. Early on April 6, he surprised the Federals at Shiloh (Pittsburgh Landing). The North was almost beaten again in the heaviest fighting the war had yet seen. Leading a reckless cavalry charge, Johnston was wounded and bled to death. On the next day, reinforcements arrived and drove the rebels off, but not before 13,000 Yankees and 11,000 Confederates had been killed. The casualty total was greater than in all previous American wars combined.

The Confederate Congress passed the first conscription law in American history to draft men between the ages of eighteen and thirty-five, though many exemptions tended to favor the rich.

In May, General McClellan began another advance on the Confederate capital at Richmond. This time he started on the east coast, at Yorktown (where the Revolutionary War had ended eighty years earlier). But President Lincoln and Secretary of War Stanton would direct his strategy. Lincoln insisted that Union troops must be left to defend Washington, and made it clear that he expected a decisive battle at the end of the campaign. McClellan took Yorktown and Williamsburg, and then, despite his great numerical superiority halted his advance, waiting for General McDowell to join him. The Federal outposts were only four miles from Richmond. He telegraphed Washington that the "decisive" battle was about to begin.

Instead, he was hit by Robert E. Lee, and they fought the Battle of Seven Days as the Yankees tried to reach a secure position on the James River. When Lee was sure that Richmond was no longer threatened, he gave up the pursuit.

McClellan informed the President that he could not go on without 100,000 fresh troops. Lincoln could not provide more than 20,000 men, and he was under political pressure to replace McClellan. Radical Republicans wanted John Fremont, but Lincoln appointed Henry Halleck as general in chief, and General John Pope was called from the west to command the retreating Union forces.

Knowing that Pope's lines of communication ran through Manassas, Lee sent "Stonewall" Jackson to seize the town. Jackson defeated the Federal garrison and captured all of Pope's supplies. He let his men carry off everything they could eat, drink, or wear. Then he burned the town and held on until Lee arrived. In two days of hard fighting, the Confederates took thirty big guns, 20,000 rifles, and 7,000 prisoners, at the same time losing 9,000 men. Yankee casualties exceeded 15,000.

General Pope retreated across Bull Run to Washington, where he blamed his subordinate officers and his superior officers and any other scapegoats he could think of, before he was sent back west. Four months earlier, Union soldiers had been within a few miles of Richmond. Now positions were reversed, and Lee was twenty miles from Washington. General McClellan was eating breakfast when Lincoln and Halleck called on him and asked him to save the city. He immediately rode out to meet what was left of his army. The men wept and cheered, for whatever the politicians thought, "Little Mac" was the general they loved.

In September, contrary to Southern policy, General Lee took the offensive. He invaded Maryland, hoping that the arrival of Southern troops would bring that divided border state into the Confederacy. More importantly, a convincing show of Southern power might convince Europeans that they should finally ally themselves with the Southern cause. In his usual cautious fashion, McClellan advanced slowly, until a copy of Lee's orders fell into his hands and revealed the rebel plans. Lee suffered terrible losses at Antietam (Sharpsburg) and had to retreat. It was the bloodiest one-day fight in modern history.

It was not a "decisive" Union victory. McClellan did not attempt to follow and destroy the weary Southern army, which had fought seven major battles in as many months. It never had enough ammunition, food, clothing, or boots. Some said you could follow Lee's line of march by the bloody footprints his men left behind. But McClellan hesitated.

President Lincoln took Lee's retreat as an opportunity to issue his Emancipation Proclamation. He had considered such a step for a long time, pressed by Radical Republicans for whom the total abolition of slavery was the whole reason for the war. It was not Lincoln's reason. He wrote to Horace Greeley, "My paramount object is to save the Union...What I do about slavery and the colored race, I do because it helps to save the Union. What I forbear to do, I forbear because I do not think it would help to save the Union."

On September 22, using his war powers, he published the Proclamation, to take effect on the first of the following year. It freed slaves in the rebel states, but said nothing about slaves held in the border states, or anywhere else in the Union or the Territories. As Lincoln saw it, their condition was a Constitutional issue. In fact, the Proclamation was almost ignored until the advance of Union armies compelled slaveowners to comply. The Democratic party in the North opposed emancipation, as did General McClellan, and many people thought the president had gone too far. That opinion was reflected in the results of the 1862 mid-term elections, and in Northern enlistments. Congress voted for a conscription act, which permitted drafting men into the Union army, unless they could pay somebody to take their place.

"Stonewall" Jackson's troops remained in the vicinity of Washington, making its citizens anxious and the politicians furious. McClellan continued to build a huge force with which, he assured the president, he would soon be able to strike the South a mortal blow. But the loudest voices in Congress were through with McClellan. They suspected him of Southern sympathies and his preference for a negotiated peace. In November, they convinced Lincoln that he had to go. He was ordered to turn over his command to General A. E. Burnside. It almost caused a mutiny among the troops, but George McClellan behaved with perfect discipline, making the transition as smooth as possible. What resentment he may have felt, he reserved for a coming political fight.

Burnside offered Lincoln and Stanton a deceptively simple strategy. He would take the shortest road to Richmond and batter the rebel capital into submission. The plan worked as far as Fredericksburg, where he got his troops over the Rappahanock River in battle order. He had 118,000 men, compared to 80,000 with Lee. But Lee had fortified the river banks with cannon, protected by logs, stone walls, and earthworks, and his sharpshooters were dug into rifle pits.

Wave after wave of courageous Northern boys stormed the slopes, yet were cut down by rebel fire. The Union losses were enormous. Burnside wanted to regroup and continue the assault the next day, but other officers realized that their position was hopeless. The Union army pulled back, having lost 15,000 casualties, while the Confederates lost fewer than 5,000. Fredericksburg was a disaster for the North, and for Burnside, who was soon replaced by General Joseph Hooker.

The western war was more or less at a standstill. The chief Confederate commander was General Joseph R. Johnston, but neither he nor President Davis could give orders to armies recruited in the separate Southern states. It would have been politically impossible for Davis to call the army of Arkansas to cross the Mississippi and join the defense of Vicksburg, the main objective of the Union campaign. Johnston held the Federals off at nearby Chickasaw Bluff where, in a single hour, the rebels killed 2,000 attackers while losing only 150 in a sturdy defense. A much bigger battle was fought at Murfreesboro, Tennessee, with a terrible death count on both sides. But the bloodshed at Murfreesboro did not achieve the Union purpose, which was to open the Mississippi Valley to Northern troops and transport.

While trying to defeat rebels on the battlefield, the president and Congress rewarded citizens who remained loyal to the Union. In May, Congress passed the Homestead Act, granting 160 acres of unoccupied western land to any family man who had not fought against the United States. For a small registration fee and a promise to live on and work the farm for five years, poor city dwellers and eastern families struggling on small plots could get a real homestead. For $1.25 an acre, they could buy the farm in six months. Such legislation had been opposed for many years by Southern Congressmen who didn't want non-slave territory settled and admitted to statehood, upsetting the balance of power they had tried to maintain since the Missouri Compromise. After Southern states seceded, the law was enacted, and 15,000 homestead claims were filed by the end of the war.

In July, President Lincoln signed another land grant bill, introduced by Representative Justin Morrill of Vermont. It gave government land to every state that stayed in the Union, 30,000 acres for each member of a state's delegation in Congress, land that could be sold to endow "at least one college" in each state. This proposal had long been the cause of Professor Jonathan Turner, at Jacksonville College in Illinois. He could see little value in the instruction offered at Harvard and Yale, at least for young men who would be farming the west. They needed instruction in modern agricultural methods, and the use of new farm machinery, in mechanics, practical chemistry, and engineering. "We wish them to read books," he said, "only that they may better read the great volume of nature ever open before them." These two men helped make possible the affordable education young Americans obtained at our great land grant colleges and universities, a system unequaled anywhere in the world. Professor Turner's curriculum (which included home economics for young women) was soon expanded to a full academic program. After reconstruction, similar grants were provided for the former Confederate states.

1863

In his constant effort to find a competent general, Lincoln chose General Joseph Hooker, whose performance at Antietam had won him the nickname of "Fightin' Joe." But the army he took over was a mess. After the slaughter at Fredericksburg, more than 300 officers and 80,000 men had gone absent without leave, or simply deserted. They might have returned to fight under McClellan, but it took the rest of the winter for Hooker to rebuild a force with which Lee could be surrounded and beaten.

For the first time, black men were taken into the Union army. Federal law had prohibited blacks from serving in the U.S. army, navy, or state militias, but now secretary of War Stanton authorized the governor of Massachusetts to recruit blacks, to the great joy of Frederick Douglass and Douglass's sometime associate, Martin Delaney. Delaney was born free in what became West Virginia (admitted to the Union in 1863) and got a good education when his family moved to Pittsburgh. For a while he attended Harvard medical school, but the objection of white students forced him to leave. Convinced that blacks had no future in America, he devoted his energy to planning, promoting, and organizing the back-to-Africa movement. But at the outbreak of the war, he and Douglass threw themselves into the enlisting of black soldiers.

Douglass's son immediately joined the fifty-fourth Massachusetts Volunteers, the first of more than 160 all-black regiments that would serve. One hundred eighty thousand men entered the army; 10,000 joined the navy. Of that number, 63,000 were former Southern slaves. In the first year of the war, Northern generals had returned escaped slaves to their masters, a policy that infuriated abolitionists but reflected the unwillingness of white officers and men to serve with slaves. The lack of Union victories and a diminishing pool of white recruits changed military minds. A song of the day endorsed "Sambo's Right to be Kilt." Frederick Douglass was too old to fight, but Martin Delaney eventually became a major, the first black to see duty as a field officer.

Some blacks tried to join the Confederate army, but they were refused. Indian soldiers were acceptable. Many from the "Five Civilized Tribes"— Cherokee, Chickasaw, Choctaw, Creek, and Seminole—sided with the South, and suffered for it when the war was over.

The war was stalled in the west, but in the east, armies fought and fought again over the same ground. Washington and Richmond—only a hundred miles apart! Yet the power of the North could not break the intrepid resistance of Southern armies.

By May, Lee's position was precarious. He was outnumbered two to one by Federals, who slashed their way through the trees and bramble scrub of The Wilderness and were met by "Stonewall" Jackson's corps. Remembering the disaster at Fredericksburg, Hooker had prepared a position at Chancellorsville and halted there. Lee divided his troops, sending Jackson to make a surprise attack from behind the Union line. With Lee in front and Jackson behind, Hooker's army might be destroyed. Jackson went forward with a few cavalry officers to reconnoiter. As they rode back, they were mistaken for the enemy and fired on by their own men.

Jackson took three bullets in his shoulder and arm, was knocked from his horse, yet clung to life. The Confederates fought savagely the next day, and the next. Hooker's army withdrew. Almost 30,000 soldiers fell in three days of fighting at Chancellorsville, including "Stonewall" Jackson. He had suffered severe blood loss, and his left arm was amputated. He knew the end was near. On May 10, he said, "Let us cross over and rest under the shade of the trees," and then he was gone, an irreparable loss to Lee and the South.

Whatever his private anguish, Lee was now asked to lead his forces on a long march west. The Southern armies that stood between Ulysses S. Grant and Vicksburg needed reinforcement. Lee refused. He would not risk losing his native state to save Mississippi. Instead, once again, the ragged rebels headed up the Shenandoah Valley. This left Richmond exposed, and General Hooker suggested another attempt to take the Confederate capital. Lincoln would not approve the plan. Privately, Lincoln and Halleck agreed that Hooker would not command in the next battle, wherever it took place. Hooker angrily resigned, and was replaced by General George S. Meade.

While Lee's army gathered in the foothills of the Blue Ridge Mountains, one of his commanders crossed to the town of Gettysburg, Pennsylvania, looking for shoes. He encountered Federal cavalry and turned back, but Lee's position was discovered. A dozen roads led to Gettysburg. Now Lee and Meade raced to gain an advantage. On July 1, 50,000 men clashed in fierce fighting that favored the South, and Union losses were brutal on the following day. Meade wanted to order a general retreat, but his Council of War urged him to make a stand.

On the afternoon of July 3, the Confederate batteries began a heavy bombardment, and under that cover General George Pickett tried to charge the Union center. A half mile of rough ground lay between the armies. Pickett led forty-two regiments out in perfect order, rank on rank, flags flying, drums beating, into a hail of enemy fire from Cemetery Ridge. They were cut down like rows of ripe corn, but they kept walking forward until they were too few to attack. Trying to get back, they stumbled over the bodies of their screaming wounded and their dead. It was the last charge at the Battle of Gettysburg. Lee lost 28,000 men, killed, wounded, or missing in action—a third of the force still under his command. General Meade spent 23,000 men. And neither side won.

At the same time in the west, 30,000 Confederate troops in the starving city of Vicksburg surrendered to General Ulysses S. Grant after a siege of six weeks. New Orleans was already in Union hands, and with the fall of Vicksburg, the Mississippi Valley was open to Northern ships and troops. The Confederacy was divided, east from west. Vicksburg was taken on the Fourth of July, just as Lee was loading his shattered Gettysburg army, and as many of the dead as he could carry, into wagon trains for the jolting sixteen-mile haul back to a Potomac crossing. The river was in flood, and Lee braced himself for a final Federal attack. It never came.

In the North, many Americans were ready to quit. Some midwest states considered recognizing Southern independence. A Congressman named Clement Vallandigham protested that this "wicked, cruel, and unnec- essary" war was being fought to free the blacks and enslave the white man. He was a leader in the Copperhead faction of the Democratic Party, named after the poisonous snake that strikes without warning. The mayor of New York City in 1862 was a Copperhead, and so was his brother, who published a newspaper and stirred up resistance to the draft. Fifty thousand rioters fought the police in mid-July demonstrations; Federal troops had to be called in to disperse the mob.

In November, President Lincoln trav- eled to Pennsylvania to dedicate a cemetery on the bloody site of Gettysburg. He was not the main speaker, and his remarks were brief, but this country has never forgotten a line of the Gettysburg Address.

Despite a valiant effort by General George H. Thomas, Union troops were defeated at the Battle of Chickamauga (Georgia). Both sides suffered horrifying casu- alties. A total of 36,000 men were listed as dead, wounded, or missing, carnage second only to the three days at Gettysburg. The remainder pulled back to Chattanooga, and Grant marched swiftly to their relief. When William Tecumseh Sherman arrived with additional strength, they made a devastating attack on Missionary Ridge above the city. Sherman then confronted General James Longstreet at Knoxville. Longstreet retreated, and the Union controlled Tennessee.

1864

The Federal general in chief, Henry Halleck, still could not run the war from Washington. President Lincoln gave supreme command to General U. S. Grant and put him in charge of all the field armies of the United States. Grant had no illusions about the cost of a Union victory. After Vicksburg, his initials had come to stand for "Unconditional Surrender" Grant, and he was ready to spend the lives of as many Union soldiers as he needed to achieve it. General Sherman, his second in command, shared that cold determination. This war would not be settled battle by battle, one great commander against another. "We are fighting a hostile people," Sherman said. His tactics would be total war.

But 1864 was an election year, and among Republicans there was growing opposition to the renomination of Abraham Lincoln. The North was tired of the war. Influential men, inside and outside the government, were critical of the President as Commander-in-Chief and wanted a more aggressive leader. Salmon P. Chase, Lincoln's Secretary of the Treasury, was approached, and agreed to accept the nomination if it was offered to him. Radical Republicans led by Representative Thaddeus Stevens held an early convention and named John Fremont as their candidate. They also called for a Constitutional amendment limiting the presidency to a single term. Horace Greeley wrote that "Mr. Lincoln is already beaten." Lincoln himself, in a private memorandum, predicted that he would not be re-elected and pledged his cooperation with the new President between the election and inauguration day.

Nevertheless, when the regular Republicans convened, it took only one ballot to nominate him. For Vice-President the convention chose Andrew Johnson of Tennessee, a man with thirty-five years of political experience as a Democrat. He had served in local offices, in Congress, and as governor before his election to the Senate in 1857. He voted against Lincoln in 1860. But though Johnson had owned slaves, he knew that the Southern cause was futile, and he opposed secession. He was the only Southern Senator to support the Union, refusing to give up his seat when Tennessee joined the Confederacy. After Tennessee was occupied by northern troops, Lincoln sent him to take over as military governor of the state. Johnson was still a Democrat in 1864, but Republicans now called themselves the "Union" party and hoped his name would win votes in the border states.

The Democratic convention was strongly influenced by the Copperhead faction of the party. Its platform called for "an immediate cessation of hostilities"—some sort of truce or armistice during which the North and South might discuss their future relationship. But their presidential nominee was General George McClellan, and he rejected the platform. He could not face the troops he once led and tell them that the Union for which they fought was abandoned.

General Sherman began his sweep through the deep South, determined to destroy not only Confederate troops but their will to fight and ability to resist. He laid waste to everything in his path, farms, factories, railroads, and supply depots, slowed only by the stubborn courage of rebel forces.In April, Lincoln gave supreme command of the Union armies to General Ulysses S. Grant. Grant set up his headquarters with the Army of the Potomac. In spite of draft resistance, the North could still get fighting men. When the last campaigns of the war began, Grant had an army of 100,000 soldiers, and he used them. In the Battle of the Wilderness, the Battle of Spotsylvania, and the butchery at Cold Harbor, Grant suffered 60,000 casualties, as many men as Lee commanded. Then he marched southeast to Petersburg, twenty miles below Richmond, trying to get control of the railroad lines that supplied the Confederate capital. P.G.T. Beauregard held him off with 2,200 troops, and Grant settled into a long siege of the entrenched city.

A small contingent of Southern forces raided in Maryland, reaching the outskirts of Washington, D.C. before they turned back into the Shenandoah Valley. Joe Johnston's dwindling rebel army beat Sherman on the rocky slopes of Kenesaw Mountain. But Sherman resumed his grim advance, and by July he was threatening Atlanta.

Old Admiral Farragut commanded the Federal fleet that attacked the port of Mobile, Alabama. Since the beginning of the war, a Northern blockade had tried to prevent foreign ships from reaching the Southern coast. But thousands of smugglers, daring blockade runners, reached the harbor at Mobile to unload their cargoes of war supplies—and luxury items for the few civilians who still had money to pay. The harbor was full of mines, called torpedoes. When one of his gunboats was sunk, Farragut shouted, "Damn the torpedoes! Full speed ahead!" And Mobile was taken.

In September, General Sherman entered Atlanta and ordered its inhabitants to leave. Then the city was set afire. Refugees moved ahead of the blaze, carrying what they could salvage, watching as railyards, factories, warehouses, and their homes were reduced to ash and rubble.

These victories insured Lincoln's re-election. John Fremont withdrew from the race, and Salmon Chase decided to support the party ticket. Lincoln won with an impressive margin of popular votes, and the electoral votes of every state but Delaware, New Jersey, and Kentucky.

A week after the election, Sherman began his famous march to the sea. He left behind him a path of destruction forty miles wide, the countryside smashed and smoking. He took Savannah, Georgia, without a fight, and telegraphed the President that it was a Christmas present.

Nevada was admitted to the Union.
The Thirteenth Amendment to the Constitution, abolishing slavery, was sent to the states for ratification in February.

President Jefferson Davis and his

Richmond government made two big decisions. Robert E. Lee was put in command of the Confederate army, and the South began to train black troops. Lee approved the plan, which had been proposed months before but was rejected as a step toward abolition. How could black men who fought for the South be sent back into slavery after the war?

Desperate Confederate representatives in France and England had already offered abolition in return for recognition of Southern independence by those countries. But they were refused; they had waited too long.

Fort Fisher and Fort Wilmington, both in North Carolina, were the last ports open to blockade runners. When they fell, the South was isolated. Sherman burned Columbia, South Carolina, grimly determined to punish the state that first called for secession. Then he moved into Charleston.

In March, President Lincoln delivered his unforgettable Second Inaugural Address: "With malice toward none, with charity for all, with firmness in the right as God gives us to see the right, let us finish the work we are in, to bind up the nation's wounds, to care for him who shall have borne the battle and for his widow and his orphan, to do all which may achieve and cherish a just and lasting peace among ourselves and with all nations."

As Southern plantations were destroyed or abandoned, slaves left behind had to find their own means of survival. Lincoln's administration set up a Freedmen's Bureau to provide temporary care for their needs, food, shelter, medicines, and most important, schools. The Bureau's director hoped to resettle many of the homeless families on land vacated by war-scattered owners, but this plan had little success. There wasn't enough money to solve the problems of almost four million ex-slaves.

White men in Pulaski, Tennessee, organized another solution. The Ku Klux Klan began as a social club for a few young

Confederate veterans who liked to dress in costumes and masks for evenings of pranks in the neighborhood, a Halloween kind of rough foolishness and often a way of settling private grudges. They found that if they rode out at night, wearing sheets and pretending to be the ghosts of dead soldiers, they could terrorize lost and wandering blacks. Soon that became their purpose. With threats and whippings and burnings, they reminded freed men and women that whites still held the power. From small local secret society, the Klan spread its terrifying influence.

In the Virginia springtime, Southern troops lost the last battle of the war. Phil Sheridan faced George Pickett at Five Forks. If Sheridan could take and hold the rail lines there, Petersburg and Richmond would be cut off from any kind of supplies. Gallant George Pickett was badly overmatched, and finally defeated. Sheridan took 5,000 prisoners and opened Grant's way through Petersburg to Richmond. Grant notified President Davis that he intended to occupy the city. Jefferson Davis, his family, and the Confederate government fled before the Union army.

Weeks earlier, Grant and Sherman had met with Lincoln on a riverboat and received his instructions for the Confederate surrender. "Let 'em up easy," Lincoln said.

On April 8, General Lee rode between ranks of Union troops to Appamatox courthouse, where General Grant was waiting. Lee's worn uniform was spotless, but his famous horse, "Traveler," was caked with mud. Surrounding the ragged rebels, Grant's men raised a cheer until Grant stopped them, "They are our countrymen now." Then, following the president's instructions, he told Lee's soldiers to stack their rifles but keep their horses, and sent them home to their families. Officers, too, could go, keeping their sidearms. General Lee, Grant's prisoner, was paroled.

Six days after Lee's surrender, Abraham Lincoln was shot and fatally wounded while attending Ford's Theater in Washington.

The assassin was John Wilkes Booth, an actor who had openly plotted for months, recruiting a band of fringe lunatics to kidnap the president. After Lee's surrender, the plan changed to murder, with Lincoln, Vice-President Johnson, Secretary of State Seward, and General Grant as intended victims. Johnson and Grant were not attacked, but Seward was wounded in a knife assault. After shooting Lincoln, Booth leaped to the theater stage and broke his leg, but managed to escape to Virginia, where Federal troops found him hiding in a barn and killed him. Eight of his collaborators were caught, and whether or not they had played an active part in the plot, four were tried and hung.

The President was taken to a boarding house across from the theater, where he died on Saturday morning, April 15. The next day was Easter Sunday. A city prepared to celebrate victory and national resurrection was plunged into grief and despair. After a funeral service at the White House, Lincoln's body lay in state while mourners passed to pay their tearful respects. Then it was taken on board a funeral train for a long last journey of 1,700 miles, through Philadelphia, New York, Cleveland, Chicago, cities where the train stopped and other services were held. At last he came home to Springfield, Illinois, where he was buried on May 4.

1865

Andrew Johnson

Andrew Johnson was sworn in as the country's seventeenth president immediately after Lincoln passed away. But it was Edwin Stanton, Secretary of War, who assumed almost dictatorial power in these confused hours.

General Sherman met with Confederate General Johnston two days after the assassination and gave his old enemy the first word of Lincoln's death. Johnston was stunned. Like Grant, Sherman had no instructions other than those he had received from the dead President, so there in a North Carolina shack, he took a piece of paper and penned his terms, which they both signed. Relentless in war, Sherman was generous in peace, agreeing to a general amnesty and further concessions, which were immediately rejected by Secretary Stanton and the War Department. New, tougher surrender terms were demanded. Sherman was angry, but Johnston complied. Mopping up operations went on for another month, until the last Confederate officers surrendered their troops. In May, it was finally over. Secretary Stanton was convinced that Jefferson Davis and Southern leaders were involved in the plot to kill President Lincoln. He was wrong, but when Davis was captured (disguised in his wife's clothes, trying to escape to Mexico), he was thrown into a cell at Fort Monroe, Virginia, charged with treason, and held for two years.

A hard war had ended. It was followed by the ten hard years of reconstruction, which forever changed the relationship between the states and their federal government.

The Constitution they had agreed upon in 1789 gave the Federal government specific powers: to provide for national defense, to regulate foreign trade, to build roads and carry the mail, to coin money, and to perform a few other duties. All powers not included in that short list were "reserved to the states exclusively, or to the people." This was the doctrine of "states' rights," for which the Civil War was fought. But Thomas Jefferson had supported the right of a state to secede, if a dispute between the state and the Congress could not be settled in any other way. Several Northern states had considered secession in the past. States' Rights had been argued out during the Jackson administration, in the long wrangle about tariffs. The doctrine is still asserted today, when a federal law is thought to interfere with the local authority of a state. But the Civil War seemed to settle any question about the right to secession: not without a fight. And the thirteenth Amendment to the Constitution settled the question of slavery. Nobody, in any state, could own slaves. Those questions had been decided by the American people.

Reconstruction was a slow and painful process. Halfway through his first term, Lincoln had formulated his Ten Percent Plan for bringing the Southern states back into the Union. It did not include men in the Confederate government, but offered all other rebels a pardon if they would accept emancipation and swear an oath of allegiance to the United States. When ten percent of the voters took the oath, they could organize a new state government, hold local elections, and apply for readmission. As military governor of Tennessee, Andrew Johnson had put such a program into effect, and similar plans were carried out in Arkansas, Louisiana, and Virginia. Now he was President.

Johnson had never belonged to the plantation aristocracy of the old South. He was a poor boy from the Tennessee back country, who worked as a tailor before he entered politics. But he shared Southern attitudes and prejudices. He didn't seem to notice, and certainly didn't interfere, when the old Southern power structure revived and took over the business of Reconstruction. New state governments were organized by former slave owners. White men determined how blacks would live and work, and what they would be paid. The night riders of the Ku Klux Klan kept frightened blacks in line. These months of Presidential Reconstruction infuriated Congress and the North. When Congress reconvened in December, it refused to recognize the new Southern governments or to seat the elected representatives they sent to Washington.

1866

Congress extended funding for the Freedmen's Bureau, and Andrew Johnson vetoed the measure. Then Congress passed a bill that gave civil rights to all persons born in the United States, regardless of race. When Johnson vetoed that bill, Congress voted again and passed it over his veto—first time in history that a presidential veto was overridden.

In June, Congress went further and proposed a fourteenth Amendment to the Constitution, giving full citizenship to all native-born (or naturalized) Americans. It specifically excluded Indians, despite their undeniable native birth, and in counting the population for purposes of representation in Congress, women were not considered "persons." It would take two years before the amendment was ratified, and meanwhile relations between Congress and the President worsened.

Many of President Johnson's conservative supporters were defeated at the midterm elections. Thaddeus Stevens now led the Radical Republicans, and began to play political hardball. He came from a Pennsylvania district with many Amish people, whose religious convictions made them longtime opponents of slavery. He had upheld the black cause for thirty years. After the war, and the assassination of his President, Stevens was cold and vengeful, determined not only to change laws and politics, but to destroy the old Southern way of life.

Ten southern states would not accept the Fourteenth Amendment. These were now divided into five military districts, each governed by a Union general. Secretary Stanton sent Federal troops and black militia to maintain order. New constitutions were written and new elections held. For the first time, black men voted, and they voted for Mr. Lincoln's party. Under Radical Republican rules, there were more black voters than qualified whites, and ex-slaves were a political majority. It was a stunning reversal of traditional Southern roles.

The economic picture for freed men was not as bright. Thaddeus Stevens wanted to divide 850,000 acres of Confederate land into forty-acre farms, to be sold for $10 an acre. This plan fell through when Andrew Johnson pardoned the rebel owners, and they reclaimed their estates. Like thousands of poor whites, black farmers became tenants, sharecroppers who rented from the owner, and bought supplies at the owner's store, paying at the end of the season with part of the crops they raised. Rarely did the owner's account book show any profit for a sharecropper; more often poor tenant farmers found themselves deeper in debt each year.

The proudest achievements of the Freedmen's Bureau came in the field of education, as it opened nearly three thousand schools to eager blacks of all ages. Many were also attended by poor whites, who had previously received little or nothing in the way of instruction. And the Bureau created black colleges where future leaders got a start. Booker T. Washington went to one of the first, Hampton Institute in Virginia. It offered industrial courses and trained schoolteachers, giving him a model on which he later based his own college at Tuskegee, Alabama. W.E.B. DuBois began at Fisk University, founded even earlier in Nashville, Tennessee. Though they later disagreed on almost everything, Washington would certainly have shared DuBois' opinion that the Bureau was "the most extraordinary and far-reaching institution of social uplift that America ever attempted."

But not all history was being made in the South.

Vitus Bering was a Danish explorer working for the Russians when he "discovered" Alaska in 1741. Of course, Alaska had been known to its own inhabitants for at least 20,000 years, since the last Ice Age. The native population of North and South America was descended from nomadic Asian people who crossed the narrow straits between the continents on ice bridges. They gradually moved down the Pacific Coast, and then east, bringing with them fire and domesticated dogs, and their own agriculture, though they did not have the wheel or the plow.

Nevertheless, Russia named the straits for Bering, and Russia claimed the Alaskan territory. In 1867, Czar Alexander II offered to sell Russian America to the United States for $7.2 million. Secretary of State William Seward jumped at the deal, acquiring 375 million acres for about 2 cents an acre. The purchase was called "Seward's Folly" until gold was discovered and, much later, enormous reserves of oil. In the same year, the expansionist secretary acquired the Midway Islands, three square miles in the North Pacific, with no native people. He thought they would have strategic importance for American shipping and the United States Navy. He was also thinking about the Sandwich Islands (Hawaii), and about islands in the Caribbean— Cuba, Santo Domingo, the Danish West Indies.

1868

Nebraska was admitted to the Union.

Secretary Seward was now one of Andrew Johnson's last political friends. The President's enemies in Congress had passed the Tenure in Office Act, which would prevent him from dismissing a Cabinet member without Senate agreement. This was insulting interference with a president's traditional right, and Johnson vetoed the bill. He had long wanted to be rid of Edwin M. Stanton, his radical Republican Secretary of War, and when the

Senate passed the Act over his veto, Johnson decided to test the law by firing Stanton, and appointing General Grant.

The House of Representatives immediately brought Articles of Impeachment against the President, which meant that he would have to stand trial before the Senate. If found guilty, he would be removed from the White House. The only important charge was Johnson's violation of the Tenure in Office Act. Congress could not accuse him, as Thaddeus Stevens suggested, on the grounds of "insanity or whiskey," but they made up eleven other trivial charges, supported by the flimsiest evidence.

In March the trial began before Chief Justice Salmon P. Chase and the entire Senate, secret proceedings that went on for two months. Seventy-six-year-old Stevens shook with hate as lawyers defended the President on each count. In the end, the Senate voted thirty-five to nineteen to convict, but this was one vote short of the two-thirds majority needed. Andrew Johnson was acquitted and served the rest of his term, a bitter and powerless man. It was the only time in our history that a President has suffered the disgrace of impeachment.

Four days later, the Republican convention met in Chicago and quickly nominated General Ulysses S. Grant as its candidate. Nobody else was considered. Grant had no political credentials; he had voted only once in his life, and that as a Democrat. But he was a victorious fighting man, a sure vote-getter, and that was enough for the cheering delegates.

Democrats assembled in New York City's new Tammany Hall, with Horatio Seymour, the former Governor of New York, presiding. One of the first speakers before the meeting read a petition from Susan B. Anthony, asking the party to support voting rights for women. Her address provided welcome comic relief, giving Democrats a good laugh before they got down to serious politics. For the next three days, there were speeches for many candidates. After twenty-one ballots, a semi-reluctant Seymour was the party's choice. The disorganized Democrats never had a chance against General Grant. He waited quietly at his home in Galena, Illinois, until informed that he had carried twenty-six states and won the election.

Ulysses S. Grant

Andrew Johnson was a poor excuse for a president, but U.S. Grant was worse, an honest man who trusted crooks. His administration came to be known as the era of the Robber Barons, the men who became fabulously rich and powerful as post-war America got back to business. Andrew Carnegie, a poor boy from Scotland, worked his way up from a job in a cotton mill to control of the steel industry. John D. Rockefeller bought out small oil producers until he owned most of the refineries, producing oil for America's lamps. J.P. Morgan was the banker, financing the growth of monopolies that kept prices high and wages low.

One sure way to get rich in America was to own a railroad. In 1867, Commodore Cornelius Vanderbilt was already a shipping tycoon, and he made another fortune with the New York Central Railroad. But it wasn't enough. He wanted the Erie line, which was owned by a shrewd old horse dealer named Daniel Drew. The two men fought their own war in the stock market. Drew's shady partners, Jay Gould and Jim Fisk, printed phony stock as long as the Commodore would buy it. When he discovered the fraud and got a New York warrant for their arrest, the three men stuffed his money in suitcases and fled across the river into New Jersey. They fortified their hotel with artillery pieces from a local militia company and hired a police guard.

Both sides bribed judges and legislators during the two-year struggle, until Vanderbilt finally gave up. The Erie gang returned a million dollars (of the millions they had stolen from him), and the Commodore concentrated on buying smaller railroad companies and extending the New York Central rail to Chicago.

By 1869, Jay Gould was a trusted friend of President Ulysses Grant. He advised the president to stop the sale of gold from the Treasury Department, telling Grant that it would help western farmers. Then he and Jim Fisk began buying up all the available gold in the country. Washington insiders and other gullible buyers followed their example, pushing gold prices higher until Gould decided it was time to sell. In the last four days of this spree, Gould and Fisk made more millions. When the president finally caught on and ordered the Treasury to start selling gold again, prices plunged. This was the "Black Friday" panic of September 24, a financial collapse that ruined many banks and businesses and led to a prolonged depression. Jim Fisk was shot and killed in a quarrel about a woman, but Jay Gould was just getting started.

Railroading in the west offered even bigger opportunities for bold investors. During the Civil War, Congress had authorized a railroad from Omaha, Nebraska to Sacramento, California. It would be an enormous undertaking, too costly for a nation at war. When peace came, two companies were chartered to organize the project. The Union Pacific would operate a line from Nebraska, heading west. The Central Pacific Company would start on the west coast and build east. For the actual construction of their rail, the men who owned Union Pacific (and one of them was Jay Gould) created another company, the Credit Mobilier, which sold stock to pay for construction. Representative Oakes Ames of Massachusetts (another partner) spread the stock around where it would do the most good. He gave or sold shares to Congressmen who voted grants of money and land to complete the plan. Eventually, Union Pacific received 9 million acres of government land.

Not until an investigation three years later was the extent of the scandal revealed. Grant's first Vice-President, Schuyler Colfax, and the second Vice-President, Henry Wilson, were both involved, as well as the Speaker of the House, James G. Blaine, and Representative James Garfield. (All four men denied any guilt; Blaine would later be a presidential candidate, and Garfield would be elected.)

Meanwhile, at the other end of the line, the Central Pacific Company ran a similar operation. The charter was given to four California businessmen: Collis Huntington and Mark Hopkins owned a Sacramento hardware store; Leland Stanford, a former governor of California, sold mining supplies; Charles Crocker had been a miner and ironworker. After they got the railroad contract, they too spent generously for government favors. Each session of Congress was said to cost Huntington between $200,000 and half a million. But it was worth it. Central Pacific was given twelve million acres of federal land.

Congress paid by the mile for railroad construction $16,000 for track laid on level ground, $48,000 for every mile through the mountains. The two companies raced each other to build mileage, because the real profit in railroading was not in providing transportation but in selling land and mineral rights along the right-of-way, and taking bribes from towns that wanted service, and otherwise cheating the public in any way the companies could devise.

Who did the actual construction work? Ten thousand Chinese immigrants were sent from California to join Central Pacific crews that cut tunnels and hacked out a rocky roadbed, freezing in the mountains, sweating on the bare plains. They were paid a dollar a day. At one time, 60 percent of the permanent pick-and-shovel crews were Chinese. Thousands of Irishmen pushed the Union Pacific line west from Omaha, driven hard in the mileage race.

On May 10, 1869, the two rails met at Promontory Point, fifty miles west of Ogden, Utah. Leland Stanford used a silver-plated sledge hammer to drive the last spike, of California gold. There were speeches and champagne, and even the exhausted workers cheered with pride in their achievement.

It has been estimated that the railroad could have been built for half as much as the government paid for it. But who can calculate its worth? While scoundrels stole millions from a willing Congress, the west was opened up for eager settlers. Soon thousands of sod houses sprang up on the plains, the homes of families that got free homesteads. Farmers bought better acreage for very little money. Millions of men and women found undreamed-of freedom, opportunity, and prosperity, sharing the abundance of the American west.

1870   But this glorious prospect depended on a final solution to the Indian problem. White developers had no intention of sharing the abundant West with its native people.

Eastern Indians had been evicted from their homelands years before, under the Indian Removal Act of 1830. In 1834, a Department of Indian Affairs was created within the War Department. Government maps showed land across the Mississippi to be reserved for Indians, and a Permanent Indian Frontier behind which Indians were to be confined. The government was slow to grasp the complexity of the "Indian problem."

The West was a vast territory, and the cultures of the tribes were vastly different. The broad expanse of the Great Plains was home to nomadic buffalo hunting people, the Sioux, Arapaho, Cheyenne, Kiowa, and Comanche. Agricultural Pueblo people lived, not always peacefully, with Apaches and Navajos in the Southwest. In the Northwest, Nisqually, Puyallup, Yakima, and Chinook were hunters and sea-going fishermen. Some California Indians were heavily influenced by old Spanish mission cultures, while others lived in independent groups.

In dealing with these diverse people, the government at first tried to make treaties, defining them as "domestic dependent nations." And many tribes were, in fact, loosely affiliated as "Nations," but not in the sense that white men used that word. Indian chiefs did not "rule" their tribes. They led by consultation and consensus. They could not speak for warrior bands that continued to resist white expansionism. For whites did not accept the idea of a Permanent Frontier. Trappers, hunters, prospectors and miners, settlers eager to stake their claims, wave after wave of whites arrived, and the fighting was bitter and bloody. The army built small forts, from which troops were expected to protect the whites, and protect Indians from further incursion into Indian Territory.

In spite of warrior resistance, it was a losing fight. More and more chiefs were persuaded to sign treaties and move to reservations. Their people were promised certain rights—limited right to manage their own affairs and to keep weapons to be used only for hunting. More importantly, they were promised food, supplies, and money with which to make a fresh start. And, of course, behind the promises, there was the military threat, even after Indian Affairs was moved to the Department of the Interior, it was still the Army's job to round up nonreservation tribes and force their relocation. As an Indian Commissioner reported to Congress in 1848, "Apathy, barbarism and heathenism must give way to energy, civilization, and Christianity." The old Indian Territory was reduced, but augmented by regional sites, and by the late 1850s most tribes were living on reservations.

Their life was hard. Reservations were managed by agents under the direction of the Bureau of Indian Affairs. Agents were often appointed by Congressmen, as political favors, because it was easy for an agent to swindle Indians and line his own pockets with government money. The system was riddled with incompetence and corruption, and treaty promises were unkept. Indians starving once more turned to raiding white settlements.

The Santee Sioux uprising in Minnesota occurred when that tribe was refused its rations. Before it was put down by the army, 400 whites were killed. New mineral discoveries brought mining into Navajo land. When Indians fought back, the army pursued Navajo and Mescalero Apache tribes and herded 8,000 Indians onto the miserable Bosque Redondo Reservation. In 1864, Cheyenne tribes were ordered to report to Fort Lyon, Colorado. Their chief, Black Kettle obeyed, because at the fort they would be fed. Soon they were told to move to nearby Sand Creek and feed themselves. But early one morning, the camp was surprised by 700 soldiers. Though the American flag flew above Black Kettle's tepee, they shot and bayoneted men, women, and children, a massacre that shocked the east. Atrocities were committed by both sides as the plains blazed up in continuous fighting.

During the Civil War, Indian warriors outnumbered regular army troops in the west. After the war, an Indian Commissioner surveyed Indian affairs and recommended that treaty efforts be discontinued. Generals Sherman and Sheridan were sent out, taking with them the concept of total war that had been so successful in Civil War campaigns. During the winter of 1868-1869, they fought the plains tribes, hitting the winter camps where the tribes were most vulnerable. Women and children, as well as warriors, died in the fighting, or starved and froze when supplies were lost.

But this warfare was costly for the government, too. An Indian Commissioner estimated that it cost a million dollars to kill an Indian (one observer said that poisoned flour would be much cheaper). So in 1869 President Ulysses S. Grant announced his Peace Policy, conquest through kindness. He was caught between the army and eastern do-gooders who, now that blacks were free, could worry about Indians. Nobody knew the horrors of war better than U. S. Grant. He sought civilian advice, particularly from Quaker leaders. Indians were no longer to be regarded as nations with whom the government could negotiate, but as wards of the nation, to be fed and cared for on reservations.

Grant appointed his old friend, Brigadier General Ely Parker, as the first Indian to be Commissioner of Indian Affairs. Parker was born Donehogawa, son of a Seneca chief, in upper New York State. He went to law school before he found that Indians were not allowed to practice law. So he got a degree in civil engineering, and at the outbreak of the Civil War, he tried to enlist in the Army Corps of Engineers. Secretary of State Seward told him the war would be fought by white men alone. "Go home, cultivate your farm, and we will settle our troubles without any Indian aid." He persevered until he got a job as Grant's military secretary.

But not even Ely Parker, Chief of the Six Nations and American patriot, could clean up the mess in the Indian Bureau. The reservations were divided up into regions, to be superintended by various Protestant denominations. They assumed the role of caretakers who would civilize and Christianize the tribes. To that end, they saw the need for government boarding schools, where children would be removed from family and tribal traditions and taught the white man's ways.

With the coming of the railroad, more thousands of white men and women traveled west, now including European immigrants and unemployed veterans of the recent war. The Indians lived by hunting bison. Huge herds roamed the plains, and the Indians killed great numbers for food and for their hides, which were made into clothing and shelter. But now white hunters came, with their rifles. They were hired to supply buffalo meat for railroad crews (one of the suppliers was Buffalo Bill Cody). And buffalo robes became fashionable accessories for the carriages of the well-to-do. Sportsmen came as well, to shoot buffalo for the fun of it. And cattlemen came, to clear buffalo herds from the grazing lands they needed. As the buffalo disappeared, the tribes that depended on those herds for survival had no choice but to accept the dubious generosity of Washington. The end of resistance was in sight.

The Fifteenth Amendment to the

Constitution was ratified in the spring of 1870. Once and for all, in two short paragraphs, it affirmed that the right of citizens of the United States to vote could not be denied "on account of race, color, or previous condition of servitude," and the new law would be enforced. The language of the Amendment was not open to any argument. Former slaves, black men in every region of the country, finally had the vote. No Indians. No women.

Former Confederate states would be re-admitted to the Union as soon as they accepted this amendment. One by one their legislatures voted, and when the Texas vote was recorded in March, the country was whole again.

1871

A great fire burned in Chicago for three days, destroying property worth $196 million. The old song says it was started when Mrs. O'Leary's cow kicked over a lantern in the milking shed. Even in the biggest cities, people still kept cows to supply their own milk. Some had pigs, many had chickens, and of course, to ride or pull a carriage, all but the poorest had a horse or two. City streets were filthy, and city air was perfumed by animal and human waste, as well as every kind of garbage, but cities continued to grow.

1872

In Washington, D.C., the stink was government corruption. The Secretary of War took bribes from traders who ran stores on Indian posts. The Secretary of the Navy was paid off by naval contractors. President Grant's private secretary made his millions from the Whiskey Ring that defrauded the Internal Revenue Department. These men, and many more, were Republican officeholders, but the Democratic leader in the House was paid off with Credit Mobilier stock, and other Democrats got their share of the loot.

Public works in Washington provided rich pickings for the Republican "Boss" Shepherd, but his theft was nothing compared to the larceny of Democratic "Boss" Tweed in New York City. William Marcy Tweed bribed everybody from the governor and mayor down to the lowest clerk in city government. Every city contractor was told to add 100 percent to his price and kick it back to the Tweed ring. He stole more than $200 million before stories in the *New York Times* and cartoons in *Harper's Weekly* led to his downfall. The cartoonist was brilliant Thomas Nast, who drew "Boss" Tweed as a ravenous tiger, tearing the heart from a bleeding city. Nast and the *Times* were offered huge bribes, but they kept up the attack until Tweed was finally jailed.

Throughout the country, reformers began to organize. Senator Carl Schurz of Missouri led a group of Liberal Republicans out of the party, calling a convention in Cincinnati to reject President Grant and choose a new presidential candidate. Fiery, red-bearded Carl Schurz had fought for decent government and civil liberties since his student days in Germany. As soon as he arrived in America, he took up the black cause, pushing President Lincoln for faster action on emancipation and he commanded black troops during the war. Now he was a power in the Republican organization, and wrote a powerful opening statement for the Liberal platform.

But his convention attracted a mixed assortment of delegates, idealists and cranks, job seekers and influence peddlers. Schurz expected the nomination of Charles Francis Adams, the son and grandson of former presidents. Like his distinguished forebears, Adams was a man with every qualification for high office, but little warmth or charm. After six ballots, Schurz lost control of the meeting, and delegates turned to Horace Greeley, the veteran of so many earlier reform battles. At sixty-one, Greeley was nationally known as the editor of the *New York Tribune*, a chubby, child-like figure with spectacles halfway down his nose, untidy gray hair, and fuzzy chin whiskers. His appearance made him an easy target for the pen of cartoonist Thomas Nast. But for all his eccentricity, he had fought many good fights. He had supported the war, but he also wanted amnesty for the South when it was over. He wanted universal suffrage, voting rights for every American. His head could not rule his heart.

Greeley brought all his old energy to the campaign against President Grant. His slogan was, "Turn the rascals out." But corruption issues were almost lost when Greeley received the endorsement of the Democratic party, for Democratic meant "southern sympathizer" to most of the northern press. Greeley was quickly accused of links to ex-Confederate leaders and to the midnight crimes of the Ku Klux Klan. A rival editor wrote, "If any one man could send a great nation to the dogs, that man is Mr. Greeley."

On election day, Grant won every northern state. He had the votes of Union army veterans, and of black men voting for the first time, and every vote that could be bought by his rich friends. Three weeks after the election, Horace Greeley died.

It was in this election that the question of votes for women first gained wide attention. Outraged because the Fifteenth Amendment did not enfranchise women, Susan B. Anthony and Elizabeth Cady Stanton had organized the National Woman Suffrage Association, and urged a Sixteenth Amendment to give their sex the ballot. In 1869 they campaigned in Kansas for a state law, getting 9,000 out of 30,000 votes cast by men. This encouraged them to believe that a national amendment might have some chance of success. In the same year, the Territory of Wyoming was organized, and the Territorial legislature gave women voting rights. It had a population of fewer than 10,000 settlers, and not enough women. Hoping to attract brave ladies, it would soon be proclaimed as the "Equality State."

But in 1872, most of the attention was focused on glamorous Victoria Woodhull, a party unto herself. She had already dazzled old Commodore Vanderbilt into backing her as an investment broker and started her own very entertaining and successful newspaper. When she announced that she would be the first woman candidate for president, she caused a sensation. She invaded the spring meeting of the National Woman Suffrage Association and held the women spellbound. Even Miss Anthony and Mrs. Stanton were carried away, but they came to their political senses just in time.

Miss Anthony not only campaigned for President Grant but decided to vote in Rochester. Since nothing in the Constitution actually prohibited women from voting, she registered herself and fifteen other women, and they marched to the polls. All were arrested. When Miss Anthony was tried three weeks later, the judge convicted her and ordered a $100 fine. She refused to pay. The judge threw up his hands and dropped the case.

Victoria Woodhull received not a single vote and would run again in four later elections with no greater success.

1873　　Nobody can explain the bank panic of 1873, or the five-year depression that followed. If you could ask the people who lived through it, you would get many answers, depending on where they lived and how they made a living.

Many people blamed the depression on a shortage of money. Before the Civil War, every American dollar was backed by gold stored in Treasury Department vaults. For convenience, the government printed paper dollars, but each paper dollar carried a written promise: if you took it to a bank, it could be redeemed in gold. The Treasury also minted silver dollars, and smaller coins. To finance the war, Congress authorized the Department to print paper money far in excess of government gold, backed only by the credit of the United States. These "greenbacks" were supposed to be withdrawn from circulation by 1879.

But farmers who needed to buy land, new farm machinery, and seed for next year's planting, wanted a plentiful supply of any kind of money, and were happy to have "soft" money to pay their debts. Small businessmen and shopkeepers also needed ready cash. These people began to organize themselves into a political party, demanding more paper money. When the government stopped minting silver dollars, it hurt the western silver mining industry and further limited the money supply. The Greenbacker Party kept growing.

Some people blamed the depression on the collapse of railroad building. As miles of track were laid in the years following the war, the railroads employed as much as 10 percent of the non-farm labor force, buying half the production of the metalworking industry. But railroads were owned and financed by speculators and outright crooks. The failure of the Northern Pacific set off a chain of failures that almost brought railroad building to a standstill, ruined the iron industry and all its suppliers, and threw thousands of people out of their jobs.

The railroads were a favorite target for the anger of farmers, who saw their profits eaten up by freight rates. A Minnesota farmer founded a semi-secret society known as the National Grange of the Patrons of Husbandry, soon called simply The Grange (an old word for barn). Its first purpose was to organize local banks, which would loan money to farmers at lower interest than eastern financiers were charging, and to form co-ops to buy farm machinery and other needed supplies. With better equipment and farming methods, production of wheat, corn, and cotton rose dramatically, while prices began to fall. There was a drastic slump in farm prices during the depression years. Farmers were infuriated by the charges they had to pay to ship their crops to market. It was cheaper to burn corn in the kitchen stove than to sell it. The Grange membership increased until it was ten times the size of the Greenbacker Party, with perhaps 800,000 members. In farm states where they held the balance of political power, Grangers won laws that set limits on rail shipping rates. Most of the Granger laws were later repealed, and a federal commission was set up to supervise railroad freight charges.

In the cities, too, there was widespread economic suffering and unrest. Workers in the shoe industry were displaced by new machines, and in the case of one Massachusetts company, by Chinese immigrant labor imported from California and willing to work for ridiculously low pay. Shoe workers organized the secret Knights of Saint Crispin, which became the largest union in the country. It was soon surpassed by the Knights of Labor, which began with garment cutters but aimed to organize all workers, farmers, and small businessmen into one big union. Factory workers saw unions as a way to win higher wages, but the Knights of Labor had a much larger dream. They wanted a country in which all laboring people got justice and dignity, a voice in government, and the recognition that honest work deserved in an America increasingly dominated by voracious capitalists, the Robber Barons.

The federal government was still trying to resolve the unfinished business of Southern Reconstruction. Radical Republicans had imposed a military occupation on ten states that were slow to swear an oath of loyalty to the Union. By 1870, all had accepted the oath and been readmitted, yet they were still governed by Republican outsiders, the hated "carpetbaggers" (so-called for their soft luggage) who came in with the military and ran public affairs. Even more despised were native-born "scalawags" who cooperated with the occupation.

Many "carpetbaggers" were certainly opportunists, looking to make a fast dollar in the shattered South. But others were serious men with professional abilities, hoping to restore the South to a functioning society. They included business people who invested in land and industrial development, agents and teachers who worked with the Freedmen's Bureau to improve the lives of former slaves, and politicians who helped organize elections and write new state constitutions.

And there was the core of the problem. Black men now had the vote, and in most Southern states, blacks were the overwhelming majority of voters. Of course, they were Republicans; they voted for Mr. Lincoln's party. With their votes, hundreds of blacks were elected to local office in small towns and counties. Six hundred served in state legislatures, and twenty-two were elected to Congress. Many were ignorant men, easily confused and corrupted by unscrupulous white politicians in both political parties, and seldom did they have notable legislative careers. But they behaved responsibly, with a clear understanding of what was needed to revive the South.

The first black elected to the House of Representatives was Joseph Hayne Rainey, of South Carolina, soon joined by John R. Lynch, from Mississippi, and Robert Smalls, also of South Carolina. Even before his election, Smalls was a famous man and a hero to Southern blacks.

John Lynch had learned to read by watching lessons through the window of a white schoolhouse, but a kind master let Smalls get some education. When the master's family moved to Charleston, he was hired out for city jobs. During the Civil War, he worked on the crew of The Planter, a Confederate dispatch and transport ship in the Charleston harbor. Outside the harbor, a line of Union ships maintained a blockade. Early on a May morning, while officers were absent from the

165

vessel, Robert Smalls loaded his wife and two children aboard, and boldly steered the ship toward the Union line. This exploit made him a free man and a celebrity. Because he knew the harbor and its fortifications, the new captain of The Planter used him as a pilot, the ship now sailing under the Stars and Stripes. When that officer deserted in the face of Confederate fire, Smalls took command and navigated out of danger. He was then made captain, and served until the ship was decommissioned after the war. He was elected to the South Carolina legislature in 1868, and to Congress in 1875.

Two black men served in the Senate, both from Mississippi. Hiram Revels was elected in 1870, to fill an unexpired term; he took the seat that Jefferson Davis had held before secession. In 1874, Blanche K. Bruce was the first black elected to a full term, and the last, for almost a century. Of course, no Southern white man, no returned Confederate veteran, would vote for the party of Lincoln and Grant. They were Democrats, and bided their time until they could regain political power. Though the Ku Klux Klan had been officially disbanded, it was now revived, and its nightriders terrorized the countryside, beating blacks—particularly black leaders and voters—but also white Republicans, carpetbaggers, scalawags, any victim they could blame for their reduced circumstances. Congress and the military joined to destroy the Klan in 1871-1872, but it would rise again.

Meanwhile, the depression distracted northern politicians from southern problems. Federal governors and troops were withdrawn from most southern states, and in many ways life returned to the bad old days. New Democratic state governments regained control and enacted the Black Codes that would dictate the lives of freedmen for generations to come. The Codes varied from state to state, but they decided where blacks could live and rent farmland, the terms of black employment contracts, and punishments for black "vagrants"—including whippings and sale for forced labor. The protection promised by the Civil Rights Act did not materialize. As black voters were kept from the polling place by threats or local voting qualifications, Democrats were elected to Congress, and in the 1873 mid-term elections, they became the majority party in the House of Representatives.

In 1873, three young farmers from De Kalb, Illinois, separately applied for patents on the same invention. The new product got far less attention than other inventions of the time, but it changed the face of the West. From Texas north to the Canadian border, from Kansas to Wyoming, stretched open range country, where more than 5 million steers had free grazing. They needed no shelter, they found water in whatever streams were flowing, and they were tended by cowboys—white, Mexican, and (almost half of them) black. Stock from many ranches moved about and mingled on the plains, until rounded up by cowboys and driven to railheads in cowtowns like Cheyenne and Abilene. From there they were shipped to Kansas City or Chicago, butchered, and sent in new refrigerator cars to markets in eastern cities. At round-up time, ranchers had to single out their animals by the brand mark. There was no way for a grower to fence his herd because fencing was too expensive on the unwooded range country.

Then, from De Kalb, came barbed wire—two strands of galvanized steel wire, punctuated by sharp points that cattle avoided. Strung between wood posts, it was the ideal material for a cattleman who wanted cheap fencing to keep his herd separate from a neighbor's stock. And it made it possible for settlers, the "nesters" who had taken up their free homesteads, to keep cattle out of their crops. They had been stopped for a generation at the edge of the plains, but now the days of the Wild West were almost over. Nevertheless, the twenty-five years of the cowboys with broad-brimmed hats, boots, and broncos, and six-guns created an image of free hard-riding and hard-living. It continued to be celebrated in dime novels and songs that we still sing.

1876   Depression and southern politics were not the concern of Indian fighters in the west. Big battles got headlines and led to shifts in government policy, but big battles were not typical of the conflict. Most soldiers spent their service time unsuccessfully pursuing the enemy over rugged terrain in blistering heat or bitter cold. Indians raided in small war parties, but rarely fought major battles.

The California and Oregon Modoc War (1872-1873) was an attempt to force the Modoc tribe back to its reservation. The small band held off nearly a thousand soldiers for several months, hiding in the lava beds of their homeland. Government attempts at peaceful negotiations ended when Modoc leaders killed the negotiators, including war hero Edward Canby. The result was a serious blow to President Grant's Peace Policy, and banishment of the Modoc from tribal land.

The Red River War of the southern plains (1874-1875) involved Kiowas, Comanches, Cheyenne, and Arapahos who had agreed to resettlement, after Medicine Lodge treaties several years earlier. They were angered by lack of food, white encroachments, and the slaughter of buffalo by white hunters. The government lifted its ban on military operations on Indian reservations. When thousands of Indians left, they were relentlessly pursued and their camps destroyed, until most of the tribes were returned to a reservation. Their leaders were jailed in Florida, and the Peace Policy got another setback.

On the northern plains, Sitting Bull was one of the leaders of Sioux, Cheyenne, and Arapaho that had refused the reservation. From the Cheyenne and other tribes came the Dog Soldiers, an elite band of warriors who scorned any peace overtures. But George Armstrong Custer was even less interested in peace. He had gone directly from West Point into the Civil War, and after the war he was assigned to a cavalry regiment at Fort Riley, Kansas, with the rank of colonel. In 1874 he ignored a treaty and led his troops into the Black Hills of South Dakota. It was sacred ground to the Indians, but when the white men found gold, all treaties were forgotten. Thousands of gold seekers invaded the Hills. Federal authorities tried to negotiate with the Sioux for the lease or sale of the huge territory. When the Indians refused, they were ordered to abandon their holy places and report to a reservation. Instead, Sitting Bull told his warriors to resist. General Sherman telegraphed Phil Sheridan, calling for a major offensive.

The most famous battle of the Black Hills War was Custer's attack in 1876. Against orders and without support, he led his regiment of 647 men against an Indian force of almost four times that strength, encamped in the valley of the Little Big Horn River, in southern Montana. He divided his troops, sending one battalion up the valley, and another to scout the left ridge. With about 250 men, he rode along rising ground on the right side of the river. On the morning of June 25, they were surrounded by Sioux warriors commanded by the brilliant Crazy Horse and Chief Gall. Within an hour, Custer and his men were all dead. The rest of his command escaped annihilation and stood off a day-long siege before they were rescued by the arrival of American troops.

This is the incident celebrated in our history and western legend as Custer's Last Stand. Crazy Horse surrendered in September, after having been promised a reservation for the Oglala Sioux. But there was no reservation. He died at Camp Robinson, in Nebraska, stabbed by a bayonet in a scrap with soldiers and police.

Colorado was admitted to the Union.

Politicians, meanwhile, turned their attention to the upcoming presidential elections, and many Republicans wanted President Grant to run for a third term. His White House performance was weak, and the two-term tradition was strong, but he still had the glamour of his Civil War victories and the loyalty of men who fought under his command. If Democrats attacked the scandals of his administration, Republicans would "wave the bloody shirt." However Grant refused to run.

The party nominated Rutherford B. Hayes, a war hero, a former Radical

Republican Congressman, and three times governor of Ohio. The Democratic convention chose Samuel J. Tilden, the former reform governor of New York, and the man who had prosecuted Boss Tweed, head of the New York City Tammany machine. The Democratic platform hammered away at a single issue—reform, reform, reform. Their prospects were very good.

When he went to bed on election night, Tilden thought he was the winner. He was ahead of Hayes by a quarter of a million votes in the popular count. But the Democrats were not sure they had carried the South. In South Carolina, Florida, and Louisiana, federal troops still guarded Republican governors who, in turn, strongly influenced election procedures and local voting. Newspapers reported that Tilden had only 184 electoral votes, one short of the majority he needed. Republican investigators were sent South to make an "inquiry." When the Electoral College met in December, it was given two sets of electoral votes from the disputed states. One set was validated by Republican governors, and one by the new Democratic authorities. There would have to be a re-count, but who would do the counting—the Republican Senate or the Democratic House of Representatives?

1877

Rutherford Hayes

Among charges of fraud, bribery, and violence during the popular voting, the argument dragged on through January and into February. It was not simply a disagreement about the official vote count. Passions ran high in the South, as Democrats realized that their election was about to be snatched away. There was talk of another war, and reports that Southern veterans were mobilizing to fight again. But behind the scene, politicians were busy with a favorite game: Let's make a deal. Republican governors in the South now exercised only a shadow power. The real power was held by Democrats, but not all of them belonged to the old plantation aristocracy. A new breed of Democratic businessmen were looking for new ways to make their fortunes. They didn't want war, they wanted—well, how about a government subsidy for a new Southern railroad, the Texas and Pacific, which would solve all the economic problems of the new South?

A special commission was appointed, consisting of five Republican Senators, five House Democrats, and five Justices of the Supreme Court. It was the last week of the Grant administration, almost Inauguration Day, before the Commission announced its findings. To nobody's surprise, the College accepted Republican electoral ballots from the contested states, giving Rutherford B. Hayes the twenty votes needed to win, or steal, the election.

This was the Bargain of 1877, in which some Southern Democrats sold the White House for Republican promises: to withdraw the last federal troops, to end all interference with the way the South dealt with ex-slaves, and to deliver favors that would benefit some Southern business interests.

Of course, many members of his party were furious, but Samuel Tilden accepted the verdict. He was not by nature a fighter, his health was poor, and he wanted to spare the country more regional strife. Hayes went on to serve four years, as an honest and moderate president, though dishonestly elected. Democratic papers always called him Rutherfraud B. Hayes. His wife, who refused to serve alcoholic beverages in the White House, was known as Lemonade Lucy.

After his inauguration, newspapers could give more space to sensational court-room reporting, as leaders of the Molly Maguires went on trial for their lives. For more than ten years the Mollies had terrorized the anthracite coal fields of Pennsylvania. They were Irishmen, and took their name from a heroine of land struggles in the old country. In America, many Irish immigrants drifted to the

coal mines, cheap, unskilled labor for the dirt-
iest and most dangerous jobs in the country.
But they began to organize, and fought the
mine owners with tactics that included threats
and assaults, the sabotage and destruction of
mine property, arson, and even murder.
Eventually they were infiltrated and betrayed
by an informer, and brought to trial. In 1877,
nineteen of their leaders were hung.

The Mollies were only the most violent
manifestation of increasing labor unrest, as
industry expanded and the monopoly power
of business combines grew. The men who
owned and managed those businesses were
angry and anxious, and it was in this atmosphere that the Great Railroad Strike of 1877
began at Martinsburg, West Virginia. During
three years of depression, the Baltimore and
Ohio Railroad had cut wages three times.
Workers struck to protest their low wages and
twelve-hour work days. The strike spread to
Baltimore, where Maryland militiamen were
called out to disperse the crowd of workers
and their families. Twelve people were killed.

But this show of force didn't stop the
strike. It spread to other cities, and the crowds
got bigger and louder. Strikers who demonstrated against the Pennsylvania Railroad in
Pittsburgh were again met by soldiers.
Millions of dollars worth of railroad property,
including 126 locomotives, were destroyed.
Rioting and shooting left fifty-seven dead. In
Chicago, the Workingmen's Association called
out 20,000 working men and their sympathizers. In St. Louis, a general strike shut down the
city for a week. National railroad traffic came
to a standstill, as the Great Strike brought
together workers from every part of the country and the economy. Mill girls and factory
hands, immigrant women in sweatshops and
farmers in the corn belt, all supported the strikers. When local militia refused to shoot their
own neighbors, President Hayes sent in regular army contingents to restore order.
Eventually the strike was broken, but not

before a hundred people had died and a thousand strikers were in jail.

1878

In an age of invention, Thomas Alva Edison and Alexander Graham Bell are stellar names. Both were born in 1847, Edison in Ohio, Bell in Scotland. Edison was severely deaf; Bell's father and grandfather had been teachers of the deaf, and with his father, he had done research on acoustics. Edison arrived in Boston in 1868, Bell three years later. Both used the facilities of an electrical shop that catered to inventors.

Bell opened a school for deaf children, and then began to experiment with the transmission of sound. He developed a device that he called the "telephone." He got a patent in 1876 (just two hours before another inventor, who was working on a similar idea) and exhibited it at the Great Philadelphia Centennial Exhibition, where it made a sensation. Hundreds of lawsuits were brought against Bell, but he went on inventing: a respirator that became the iron lung; boats, airplanes, and, with Edison, improvements for a commercially practical phonograph.

In Boston, New York, and in the famous labs he built in Menlo Park, New Jersey, Tom Edison worked on hundreds of inventions. His first patent was for an automatic vote counter (perhaps he had followed the furor during the Tilden-Hayes contest) but we hail him for the electric light. After endless experimentation, he found a bamboo filament that would glow inside a glass bulb, in a vacuum, for hours. Nine years later he invented the Kinetoscope, which became movies, and much else in between. When he turned to problems of electrical generation and transmission, he suffered a defeat. After a long lawsuit, George Westinghouse (inventor of the air brake) proved that alternating electric current was much more sensible for long distance transmission than Edison's direct current.

The first telephone exchange opened

in New Haven, Connecticut, in 1878, the same year that Edison founded the Edison Electric Light Company.

1880

Because neither President Hayes nor Samuel Tilden wanted the job, the political parties scrambled to find presidential candidates. The Republican party had been born thirty-five years earlier to confront the great issue of slavery. It had freed the slaves, led the Union to victory in the Civil War, and undertaken the almost impossible tasks of Reconstruction. But now the country was tired of Reconstruction, and wanted to get on with national expansion.

The depression had lifted, and money was not a major concern. The government started minting silver dollars again, and buying enough silver to appease western miners. Greenbacks could again be redeemed for gold, but Americans had such confidence in their government that on the redemption date only $125,000 in paper money was exchanged for gold, while $400,000 in gold was turned in for paper. With no great issues to argue, both party platforms were a hash of political cliches and tired propaganda.

The former Confederate states were now Democratic, the Solid South. The north and west were mainly Republican, and many in the party wanted to send their star player, former President Ulysses Grant, back into the game. But a dozen other candidates volunteered to take his place. Thirty-seven ballots were required before the convention agreed on Senator James Garfield of Ohio, with Chester Arthur, the handsome boss of New York, as his running mate. They narrowly defeated a Democratic ticket headed by Winfield Hancock, a famous Civil War general. The Republicans won by fewer than 10,000 votes.

In July, President Garfield was shot at the Washington railroad station, as he was about to leave for his college reunion. Wounded in the back, he hung on for almost ten weeks of

1881

James Garfield

Chester Arthur

1884

terrible suffering before he died on September 19. His assassin was Charles Guiteau, who had been seen at the White House for many months, as he tried to wheedle an appointment as the American consul in the port of Marseille, France. He was executed by hanging the following July.

Chester A. Arthur was sworn in as the twenty-first president. He was a tall, elegant gentleman, who liked to sleep late and dine well, a sportsman, and an able administrator. Though he had come up through the New York Republican machine, he was willing to consider reform proposals and, when it made political sense, to support them. So when Congress passed a bill to clean up the Civil Service, substituting competitive exams for political favoritism, Arthur signed it. He also favored government regulation of railroads and, above all, a modern navy. During his administration, the navy built three new and powerful warships, and acquired Pearl Harbor, Hawaii, as a base for Pacific operations.

President Arthur wanted a second term, but faced strong opposition at the Republican convention. The darling of the party was James G. Blaine, who had served as Speaker of the House of Representatives, as Senator, and as Secretary of State. He had sought the nomination in 1876 and in 1880, and did not intend to be passed over again. John Lynch, one of the first blacks to serve in Congress, chaired the Convention, and when Blaine was nominated, it set off five hours of riotous celebration, marching, cheering, more speeches, more demonstrations—one delegate called it "a disgrace of decency." Never mind that during his 1876 try for the office evidence had proved that Blaine took more than $100,000 for selling his influence in Congress. The past was forgotten, and he was once more the "Plumed Knight" of the party. Chester Arthur never had a chance.

The Democrats nominated Grover

Cleveland, the reform Governor of New York. Reform elements in the Republican party broke away to join the Democrats. They were called "Mugwumps," but with their votes and the Solid South, a Democratic victory seemed certain, until Republicans dug up the story of Cleveland's illegitimate child. The candidate admitted that he had an earlier affair with a widow of dubious reputation, and she had born a son. Cleveland had given the baby his name and supported it until the mother placed it in an orphanage.

So the Democrats jeered at "Blaine, Blaine, James G. Blaine, the continental liar from that state of Maine," while Republicans chanted, "Ma, Ma, where's my Pa? Gone to the White House, Ha! Ha! Ha!" Voters had a choice of scandals to enjoy, until one last blooper settled the question. A New York minister, announced that he would never leave the Republicans and join the party of "Rum, Romanism, and Rebellion." It was an insult to all Catholics, and gave the election to Grover Cleveland.

1885

Grover Cleveland

The Statue of Liberty arrived in New York in 214 sturdy crates ready for assembling. It was a gift from the people of France to the people of the United States, in recognition of their long friendship. Designed by the French sculptor, Frederic Auguste Bartholdi, it was to be erected on a pedestal constructed by American engineers on Bedloe's Island in the New York harbor. Americans were slow in contributing to the project until Joseph Pulitzer, publisher of the New York World, appealed for contributions and raised money.

The giant figure of Liberty, copper-sheathed, 151 feet tall and weighing 225 tons, was dedicated the following year by President Cleveland, to celebrate the 100th anniversary of the American Revolution. When nearby Ellis Island became the port of arrival and processing for millions of immigrants in the next decades, the sight of Miss Liberty lifting her lamp "beside the golden door" (as the poet Emma Lazarus would write) brought inspiration, joy, and hope.

Although the Chinese constituted only .002 percent of the population, and didn't represent much of a threat to American working people, their immigration was resented in the west. So on economic grounds, and expressing concern about white "racial purity," Congress passed the first major law restricting immigration. The 1882 Chinese Exclusion Act suspended their entry for ten years, and was renewed ten years later. In 1902 Chinese immigration was made permanently illegal and they were ineligible for citizenship until 1943.

President Cleveland was a huge man, 260 pounds, with a huge capacity for hard work. Except for the constant pestering by office-seekers, he liked the job of President and sincerely believed that "a public office is a public trust." He appointed capable men to his Cabinet. He fought corruption and wasteful government spending. He even answered his own phone. The Treasury had a surplus of $100 million during his term.

That money was mainly the result of very high taxes on foreign goods imported into the United States. Cleveland opposed such tariffs. They protected northern manufacturers from foreign competition but meant higher prices for American consumers. The president argued for a reduction of all tariffs, particularly the tariff on raw materials. This became the major issue between Republicans and Democrats in Congress, though neither party wanted to offend wealthy industrialists who could contribute to political campaigns. Safe behind the "wall" of a protective tariff, big business got bigger.

Working people continued their struggle for higher wages, better working conditions and an eight-hour work day. In May, 340,000 union members took part in a nationwide strike to call attention to their demand for "eight hours." In Chicago, picketers continued to march in front of the McCormick Harvester Machine Company. The demonstration was peaceful until police fired into the crowd, killing one picket and wounding several more. The next night, 3,000 union members and radical agitators turned out for a protest meeting in Haymarket Square. One hundred eighty policemen were on the scene, as the speeches became more violent and the temper of the crowd got uglier. When the police started to move in, somebody threw a bomb. Seven policemen were killed, and sixty-six others were wounded. In the riot and shooting that followed, many more working men died.

The bomb-thrower was never identified, but eight anarchists were arrested. Four were hanged, one committed suicide, and three were eventually pardoned by Governor John Peter Altgeld of Illinois, who (like many others) thought their trial had been unfair. But the bloodshed of Haymarket Square caused a sharp decline in the membership of the Knights of Labor, and in December, twenty-five craft unions founded the American Federation of Labor.

1886

Like his father, the immigrant Samuel Gompers was a cigar maker, and belonged to a national cigar maker's union that was affiliated with the Knights. The Knights dreamed of one big union for all workers, skilled and unskilled, in all trades. They were willing to include small businessmen, but emphatically excluded "bankers, lawyers, liquor dealers, professional gamblers, and stockbrokers." They reached a membership of 700,000 before the Haymarket incident.

But the Knights of Labor asked every working man to identify with the interests of all working men; railroad conductors were expected to support a strike by women in the garment industry, and vice versa. Samuel Gompers thought it was impossible to create or sustain that kind of common cause. Instead, he wanted to organize each trade and craft into its own union. Coal miners, carpenters, and clerks in their own unions could agree on their own economic objectives and work to achieve them. He was not interested in politics, nor a Labor Party. He took the cigar makers to a new union, reorganized in December, 1886, as the American Federation of Labor, which represented his own practical conclusions.

Gompers became the first president of the AFL, and filled that office every year but one until his death. He rewrote its constitution and the rules that emphasized the complete autonomy of each trade. And he stuck to his rules. He was not a dictator. He was a conservative man who tried to keep the diverse and fractured labor movement focused on "pure and simple" unionism, their own business: wages, hours, and working conditions; organizing for strikes, picket lines, and boycotts, any action where union strength could be effective.

But when it became clear that government power was often used against unions—when companies got court-ordered injunctions against strikers, and those orders were enforced by police, sometimes by soldiers—Gompers had to become more political. He supported Woodrow Wilson in 1912 and eventually became the elder statesman of the labor movement. Wilson appointed him to the Council of National Defense in 1917, and after World War I to the Commission on International Labor Legislation. By 1920 the AFL had four million members. The railroad unions, with about half a million members, never joined the AFL, nor did the Amalgamated Clothing Workers, another large union. But AFL locals grew, even though most excluded blacks, women, eastern European immigrants, and Asians. Progress slowed when the country moved into a ten-year depression, picked up again when recovery began. Sam Gompers served the labor movement for almost fifty years, and died in 1924, on his way home from his last

AFL convention.

President Cleveland lost his bid for re-election to Republican Benjamin Harrison, the grandson of old "Tippecanoe" Harrison. Business money was spread around lavishly to defeat Cleveland and his efforts to reduce the tariff. He got more popular votes, but lost in the Electoral College.

Benjamin Harrison

Two million acres of the old Indian Territory were bought from the Indians for a ridiculous price. It was opened up to white settlement, and on April 22 the Land Run began. In twenty-four hours, 50,000 settlers staked their claims.

Government policy was now set forth in the General Allotment Act of 1887. Tribes would no longer have any legal standing, and tribal lands would be broken up into individual allotments, 160 acres for Indian families, half that for single people. In return, Indians who gave up tribal rights would become American citizens, self-supporting, exchanging their heathen life style for private property and civilization. It sounded good to reformers concerned about the suffering of reservation Indians, and it sounded even better to the government, which would be relieved of treaty obligations and the cost of supporting Indians as dependent wards of the nation. Best of all, the Native American population was rapidly declining, and after surveys, officials calculated there would be much more land left over than Indians could possibly need. Tribal lands could be auctioned off to the highest white bidders. And those calculations were right. In five years the Indians lost half the treaty lands they "owned." North Dakota, South Dakota, Washington and Montana were admitted to the Union.

In this year, the Western Frontier officially vanished. The last great herd of buffalo was gone, and the Indian population dropped to fewer than 300,000. The great Apache chief, Cochise,

180

had died on a reservation, but Geronimo, still resisting, led attacks in the Apache War against Arizona settlers. After his surrender, he and the rest of the tribe were sent to a Florida prison. When gold was discovered in Oregon, the government seized much of the Nez Perce reservation. Chief Joseph put up a fight before leading the tribe north into Canada. He then recrossed the border into Montana, where they were forced to surrender and were relocated in Oklahoma. The many tribes of the great Sioux Nation were now scattered on the northern plains. Sitting Bull gathered the remnants and they, too, briefly found refuge in Canada. Eventually he gave up and was sent to the Standing Rock Reservation.

Most Indians did not die in fighting. They died of disease: cholera, typhus, tuberculosis. They also died of hunger and exposure on their long flights ahead of the army, or of exhaustion in long marches to relocation sites. A Paiute prophet named Wovoka began preaching Indian deliverance through non-violence and the Ghost Dance. His new religion brought hope: The whites would go, the buffalo would come again, the dead would reappear, and life would be as it once was. He found many believers among the Sioux, Cheyenne, and Arapaho, who gathered to sway and chant and see visions in which his prophecies came true. Not all were converted to non-violence. The growing number of Ghost Dancers made settlers and reservation agents nervous. In South Dakota, at the Pine Ridge reservation, they called in the army.

Three thousand Sioux had gathered in what was suspected to be a Ghost Dance uprising. Cavalry, infantry, and Buffalo Bill arrived. Sitting Bull had been a main attraction in Bill's Wild West Show, and he thought he could ask the old chief to help avert violence. But the reservation agent sent him away, and Sitting Bull was shot by Indian police who tried to arrest him. Big Foot was another chief, camping with 350 Miniconjous near Wounded

Knee Creek. He, too, wanted to counsel peace, but the army thought he was part of the rebellion. His people, mostly women and children, were rounded up and spent the night on the bank of the frozen stream. On the morning of December 29, the warriors were separated into a group and disarmed. Soldiers entered the camp and began to search tepees for weapons.

As a medicine man began dancing the Ghost Dance, a shot rang out, and troops began firing on the Indians. Surrounded by 500 soldiers, with heavy guns mounted on the ridge above them, Indians fought back with whatever rocks and lengths of wood they could find. Twenty-nine soldiers fell. In an hour, 200 Indians were dead or fatally wounded. As survivors fled, they were run down and slaughtered. About a hundred escaped through falling snow, but froze to death in the surrounding hills. The bodies in the camp, including the body of Big Foot, were thrown into a mass grave. New snow covered the campsite, the blood, and the grave, but the massacre at Wounded Knee cannot be obliterated from the American record.

Idaho and Wyoming were admitted to the Union.

1891

President Benjamin Harrison certainly had the credentials for his high office—great-grandfather who signed the Declaration of Independence, a grandfather who was president, a father who served in Congress. Harrison was a lawyer with a distinguished war record, and he went to the White House after a term in the Senate. He served the Republican Party well, but the country suffered.

Real power was exercised by the House of Representatives, where the Republicans had a majority of just three votes. But they had Speaker Tom Reed in the chair, and that was all they needed. Under "Reed's Rules," they managed to get rid of the enormous Treasury surplus, mainly by voting generous pensions to Union Civil War veterans. They also raised tariffs on almost everything any Congressman could think of, which delighted manufacturers, but set off a nationwide buyers' strike as the cost of living shot up. The President obediently signed all the bills they put before him, with the result that this was the first administration to spend a billion dollars in peacetime. "Why not?" asked Speaker Reed. It was a billion dollar country.

While politicians enjoyed the spoils of office, and industrial tycoons reaped huge profits, ordinary citizens were picked clean. After two years, they had enough. At the midterm elections, the Republicans were decisively defeated, and by 1892 a full scale revolt was sweeping the West.

1892

One of the organizers was Mrs. Mary Elizabeth Lease, a militant woman who came out of Kansas with considerable political experience. Her father was an Irish immigrant, and she had toured the state speaking for the Irish National League. She favored Greenback politics. She joined the Knights of Labor and the Kansas Farmers Alliance. She was a lawyer and a strong proponent of women's suffrage. She was also six feet tall. When Mrs. Lease spoke out, people listened.

The early 1880s had been boom times for farmers, but hard times followed. Between grasshoppers and drought and debts, many homesteaders gave up and went back east. Mrs. Lease had seen the whole cycle. She went to St. Louis in 1892 to attend the first convention of a new political party, the National People's Party, soon called the Populists. It represented Grangers and what was left of the Knights of Labor, and its platform went far beyond any earlier reform efforts. It called for a graduated income tax, and government ownership of the telephone and telegraph systems, as well as the railroads. During the presidential campaign, she stumped the country, drawing enthusiastic crowds in western states, but being pelted with eggs in Democratic Georgia. Reporters called her the Kansas Pythoness, a "miserable caricature upon womanhood." But she kept going, telling farmers to "raise less corn and more hell."

City people did not respond to the People's Party, though James B. Weaver, the Populist presidential candidate, tried to explain their common cause. They were all at the mercy of corporate and financial giants. He was proven right in July, when the quarrel between workers and management of the Carnegie Steel Company came to a head.

Though protected by a tariff that increased its profits, the company reduced wages. Its employees were represented by the Amalgamated Association of Iron and Steel Workers. The union refused to accept the pay cut and tried to negotiate, but the Pittsburgh plant was closed and thousands of men were laid off. After hiring 300 Pinkerton guards for protection, the manager tried to re-open with non-union employees. (The Pinkerton Agency provided private detective and security services; it had helped break the Mollie Maguires years before.) When they arrived, 5,000 steel workers were waiting on the riverbank. The strikers had guns and dynamite, and they pumped oil into the water, trying to set it on fire to burn the barges from which heavily armed Pinkertons kept up a steady barrage. The battle lasted two days, with many dead and injured, until 8,000 state troops were sent to the scene and the strikers were defeated.

Public opinion turned against the tactics of the Carnegie Company, and as the election approached, nervous Republicans appealed to the manager for a more reasonable approach to labor disputes. The Democrats again nominated Grover Cleveland, and in accepting the nomination, Grover Cleveland said flatly that the company owners had been made "selfish and sordid by unjust government favoritism."

The Populists took votes from both

parties, but on election day Cleveland was the winner, Harrison the loser, and the Populists in a distant third place. Cleveland was the only president elected to two non-consecutive terms.

As thousands of Americans made merry at the grand Columbian Exposition in Chicago, the country plunged into another depression. Maybe business had natural cycles, like farming, or like the fair's giant Ferris wheel, that took you up only to drop you from the top in a frightening descent. While some men stood in line to see the hoochy-coochy dancers, others stood in breadlines to get a handout.

Once more, money was scarce. There was less of it than before the Civil War, although the population had doubled. But instead of the Greenback solution—just print more money—debate centered on silver. The Silver Purchase Act of 1890 authorized the government to buy four and a half million ounces of silver every month from western mines, at the rate of sixteen ounces of silver for one ounce of gold. Now President Cleveland called an emergency session of Congress to repeal that law and protect the government's dwindling gold reserves. But why did America have to be tied to the Gold Standard, the idea that all money in circulation must be backed by gold in Treasury vaults? Why not both gold and silver to back the country's currency?

This was not a new financial proposal. It had been put forth during earlier depressions, and had strong appeal to Populist reformers. But President Cleveland insisted that every major economy in the world was based on gold. So the special session of Congress turned into a fierce debate which pitted the agricultural west and south against the industrial and financial east. Farmers needed silver money to pay their mortgages; bankers wanted their gold to retain its value. William Hope Harvey, a westerner, wrote a little book that sold for a quarter. He called it *Coin's*

Financial School, attributing it to a fictional young financial genius named Coin. It sold a million copies and became the bible of the Populist and Free-Silver movements. Free Silver was increasingly taken up by western and southern Democrats, who deserted their president as the depression deepened. Nevertheless, the Silver Purchase Act was repealed, and the Gold Standard prevailed, to be debated by future generations.

1894

Millions of men and women were out of work. Half a million employed workers were striking to protest wage cuts. The strikes failed because so many people were willing to work for any wage they could get. In March, "Coxey's Army" began to march on Washington.

What an army! At the head of the line was a black man waving the American flag. He was followed by about a hundred shabby marchers, carrying bundles of food and blankets. They left from Masillon, Ohio, where Jacob Coxey was a rich man. He owned a profitable sandstone quarry, and a farm where he raised racehorses. Coxey was a Greenback Democrat, a mild man with gold-rimmed glasses, a dimple in his chin, and a social conscience. During the depression he had to lay off some of his help, and it worried him. He thought the government should print money, but more importantly, it should hire the unemployed to build a national road system. He might have stayed home and expounded these ideas in Masillon, but he met Carl Browne, an old radical and a former sideshow barker, and together they conceived the march.

Coxey, the general, rode in a carriage, with his wife and an infant son named Legal Tender Coxey. He expected to be joined by thousands of the unemployed and their sympathizers. And he did attract publicity, as well as curious crowds. In small towns onlookers worried, because there were many bands of vagrants moving through the countryside, begging at farmhouse doors, camping in hobo "jungles," warming themselves around fires at the railyard. But eventually Coxey had an army of about 500, and they reached Washington, where neither President Cleveland nor the Congress would meet with them. Coxey was arrested and sentenced to twenty days in jail for walking on the grass.

Coxey got a hearing before a House committee chaired by Congressman William Jennings Bryan, already a rising man in the Free Silver faction. But a bill for his plan was buried. Perhaps 1,200 men in various armies camped around Washington all summer, and then dispersed. The general remained active in politics, running for many offices but only being elected to one term as mayor of Masillon. He returned to Washington several times. At 90, he read his petition again on Capitol Hill. He died in Masillon, in 1951, at the age of ninety-seven.

Eugene V. Debs led a bloodier action in Chicago. The Pullman Palace Sleeping Car Company had its factories and a company town for its workers on the south side of that city. Most of the workers belonged to the new American Railway Union, but in May, both union and non-union men spontaneously laid down their tools and walked off the job.

Debs had organized the ARU, and he thought it was the wrong time and place for a strike. Born and raised in Indiana, he got a railroad job as a fifteen-year-old boy, first as a locomotive cleaner and then as a fireman, shoveling coal into the firebox. It was dangerous work. He turned to bookkeeping, was elected to be the city clerk of Terre Haute, and then was elected to the state legislature. But his experience in railroading gave him a lifelong interest in rail unions and their efforts to improve conditions and wages for railroad men. He joined the Brotherhood of Locomotive Firemen and worked his way up in that organization, urging the importance of creating a federation of all rail unions into one big

187

enough to negotiate with the huge railroad companies.

His efforts created the American Railway Union (ARU), which had 150,000 members when the walkout at the Pullman Company began. The company had laid off most of its workers late in 1893 and then began hiring them back for a 25 percent lower wage. But the company did not reduce rents or utilities charges in its "model" company town— charges that were already higher than people paid in other parts of Chicago. When those deductions were made from his paycheck, one worker reported that his check was for seven cents. George Pullman said, "The workers have nothing to do with the amount of wages they shall receive."

The workers struck, and a month later the American Railway Union called for a boycott of all railroads that used Pullman cars. Most rail traffic between Chicago and the west coast came to a standstill. Debs told the union men to avoid violence, but President Cleveland sent troops to Chicago, and during the summer riots broke out. As many as thirty civilians were killed and more than twice as many were injured.

Gene Debs was indicted for conspiracy to interfere with interstate commerce, but was defended by the famous lawyer Clarence Darrow. Eventually the case went to the Supreme Court, where they lost the decision. Debs was sent to jail in Woodstock, Illinois. The court's ruling in the Debs case stood for the next fifty years, giving the government the right to step in and prohibit a strike that appeared to threaten a national interest. With Debs in jail, the strike and the ARU collapsed. But it made him a national hero to working men, a socialist, and a significant figure in politics for the rest of his life.

Depression, Free Silver, and labor strife were not the only problems President Cleveland had to wrestle with. The Democrats had promised tariff reductions, which would mean a loss of revenue to the federal government. To make up for that loss, the tariff bill proposed, for the first time, an income tax of 2 percent on incomes above $4,000—a good income in those days. Of course, that idea was bitterly fought by affluent people, and politicians who represented affluent people. In any case, the tariff reduction bill had been so changed by exempting hundreds of imports from the list of products originally included, that Cleveland refused to sign it. It became law without his signature, but the income tax provision was struck down by the Supreme Court as unconstitutional.

1895

Though many Democrats had now been converted to the cause of Free Silver, the President bravely and stubbornly stuck to his insistence on gold to back the country's money. But very little gold was left in the Treasury's reserves. Where was it? Well, here's a clue: President Cleveland and members of his cabinet met with the Wall Street banker, J. Pierpont Morgan, and arranged to buy $65,166,000 in gold, paying the bank with government bonds. Morgan and his syndicate agreed to use their influence to protect the government from further bank withdrawals of Treasury gold, and then made a nice profit by re-selling the government bonds to the public at a much higher price.

So Cleveland saved the Treasury, and lost most of his party support.

1896

In May, the Supreme Court handed down an opinion in the case of Plessy v. Ferguson, which would stand as law and shape the lives of southern black Americans for the next half-century. It grew out of a bill "to promote the comfort" of railroad travelers, passed six years earlier by the Louisiana legislature. Railroads were required to provide "separate but equal accommodations for the white and colored races."

Southern Reconstruction had ended with the "stolen election"

189

of Rutherford B. Hayes. In that political deal—dressed up as the Compromise of 1877—the Hayes Republicans got the electoral votes they needed, in return for withdrawal of the last federal troops from former Confederate states. Northern administrators packed their carpetbags and departed, leaving southern government to local control. Almost immediately, the small achievements of Reconstruction were wiped out. State laws and municipal ordinances began to build the wall of racial separation that was defined by a Richmond Times editorial, "It is necessary that this principle be applied in every relation of Southern life. God Almighty drew the color line, and it cannot be obliterated. The Negro must stay on his side of the line, and the white man must stay on his side, and the sooner both races recognize this fact and accept it, the better it will be for both."

Ex-slaves who had gotten a taste of freedom at post-war schools and polling places were now pushed back into the social, political, and economic realities of a segregated society. Black men were prevented from voting by the intimidation of the Ku Klux Klan, and then by increasingly discriminatory poll taxes, property requirements, and literacy tests. Not only schools were segregated, but also churches, theaters, lunchrooms, transportation, poor houses, prisons, even cemeteries. Of course, promoting the comfort of white people required many exceptions to God's color line. Black nursemaids were needed to tend white babies, and black laundresses to do the white folks' washing; black men waited on tables in the best hotels, and worked as porters (not conductors) on the railroads. Blacks and whites shared dozens of intimate daily contacts, and got along, as long as blacks understood their place. At the least sign of misunderstanding, there was the grim reminder of a lynching. There were 230 recorded lynchings in 1892 (161 black, 69 white), and usually more than 100 each year until the turn of the century; thereafter somewhat fewer.

Segregation laws were local laws, and when the Louisiana legislature passed the railroad accommodation bill, it infuriated the sophisticated black people of New Orleans. That city was home to a large community of educated and relatively well-off "people of color." Many could trace their ancestry back to the years of French law. Their attitudes were shaped by Creole traditions and by life in a great cosmopolitan port city. Some black men still voted in New Orleans or served in local elective offices. They now decided to test the railroad bill in the Supreme Court.

It took several years to pursue the matter. First they had to collect enough money for a prolonged legal action. They contacted a well-known civil liberties lawyer in Mayville, New York, to represent them. Albion Tourgee was a Civil War veteran, active in Reconstruction politics, and formerly a judge on the North Carolina Superior Court. Then Homer Plessy agreed to be the test case, which began when he bought a ticket on the East Louisiana Railroad to travel from New Orleans to Covington. He took a seat in the white coach, and when the conductor told him to move, Plessy refused. This incident had probably been arranged with the railroad authorities, because the conductor immediately called a detective and Plessy was taken away.

Tourgee represented Plessy before John H. Ferguson of the Criminal District Court for the Parish of New Orleans. He argued that the Louisiana Jim Crow law was null and void because it was in conflict with the Constitution of the United States. Judge Ferguson overruled him, setting in motion the long process which finally brought them all to the Supreme Court. There, despite Albion Tourgee's eloquence, they lost the case.

Delivering the majority opinion, Justice Henry Brown said that the Louisiana railroad law was perfectly "reasonable." If the colored race chose to interpret it, and other Jim Crow laws, as discriminatory—well, that was their interpretation. The court viewed such laws as neutral. Segregation was not, of itself, a "badge of inferiority." It simply drew a line. On their side of the line, white people felt perfectly comfortable. If blacks were unhappy on the other side of the line, that was a problem for black people, not for the Supreme Court.

Only one Justice, John Marshall Harlan, dissented from the majority opinion. He was a Kentuckian; he had owned slaves; he was exactly the kind of conservative Democrat who might have been expected to uphold segregation. But Justice Harlan saw that the United States, could not recognize two classes of equality. Once black men became citizens of the United States, they had all the rights and freedoms guaranteed by the Constitution. State laws could not decide that some men were more equal than others. The Constitution defined equality, and it applied to all Americans, whatever their color, wherever they lived.

Harlan was alone in his opinion. The Louisiana law and other Jim Crow laws stood for the next fifty-eight years. There was almost no comment on the case in the white press, because northern liberals were simply worn out with black problems and civil rights issues. Everybody wanted to get on with the fun of an election year.

At the Democratic convention, Silverites took over. Their platform asserted that the Gold Standard had led to "the enrichment of the money-lending class at home and abroad, the prostration of industry, and the impoverishment of the people."

A minority of the committee agreed that America should work to have both silver and gold established as the basis for money values in every country, but until that could be accomplished, America should remain on the Gold Standard to which all major nations were pledged. The convention paid them no attention. A South Carolina delegate shouted that Grover Cleveland was "the tool of Wall Street," and called for the president's impeachment. Temperatures in the convention hall began to rise.

And then William Jennings Bryan, a delegate from Nebraska, mounted the platform to make one of the most memorable speeches in American political history. "Mr. Chairman and Gentlemen of the Convention," he began, "...I come to speak to you in defense of a cause as holy as the cause of liberty—the cause of humanity." With spellbinding oratory he spoke for the west, for "the hardy pioneers who have braved all the dangers of the wilderness, who have made the desert blossom like the rose...who rear their children near to Nature's heart, where they can mingle their voices with the voices of the birds...You come to us and tell us that the great cities are in favor of the gold standard, we reply that the great cities rest upon our broad and fertile prairies..."

He challenged his opponents to come out " and defend the gold standard as a good thing..." and he would fight them. "Having behind us the producing masses of this nation and the world, supported by the commercial interests, the laboring interests, and the toilers everywhere, we will answer their demand for a gold standard by saying to them: You shall not press down upon the brow of labor this crown of thorns, you shall not crucify mankind upon a cross of gold!"

Then he stood silent with his arms outstretched until 20,000 delegates found their voices and shouted, "Bryan, Bryan, Bryan!" And the next day he was nominated as the Democratic candidate for the Presidency. Halfway through the speech, Governor John Altgeld of Illinois asked Clarence Darrow,

"What'd he say, anyway?"

The thirty-six-year-old Bryan was the youngest man ever nominated. He needed all his youthful energy for the campaign, which took him on a tour of twenty-nine states, making dozens of stops and fifteen or twenty speeches a day until he had spoken to five million Americans, trying to convince them that their hard lives and hard times could be blamed on eastern money men and the gold standard. Nineteen hundred years ago, he told them, God's house had become a den of thieves; Jesus threw the money-changers out of the Temple, and now it was time to throw them out of American government. His audiences listened, wept, and cheered.

1897

William McKinley

But Mark Hanna, a Cleveland millionaire, simply opened an office in New York City and began to shake contributions out of the money-changers, the rich Republicans, banks, and corporations who supported the Republican party. The Republican convention in St. Louis had nominated Governor William McKinley of Ohio. "Uncle Mark" told the candidate to go home, forget the exertions of a campaign, welcome delegations that Hanna would send to visit him, and shake hands with any voters who stopped by the front porch. Mark Hanna believed in the gold standard and a sound dollar, spent where it would do the most political good. With this no-nonsense approach, he raised millions, and McKinley was elected, with a comfortable Republican majority in both houses of Congress.

1898

The country had plenty of unfinished domestic business, but no political enthusiasm for dealing with those matters. The silver issue vanished after new gold discoveries in Alaska, Australia, and South Africa, and new technologies for gold extraction, doubled the world supply. The Treasury printed more gold-backed money, and there was no further demand for expanded silver coinage.

American industry was thriving behind a high protective tariff. The untaxed rich got richer, but it seemed impossible to unite working people in any effective protest. It's always easier to find a foreign target for national irritability, and in 1898, a feeble foreign enemy was close at hand.

The great Spanish empire that had dominated the New World was long gone. Only a few scraps of global real estate remained as evidence of the generations during which Spanish galleons ruled the seas. Among those bits and pieces was Cuba, a hundred miles off the coast of Florida, and Puerto Rico, a thousand miles farther east. On the other side of the world, Spain still held the Philippine Islands.

Since 1895, the Cubans had been trying to win their independence. The fighting was well covered in the American press. Papers like Joseph Pulitzer's *World* and William Randolph Hearst's *Journal* printed columns of lurid stories and horrifying pictures of atrocities in Spanish concentration camps. And behind the tabloid journalism were the hard facts of American investment in Cuba, starting with the $50 million American interest in its sugar industry.

President McKinley did not want a war, which might interrupt the country's recovery from the last depression. He offered his services to the Spanish government, to negotiate a peace with the Cuban revolutionaries. The pocket battleship Maine was sent to Havana as "a friendly act of courtesy." Everybody knew the ship was there to protect American citizens and property if the revolution escalated, but for three weeks, the officers of the Maine and authorities on the island exchanged civilities. Then, on the night of February 15, the Maine blew up.

Nobody has ever determined what caused the explosion. The ship sank, and 266 Navy men were lost. The World, the Journal and Theodore Roosevelt, Assistant Secretary of the Navy, assumed that the disaster was caused by hostile Spanish action, a torpedo or a hidden mine. The Spanish government protested innocence and sent condolences, but war fever rose in the United States. McKinley delayed as long as he could, but as of April 21 a state of war existed, and on April 22 Congress passed the Volunteer Army Act, calling for men to fight in Cuba. Teddy Roosevelt immediately left his desk job with the navy and was commissioned a lieutenant colonel in the elite cavalry dubbed the "Rough Riders." Many of them were genuine cowboys, used to rough riding, but many were college kids whose previous combat experience was gained on the football gridiron or the polo field. And in any case, their horses had to be left behind in Florida.

But the real war began in the Philippines when, on May 1, Commodore George Dewey fought a seven-hour battle outside Manila Bay, sinking the Spanish fleet stationed there. Spain lost 300 men; Dewey suffered a few casualties without losing a single ship. Puerto Rico was bombarded on May 12, and taken without further resistance.

In June, an American army landed in Cuba and there was major action, marked by considerable confusion and ineptitude on the part of American commanders. The army suffered serious losses inflicted by smaller Spanish forces. On foot, the Rough Riders followed Teddy up San Juan Hill in fighting that made a name for the outfit, and a heroic reputation for young Roosevelt. But with the final destruction of the Spanish fleet, the end was in sight. By the end of the month, Spain capitulated. On August 9, the war was over.

More than five thousand Americans died in Cuba, most from tropical diseases. The usual count for battle casualties was 379, including eighteen sailors. "It has been a splendid little war!" said John Hay, the American Ambassador to England, to his friend Theodore Roosevelt. And indeed it was—ten weeks of fighting that gave America an overseas empire: Puerto Rico and Cuba; the Philippines, Wake Island, and Guam; and also, almost incidentally, Hawaii.

Those islands in the middle of the North Pacific belonged, for all practical purposes, to American sugar producers. They had ousted Queen Liliuokalani and created a "republic" with Sanford B. Dole as president. They petitioned the United States for annexation, but Grover Cleveland had insisted on an investigation of island affairs, which indicated that most Hawaiians were not interested in becoming part of the United States and, on the whole, would prefer to have their queen back again. President Dole refused to give way. President Cleveland let the subject drop. But the use of Pearl Harbor as a base during the Spanish-American War renewed interest in its annexation, which was accomplished by a Joint Resolution of Congress on May 17. On August 12, the American flag was raised in Honolulu.

1899

Though he had limited experience with naval warfare, Captain Alfred T. Mahan wrote several books that made him an international authority on the subject. His conclusions were really fairly simple. Big ships could beat little ships in a naval engagement; a large navy with many big ships could whip a small navy; a country with a large fleet of big ships would be a dominant power in world affairs. He was an ardent expansionist. America had to take over islands in the Caribbean to defend the canal it had to build to link the Atlantic and the Pacific and to permit passage of its fleet of big ships from one ocean to the other. America had to be the greatest naval power on the planet, not only for the security and prosperity of the country, but for the future of mankind. American naval strength would decide whether the Anglo-Saxon race and western values would rule the world, or whether it would fall to the domination of Asian people.

Mahan believed that a small war was always good for national health and spiritual vitality. So the Spanish-American War and its territorial rewards was a very satisfactory development for him, as it was for other expansionists, like Roosevelt and Senator Henry Cabot Lodge. But there were many men in Congress who opposed this expansionist policy. An Amendment was attached to the war resolutions in Congress, making it clear that the United States had no intention of exercising "sovereignty, jurisdiction, or control" over Cuba. As soon as the island was pacified, its government would be left to its people. The same men objected to the annexation of Hawaii, because the America defined by the Constitution had no imperialist character. But they couldn't argue with the happy outcome of the summer action in the Caribbean.

The American victory also delighted a Filipino patriot named Emilio Aguinaldo, who quickly set up a revolutionary government and proclaimed the independence of his country. But though Congress guaranteed Cuba for the Cubans, there was no such agreement on the future of the Philippines. President McKinley proclaimed that America now had "duties and responsibilities" there, and also (in case anybody missed the point) "commercial opportunities to which American statesmanship cannot be indifferent."

So began another kind of war, three years of dirty and costly guerrilla fighting in the jungles of the Philippines. Aguinaldo held out until he was captured. Four thousand three hundred American soldiers died, and 600,000 Filipinos. Countless thousands were maimed and left homeless as their small villages and farm plots were destroyed.

But expansionists could celebrate when President McKinley and Germany's Kaiser Wilhelm II divided the Samoa Islands without hostilities. And John Hay, now Secretary of State, announced that he had secured international agreement to an

Open Door policy regarding China trade. All nations, he said, would have equal trade and development rights in that huge and troubled country. In fact, there was as yet no such agreement, certainly no arrangement to which the Chinese had agreed.

But America had an island empire, and the Asian mainland was now on the national agenda. In the hundred years since the country was founded, Americans had steadily moved west. They could not be stopped by a large pond called the Pacific Ocean. The war in the Philippines taught Americans that empires did not come cheap, but the country was excited and invigorated, looking forward to the international challenges (and commercial opportunities) of the twentieth century.

THE TWENTIETH CENTURY

America came late to the age of empire. Not much foreign real estate was left to grab. South American patriots had evicted Spain and Portugal from that continent; only a few British, Dutch, and French colonies remained on the northwest coast. Most of Africa, the Middle East, and India "belonged" to various European powers—primarily the acquisitive British. Canada was a British Dominion and Australia was a British colony with its own government. Russia was expanding into Asia, and Japan into China, where European and American trading companies had negotiated leases and agreed to respect each other's "spheres of influence". European powers seized islands in the Atlantic and Pacific oceans, which served as coaling stations for the great trading fleets.

But America spent the nineteenth century conquering its own domestic empire, a country so vast and so rich in resources that it had little need for food or iron or oil from abroad, or for land on which to settle its growing population. The country now had more than 92 million inhabitants, of whom ten million were blacks and Indians, most of the latter confined to reservations. Another ten million arrived as European immigrants in the first decade of the century. Most stayed in northern cities. Some midwest legislatures set up recruiting offices in the east, urging newcomers to move on and take jobs in the midwest, but three out of five Americans, old and new, were city dwellers, in housing from grand to grim. New York and Chicago ranked third and fourth among large cities of the world. Immigration had come under federal control. There were new laws to prohibit the entry of idiots and the insane, people suffering from "loathsome or contagious disease," paupers likely to become a public charge, and Chinese laborers. The main eastern point of entry was now the federal processing center at Ellis Island, New York; on nearby Bedloe's Island, the Statue of Liberty raised her lamp.

As Republicans prepared to campaign for the re-election of President McKinley, Democrats opposed Republican expansionist policies. Small wars had satisfied the nation's need to flex its muscles, and there was strong resistance to the idea of the United States as an imperial power. The Democrats once more nominated William Jennings Bryan, with Adlai Stevenson of Illinois as his running mate. The first plank of their platform took a stand against militarism which meant "conquest abroad and oppression at home."

But when the Republican convention chose Theodore Roosevelt as its candidate for Vice-President, the outcome of the election was settled. By tradition, President McKinley did not campaign for himself. It was Teddy, the Rough Rider, often wearing his battered old Cuban sombrero, who represented the party and drew cheering crowds.

As he had done four years earlier, Bryan made hundreds of speeches in a tour that covered twenty-four states, but the country was used to his eloquence. Teddy was a new voice, and though Republican bosses feared his maverick energy, he proved to be a vote getter. Republicans easily won the election.

1901

Theodore Roosevelt

In September, President McKinley was in Buffalo, New York, shaking hands at a public reception. He was approached by a young man whose right hand was wrapped in a handkerchief, as if he had just received a slight injury. While greeting the president, Leon Czolgosz shoved a revolver against McKinley's stomach and shot twice. He was an American anarchist, determined to kill some "great ruler." McKinley died a week later. Czolgosz was executed by the State of New York. Forty-three-year-old Theodore Roosevelt became President of the United States, the youngest man ever to hold the office.

Roosevelt came from an old and wealthy New York family. He was a sickly boy who suffered from asthma and wore thick glasses to correct his nearsightedness. So he worked at physical fitness all through his school years, and loved sports at Harvard, where he was a tough little boxer. He also loved books, read widely, wrote a history of naval warfare in the War of 1812.

After Columbia Law School he entered public life, served a term in the state legislature, and then went west to work on a North Dakota ranch. Teddy had always enjoyed and studied nature, but in the west he developed a passion for its landscape and wildlife. He returned to politics as a reform Republican, and was serving as Assistant Secretary of the Navy when he left Washington for the Cuban War and his famous charge up San Juan Hill. Now he was President—"that damned cowboy!" snarled Republican Boss Mark Hanna. Roosevelt installed his family and his wrestling mats in the White House and prepared to take on all comers, starting with the Robber Barons of Wall Street.

Big corporations operated under protective laws which limited their liabilities. They could take risks that individuals and partnerships could not afford. Now Americans were getting nervous about the growing power of corporate trusts, the combines and agreements in many industries, which used their financial resources and marketing strength to squeeze out their smaller competitors. With the monopolies they created they could set their own high prices. Consumers suffered, and so did independent businessmen. The Sherman Antitrust Act of 1890 was an attempt to control the trusts, which states could not regulate because they were interstate operations. The trusts found other ways to retain their monopoly control.

And so the years after the Civil War came to be known as the Gilded Age, during which great tycoons built fortunes that any foreign monarch might have envied, and used their wealth to buy political influence. The biggest tycoon on Wall Street was John Pierpont Morgan. He had inherited a fortune and a powerful international bank from his father; by the turn of the century he controlled the money business associates needed to finance their growth. Andrew Mellon was the Pittsburgh coal and iron tycoon, big enough to have his own bank—but he wasn't Morgan.

Andrew Carnegie, another Pittsburgh giant, consolidated his Homestead Steel works with seven other companies he owned to form the Carnegie Steel Company, then merged with the United States Steel Company. Tight-lipped John D. Rockefeller of Cleveland built the Standard Oil Trust, which was dissolved by the courts; but he continued to dominate the oil business. Phillip Armour made his fortune with the Chicago beef trust, but there was room for Gustavus Swift, who invented the refrigerated railroad car. Meat packers used every ounce of a beef carcass for a range of products, from prime cuts to sausage, glue, and fertilizer, using methods that would be exposed in a famous novel and make the country gag. In the west, the Guggenheims got rich from copper and gold, adding mines in South

America and rubber from Africa. William Randolph Hearst inherited a mining fortune and made another by publishing newspapers and magazines.

The railroads had easily eluded provisions of anti-trust laws. Edward Harriman controlled the Union Pacific and had his eye on the Burlington Line, which was also coveted by James J. Hill, who owned the Great Northern and the Northern Pacific. After a fierce battle on Wall Street, the two contenders called a truce and pooled their stock to create the Northern Securities Company, a huge railroad monopoly, financed and sponsored by J.P. Morgan. This combine was Teddy Roosevelt's first target, and he promised to wield a Big Stick.

1902

In February, the president announced that Northern Securities would be prosecuted under the Sherman Anti-Trust law, which had been on the books for ten years but was largely ignored by the business world. Morgan and others hurried to the White House, sure they could make a deal with the new young president. They didn't know their man. The case was successfully prosecuted and the rail monopoly prevented.

While proceedings began against Harriman and Hill, Roosevelt was confronted with another business crisis. Hard coal miners in eastern Pennsylvania walked off the job, and the mine owners (railroad men and J.P. Morgan) would not negotiate. The miners refused to go back to work in miserable and dangerous conditions for an average wage of $560 a year. The long strike was a crippling blow to many industries, and to city dwellers who depended on coal for heating and cooking. Roosevelt had no power to compel arbitration, but as winter came on he called the head of the United Mineworkers to the White House, pleading with him to consider the welfare of his fellow citizens and end the national emergency. The president of the union agreed to talks, but the representative of the coal companies coldly refused, characterizing the strikers as anarchists and criminals.

The angry president took one more step. He called J.P. Morgan and told him that the United States Army would be ordered to take over the mines; the army would operate the mines as long as the strike continued. Morgan put pressure on the mine owners until they accepted an arbitration commission. Eventually the miners got a 10 percent wage increase. During earlier labor disputes, the army had often been used to support management and break a strike. Roosevelt was the first president to use the threat of army action to compel arbitration, a significant victory for American working people.

And meanwhile he pursued another scheme. Since the eighteenth century the world had waited for a canal across the Isthmus of Panama, a way to link the Atlantic and Pacific Oceans. It was needed to serve world trade, and now the United States saw it as a military necessity. During the Cuban war, it had taken seventy-one days to move the battleship *Oregon* from its Pacific duty to the fighting in the Caribbean. Engineers debated the best route for a canal: the high route, across Nicaragua, or the shorter route through the swampy and fever-ridden jungles of the Columbian province of Panama?

A French company attracted thousands of investors and spent millions of francs on a dig across the Isthmus before they were defeated by the terrain, the climate, and disease. They abandoned the Nicaragua route, leaving behind the bodies of dead workmen and their rusting equipment, which they offered to an American company for the bargain price of $40,000,000.

1903

Congress voted to pay the French price. The Panama Canal Company, with money from Wall Street bankers, would undertake the enormous construction project. There was only one hitch. No agreement had been reached with the government of Colombia.

Roosevelt suggested a cash payment of $250,000, plus an annual rent of $250,000, for 300 square miles to be put under perpetual American control. Columbia considered the

203

offer, then turned it down. Teddy was ready to send troops to seize and occupy the canal route and protect construction workers.

But Phillipe Bunau-Varilla saw a simpler solution. He was a French engineer who had been in Washington for some time, trying to peddle the French investment. Now he put together a revolution in the Panama province, helped by connections in Panama, backed by American bankers, and tacitly supported by the Roosevelt administration. He supplied a "liberation fund," a flag, and a declaration of independence, which the secessionists quickly proclaimed. When a U.S. Navy gunship arrived, the new nation of Panama was born, immediately recognized by the American government but not by Colombia (until 1921, when America paid Colombia $25 million for the theft). Panama collected the money and gave America a 300 mile wide strip across the country. The Canal Zone comprised most of the new nation, and was guarded by American troops. Teddy was right when he later boasted, "I took Panama." Bunau-Varilla signed the treaty and became Panama's first minister to America.

But now the real work began, and success depended not on soldiers, or even army engineers, but on the efforts of doctors, for the enemy was disease. One of the most thrilling stories in medical history is the discovery in 1900 of the cause of yellow fever, and its transmission by mosquitoes—the fatal Yellow Jack. Dr. Walter Reed, a major in the medical corps, proved the mode of transmission, and Dr. William Gorgas eradicated Yellow Jack (and the less often fatal but terribly debilitating malaria) during the American occupation of Havana. Now Gorgas was made Chief Medical Officer of the Panama Canal Commission. His strict enforcement of methods for mosquito control were applied to the Canal Zone. At first there were men who interfered, rejected the scientific evidence, but finally Gorgas was given a free hand and quickly reduced the incidence of disease. Construction went forward.

Teddy Roosevelt continued to attack business monopolies and trusts in fiery speeches around the country. He created a

Department of Commerce and Labor. In wielding his Big Stick he always distinguished (by some standards of his own) between good trusts and bad trusts. In general, he preferred regulation to harsher court action; in dealing with legislators, he used the people to pressure their Congressmen.

Thus he accomplished stronger regulation of the railroads, and of the food and drug industries. He saved millions of acres of public land in forest preserves, national parks, national monuments, and wildlife preserves. When critics objected to his own love of hunting he fought back, calling them "nature-fakirs"; he himself was a nature lover. (A popular new toy, the Teddy Bear, was introduced in admiration of Teddy the Hunter.) In response to the demand for agricultural land, he undertook irrigation projects in the far west. An act of Congress earmarked money from the sale of public land to be set aside for that purpose, and sold the irrigated land to small farmers. The government kept title to the reservoirs and irrigation systems, and reserved timber and coal rights and what it needed for irrigation construction. Former deserts were brought under cultivation, with new farming methods and suitable crops. This reclamation yielded more than $60,000,000 in revenue for the federal treasury.

In December, at Kitty Hawk, North Carolina, Orville Wright lay down on his stomach between the wings of the biplane he had built with his brother Wilbur, and flew it, keeping the 750-pound craft in the air for twelve seconds and covering 120 feet. The brothers made three more flights that day; the longest was Wilbur's fifty-nine-second effort, which traveled 852 feet. And this was the start of aviation, the first flights by a heavier-than-air, powered, and controlled airplane—the power supplied by their home-built twelve-horse-power engine.

Wilbur was thirty-six years old, Orville was thirty-two. But they had worked together for fourteen years, doing moderately well in a series of ventures in Dayton, Ohio. They ran a print shop, then published small local papers. In 1892 they began to build and, later, to manufacture bicycles. Profits from that modest enterprise financed their growing interest in flying machines. Experiments with kites and gliders and wind-tunnels at last produced the plane they took to Kitty Hawk. They continued to experiment with steering and equilibrium controls until in 1905, Orville could keep a plane in the air for more than half an hour. Public demonstrations followed, attracting more interest in England and France than in the U.S. Not until 1908 did the government award them a $25,000 contract if they could build a plane that could reach forty miles an hour in sustained flight for an hour, carrying two men and enough fuel for 125 miles, and land safely. The first plane crashed and killed the passenger. The next year they re-built it and passed the army's test. They founded the American Wright Company in 1909. But by then other pioneers like Glenn Curtis (who loved motorcycles and manufactured engines) and others were making a reality out of man's old dreams of flying.

1904

But what Teddy wanted most was election to the presidency in his own right. His worst opponent was Boss Mark Hanna, who had more docile candidates in mind. Big businessmen wanted Hanna to make his own run for the office. But early in the year it was clear that the convention would nominate Roosevelt.

The Democrats turned away from William Jennings Bryan, a two-time loser, for a New York judge. It was not much of a contest. Even the *New York Sun*, usually the voice of business interests, endorsed Roosevelt in a five-word editorial: "Theodore! With all thy faults!" And Theodore won by a large margin.

One of his faults was his blindness to rising racial tensions in America. Yes, he had invited Booker T. Washington, a distinguished black educator, to lunch at the White House, but in his campaign tour through the South, his speeches made it abundantly clear that he would not use any Big Stick on white supremacy. Northern black voters would support him because they stuck to the Republican party, Mr. Lincoln's party. Southern Blacks could not vote, no matter what the Constitution said; intimidation kept them from the polls. Roosevelt was trying to win votes in the solidly Democratic South. A few white voters might change parties if he used enough charm and coddling.

Then came the Brownsville incident. A white officer marched his black troops into that dusty Texas town to find some recreation. They were members of a crack battalion that had served in the Indian wars, in Cuba, and in the Philippines; they were now stationed at nearby Fort Brown. Some soldiers got drunk and allegedly "shot up the town." Certainly a bartender was killed and a policeman wounded.

After a brief investigation, but without any court martial proceedings, Roosevelt signed an order discharging 167 infantrymen—almost the whole strength of the battalion—without honor and without military pensions. Some of those men had twenty-five years of service; six had won the Medal of Honor. The order was kept secret for a few days while the president left to inspect progress in Panama and have his picture taken on a huge dredge. He did tell Booker T. Washington of the decision, and Washington was shocked. William Howard Taft, serving as Roosevelt's Secretary of War, suspended the order until the newly elected president returned, rightly fearing the political consequences of such unfair proceedings. But Roosevelt would not heed any warnings or protest. When the order was made public it stood, though the *New York Times* could find "not a particle of evidence against the First Battalion," and the *World* called it "lynch law."

1905

When Japan attacked Russia, Roosevelt was pleased, but when Japan appeared to be taking too much territory, he stepped in to stop the war. Japan was allowed to keep Korea, and Teddy won the Nobel Prize for his peace making. Construction of the Panama Canal moved ahead, and Teddy treated the nations of Central America and the Caribbean as if they were his own private domain.

But he had plenty of time and vigor for trust busting, or at any rate, regulation. This was the era of reform. Popular magazines printed hundreds of articles about corporate abuses of the public interest. Ida Tarbell was piling up thousands of facts for her *History of the Standard Oil Company*. Lincoln Steffans wrote *The Shame of the Cities*. Ray Stannard Baker took a hard look at crooked labor leaders. Upton Sinclair, in *The Jungle*, described the processes and practices of the meat packing factories so vividly that he turned the national stomach. These were the "muckrakers" who exposed the seamy side of capitalism.

1906

The President could not control acts of nature. In April a devastating earthquake, and the fires that followed it, destroyed the city of San Francisco. It was the greatest natural disaster in American history until that year.

But the President could enhance the image of America as a world power, sending sixteen battleships and 12,000 men around the world on a goodwill voyage. It was dubbed the Great White Fleet, for the gleaming paint on the ships.

He had to act quickly when a combine of copper companies, banks, and other business interests collapsed, tying up the money supply for many months. Financial panic and depression resulted, and financial stability was not restored until J.P. Morgan joined government efforts to make bank funds available and revive national confidence.

1908

William H. Taft

After his election in 1904, Roosevelt had announced that "under no circumstances" would he be a candidate or accept another nomination. Now he said he would cut off his hand if he could recall that pledge. But he couldn't, so he chose his successor, William Howard Taft. They had been friends since their earliest days in public office. Teddy not only liked Taft, but trusted him as a man of sound judgment. He had served as the first governor of the Philippines, and then as Roosevelt's Secretary of War, an office his father had held under President Grant.

Taft was a genial man. He had a ready and infectious laugh, and a heart almost as big as his 350-pound body. He was nominated on the first roll call at the Republican convention, and the cheers lasted for twenty-nine minutes. The cheers for the retiring President lasted forty-five minutes, and threatened his refusal to run again. The Democrats once more nominated William Jennings Bryan, and the cheers of his loyal western supporters lasted for an hour and a half. Nevertheless, most Americans felt that a vote for Taft was an endorsement of Teddy's policies. Taft won by 30,000 more votes than Roosevelt had received. Whatever his private regrets, Teddy beamed through the inauguration ceremonies and went home to plan an African safari.

But just before the election, another event occurred that would influence the country more than the election results. Henry Ford introduced his Model T automobile, priced to sell for $850. Ford was one of many inventors who had been working on motorcars since the end of the nineteenth century. The first modern car was produced by German engineers in 1901, and an automobile crossed the United States from San Francisco to New York—in a mere sixty-nine days—in 1903. Glenn Olds motorized a horse carriage and manufactured more than 5,000, priced at $650. In the first ten years of auto manufacturing 485 companies got into the business. In 1908, William C. Durant, who owned the Buick Company, organized General Motors.

Ford was a Detroit machinist by trade, but he had worked at many jobs, eventually becoming an engineer for the Edison Illuminating Company. Meanwhile he tinkered with internal combustion engines in his home workshop. He produced his first car in 1896, and went into business as the Henry Ford Company. It failed. He turned to designing and building a prizewinning racing car, the Ford 999. But he wanted to produce a sturdy and dependable car for the masses, at a price almost any American could afford. He formed another company, and his "Tin Lizzie," as the

Model T was affectionately known to millions of buyers, dominated the market for many years. As production increased, the price dropped. A bitter enemy of labor unions, Ford paid the unheard of wage of $5 for an eight-hour day, which made him a hero to working people, even in communist Russia. Five years later, he introduced the idea of profit-sharing for his more than 100,000 employees. As he got richer and more powerful, he involved himself in a dozen causes: He was a philanthropist, an anti-Semite, a pacifist, a candidate for the Senate (he lost); he had little interest in books or art, but believed in exercise, a healthy diet, the avoidance of strong drink, and plenty of hard work.

As more and more people crowded into cities, the cost of land increased. Masonry construction gave way to taller buildings, with more office tenants stacked inside steel skeleton "skyscrapers." In Chicago, Louis Sullivan and his German-born partner, Dankmar Adler used new materials in new ways. "Form follows function," said Sullivan, and within a decade, steel buildings would define modernity in cities around the world.

1909

In many ways, the presidency of Teddy Roosevelt had been the high point of the office. No matter what qualities earlier presidents had possessed, he gave America a young leader whose energy and exuberance meant constant excitement. He communicated a new vision of America as a great power, with a new role to play in the future of the world. Taft could not provide that kind of glamour. He took a sound Republican position on a new protective tariff, but he couldn't or wouldn't grapple with the social concerns of the American people.

In the opinion of many historians, the condition of black Americans was worse than ever. During slavery, their labor was essential to the agriculture of the South; there were simply not enough white men to work the cotton plantations and tobacco fields. Slaves were bought and sold and bred, but given basic care because they represented wealth for their owners. The Civil War brought emancipation, and twelve years of Reconstruction gave former slaves a glimpse of freedom. While federal troops occupied the South, former Confederate soldiers and office holders could not participate in government. Until Southern states qualified for readmission to the Union, local blacks voted and held office. Though most former slaves were displaced people, taking whatever jobs they could get, for whatever pay, Reconstruction provided education, and some began to find a foothold on the economic ladder. A few managed to buy land, or start a small business.

Predictably, the rage of humiliated white men festered. When the last federal troops were withdrawn, they returned to power and wiped out any gains the black population had won. Blacks no longer voted; they were barred from the polls by threats and new laws. They had no civil rights, and rigid segregation became the community rule. If cotton prices fell and hard times hit everybody, armed white mobs took it out on struggling black enterprises. The black grocer or carpenter or printer was driven out of town. If they resisted they could be lynched as a warning to other "uppity" blacks.

Those who moved north certainly had a better chance. They could find jobs, and they could vote. A few served on city councils, in state legislatures, and in Congress. By the turn of the century, a class of secure and prosperous blacks emerged, businessmen, teachers, doctors, lawyers, scientists, and inventors. Lewis Latimer was a gifted draftsman who drew up the patent applications for Alexander Graham Bell's telephone. He began his own work on electric lighting and got his own patents before he worked with Thomas Edison. Granville Woods, who was known as "the black Edison," held more than sixty patents for everything from railroad telegraphy to chicken hatcheries. Elijah McCoy was the inventor of automatic lubrication devices for all kinds of machinery, particularly steam locomotives. Manufacturers in the market for new industrial equipment looked for his attachments, and made sure they were "the real McCoy"—a phrase we still use.

But full acceptance into the white community was still rare, and the worst manifestations of race hate lay just under the surface, even in the north. Springfield, Illinois, Abe Lincoln's hometown, had a black population of just over a hundred, getting along in various trades. But during the hot days of August, 1908, a white woman was allegedly raped by a "well-spoken" young black man, and the town exploded. A white mob rioted and did thousands of dollars in damage. There were at least eighty injuries and six fatal shootings. Two black men were lynched, one a clearly innocent elderly citizen.

This incident, and Roosevelt's handling of the Brownsville

Raid, were among the events that led to the formation of the National Association for the Advancement of Colored People. A small committee of New York whites chose Oswald Garrison Villard as their chairman. He was the grandson of William Lloyd Garrison, the abolitionist leader who had lectured with Frederick Douglass. Villard's mother inherited her father's reform zeal, but his father was a tycoon, owner of the Pacific railroad and backer of Edison's General Electric Company. Oswald published the *New York Evening Post*, and a political journal, *The Nation*. So he had money and social standing, both of which he used to recruit hundreds of concerned and effective people, black and white leaders who saw the need to confront race issues.

Absent from their meetings was Booker T. Washington, the best-known and most respected black educator of the day. Born a slave, he was educated during Reconstruction and taught in Atlanta before he founded his own college at Tuskegee, Alabama. He ran his "Tuskegee machine" with an iron hand for thirty years, and his policy was accommodation to the realities of southern life. One of his most prominent faculty members was George Washington Carver, who held a master's degree from Iowa State. At Tuskegee, Carver directed an agricultural experimental station, trying to persuade black and white farmers to adopt new methods and new crops. Because cotton exhausted the soil, he promoted protein-rich peanuts and invented new uses for peanuts. He was taken up by the National Peanut Growers Association and lobbied for them before Congress. Stooped (though not old), shabby, and humble, he was in general agreement with Booker T. Washington's views, and he certainly represented the white man's idea of a useful and undemanding Negro.

Washington advised his students to accept their status and prepare for employment as agricultural laborers, teachers, or factory hands. His insistence on vocational education got support from many rich men, including Andrew Carnegie. But most black (and white) farmers were sharecroppers, renting from white owners and paying for rent and supplies with a share of the crop. Most were always heavily in debt to their landlords. The number of black landowners did not increase. And though Tuskegee trained students for industrial jobs, there was little demand for skilled industrial labor in the South, or in the north, where there was plenty of cheap immigrant labor. Blacks were denied membership in the American Federation of Labor.

Bitterly opposed to the Tuskegee philosophy was W.E.B. DuBois, a founding member of the new NAACP and editor of its journal, *The Crisis*. DuBois was born in Massachusetts, educated at Harvard and the University of Berlin before he became a teacher of economics and history. He was a prolific writer, and he saw black Americans in the context of people of color everywhere. During his many, and often quarrelsome, years with the NAACP, he served as a brilliant organizer and speaker, with an eloquence few could equal. He despised Tuskegee and everything it stood for, the submission of blacks to conditions he could not, and never did accept.

Villard had raised $150,000 for Tuskegee, and did not want Washington excluded from the organization. It was still run mainly by whites, because Villard did not think blacks were ready to lead the NAACP, and he was afraid of black radicals who might upset its agenda of legislative and legal action. Booker T. Washington, who had been welcomed by President Roosevelt at the White House, and had met with President McKinley at Tuskegee, kept his distance, wanting no part of northern hotheads like W. E. B. DuBois.

Another problem that successive presidents tried to ignore was the rising demand for woman suffrage—votes for women. Like the black movement, it had long been split; the conservative American Woman Suffrage Association worked state-by-state, the hard-line National Woman Suffrage Association (NWSA) insisted on a Constitutional amendment. The two groups were reconciled in 1890, but even their combined strength carried no weight with politicians.

NWSA was founded by Mrs. Elizabeth Cady Stanton and Susan B. Anthony in 1869. They were furious when the Fifteenth Amendment gave black men voting rights that women were still denied. They spent the rest of their lives in the movement. Miss Anthony headed the new National American Woman Suffrage Association until she resigned, but still continued in an active role, making her last speech to the national convention in 1906, a month before she died at eighty-six. Mrs. Stanton had already passed away, and her place was taken by her daughter, Harriet Stanton Blatch.

Married to an Englishman, Harriet Blatch worked for woman suffrage in England, where their tactics were much more aggressive than anything yet seen in America. English suffragettes chained themselves to the fences outside Parliament. When they were arrested, they went on hunger strikes, and were cruelly force-fed by their jailers. Good heavens, English suffragettes cut up golf greens! On her return to New York, Mrs. Blatch went to live on the lower East side, where she found tremendous support among poor women. She founded the Equality League of Self-Supporting Women, which sponsored the first suffrage parades and demonstrations. Joined by many professional women, they took to the streets. For their "unladylike" behavior, they were jeered and spit on by men who watched. But they marched,

marched, marched, and the movement grew. NAWSA was now led by Carrie Chapman Catt, a widow with considerable means. She finally put the rather personal and haphazard efforts of the Association on a firmer footing, with state headquarters, local study and action groups, and instruction manuals supplied by national financing. It should be noted that no black women were invited to join the campaign.

1912

President Taft, pledged to carry on Roosevelt's reforms, was thwarted by Congressional Republicans, still representing the interests of big business. He did initiate more anti-trust actions, and won both a corporate and a personal income tax. Also—a long step toward more open elections—he achieved a constitutional amendment for the direct election of Senators, who had previously been chosen by state legislatures. But he never got TR's kind of public loyalty, and never cut a dashing figure in foreign affairs, as Teddy had done. On the sidelines, Teddy watched and fretted. Their long friendship was forgotten as he began to plot his return to the game. Encouraged by several governors, Roosevelt finally made the announcement: "My hat is in the ring!"

As the Republican convention aproached, the growing bitterness between the two men made them blind to the damage they were doing to their party. When delegates gathered in Chicago, Teddy was already speechifying on street corners. The party-controlled convention nominated Taft, but Roosevelt wasn't finished. His supporters organized another Chicago convention, where 20,000 people chanted and cheered. "I feel as strong as a bull moose," he told reporters, so his new Progressive party was called the Bull Moose party in all the papers. Its platform included regulation of trusts; better working conditions, with a minimum wage and an eight-hour day, and the elimination of child labor; tariff reduction; easier credit for farmers; votes for women—popular reform issues, and not very different from the ideas of the Democratic candidate, Woodrow Wilson.

Wilson was born in Virginia. He was a

Democrat because he was a Southerner, but more than that, he had seen the cost of the Civil War to his homeland. For the rest of his life, he would hate the waste and pain of war. After graduation from Princeton, he studied law at the University of Virginia and briefly practiced that profession before he decided to get a degree in political science from Johns Hopkins.

He was an inspired teacher at Bryn Mawr and Wesleyan, and wrote a brilliant textbook on government. He returned to Princeton to teach and write, developing his arguments on behalf of active government, concerned with the larger questions of the country's economy and condition—a position contrary to the Republican preference for a government that kept its nose out of the nation's business. As president of Princeton, Wilson set about reforming academic and social life. He was opposed by influential faculty and trustees, and was forced to resign after eight years of leadership.

His articles and speeches attracted attention, and he won election to the governorship of the state of New Jersey in 1910. There, too, he accomplished fundamental reforms and began to build a following in the Democratic Party. But it took many ballots before the presidential nominating convention accepted him as its candidate. Party conservatives distrusted Wilson, and he was not nominated until William Jennings Bryan announced that his people would never accept a machine candidate.

President Taft stayed out of the election campaign, and let the Republican regulars oppose Teddy Roosevelt's Progressive platform. The old Bull Moose campaigned hard, and when the votes were counted, Taft carried only two states; Roosevelt captured six; and Woodrow Wilson won the rest. Eugene Debs, the Socialist candidate, got 6 percent of the total vote.

Alice Paul was another militant feminist,

Woodrow Wilson

1913

trained in the guerrilla-warfare tactics of English suffragettes. She formed her own organization and brought 5,000 women to Washington for Wilson's inauguration. Set upon by the celebrating crowd, they had to be rescued by police and army cavalry. No arrests were made, and the ceremony proceeded.

The new president broke with tradition when he came before Congress to deliver his first State of the Union speech in person. He called his program The New Freedom, and soon demonstrated his political skills in pulling Congressional Democrats together to endorse it. He set forth a clear, positive agenda, combining idealism with practical legislative management. He quickly won reductions in the Republican protective tariff, which prevented foreign competition and kept consumer prices high. Tariff reduction meant a loss of revenue to the federal government, but a graduated personal income tax—now permitted by a Constitutional amendment—would make up the difference. The Federal Reserve System created a system of regional federal banks, which local banks could choose to join (or not) and which created new paper money. A Federal Trade Commission began to investigate trusts in the continuing effort to ensure fair competition in American business.

It was a time of great labor unrest—as the high election day turnout for Socialist Gene Debs had demonstrated. Labor unions had grown in size and strength; there were more strikes during Wilson's first term than ever before in our history, and they were more violent. Union men were pitted not only against their hard-nosed employers, but against non-union men, in long struggles that tore whole communities apart. The president needed to convince Congress that it was time for the federal government to intervene.

1914

But he was about to be overwhelmed by foreign affairs. In early summer, the Archduke Francis Ferdinand, heir to the crown of

Austria-Hungary, was assassinated by a young Serbian nationalist, a member of a radical student group. This bloody deed in a small central European city would plunge all of Europe, and eventually the United States, into World War I, the Great War that was called the War to End Wars.

The powers of Europe were itching for a fight. Tremendous quantities of munitions were available. Armies numbered in the millions; great fleets of battleships had been launched. Germany dominated Europe industrially but was determined to regain territory lost to France in an earlier war. France was allied to Britain and Russia against Germany and Austria-Hungary. So when the assassination of the Archduke gave Austria-Hungary an excuse to attack Serbia, and Russia backed the Serbs, Germany immediately attacked France. German troops advanced swiftly through Belgium and across the French border, almost reaching Paris before they were stopped by French and British armies in the first Battle of the Marne. Within months, Turkey, Bulgaria, and Italy were combatants. Europe was in flames.

President Wilson and William Jennings Bryan, his Secretary of State, were deeply committed to peace. Bryan had been working on plans that would have pledged all nations to settle conflicts by international arbitration. Wilson now issued a proclamation of neutrality, and restated the principal of "freedom of the seas," the right of all nations to trade with warring countries. Americans, whose sympathies certainly favored Britain, France, and their allies, responded generously to relief appeals. A successful engineer named Herbert Hoover was put in charge of the American Red Cross in Europe.

The country was not prepared to do more. America didn't have a single airplane; only four field guns; and no way to transport heavy weapons on a battlefield. It had an army of 80,000 men. The navy had Theodore

Roosevelt's Great White Fleet, but no small, fast fighting ships and few submarines. Wilson's policy of neutrality expressed his moral convictions (he would say, "There is such a thing as a nation being too proud to fight"), but also reflected the realities of his military weakness. Besides, if freedom of the seas could be sustained, a European war would be very profitable for American business and farmers.

1915

Britain had no intention of letting American factories supply the enemy, and a British blockade soon cut off trade with Germany. But trade with Britain, France, and Italy tripled. The threat to this rich commerce was German submarines, which followed none of the old rules for naval warfare. The dreaded U-boats sank merchant ships without warning. When the British liner *Lusitania* was torpedoed and went down with 124 American passengers among the 1,198 lost, Wilson sent a strong diplomatic protest to Berlin, but maintained American neutrality.

Meanwhile, most men stuck to business. Radio had many inventors, but David Sarnoff wasn't one of them. His genius lay in his ability to conceptualize a corporation that would do it all, from transmission to the manufacture of the receiving sets, from creating programs to selling advertising. All this was included in the "Radio Music Box" memorandum the twenty-four-year-old Russian immigrant sent to his supervisors at the American Marconi Company in 1915, a memo that is generally regarded as the beginning of the American radio industry.

1916

There were other foreign matters to distract the President from his domestic agenda. He had a small Caribbean empire to administer. Haiti and the Dominican Republic were now under American military control; Puerto Rico was an American possession, and its people became American citizens; the Virgin Islands were purchased from Denmark; the Panama Canal opened; and the little Republic of Panama was virtually an American protectorate. But the most urgent problems involved relations with troubled Mexico.

In 1913, the President of that Republic had been murdered and replaced by Dictator Victoriano Huerta, who was soon ousted by Dictator Venustiano Carranza. In 1914, a very minor incident about a salute to the American flag provoked an overblown American uproar, in which the United States Navy attacked and occupied Vera Cruz. But Wilson resisted pressure from businessmen with Mexican interests to intervene otherwise in Mexican affairs.

Pancho Villa called himself one of Carranza's generals, but in fact he was little more than a border bandit who killed Americans in northern Mexico. Not until he raided in Columbus, New Mexico, was General John J. Pershing ordered to pursue him into the Mexican interior. It was a fruitless chase. Eight months later, the army was recalled without having recaptured Villa or achieving any other objective.

It was still the European conflict that dominated newspaper headlines and political party reactions in this election year. Teddy Roosevelt was one American who wanted to get into it. His Progressive Party faithful met again in Chicago, hoping to swing the regular Republicans behind his nomination and bring the party together. But they failed, and the Republican convention named Supreme Court Justice Charles Evans Hughes to run against Wilson. Both the Republican and Democratic conventions endorsed votes for women.

Wages were soaring for thousands of men employed in munitions plants; but consumer prices also soared, as huge quantities of farm produce were shipped overseas. There was little competition for jobs from immigrant labor because immigration had fallen off, but there were continued outbreaks of labor violence. When a bomb exploded during a Preparedness Day parade in San Francisco, ten people were killed and forty wounded. Tom Mooney, a labor organizer, and Warren Billings, a shoe worker, were among labor and radical activists arrested. Though both insisted they were innocent, both were convicted, and Mooney received a death sentence. After months of union demonstration and several investigations, Mooney's sentence was reduced to life imprisonment; years later both men would be pardoned and released.

Meanwhile, Democrats rallied behind Woodrow Wilson and their slogan, "He kept us out of war!" Wilson won a close election.

Republican Jeannette Rankin became the first woman in Congress when she became Montana's only member of the House. By now many states allowed women to vote in some local elections, mainly connected with the schools. Wyoming had given women the vote when it was still a territory. When Wyoming applied for statehood in 1890, its admission was stalled while Congress argued whether it was possible to admit a territory whose constitution permitted female suffrage. The Territory said it would stay out of the Union "for a hundred years" rather than deny its women that right. Women voted in Colorado, Utah, and Idaho, but the national suffrage effort was now divided between the mainstream group headed by "General" Carrie Chapman Catt and the more militant followers of Alice Paul. Southern Congressmen were hostile to a federal law because they didn't want black women to vote, and the last thing Woodrow Wilson had on his mind was the issue of votes for women.

Closely connected to the suffrage cause was the question of prohibition. Booze—and the domestic suffering, crime, and political corruption associated with the consumption and sale of hard liquor—was a serious issue with many Americans, and particularly for women. Organizations like the Woman's Christian Temperance Union and the Anti-Saloon League were active in the suffrage movement. They wanted to vote so they could elect "dry" local and state officials. By 1916 twenty-one states had banned saloons, and in 1917 Congress submitted a Prohibition amendment to the judgment of the country.

1917

German submarine warfare had subsided for some time after the Lusitania incident, but as the British navy strangled its foreign trade, Germany declared unrestricted war on all shipping headed for Britain. Wilson broke diplomatic relations with Germany and began to arm merchant ships, hoping to avert further attacks. Then the British Secret Service intercepted a telegram from Alfred Zimmerman, the German Foreign Minister, to the German Ambassador in Mexico. The message urged him to encourage a Mexican invasion of America, and promised help in a Mexican recapture of territory it had lost to the United States in the Mexican War. Americans were already furious about the loss of lives and cargoes when U-boats sank merchant ships. Now publication of the Zimmerman Note fed their anger.

On April 6, Congress voted a declaration of war. Jeannette Rankin joined fifty-six other members in opposing the declaration, and she would be a committed pacifist for the rest of her life. A conscription law followed, and the first American troops arrived in Europe in June, led by General John J. Pershing. They were in time to fight the Battle of Chateau Thierry, on the River Marne, in northeast France, where a massive German advance toward Paris was halted.

On the homefront, a passionate burst of patriotism brought citizens together to buy Liberty Bonds, to observe meatless and wheatless days, to dim the lights and turn down the furnace, to collect fruit pits for the manufacture of gas masks. Four million men volunteered for or were drafted into the army. Women replaced them on farms, in factories, and in dozens of other occupations. Citizens of German birth or parentage were targets of suspicion and insult; schools no longer taught the German language.

Two million Yanks went to France, and 1.39 million saw action, mainly on the western front, where the Germans had fortified the dense Argonne Forest along the Meuse River. The navy went after the U-boats, putting an end to German depredations in the Atlantic. Under pressure from an American propaganda campaign which hammered the bad news into the consciousness of the German people, their morale crumbled. Their allies in Austria-Hungary, Bulgaria, and Turkey caved in.

President Wilson, who had resisted involvement for three years, now set forth his war aims with Wilsonian precision and clarity. The Germans were willing to discuss Wilson's Fourteen Points, but the Republican majority in Congress were not. Wilson's utterances, said Teddy Roosevelt "have ceased...to be expressive of the will of the American people."

1918

The fighting went on, as the Germans retreated to their defensive line in Belgian Flanders. The biggest American force in history helped push them back, and the Allied attack led by general Pershing at the Battle of Meuse-Argonne was one of the last offesives of the war. Germany surrendered on November 11.

In December, Woodrow Wilson sailed for Europe, to receive a tumultuous and tearful reception from its people. In every city he was mobbed, cheered, pelted with flowers, hailed as a new kind of war hero, the hope of the future, the man who wanted peace without victory. He was also wined and dined by European diplomats and politicians who had quite different ideas because they had fought a different war.

The Allies had been at war for three

years before the first American troops landed, had seen terrible slaughter as their mud-and-blood-soaked trenches were blown up by heavy bombardments and their young men died on their own barbed wire defenses. Poison gas was introduced early. Americans suffered more than 320,000 casualties (half as many as the total casualties in the Civil War) and lost 53,513 men killed in battle. (A greater number later died of their wounds.) The Allies had more than four million dead. Total Allied casualties were more than nine million. The great flu epidemic of 1918 killed more than half a million Americans, far more than were lost in the European fighting. As for the enemy: the human cost of the war was even higher. Germany and Austria-Hungary each had total casualties of more than seven million; more than 1.73 million German soldiers laid down their lives for the Kaiser, their last, who was deposed before the year was out.

Wilson's Fourteen Points began with a call for "open covenants, openly arrived at." He wanted all the cards on the table, no secret deals, the claims of all countries set forth and considered, the rights of all people respected. He wanted freedom of the seas, freedom of trade, the fair adjustment of national boundaries and settlement of colonial questions. Above all, he wanted self-determination by "the people immediately involved" in any international dispute, and to that end "the establishment of an organization of peace"—a League of Nations strong enough to guarantee political independence and territorial integrity to great and small states alike.

The Paris Peace Conference got underway with twenty-seven great and small countries represented, but it soon boiled down to the Council of Four: Wilson, and the delegates from France, Great Britain, and Italy, determined to wring the last drop of revenge out of any treaty with Germany. They let Wilson labor away at his plans for a League of Nations, while they calculated the huge reparations Germany would have to pay, the resources and German colonial possessions that would be seized, the compensation they would demand for the losses the Allies had suffered.

One by one, Wilson's Fourteen Points were rewritten, or simply written off. He gave way, compromised, but stuck to his major objective, a League of Nations as part of the final document. Then he had a nervous breakdown.

1919

At home, the Eighteenth Amendment to the Constitution was ratified, and Prohibition became the law of the land. Mrs. Catt and her suffrage activists could begin the last push for a Nineteenth Amendment, and votes for women. They narrowly won the Congressional vote. Seven Senators had attached riders which would have allowed southern states to discriminate against black women. But at last the Amendment was approved and went to the states for ratification.

Both the peace treaty and American participation in a League of Nations had to be approved by a two-thirds vote in the Senate. Wilson had a tough opponent in Republican Henry Cabot Lodge, chairman of the Foreign Relations Committee. Lodge was an expansionist, a skillful veteran after twenty-five years in the Congress, and a close friend of Teddy Roosevelt. He now offered his fourteen reservations, based on what he perceived as a political reality. No nation would fight for the rights of another nation unless its own interests were at stake. He would not pledge American troops to the defense of others in Wilson's League, without Congressional approval in each particular circumstance. Wilson stood his ground. The treaty and the League covenant had to be approved as submitted.

He set out on a national speaking tour to sell his treaty to the country. After delivering forty speeches to enthusiastic crowds, he

224

collapsed in Pueblo, Colorado, exhausted and semi-paralyzed. He was taken back to Washington, where his devoted wife, Edith, tried to cover up his condition. He saw no visitors, refused communication with even his closest friends and advisors. The rumors spread that Wilson was incoherent, insane.

1920

No matter that Woodrow Wilson had received the Nobel Peace Prize in 1919, his career in American public life was over. Henry Cabot Lodge triumphed in the Senate. The League of Nations was voted down in a close balloting. Democrats and Republicans could throw themselves into their convention excitement unhampered by any international idealism. The country was ready for a change, eager to get back to business.

The Republicans had more than a dozen potential candidates, including Teddy Roosevelt. Plenty of money poured in to win delegate votes for various favorite sons. In the end, party leaders got together at the Chicago's Blackstone Hotel, and in a "smoke-filled room" settled on Warren G. Harding as their choice. Harding was a very dark horse, a newspaper editor in Marion, Ohio, an unsuccessful candidate for governor, but delighted to have won a Senate seat. He had no further political ambitions, but his wife, Florence—"the Duchess"—and Harry Daugherty, his old friend and new manager, had plenty.

When Harding expressed his personal doubts, asking "Am I big enough for the task?" Daugherty reassured him. "Don't make me laugh. The days of giants in the presidential chair (are) past. Greatness is largely...an illusion of the public." The presidency was an easy job, Daugherty said.

The Democratic convention met in San Francisco, and the leading contender was Wilson's son-in-law, William McAdoo. But he was passed over for James M. Cox, another Ohio editor. His running mate was the handsome young New Yorker who had served ably as assistant Secretary of the Navy during the war, Franklin D. Roosevelt.

Thirty-six states were needed to ratify the Nineteenth Amendment. The last year of the effort required grueling exertions. During the war, Carrie Chapman Catt and her ladies of the National American Woman Suffrage Association had done war work, folded bandages and hoped to win public approval and Congressional support. Alice Paul and her more militant Congressional Union for Woman Suffrage picketed the White House. Every day, six dignified but determined women walked the picket line, wearing white dresses, carrying purple banners. Men attacked them; they were arrested for "obstructing traffic"; 168 suffragists were jailed, some repeatedly, and went on hunger strikes in prison. Alice Paul was confined in a psychopathic ward until friends could secure her release.

But let Mrs. Catt tell the whole story. They had spent fifty-two years "in pauseless campaign. During that time we were forced to conduct fifty-six campaigns of referenda to male voters; 480 campaigns to urge legislatures to submit suffrage amendments to voters; forty-seven campaigns to induce state constitutional conventions to write woman suffrage into state constitutions; 277 campaigns to persuade state party conventions to include woman suffrage planks; thirty campaigns to urge presidential party conventions to adopt woman suffrage planks in party platforms, and nineteen campaigns with nineteen successive Congresses. Millions of dollars were raised, mainly in small sums...Hundreds of women gave the accumulated possibilities of an entire lifetime, thousands gave years of their lives."

And all that brought them to Nashville, Tennessee, in the summer of 1920. Thirty-five states had ratified the Nineteenth Amendment; they had lost the vote in Delaware and needed to find one more state—southern state—to accept the Constitutional change. They assaulted the Tennessee legislature, and so did their opponents. Independent legislators were bribed with illegal booze and more material inducements, by factions determined to defeat ratification. It came down to one vote, and one Representative received a note from his mother. "Hoorah!" she said. "—vote for suffrage and don't keep them in doubt—be a good boy." "I always mind my mother," said twenty-four-year-old Harry Burns, and the thirty-sixth state was won.

Twenty million women became full citizens of the United States. They could vote.

General Catt founded a new organization, the League of Women Voters, to provide non-partisan political education for these new voters. But it should be noted that the heroic suffrage leader did not approve of extending that right to blacks, Indians, or foreigners. She shared the white, Protestant, native-born American's suspicion and fear of the immigrant poor in the slums.

This was the year of the great Red Scare, which built on the fears of Carrie Chapman Catt and many others, now greatly intensified by the 1917 Russian Revolution. Military defeats and disastrous casualties (Russian figures were much higher than those of any other Allied power, a total of 9.15 million dead, wounded, and missing) led to the overthrow of the government and a separate peace with Germany. Civil war followed, as the Bolsheviks ruthlessly consolidated their power.

Bolshevism terrified American government. A rising young bureaucrat named J. Edgar Hoover was made head of the Justice Department's General Intelligence Division, charged with tracking down anybody suspected of subversion. He accepted the assignment with zealous enthusiasm. Immigration officers rounded up thousands of foreign-born radicals; 2,700 were arrested and deported.

Many people blamed communist influence for the widespread social discontent that found one expression in the growth of labor unions. Millions of patriotic workers had set aside their grievances during the war. Now a wave of strikes expressed their anger and determination to organize. Steel companies were targeted by men who were still working twelve-hour days for pay that was ridiculously low, disgraceful in the light of wartime profits enjoyed by the industry. Though big companies called in federal troops to break the strikes, the American Federation of Labor continued to recruit skilled workers in many trades. Gene Debs' Industrial Workers of the World dreamed of one big union which would overthrow capitalism and bring in a golden age of brotherhood for all working men and women everywhere. Because it welcomed blacks, immigrants, migrants, the lowest and poorest of the working class, the IWW never attracted the majority of labor sympathizers. Nevertheless, though small, the IWW was loud, and its rhetoric was disturbing. Surely such radical notions were inspired by foreign agitators? Socialists and communists (law enforcement made little or no distinction) became the targets of Congressional investigations, and Wilson's Attorney General led the witch-hunt.

Nicola Sacco, a shoemaker, and Bartolomeo Vanzetti, a fish peddler, were young radicals, Italian aliens, and self-proclaimed anarchists, accused of killing two men in a Massachusetts payroll holdup. They were identified by witnesses, in spite of Sacco's corroborated testimony that he was nowhere near the scene on the day of the crime. But they fit the jury's idea of Reds, dangerous radicals whose politics could infect the whole working class and undermine the foundations of American society. They were found guilty. The trial and their subsequent death sentences aroused a storm of protest among liberals, and appeals for clemency from around the world. In 1925, another man, a convicted murderer, confessed to his involvement in the crime, as a member of the Joe Morelli gang, but all motions for a retrial were denied. Sacco and Vanzetti sat in prison for the next six years, waiting for a final decision. The case has never really been closed, and is still argued, more than half a century after they died in the electric chair in 1927.

When the panic of the great Red Scare cooled down, the activities of the Justice Department were examined and the Attorney General was accused of abusing his power. But none of those charges touched J. Edgar Hoover, who won promotion and became head of a reorganized Bureau of Investigation. He was launched on a career that made him one of the most powerful men in America.

1920

Warren Harding

Prohibition, votes for women, labor violence, the Red Scare—it was an era of great change, but Warren Harding said it was time for the country to get back to "normalcy." He was a tall, handsome man, with silver hair and dark eyebrows, blue eyes vivid against his tan skin. He was genial and gregarious, a glad-handing, small-town type with whom the country could feel right at home. He liked golf and all-night poker games with his cronies, and he liked the ladies.

Harding's fifteen-year affair with the wife of a friend, a Marion shopkeeper, was over, but his relationship with Nan Britton was much more complicated. She had fallen in love with him when she was in high school, and threw herself at him until he succumbed. She was already pregnant when the Republican convention nominated him—an adoring spectator in the convention gallery.

With Calvin Coolidge as the candidate for Vice-President, Harding was elected by an overwhelming majority, and swept the electoral count. Eugene Debs, the Socialist candidate, though in prison for seditious activity in wartime, got more than a million votes, 3.5 percent of the total count. And Nan Britton's baby was born before Harding's inauguration.

He promised to appoint the country's "best minds" to his Cabinet. He chose Charles Evans Hughes as his Secretary of State and Andrew Mellon as his Secretary of the Treasury. Herbert Hoover, who had served as food administrator during the war, became Secretary of Commerce. But the president also made room for Harry Daugherty and other old pals. His administration was conservative, anti-spending, anti-taxation, favoring high tariffs and restrictive immigration policies, but constructive measures were passed to help farmers and other sectors of the economy.

He had been promised an easy job, but Harding took it seriously and worked hard. Somehow he found time for Nan, writing her long, gushy letters and romantic poems, and meeting her whenever possible, even in the White House. He supported her as well as he could, though not in the style she wanted. Poor Florence, "the Duchess," enjoyed Washington high life. She was five years older than her husband, and couldn't match Nan's youthful charms, but she welcomed his poker players, poured their drinks, and shared their rough jokes. For his stag parties, she provided dinners of wieners and sauerkraut. She put up with a lot; so did Nan.

1923

President Harding, accompanied by Mrs. Harding, set out for a summer speech-making tour through the west and Alaska, but he suffered a heart attack in Seattle. Rushed back to San Francisco, he appeared to be resting comfortably at the Palace Hotel when he suddenly died. It may have been the last stroke of good luck in a lucky life, for he died before the exposure of one of the country's major political scandals.

Calvin Coolidge

Calvin Coolidge was sworn in as the new president while a Senate committee was beginning its investigation. It would take years of legal action to reveal all the rascality. Massive frauds and thefts were uncovered in Harding's Veteran's Bureau and the Alien Property Department. In what came to be known as The Little House on H Street, Attorney General Harry Daugherty saw between 50 and 500 visitors a day. It was a borrowed house, staffed with many servants, stocked with plenty of bootleg booze. Daugherty and his sidekick, Jess Smith, shared household expenses of $50,000 a year. Daugherty took care of the important deals; Jess, now also close to the Hardings, handled the smaller stuff and acted as Harry's gofer. No one will ever know the extent of their crimes, because Daugherty burned bank records and pleaded the Fifth Amendment when he was brought to trial. Jess committed suicide.

But the real tempest blew up during the Teapot Dome scandal, involving the sale of oil fields in Wyoming. For a long time there had been honest disagreement and heated debate over the development of public lands in the west. Conservationists wanted to preserve open space; developers wanted to prospect for minerals and oil, and to buy or lease rights to extract what they found. Experts from the Navy Department predicted (wrongly, as it turned out) that American oil would soon run low and that western oil should be reserved for navy requirements, perhaps nationalized. Before World War I, reserves at Teapot Dome and Elk Hills, California, had been set aside for the navy.

President Harding wanted Albert Fall, a New Mexico rancher, for his Secretary of State, but Fall asked for the Interior Department, which had authority for disposing of public land. Fall thought the whole idea of public land was absurd, and the question of reserves for naval needs was nonsense. He persuaded the Secretary of the Navy to transfer oil land to the Interior Department. He then proceeded to negotiate secret deals, leasing Elk Hills to the Pan-American Petroleum Company and Teapot Dome to the Mammoth Oil Company. He was paid off with a $100,000 interest-free loan, cash, bonds, and fancy breeding stock for his huge New Mexico ranch holdings. In 1922 he retired and went home to the ranch, where he spent the bribe money so freely that people began to wonder about the source of his new wealth. The Senate investigators were already looking into oil lease shenanigans before Warren Harding died, but until the end of his life, Albert Fall would maintain his innocence. The money from big oil men consisted of personal loans, he said, and had nothing to do with oil reserves. The oil executives were sued by Congress for cancellation of the leases, but acquitted of fraud. Harry Sinclair, president of Mammoth Oil was convicted of jury-tampering and imprisoned. Albert Fall, who had also been given a lucrative job with Sinclair's company, was convicted of accepting a bribe and sent to jail six years later.

(As for Nan: she and Harding's daughter, Elizabeth Ann, were not mentioned in his will. Nan worked, holding various secretarial jobs and living beyond her means while she harassed the Harding family and friends. She wrote a book that no reputable publisher would touch; privately printed, *The President's Daughter* became a best-seller. To answer her detractors, she wrote another book, which failed. She married a Norwegian ship captain because she thought he was rich. He wasn't, and the marriage was annulled. Elizabeth Ann grew up, married, had a family, and tried to forget the past. Nan lived out her life in Evanston, Illinois.)

1924

But none of this mud ever stuck to Calvin Coolidge. He was born in Vermont, graduated from Amherst College, and held many city and state offices before he became Vice-President.

As governor of Massachusetts, he gained national prominence when he put down the 1919 Boston police strike, asserting that "There is no right to strike against the public safety by anybody, anywhere, any time." As President, he quickly restored public confidence during an administration distinguished for its pro-business stance. Taxes were cut further, high tariffs were maintained, government spending was held down, and the growing prosperity of the country seemed to prove that "Silent Cal" knew what he was doing. So he was easily re-nominated to lead the Republican ticket in 1924.

The Democrats seemed to have a ready-made campaign issue, the betrayal of the public trust by so many men close to President Harding, evidence of Republican corruption on a scale unmatched since the time of President Grant. But they were torn by internal party disputes over Prohibition and the re-emergence of the Ku Klux Klan. Since the end of the Great War, the Klan had grown in membership and political power. Klan members were mainly lower-middle-class white threatened by newly arrived immigrants (Catholics, Jews, radical riff-raff), by blacks moving north in search of jobs, by labor unions, and by any perceived threat to their confused values.

Franklin Roosevelt, crippled by polio four years earlier, returned to the political scene and took the podium in Madison Square Garden to nominate Alfred E. Smith, the four-time governor of New York. Smith was a "wet" who opposed Prohibition, and an outspoken enemy of the Ku Klux Klan. He was also a Roman Catholic, the first ever nominated for the presidency. He was opposed by southern and mid-west "drys," who won the first fight on the convention floor.

Smith and many other delegates representing the big cities and their changing populations, wanted an anti-Klan resolution, to put the party on record as opposing its bigotry. The resolution was defeated by one vote.

When balloting on the candidates began, votes were almost equally split between Smith and William McAdoo of California. Voting went on for nine sweltering days until, after 102 roll calls, it became obvious that the convention was hopelessly deadlocked. McAdoo could not command a majority, and the convention would not accept a Catholic. Worn out, delegates turned to John W. Davis, a Wall Street lawyer.

True reformers gathered in Cleveland to organize a new Progressive Party. Unhappy with both the Republicans and the Democrats, the Progressives had first appeared on the ballot in Wisconsin, opposed to the 1912 nomination of William Howard Taft. When Teddy Roosevelt came into the fight, they had abandoned their leader, Senator Robert LaFollette, and helped Teddy win more than a quarter of the vote. In 1916 they nominated Charles Evans Hughes. In 1920 they backed Harding. But in 1924 they were thoroughly disgusted and again nominated old Bob LaFollette, with Burton K. Wheeler (one of the Montana Senators who pursued the Teapot Dome investigation) as his running mate. They stood for conservation, for higher taxes on the rich, for an end to child labor, and for direct election of the President. This time the party got almost five million votes.

But Calvin Coolidge got more than twice as many votes as the Progressives and Democrats combined. Nellie Tayloe Ross was elected governor of Wyoming, and Miriam (Ma) Ferguson was elected governor of Texas.

And in this year, native Americans finally became American citizens. This was partly in recognition of Indian contributions to the war effort, when many native Americans enlisted and fought, and many died.

The first quarter of the twentieth century saw great progress in science and technology. The country produced Nobel Prize winners—Albert Michelson for physics, in 1907; and Theodore W. Richards for chemistry, in 1914. A 100-inch telescope, the most powerful in the world, was installed at Mount Wilson, California. A controversial report, written by Abraham Flexner and issued by the Carnegie Foundation, called for a complete overhaul of medical research and education.

Ten million telephones were in daily use. Twenty-five million Americans watched actual motion pictures in the country's nickelodeons, and *The Birth of a Nation* became a film classic, and a scandal for its romantic view of the Ku Klux Klan. Sound was first added to film in 1923, one of the many contributions of Lee De Forest, the radio pioneer. He broadcast Enrico Caruso's voice over the radio in 1910, and radio news in 1916.

Woodrow Wilson was the first president to ride to his inauguration in an automobile, and the country was soon producing four-fifths of all the motor vehicles in the world. After Henry Ford introduced the moving assembly line (1913-1914) other manufacturers quickly followed. Mass production methods might have swamped the market if the industry had not introduced model changes and the idea of trading up to bigger, faster cars—bought on credit. The oil industry provided better gas, efficiently distributed to the whole country in company service stations.

After the Wright brothers made their first short flight in 1903, they continued to experiment and improve their flying machines. They began to build and sell planes in 1909, but the major manufacturer was another aviation pioneer, Glenn Curtiss, and the two companies were almost constantly involved in legal battles over patents.

In 1927, Captain Charles A. Lindbergh thrilled the nation and the world with his non-stop flight from New York to Paris. Amelia Earhart would make an Atlantic crossing the following year. Dr. Robert Goddard began to write about a rocket capable of reaching the moon in 1921; in 1925 he launched the first liquid fuel rocket at Auburn, Massachusetts. It traveled 184 feet in 2.5 seconds (about fifty miles an hour).

The aviation industry was a good example of the crucial role played by government in scientific and technological development. It not only conducted basic research and stimulated design improvement, but provided a market; contracts carrying the mail supported the country's first airlines—Charles Lindbergh was an airmail pilot. The Air Commerce Act (1926) provided federal aid for airlines and for airport construction.

Car sales depended on access to good roads, a need recognized by the Federal Aid Road Act (1916) and the Federal Highway Act (1921). Radio transmission depended on the electromagnetic spectrum, and "air waves" were a natural and limited public resource. The government began to license broadcasters and allocate wavelengths; without this control, no broadcasting industry would have been possible. The Department of Agriculture was responsible for much of the science that resulted in improved plant varieties, in animal breeding and nutrition, in fertilizers, and much other information that was widely disseminated to American farmers. World War I increased the need for new discoveries and stimulated the growth of research and productive technologies, which led to creation of the National Research Council (1916).

Nevertheless, Republican presidents continued to insist the government had nothing to do, and should have nothing to do, with business, and no role in the American economy.

1925   And while science and technology were making these tremendous changes and improvements in the lives of the American people, the country was experiencing one of its periodic revivals of fundamentalist religion.

The State of Tennessee passed a new law. Henceforth, it would be unlawful for any public school or any university to teach "a theory that denies the story of the divine creation as taught in the Bible, and to teach instead that man has descended from a lower order of animals."

Religion had always been an active force in America, providing much of the social organization, a large part of the education in private schools and colleges, and almost all of the charity the nation offered. About half the population counted themselves as regularly-attending church members. The number of denominations increased and diversified. Early in the century there were perhaps ten thousand Catholics, and many more arrived with each wave of European immigration. The Mormon church also grew with European recruits. A 1906 religious census identified fewer than 150,000 Jewish families, another group augmented by immigration. The same census counted about 33 million Christians, who lived together in a general community atmosphere of tolerance and mutual respect, and, of course, the government did not interfere with what anybody chose to believe.

But for a state to pass a law dictating what public schools could or could not teach was something else. The American Civil Liberties Union decided to challenge the constitutionality of the Tennessee law, and John Scopes, a high school biology teacher, agreed to be their test case. The ACLU brought in a blue ribbon team of defense lawyers, headed by Clarence Darrow, the most famous defense attorney in the country. Sixty-five-year-old William Jennings Bryan, the perennial presidential candidate and a devout Christian, assisted the local prosecutor. So the stage was set for high drama in the small town of Dayton, Tennessee.

For eleven days the trial drew wide attention in the United States and the world. Reporters flocked to the scene, and millions of readers followed the case in the newspapers. It was the first jury trial ever broadcast on the radio. Despite temperatures that reached 110 degrees, the courtroom was jammed, and the courthouse grounds swarmed with men and women who loved the entertainment. Country preachers sold Bibles and preached to perspiring listeners; vendors did a lively business in hot dogs, Coca-Cola, and lemonade. Toy monkeys were peddled as souvenirs of "the Great Monkey Trial."

The judge prevented Bryan from making the long oration he had planned to deliver, so Bryan took the stand as a prosecution witness. Clarence Darrow, in a sarcastic and unrelenting cross-examination, succeeded in making a monkey out of the faltering old man. The humiliation may have caused Bryan's death five days after the trial adjourned.

In the whole proceeding, there was no discussion of evolution theory or the Constitution. The only question was, did Scopes actually teach evolution in his classroom? And, of course, he was guilty. The judge fined him $100, but he was later cleared when the appeals court overturned the decision on a technicality. The law remained on the books, but no further efforts were made to enforce it, and evolution continued to be taught in

Tennessee schools.

1926

In an era of national prosperity a lot of people were getting very rich. Corporate directors got rich gambling in the stock market; speculators got rich in the Florida land boom (that bubble would burst after the hurricane of '26); gangsters got rich in the heyday of Prohibition. And even the less rich were enjoying a spending spree with new retail credit, the department store charge-plates. Calvin Coolidge was determined not to rock the boat. It was reported that he often slept eleven hours a day.

Of course, the farmers continued to lag economically behind the rest of the country. Farm belt Congressmen offered bills for farm aid. Some wanted to separate farm produce for export from the domestic market, but failed to get enough votes for passage. When a farm bill was finally approved by both Houses in 1926, it was vetoed by President Coolidge as unwarranted interference in the country's economic life. When it was passed for a second time, he vetoed it again.

Coolidge gave some support to the idea of American participation in a World Court, but not enough to sell it to isolationist Senators. The administration had more success in backing the Kellogg-Briand Treaty, which brought fifteen nations to Paris to renounce war "as an instrument of national policy." But there was no way to enforce that solemn declaration.

1927

From his summer White House in Rapid City, South Dakota, the president unexpectedly announced that he did not intend to run for re-election in 1928. Coolidge said that the expansion of the stock market was a national expression of economic opportunity, but perhaps some Vermont instinct warned him that it was dangerous. Certainly Wall Street brokers knew that much of the trading was done with borrowed money—more money than the country had in circulation.

1928

Herbert Hoover

The Republican convention in June nominated Herbert Hoover on the first ballot. Born in West Branch, Iowa, Hoover received a degree from Stanford as a mining engineer, and worked in that profession for many years, in many parts of the world. He made big money when he left his London-based company to join ventures in Burmese tin and Russian oil. His first experience in public life came with relief efforts in London during the war, soon becoming chairman of the Commission for Relief in Belgium, until President Wilson made him head of the Food Administration Board in the United States. In 1921, President Harding had appointed him Secretary of Commerce.

The convention offered few surprises and little excitement. Its platform was an endorsement of Coolidge policies. As usual, it pledged the party to government economy and tax reduction, to high tariffs, and to the Prohibition law. When farm state delegates offered a plank endorsing farm aid, it was rejected. But Charles Curtis, a Kansas Senator and a Kaw Indian with a following in the farm block, was nominated for Vice-President.

The Democrats met in Houston, still divided on many issues but now united in support of Governor Al Smith. Like the GOP, they promised to enforce Prohibition, the Eighteenth Amendment to the Constitution.

In fact, of course, Prohibition had been a bonanza for bootleggers and racketeers like Al Capone. The Capone gang controlled gambling and prostitution in Chicago, but spread its terror to other cities, where rival gangs fought for control of the liquor market. Americans who could not afford good whiskey (smuggled across the Canadian and Mexican borders and sold in speakeasies, some glamorous, most sleazy), drank various poisonous home brews, "bathtub gin." During the Roaring Twenties, Capone and other gang leaders became folk heroes, known to every cop and reporter but immune from prosecution because of lavish payoffs to politicians.

While many rural people still supported Prohibition, those who lived in cities were disgusted by the corruption and violence that came in its wake, but America had never repealed a Constitutional amendment and was slow to consider the possibility.

Otherwise, the Democratic platform wanted farm relief and tariff reform, and cautiously proposed a "constructive" foreign policy. It was not much for candidate Al Smith to run on, but he campaigned across the country, calling for "modifications" in the Prohibition laws and making what appeals he could to farmers and working men and women. He was the target of vicious anti-Catholic propaganda.

At the peak of Coolidge prosperity, the Republicans promised "two cars in every garage, two chickens in every pot." The election was a Republican landslide. Hoover won in forty states and overwhelmingly in the electoral college.

The new President was inaugurated as the nation continued to enjoy the best of times, booming business, and a stock market barely able to keep up with the appetites of speculators. Predictions of greater gains and bigger profits blinded many to the underside of the boom. A million and a half Americans were unemployed; those who held jobs were still not sharing in the wealth; wages were low, and living conditions for working families showed little improvement. Farming families found that their incomes dwindled, their debts mounted, and the predicted brighter days did not arrive. More than half of American households still had no electricity, no running water, no toilets.

Un like most presidents who came to the office from a background in law, Hoover was a technician. People trusted him to apply engineering know-how to the economy. He had been an active and innovative Secretary of Commerce, interested in new products and processes, open to new approaches for getting cooperation between the public and private sectors. Unfortunately, if Hoover had any good presidential ideas, he didn't have time to think them through before the bottom fell out of everything.

1929　Although Hoover called Prohibition "a noble experiment," the nation was shocked by the Saint Valentine's Day massacre. Seven members of the Bugs Malone gang were lined up along a garage wall in Chicago and shot by the rival Capone gang. That left Scarface Al as undisputed boss of the Chicago crime scene, and dramatized the arrogance of criminals who now controlled not only the illicit trade in bootleg alcohol, but city government and state legislatures.

Worse shocks were ahead. Much of the feverish activity on Wall Street was simply gambling. People were not investing in new business ventures, creating new factories, new jobs. They were buying shares in old companies that were rising suddenly, hot because they had been profitable in the past, and now somebody else wanted a piece of the action. Speculators bought with borrowed money. It was like getting a loan to buy more poker chips and stay in the game.

When new issues found takers, expansion of the country's industrial capacity produced goods that nobody could buy. Unemployment, low wages, and the starving farm economy resulted in a lack of the purchasing power that healthy commerce required. High tariffs prevented any growth of foreign trade. Europe failed to recover from wartime devastation. In desperate Germany, a comical-looking man named Adolph Hitler was haranguing audiences who looked to him as a national savior.

The stock market crashed on October 29. Heavy trading in the morning made brokers apprehensive, for they could not explain the large volume of "sell" orders. By eleven o'clock, the sell orders had increased to the point where stock tickers were swamped, running far behind; customers could not get market prices. Panic set in. Efforts by traders for J.P. Morgan and Company steadied the market for awhile. Morgan had raised $240 million and between $20 and $30 million was now used to place "buy" orders, restoring a measure of confidence. The market had suffered a loss of $11 billion, but it looked like the worst was over.

On Monday morning, heavy selling began again, prices fell and kept falling despite a two-day closure of the Stock Exchange. Hopeful words from John D. Rockefeller and other financial experts were reported by the press but ignored by the public as men watched the value of their portfolios plunge. By November 13, hope was lost. Prices had fallen past any possibility of recovery. Some $30 billion in the market value of securities had been wiped out, had disappeared. Millions of investors, large and small, were ruined. Banks and businesses folded. The game was over.

1930

Investors who held on to their shares in steel or copper or General Motors continued to collect interest and dividends, even though the value of the stock had declined drastically. Ordinary citizens with no such source of income watched the country slide into a long Depression. As jobs vanished, the ranks of the unemployed swelled to three million, then to ten million, eventually to fifteen million. Farmers were not bad off any more; they were busted, their farms sold for taxes.

President Hoover issued continual reassurances to the public, and privately conferred with business leaders, begging them to devise a recovery program. The Great Engineer could not engineer a way out and stood by helplessly as conditions worsened. The resources of state and local governments were soon exhausted. The poor waited in breadlines before charity kitchens until those, too, ran out of crumbs to offer. Men who had proudly worn army uniforms ten years earlier now peddled on street corners, hoping passers-by could afford to buy an apple for a nickel. Or they simply begged, "Brother, can you spare a dime?"

The mid-term elections seated a Democratic majority in the House, but the

Senate remained divided, and proposals for some kind of relief for the unemployed were stalled. The president opposed "a direct or indirect dole."

Finally a Reconstruction Finance Act was passed, and the president signed it into law— a measure which would lend money to banks and railroads, to farm agencies, and to local governments to stimulate recovery.

But in May, an army of veterans marched on Washington, gaining recruits as they crossed the country. These men held certificates, issued under a post-war bonus law, which promised to pay each veteran a thousand dollars in twenty years—roughly the differences between their service pay and the wages of civilian war workers. They needed the money now. Through June and July they continued to arrive, many with wives and children, first camping on the Capitol lawn, then moving to shacks and lean-tos at Camp Marx on Anacostia Flats.

Ten thousand waited on the Capitol steps while the Senate voted on their demands. When the Senate voted "No," many began to drift home, but just as many, with nowhere else to go, stayed on in desolate Camp Marx. President Hoover's frayed nerves gave way. He ordered General Douglas MacArthur and his aide Major Dwight Eisenhower to clean them out and burn the camp. The army advanced with tanks, cavalry, bayonets, and torches. Two veterans were killed, dozens of campers injured; a baby died of tear gas. The country was sickened by newspaper accounts, and though Hoover defended his decision and the army action, the President lost his last credibility with millions of citizens.

Still, Hoover was re-nominated on the first ballot at the Republican convention. The party platform had nothing useful to say about economic conditions, and fudged the Prohibition issue.

The Democratic convention was a

boisterous affair. They smelled a victory, and the only question was, who would lead them? Of many contenders for the nomination, two favorites emerged: former New York Governor Al Smith, still the choice of party regulars, and former vice presidential candidate and present governor of New York, Franklin Roosevelt.

But before voting on the candidates began, the party adopted a bold platform. It promised unemployment relief, state insurance against unemployment and old-age destitution, new labor laws, farm aid, and regulation of the stock market. They would also support conservation measures and develop power resources, and replace high tariffs by reciprocal trade agreements with foreign countries. The convention cheered a platform plank proposing repeal of Prohibition. Powerful drys argued for submitting repeal to state decision, but the repeal plank remained part of a platform that promised so much to so many. And it could be done, the platform asserted, while balancing the budget and maintaining a sound currency.

Franklin Roosevelt

On the following day, after much deal-making and four ballots, Franklin Delano Roosevelt was nominated. To balance the ticket, Texas Representative John Nance Garner was named for Vice-President. And then the celebration began.

Roosevelt flew from Albany to Chicago to accept the nomination, and for the first time Americans were electrified by the phrase that would define his administration. He pledged himself to "a New Deal for the American people." It was a clear break with Republican philosophy. The Democrats promised to help "the forgotten man," and Roosevelt was full of optimism, impatient to get on with the tasks ahead. For the first time in many years, a presidential candidate communicated zest, the sheer excitement of meeting an enormous challenge. Campaign manager Jim Farley was candid with a radio audience about the candidate's disability. Ten years earlier, infantile paralysis had left him unable to stand or walk without support. He might be handicapped in a footrace, said Farley, but he was strong in every way that mattered.

On election day, forty million voters went to the polls. Herbert Hoover knew his chances were very slim. "We are opposed by six million unemployed (actually there were twice as many), ten thousand bonus marchers, and ten cent corn." When the ballots were counted, the Democrats won forty-two states and both Houses of Congress. The Republicans were whipped.

1933

Franklin Roosevelt was Theodore Roosevelt's fifth cousin. His wife, Eleanor (of whom the country would learn more later), was Theodore Roosevelt's niece. As a noted historian observed, —"there was something about that family!" And there certainly was.

Franklin had been the Democratic candidate for Vice-President in 1920, running with James Cox against Harding and Coolidge, in a year when the Democrats took a beating. The following year, at thirty-nine, FDR was crippled by polio. He might have retired to the huge family estate in Hyde Park, New York, but his wife and Al Smith urged him to run for governor. He proved to be an energetic liberal, with a public appeal that won his nomination for President. Now he was expected to lead a country that seemed to be on the verge of collapse or of revolution.

There were many fringe parties and personalities offering solutions to the economic crisis. Norman Thomas was the dedicated and eloquent head of the growing Socialist party. William Z. Foster, a veteran of years in the labor movement, ran in 1932 on the Communist ticket, with James Ford as the vice presidential candidate, the first black man ever nominated to that office. Father Charles Coughlin preached to millions every Sunday morning, broadcasting from his Shrine of the Little Flower Church outside Detroit, and passing a kind of radio collection plate which netted him thousands of dollars in contributions. First an admirer of Franklin Roosevelt, then a violent critic, Father Coughlin had a scheme that involved "mobilization of all Christianity" against the gold standard.

In California, Francis Townsend was a doctor who saw his practice wiped out by the Depression, and brooded about the plight of other impoverished old people. He developed his Old Age Revolving Pension Plan, which promised them "$200 every Friday" and attracted as many as 2.5 million people to local Townsend clubs. Memberships cost only 25 cents, but it added up, and his political influence grew. Governor Huey Long of Louisiana was a canny political boss, "the Kingfish." He had his Share the Wealth Plan for confiscating the incomes and inheritances of millionaires and giving every American $5,000 a year. "Every man a King!" was his rallying cry while he built many miles of Louisiana roads, a hundred bridges, hospitals, and other public works, and provided free textbooks for the state's schoolchildren. He was elected to the Senate in 1932 and confidently eyed the presidency; he wrote a book, *My First Hundred Days in the White House.*

A possible merger of these forces worried Franklin Roosevelt, because such coalitions had brought Fascist dictatorships to power in Germany and Italy. But meanwhile, he was president, and in his own First Hundred Days, he established a record of administrative and Congressional action that has never been equaled. Between the election and his inauguration, Roosevelt conferred with outgoing President Hoover, who still believed that measures undertaken late in his term would work, if given enough time. He wanted Roosevelt to endorse that program, and throw out the dangerous nonsense proposed by the Democratic platform.

Roosevelt refused.

Just after 1 P.M. on a rainy Saturday, March 4, the President delivered his memorable inaugural address from the Capitol steps. "The only thing we have to fear," he said, "is fear itself.... This Nation asks for action, and action now." A few hours later he met with William Woodin, his Secretary of the Treasury, to agree on a plan to handle the banking emergency (the banks in Michigan had already been closed for two weeks). On Sunday, March 5, Roosevelt called his Cabinet together and issued two proclamations. All the banks in the country would be closed, there would be no financial transactions whatsoever, and depositors could not get at their money. And Congress would be called into emergency session five days later.

Citizens took the bank closing with surprising calm, but bankers were frantic. Many assumed that there was not enough currency in American banks to meet the country's needs. They wanted the government to offer scrip, any bits of paper that a housewife could use at the grocery store. But after repeated meetings with bankers and all night sessions of writing and rewriting, a bill was finally drafted and a schedule for reopening the banks was prepared. On Thursday, March 9, the bill was read to the Congress—only one copy was available—and passed unanimously by the House. In the Senate, Huey Long protested, but the bill passed seventy-three to seven, and on Monday the banks reopened. Deposits and gold began to come in.

A new Constitutional amendment was proposed, repealing the 1917 Prohibition amendment. (When ratification was completed in December, 3.2 percent alcoholic beer became legal.) A government economy bill was passed, cutting federal salaries and pensions. A Civilian Conservation Corps was created to employ young men in re-forestation and other conservation works. The gold standard, which established the value of money and provided that all paper money could be redeemed for gold on demand, was abandoned. A Federal Emergency Relief Act was passed to authorize a national relief system. That was the first week.

The New Deal now got into high gear. Hard times had hit not only farmers and industrial workers, but law firms and colleges. Unemployed men and women from many professions and all parts of the nation now headed for Washington, looking for jobs and more than that—wanting to be part of the most exciting social transformation of their lifetimes. They were often impetuous and arrogant, not much interested in the collective experience of longtime legislators and government employees, often ignorant but open to new ideas, willing to take chances, non-stop talkers. Some soon learned the political ropes, the cynical tricks that served political ambition. But an astonishing number were dedicated to service and to a shining future for the United States of America. It is worth noting that in Roosevelt's three-full-terms-plus not a breath of scandal touched his administration. Whatever else the New Dealers may or may not have been, they were honest.

By the middle of June, Roosevelt pushed Congress to more legislation: an Agricultural Adjustment Act, to set agricultural policy; the emergency Farm Mortgage Act, to help farmers refinance their mortgages; the Tennessee River Valley Authority Act, a visionary plan for redevelopment of the Tennessee Valley; the Truth-in-Securities Act, requiring full disclosure in the issue of new stocks and bonds; the Home Owners' Loan Act, offering others the same refinancing benefits that farmers had received; the National Industrial Recovery Act, which would get the government deeply involved in questions of industrial management and fund a $5.5 billion program of public works; a bill to guarantee bank deposits and separate commercial from investment banking; the Farm Credit Act, giving farmers easier access to loans for seeds and equipment; the Railroad Coordination Act, creating a federal Coordinator of Transportation.

This was the work of the First Hundred Days, Franklin Roosevelt's revolution, watched not only by Americans but by people in other depression-wracked countries. His counselors were called his Brains Trust, and he welcomed their advice. His heart was full of optimism and extravagant hopes. He genuinely believed in that Declaration of Independence which said the American people had a God-given right to "the pursuit of happiness." The government was entrusted with their well-being. They were entitled to enjoy the fruits of what their forefathers had planted, and their children should inherit not only a healthy economy but all the natural resources with which the Republic had been blessed. Why should the government be stingy, in the name of careful accounting? Why should government be repressive, in the name of public order? And why, above all, should government be dull? Why not make it the highest and most satisfying and most exhilarating sphere of human activity?

Of course, new laws meant the proliferation of new government offices and agencies to implement the laws. Some of the most important included: The Agricultural Adjustment Administration; the Securities and Exchange Commission; the Federal Deposit Insurance Corporation; the Federal Emergency Relief Administration; the Public Works Administration; the Civil Works Administration; the National Labor Relations Board; the Federal Housing Administration; the Resettlement Administration—and more, the "alphabet soup" (AAA, NRA, SEC, FDIC, etc.) which drew so much derision. The Reconstruction Finance Corporation was brought to life and broadened.

The heads of these departments and agencies soon became familiar figures to every

American who read the papers. But before we meet the men who helped Franklin Roosevelt make the New Deal, we should talk about his wife, for Eleanor Roosevelt played a role that nobody else could have filled. She was a shy, gawky girl, from a wealthy but not very happy family, educated at private schools in America and Europe, raised to a life of privilege. (Though she never got the braces she needed for those terrible front teeth; people didn't yet know about orthodonture.) Eleanor was drawn by deep personal conviction to the reform causes of her time, and after she married her handsome cousin Franklin she was quickly caught up in his political career. He was a rising star in the Democratic party, after serving in Woodrow Wilson's Cabinet and despite losing for Vice-President in 1920. The following summer he was stricken by polio, permanently crippled and, of course, profoundly depressed. But it didn't last long. Unlike friends who suggested that he retire to his estate and live the life of a country gentleman, Eleanor urged him to get back into the action.

Theirs was not a conventionally good marriage. Roosevelt was attractive to women, and attracted by women all his life. There was not much downright infidelity, but Eleanor eventually learned of a serious love affair, and that ended their married intimacy. Nor were they conventionally good parents. Eleanor bore seven children, and could never cope with them; in the end she left all that to her mother-in-law. But after his illness, she became her husband's eyes and ears and legs. She helped him with the governorship of New York in 1928 and 1930; she toured with him during the presidential campaign. It became an astonishing partnership, because Franklin could reassure people with his warm, resonant voice, but Eleanor could listen.

During the next years, she would travel tens of thousands of miles, listening to people whose lives had been wrecked by the

Depression. Even more importantly, she listened to those who had never had much of a life, even in the country's most prosperous years. She was committed to the cause of human rights and of economic justice. Her husband was certainly a liberal, but he was keenly aware of the political consequences of any action he took. Eleanor did not have the constraints of office; she acted unofficially, and she never wavered. She was the president's conscience, and in later years the conscience of the world.

Harold Ickes had been a reform Republican for most of his political life, going back to the days of the Bull Moose party. Franklin Roosevelt made him secretary of the interior, an office he occupied for longer than any other Cabinet member has ever served. For six years he ran the Public Works Administration, dealing with conservation and environmental programs, public electric power, slum clearance and public housing, and many other long-term, heavy investment projects for military and civilian purposes. Others in the administration were impatient with Ickes, because he did not come up with programs that offered immediate relief to the unemployed, but job creating was not the secretary's first priority. He was spending big money, and he was determined that every penny should be spent carefully. Each contract was gone over with a fine-toothed comb. In a department too often exploited by crooks, no hint of corruption would be tolerated by "Honest Harold" Ickes. (He was not so honest to the many women in his life.)

Henry Wallace, Roosevelt's secretary of agriculture, hailed from Iowa. His father had been agriculture secretary in the Harding administration and continued to be an important voice in midwest agriculture as editor of his paper, *Wallace's Farmer*. Young Henry went to Iowa State Agricultural College at Ames, where one of his teachers was George Washington Carver. He began to experiment with plant genetics and hybrid corn, until he took over the family paper.

After the Congress passed a farm bill, the president had moved quickly to consolidate a Farm Credit Administration, which loaned $100 million to help farmers pay mortgage debt, for marketing loans, and to strengthen farm cooperatives. But Henry Wallace understood the basic problem, the bottom line. "In agriculture, supply sets the price. In industry, price sets the supply." Half a century of spectacular improvement in American farming methods had caused tremendous increases in productivity. Farm surpluses depressed farm prices and farmer's incomes. There was not much possibility of selling those surpluses in foreign markets; high tariffs and economic conditions in Europe limited that option, though a considerable amount of wheat was sold to the Far East.

In any case, the first step in a successful farm program was to convince farmers that to raise prices they must end surpluses, reduce crop acreage and take part of their land out of production. In the last year of the Hoover administration, two midwest Congressmen had introduced bills for land allotments, which would tell farmers how much land they could use to grow crops for market; nobody had to accept the plan, but farmers who signed up would be paid for part of their lost production. The plan was revised to focus on wheat, cotton, hogs, and tobacco, but still got nowhere in the Senate. Now farmers threatened by foreclosures and eviction notices were taking their problems into their own hands. In Henry Wallace's home state, an angry mob dragged a judge from his bench and from his courthouse and got ready to lynch him. They threw a rope over a branch and tightened the other end around his throat, but after hours of humiliation and rough handling, they let him go.

The new farm bill included an allotment plan, and benefits for farmers who accepted it, to be paid out of a tax on food

251

processors—flour mills, meat packers, and so on. All that remained was to sell the idea to farmers, and that became the job of the Agricultural Extension Service provided by the land grant colleges. County agents who worked for the service knew the problem and knew the people. They were soon able to persuade thousands of farmers to destroy standing crops in return for benefit payments, and to reduce planting over the next three years. Cotton and wheat crops were brought under control. There was little public outcry about taking forty million acres of productive land out of cultivation (though many people saw the irony of plowing up wheat while millions of Americans couldn't get bread) but pigs were something else. The only way to limit hog production was for the government to buy and slaughter five or six million little pigs, and the squealing of those piglets was almost unbearable. Despite widespread protest, the pigs were killed; the Federal Surplus Relief Corporation bought over 100 million pounds of pork to feed hungry families.

But whatever help Henry Wallace was able to give the country's farmers, the core of the economic crisis was industrial. The goal of the National Industrial Recovery Act (NRA) was to reopen factories and rehire workers, but it would require a degree of government control over major industries, a serious infringement of the capitalist freedom that Americans had always cherished. Chain-smoking, harddrinking General Hugh Johnson was put in charge of the NRA. He was a tough military administrator who had devised plans for the 1917 Selective Service draft and helped mobilize industry for the production efforts of World War I.

As a result of that wartime experience, Johnson became a firm believer in government-industry cooperation, and quickly identified the industries that had to be involved—textiles, coal, oil, steel, automobiles, construction, and others, whose representatives were invited to Washington to confer—i.e., to get the General's orders. He wanted regulation by trade associations in each industry. They would write their own fair practice codes, which government would enforce. There were still no state laws governing minimum wages, and not many to limit working hours. Sweatshops and child labor came back as the Depression worsened and desperate employers struggled for marginal profits. Trade association codes would set minimum wages and maximum hours and determine working conditions to abolish the worst abuses of factory labor; they gave labor unions bargaining rights; but Johnson did not get the kind of production planning he hoped for, nor the complete compliance on which success depended. More than 700 codes were drawn up, but many industrialists refused to join an association (Henry Ford, for one) or accept any code. The president tried to impose a blanket code on those that dragged their feet, but it was slow going.

At last Hugh Johnson got the president's approval for a massive publicity and selling campaign. He designed a logo, the Blue Eagle, a symbol for business cooperation awarded manufacturers who abided by fair practice codes and shopkeepers who sold only the products of those companies. Factories flew the Blue Eagle flag and stamped the symbol on their products; merchants proudly displayed Blue Eagle signs in their windows. Two million employers signed up and almost a million workers marched in a New York parade to celebrate. In the ninety days after it was hatched, the Blue Eagle grew strong wings and soared over the first summer of the New Deal.

1934

Farm incomes rose and foreign trade increased. The upturn in business was noticeable, if not very fast. Railroads, banks, and insurance companies began to pay back their government loans. Wages and salaries went up, investments began to pay dividends. But economic growth was far exceeded by federal expenditures on relief and public works; the Treasury showed staggering deficits.

And far from Washington, D.C., the skies darkened with a new disaster. In 1931, after a seven-year drought, dust began to blow in part of west Kansas and eastern Colorado, and got worse in 1932. The AAA suspended plans to plow up wheat fields. Nature was starting to limit the over-production of wheat, which began when wheat prices were high after World War I. In those years, farmers on the southern Great Plains broke more sod every year; wheat acreage had increased 200 percent, in some counties as much as 1,000 percent. This not only depressed the market price, but wore out the soil in a region that had always known cycles of drought. There was little snow and less rain in 1933. In 1934 the spring rains failed again and the winds rose during the 'blow months"—February, March, and April.

The huge dust storms began in May. The Dust Bowl, as reporters began to call it, included ninety counties in Kansas, Colorado, Oklahoma, New Mexico, and Texas, 97 million acres, of which 32 million were under cultivation. But the dust soon blew across much of the Dakotas, Nebraska, Arkansas, Missouri, Mississippi, and farther east. Across the plains, the black clouds towered a thousand feet high, coming in "like a wall of muddy water." Frightened birds flocked before the wind. The black blizzards drifted dust along fence walls, on country roads, on city streets where streetlights provided eerie illumination in a noon-day twilight. Schools closed; housewives stuffed rugs under the doors and rags around the windows, even plugged keyholes, but the dust seeped in. People went out with wet towels over their faces, but it was almost impossible to breathe. Millions of acres were still in pasture, but overgrazing and drought had already damaged the land, and native grass was smothered in dust. Livestock choked and starved. Without Red Cross food parcels, people might have starved.

The Soil Conservation Service advised farmers on methods to save the land, but the storms got worse in 1935 and each year until 1938, when the long drought broke. Rain returned, and for the next decade the rainfall was above average. But it came too late for half a million refugees who had already given up and started west on Route 66, in wagons, trucks, old flivvers, on foot, taking with them as much of their household goods as they could carry. Wherever they came from, they were called Okies. Along the road they worked if they found work and got handouts from general stores or gas stations where the owners took pity, on these shame-faced strangers. Those who made it to the promised land in California didn't get much pity and were often driven off by gun-toting land owners and local sheriffs. But they could go no further, so they took any job in the cotton or potato fields, or picked fruit, ate semi-rotten produce and sometimes "Hoover hogs"—jackrabbits. Lucky families found shelter in camps run by the Farm Security Administration, clean cots, drinkable water. And eventually the Okies and their kids became Californians.

Of course, this natural calamity greatly complicated the task of Harry Hopkins, who headed the Federal Emergency Relief Administration. Hopkins had no patience with the Public Works projects of Harold Ickes. PWA would eventually employ thousands in construction. Between 1933 and 1939 PWA built 70 percent of the country's new schools, 65 percent of the courthouses and city halls, 10 percent of the roads, bridges, and subways, and even ships for the navy—the aircraft carriers Yorktown and Enterprise—but the magnitude of such programs, and the meticulous bookkeeping of Harold Ickes meant that PWA was slow.

Harry Hopkins came to the New Deal as a social worker. He relaxed with tennis and poker and an occasional afternoon at the racetrack, but he didn't relax very often. A tense, nervous man, he drank gallons of coffee and smoked innumerable cigarettes while he pushed his small staff to greater efforts on behalf of the poor. He pushed the states, too, intending to spend one federal dollar for every three dollars spent by the states in public assistance. The Ohio Unemployed League had already marched on the State House in Columbus, demanding action, but the states were too slow for Harry Hopkins, who insisted on jobs, not relief that destroyed the self-respect of decent Americans. But on what kind of programs could they work, with what tools? With astonishing speed, he organized the Civil Works Administration (CWA, 1933-1934) and the Works Progress Administration (WPA, 1935-1943). The workers were widely ridiculed as "leaf-rakers" and "shovel-leaners," but by January, 1934, more than four million people were hired. Like Ickes, Hopkins built roads and schools, but there were smaller projects—parks, playgrounds, community swimming pools, insect control, sewers. Fifty thousand teachers were sent to country and city schools to organize classes for adult education. Small airports were built or improved. Even artists were hired to brighten the walls of railroad stations and other public buildings with decorative murals.

States did what they could. Ohio Relief Production Units took over vacated factories and created jobs for people who made mattresses and clothing, or canned food. In Kansas, Governor Alfred Landon cooperated and applauded New Deal efforts like the FERA Rural Rehabilitation Division which supported state and private self-help cooperatives. But there was a lot of opposition from businessmen who called this kind of competition a socialist, even communist, intrusion into the market economy. In the south, cotton planters complained that they couldn't get black crews to work for 50 cents a day if relief jobs were available.

The federal government stuck to the New Deal agenda and found time for other national concerns. The General Allotment Act of 1887 had given a "white man's title" to Indian farmers, but tribes lost their legal standing. Surplus land was distributed to white settlers. The American Indian population reached its low point in 1890, when only 228,000 native Americans survived. But in 1934, after bitter debate, Congress passed the Indian Reorganization Act. John Collier, the Commissioner of Indian Affairs, had founded the American Indian Defense Association, and he drafted this sweeping reform whereby tribes were given legal recognition. Unsold allotments were returned to the tribes and provision was made for the purchase of new lands. He encouraged tribal constitutions and expanded political and judicial authority. Indians got easier access to credit; corporations brought new economic opportunities; and new educational facilities provided reservation day-schools instead of sending Indian children away from home to boarding schools.

Under Collier, the bureau hired Indians and involved Indians in management and policy-making. Another act allowed the Secretary of the Interior to contract with state and territory agencies to provide social, educational, agricultural, and medical services which improved Indian standards of living. Collier had visions of an "Indian Renaissance" after which Indians, though still legally and financially dependent on the federal government, would be healthier and more prosperous. Unhappily, later Congresses did not share his vision, and many gains made by Native Americans were reversed. Ten years later there would even be charges that the traditions of tribal life looked suspiciously like the communism practiced in Red Russia.

1935

In May, the New Deal got a real setback. Four young brothers in Brooklyn owned the Schechter Poultry Corporation: they were charged with violation of the Live Poultry Code, the NRA fair practice rule that was supposed to be observed in that industry. They were accused of selling "unfit" chickens, and paying lower wages than the code called for. The Schechter brothers maintained that theirs was not an interstate business, and therefore not bound by any of General Hugh Johnson's trade association codes. What's more, the NRA was unconstitutional because it granted legislative powers to the executive branch of government. There had been increasing objection to the Blue Eagle program from big companies (at first cooperative) and labor (at first enthusiastic about the worker protection and union recognition provisions of the association codes), and even more hostility from small business. *Schechter Poultry Corp. v. United States* was the case that came before the Supreme Court in May, and the court agreed unanimously with the plaintiffs. The National

257

Recovery Act was finished. The high-flying Blue Eagle was brought down by a dead chicken.

Senator Frank Norris was seventy-four years old when he traveled to Knoxville, Tennessee, for his first look at the nearly-completed Norris Dam, the first dam built by the Tennessee Valley Authority. The veteran Nebraska legislator had worked for public development of the Tennessee River since the 1920s, pushing two bills through Congress. Presidents Coolidge and Hoover vetoed the bills. Not until the first Hundred Days of the Roosevelt administration did a TVA get approval.

The Tennessee is a major river, fed by the heaviest rainfall in eastern America. It flows through seven states—Tennessee, Alabama, Kentucky, Virginia, North Carolina, Georgia, and Mississippi—an area about as big as England and Scotland, with a population (then) of about six million people. It has five mountain tributaries, each a fairly big stream. Before the TVA, in the rainy season, water rushed out of the mountains and overflowed the banks of those branches, eventually swelling the Tennessee to flood stage. Centuries of flooding had badly eroded land in the valley, and silted the river so it was only navigable for short stretches. Farms in the Tennessee Valley were typically small, the families big. Each acre supported more people than in any other part of the country. Thousands of families never saw more than $100 cash income a year; only two out of a hundred farms had electricity.

The government had already built two dams at Muscle Shoals, miles of river where rapids made navigation dangerous during the winter flood season and impossible when the water was low. During World War I, under the National Defense Act, federal dams harnessed the flood waters to generate power and constructed two plants to produce fertilizers and materials for high explosives. Those projects were put up for sale after the war, and the argument about public versus private development dragged on for years. Henry Ford made a ridiculously cheap offer to take over the operations at Muscle Shoals; Wendell Willkie, president of the Commonwealth and Southern Company, headed a group of utility executives opposed to the TVA, because if the government dams produced cheap electric power at Muscle Shoals, it would compete with private power generation and transmission. Anyway, there was no market for more power; poor farmers couldn't afford electricity. And of course, conservative

Congressmen roared their disapproval of an idea that smacked of communism, fascism, every kind of radicalism, and was just generally no good whatsoever.

But Senator Norris fought it through Congress again, and Franklin Roosevelt appointed a chairman who shared Norris's vision. He was Arthur E. Morgan, an engineer with sound experience in flood control and a broad philosophical approach to public responsibility. For ten years he had been president of Antioch College in Ohio. Now he was joined on the TVA board by another Morgan, an agricultural scientist, well-known in the valley because of his long career as head of the Agriculture Department and then president of the University of Tennessee. With Harwell Morgan would serve young David Lilienthal, a lawyer who worked with Governor Philip LaFollette as chairman of Wisconsin's Public Service Commission. These three men would implement the Norris dream. Arthur Morgan would build the power-producing dams; Harwell Morgan would direct agricultural policy and fertilizer production; Lilienthal would manage power policy.

As these men and the president conceived of the Tennessee Valley Authority, it would lift millions of people out of dire poverty by building dams on the tributary rivers to provide flood control and prevent soil erosion; it would restore eroded and exhausted land and start reforesting steep hillsides; it would produce and transmit power, and build plants to refine the high-grade phosphate ores of Tennessee into fertilizer for valley farmers; cheaper electric power would also attract private industrial development and offer new work opportunities.

Eventually, TVA constructed twenty-five dams on the upstream tributaries. Five more were privately constructed. All held water back during the winter floods and released water during the last half of the year to maintain an eleven-foot navigation channel in the river. Nine more mainstream dams created a long chain of navigable lakes for good fishing and recreational uses. Those dams generated the hydroelectric power which transformed valley life; families displaced by dams and lakes were resettled on new farms and worked their own transformations. More than fifty thousand private farms became demonstration operations, experimenting with and teaching new methods to raise more corn, better pastures, more beef cattle and milk cows, more hogs and chickens, which in a few years were translated into healthier and smarter kids. Thus the New Deal's most controversial proposal became a success story, run not from Washington but from modest headquarters at Muscle Shoals and other decentralized offices. And Senator George Norris, for whom the first dam on the Clinch River, and the broad lake behind it were named, lived to see his dream come true.

In 1935, the tremendously important Social Security Act became law. Labor Secretary Frances Perkins, the only woman in Roosevelt's Cabinet, came from a career in social work, and had told Franklin Roosevelt that her personal agenda included old-age pensions and unemployment insurance. Neither was a new idea. Britain already had a system of unemployment insurance, as did the state of Wisconsin. Since the days of the Progressive Party old-age pensions had been under discussion, and some states had passed mandatory pension laws. The president wanted a single package and Frances Perkins was directed to develop a plan for his consideration.

Again there was widespread conservative objection. Since the proposal that emerged called for funding by employer and employee contributions, businessmen deplored a scheme that would wreck the private enterprise system and drive them into bankruptcy. Employees were suspicious and wanted federal funds, or state funds, or a tax on future wage earners, or almost any formula that did not tap them for their future security. On the other hand, liberals tried to tack on many health measures relating to assistance for mothers and dependent children, the blind, and so on. These were opposed by the American Medical Association and others, and were dropped in later bills. Finally, in August, emerged the law with which all Americans are now familiar. The Social Security Board was chaired by John Winant, formerly governor of New Hampshire, who had supported the idea since his 1912 days with the Bull Moose party. The Board managed funds (initially 1 percent) deducted from workers' paychecks and company earnings, paid out when the workers reached age sixty-five or to their survivors. Part of the money was returned to the states, which administered unemployment insurance. No government program ever affected so many Americans so directly.

Huey Long, who filibustered against the act, was assassinated in Louisiana, in the state capitol at Baton Rouge, by the son of a local political opponent, who in turn was shot by the senator's bodyguard.

John L. Lewis, president of the United Mineworkers, wanted to unionize both skilled and unskilled workers by industries, rather than by their particular trades as in the American Federation of Labor. These "vertical" unions came close to the One Big Union envisioned by the IWW a generation earlier. The Congress of Industrial Organizations (CIO), grew rapidly after the CIO split from the AFL and was successful in recruiting members in mass-production industries like steel, automobiles, and textiles.

1936

In Roosevelt's first terms, millions of dollars were spent to put people back to work and relieve the suffering of the poor. Many people in and out of the administration were horrified at the cost of the New Deal, including Roosevelt's director of the budget. He hated the NRA and the PWA and programs like the Civilian Conservation Corps (CCC) which took young men from the slums and put them in camps from which they planted trees, fought forest fires, built small dams for erosion control, and added seventeen million acres to the country's forest land; or the National Youth Administration (NYA), which put other unemployed young men and women into occupational training and helped them find jobs. Most historians agree that these programs were important contributions to national recovery and a needed reform of a failing economic system. They not only gave victims of the great Depression immediate assistance, but enriched the nation with public works of lasting value and helped salvage national resources. But the budget director viewed that spending with genuine alarm because the New Deal greatly increased the national debt. Between 1933 and 1937 the debt grew from $22 billion to $36 billion. The director resigned, but he kept his mouth shut during this election year.

The Republican convention was a dull affair. The party's platform promised to restore and preserve free enterprise, and to provide "encouragement rather than hindrance to legitimate business." Republicans would certainly put an end to "uncontrolled spending," and would stoutly resist American participation in the League of Nations. They nominated Alfred E. Landon, a wealthy oil man and governor of Kansas.

To nobody's surprise, the Democrats re-nominated Franklin Roosevelt and John Garner. Then delegates enjoyed a day and night of fifty-seven speeches, impromptu singing and dancing, parades that included a balky donkey, and a general hoopla in celebration of the election victory they saw ahead.

There were other candidates. The Union party was endorsed by Father Coughlin and Dr. Townsend. The Socialists again nominated Norman Thomas. The Communists named Earl Browder. Even the Prohibition Party got into it. Al Smith left the Democrats and came out for Alf Landon. Senator Frank Norris left the Republicans and ran as an Independent. The AFL was officially non-partisan, but labor supported Roosevelt; most of the national press supported Landon and predicted a Republican win.

Alfred Landon had no taste or talent for the kind of dirty campaign waged in 1936, during which Republicans targeted the Social Security Act. But even their darkest accusations made little difference. When the votes were counted, Governor Landon suffered the worst defeat in American political history, carrying only the states of Maine and Vermont, eight electoral votes. Roosevelt's popular vote was almost five million more than he got four years earlier. The stock market was up, farm prices were up, steel production was up—the recovery led by the New Deal was real and measurable.

1937 But in his inaugural address, Roosevelt reminded his audience that one-third of the nation was still "ill-housed, ill-clad, ill-nourished," and there was still a long way to go.

The Supreme Court had nullified nine New Deal measures, including the NRA, the AAA, the Railroad Retirement Plan, the Municipal Bankruptcy Act, and others, struck down as unconstitutional. Franklin Delano Roosevelt wanted a court more favorable to his purpose, and proposed to enlarge its membership. Those nine old men, he said, were overworked and tired; one Justice was seventy, four were approaching seventy-five, and he had not had an opportunity to appoint even one new Justice during his first term. The number of Justices had been changed before (it was not fixed by the Constitution); Presidents Adams, Jefferson, Jackson, Lincoln, and Grant had changed it in their time. Roosevelt offered a plan by which, depending on the retirement of Justices over seventy, new judges would be appointed, to a limit of fifteen. It was not quite as radical a plan as his opponents charged, but this "court-packing" scheme outraged the public. Even many of his most ardent admirers opposed him, and the plan was defeated by Congress in July.

However, he had gotten the attention of the "nine old men," who in the next months handed down decisions that approved progressive legislation, including the Social Security Act and the Labor Relations Act. In the next year, death and retirements gave Roosevelt a chance to appoint seven more liberal Justices to the court.

There were still eleven million Americans unemployed, and more than five million only partially employed. The ranks of labor were split between the AFL and the new CIO. Neither the president nor the secretary of labor would take sides, hoping the National Labor Relations Board (NLRB) could arbitrate between industrial unions as it had handled similar disputes among railroad unions.

But more than five thousand strikes flared up during the year, none bloodier than the fight at the Republic Steel plant in Chicago. When cops attacked picketers, ten workers were killed, eight shot in the back. The CIO developed a new tactic, the "sit-down" strike, during which union men settled into a factory and refused to work, or let others enter to work. General Motors and United States Steel, the two biggest mass production companies in the country signed up. CIO membership grew to 2.5 million, and the number of strikes began to decline.

1938

Though the NRA had been abolished by the Supreme Court, some of its objectives were met by the Fair Labor Standards Act, which established a work week of forty hours and a minimum wage of forty cents an hour. Congress was increasingly concerned about the national debt and began to slash hundreds of millions from administration appropriations bills. But efforts to balance the budget led to a new recession, which lasted almost a year. FDR launched another $500 billion federal spending program.

Coping with their own problems, most Americans had ignored a decade of bad news from abroad. In 1931, Japan invaded Manchuria; Benito Mussolini, the Fascist dictator of Italy, sent his forces into Ethiopia in 1935; a civil war began to tear Spain apart in 1936, one side armed by Fascist Germany, the other by Communist Russia; Japan hit China and moved south in 1937; Germany's Adolph Hitler annexed Austria in 1938, and took the Czechoslovakian Sudetenland, which had been German before World War I; England and France agreed to that theft by signing a pact with Hitler, hoping that his territorial appetite was appeased and the Munich agreement would avoid a larger war. The prime minister of England returned to assure his anxious countrymen that the pact would mean "peace in our time."

This policy of appeasement was matched by American determination to stay out of another European conflict. Americans had rejected Woodrow Wilson's call for "a general association of nations—for the purpose of affording mutual guarantees of political independence and territorial integrity to great and small states alike." The United States did not join the League of Nations, and without Wilsonian resolve, that organization was not prepared to deal with the aggressions of the 1930s.

Congress made no distinction between aggressor nations and their victims. Four Neutrality Acts were passed between 1935 and 1939, the first after Italy's attack on Ethiopia. It let the president embargo arms sales to belligerents, but did not interfere with trade in essential war materials like copper, steel, and oil. The neutrality policy was applauded by Henry Ford, Charles Lindbergh, Father Coughlin, and millions of isolationist

Americans who wanted to steer clear of foreign "entanglements."

Perhaps it was this charged atmosphere, the war headlines, the constant news bulletins from abroad, that made it possible for a twenty-three-year-old radio producer to terrify the nation with a Halloween broadcast. Orson Welles opened his show with dance music, the kind of easy listening familiar to audiences then and now. It was interrupted by a news flash reporting a mysterious occurrence in a New England town, and then the music returned. After a couple of such interruptions the music was pre-empted and the time given over to increasingly frightening descriptions from newsmen at the fictional scene, and interviews with hysterical eyewitnesses to the fictional disaster. Millions of Americans were convinced that the United States was being attacked by spaceships, invaders from another planet, using devastating weapons. Telephone lines were swamped. The roads were jammed with panic-stricken families trying to escape to somewhere, anywhere, away from certain doom. Welles based the script on a story by a famous British writer, but so brilliant was his production, so blood-curdling the details and so stunning the performances of his cast, that the whole country was taken in by his Halloween prank. It made the young prankster famous; Orson Welles became a great name in the history of American radio, theater, and films.

1939

Fascist forces won the civil war in Spain, and America recognized the new government of dictator Francisco Franco. Hitler swallowed the rest of Czechoslovakia and signed a non-aggression pact with Russia. On September 1, that country joined his brutal attack on Poland. England and France could stand by no longer; they declared war on September 3.

President Roosevelt got an increase in the national defense budget and declared a national emergency. He called for revisions of the Neutrality Act to permit weapons sales to nations that could pay cash and transport arms in their own ships. This "cash-and-carry" provision was meant to help England; there was no question about which side America intended to support, but a deep split developed over how much support it would provide.

In this year Eleanor Roosevelt fought a small battle of her own. She belonged to both the National Association of Colored People and the Daughters of the American Revolution; now she had to choose sides. Marion Anderson was a well-known black contralto. She broke the color line in grand opera when she signed a contract with the Metropolitan Opera in New York. But when she planned a concert in Washington, the DAR refused its permission to perform at Constitution Hall. Eleanor arranged for Miss Anderson to sing on the steps of the Lincoln Memorial, to an audience of seventy-five thousand people who loved music and justice for all.

After Hitler's lightning victory in Poland, his storm troopers swept into Denmark and Norway. FDR urged a conscription law that would draft young men into what had been for twenty years a volunteer army. He did not inform the country about the letter he received from physicist Albert Einstein, warning him about German progress in developing a devastating new kind of weapon, an atomic bomb.

The President set up an Advisory Council on National Defense, consisting of six Cabinet members and seven representatives of industry. He gave England fifty old destroyers in exchange for leases on eight naval bases on the Atlantic coast from Newfoundland to British Guyana. Latin American countries had already pooled their navies and were patrolling 6,000 miles of South Atlantic coast. But Germans sank American merchant ships, thousands of tons of cargo and hundreds of men, as well as launching three unsuccessful torpedo attacks on patrol ships in the North Atlantic.

America was still selling war material for Japan's armies in China, but after the Japanese invasion of Indochina, shipments of scrap iron and steel were embargoed, and Japan signed military alliances with Italy and Germany.

As war raged in Europe and Asia, Americans welcomed the distraction of the New York World's Fair. David Sarnoff, now president of the Radio Corporation of America, (RCA) used the occasion to demonstrate a new technology that would transform American life. Like radio, the development of television was the result of decades of work by many scientists and engineers. But when another young Russian immigrant, Vladimir Zworykin, went to Sarnoff with his all-electronic concept, Sarnoff immediately grasped its superiority and focused RCA's research on television. As with radio, the Federal Communications Commission played a crucial role. An earlier agency had allocated broadcast frequencies among station owners and issued licenses to operate for "the public interest, convenience or necessity." Now it had to establish technical standards and channels for television service, so that set owners could get pictures from every channel instead of being limited to the transmitter with which their sets were aligned. Within two years of its World's Fair debut, RCA launched the first commercial telecasting, and sold advertising time for four dollars a minute.

1940

In the summer of 1940, the bleeding remnants of British and French armies were driven from Europe, evacuated from the small coastal town of Dunkerque. Under heavy German shelling, more than 300,000 troops were rescued from the beaches of the Dover Straits by the Royal Navy and a flotilla of small boats—merchant vessels, fishing ships, even pleasure craft. Ten days later, Paris fell and France surrendered. General Charles de Gaulle formed a Free French government and announced from London that it would continue to resist. Now in control of the English Channel, Hitler began the Battle of Britain.

From August until October, German bombers attacked London and other cities. Death rained down on civilians who took shelter in churches, cellars, and subways, where they joked and sang to keep up their spirits. When the "All Clear" sounded they crawled out and tried to clean up. Only the courage and sacrifice of Royal Air Force fighter pilots, facing German planes in daily dog-fights, saved England from invasion. Winston Churchill, the new Prime Minister, said, "Never have so many owed so much to so few."

In September, Congress passed the Selective Service and Training Act, and American men between twenty-one and thirty-five were ordered to register. The first draftees reported for duty in October.

The Republican convention met in Philadelphia and produced a platform that called for "Americanism, preparedness, and peace." They cautiously agreed on aid to countries that were victims of Fascist aggression, but otherwise maintained a position of nonintervention. And, of course, they were committed to the long tradition of two-term Presidents.

The GOP had gained Congressional seats in the mid-term election and now had many strong contenders for the presidential nomination. The front-runner was Thomas E. Dewey, who had gained national attention as the crime-busting district attorney of New York City, but behind him were a number of governors, senators, and other public men.

Less well known was Wendell Willkie, a Wall Street lawyer who, as president of the billion dollar Commonwealth and Southern Company had opposed TVA plans for producing cheap electric power for the Tennessee

Valley. He was a big, energetic, handsome man with no previous political experience. He had been a lifelong Democratic voter and held far more liberal views on many domestic issues than most Republicans. He thought that labor unions had a useful role in industry, and he believed that the government should provide minimal economic security for working people. As the war in Europe escalated, Willkie favored aid to the Allies and emphatically differed with the isolationist wing of the party. He was backed by like-minded businessmen, newspaper publishers, and others who were tired of Republican politics as usual. They organized and financed a "spontaneous" Willkie boom which attracted thousands of enthusiastic independents, who now packed the convention hall galleries while pro-Willkie letters and telegrams swamped the delegations on the floor. And they beat all the party bosses and deal-makers. On the sixth ballot, Wendell Willkie was nominated.

Early in the year Roosevelt had no plans to run for a third term. He told close associates that he would issue a statement removing himself as a candidate. But the war changed his mind. As German armies occupied Holland, Belgium, and France, it was obvious that America would have to be united under strong leadership. The Democrats certainly could not find another candidate of equal stature. For Vice-President, Roosevelt wanted Henry Wallace, his secretary of agriculture. There was much objection to the lanky Iowan from both sides of the party. He was too "mystic" and idealistic for the conservatives, while liberals criticized his AAA program as concerned only with commercial farmers, too little interested in the rural poor. But FDR insisted. "Dammit to hell," he told Harry Hopkins, "they will go for Wallace or I won't run,"—so they did.

The platform promised the Allies "all the material aid at our command" but said that no American forces would be committed unless the nation was attacked. Roosevelt repeated the pledge in a Boston campaign speech, "I have said this before and I will say it again and again and again. Your boys are not going to be sent to foreign wars."

Willkie challenged the President to a series of debates. Roosevelt declined and limited himself to a few speeches before the election. Willkie emphasized his agreement with much of the New Deal program until veteran GOP campaigners told him to get tough. There were really only two big issues: the war, and the dictatorial ambitions of a president who wanted three terms. So Willkie began to jeer at That Man in the White House, the so-called "indispensable" man who had failed to build a system of national defense. Americans lacked planes, tanks, guns, and ships, and didn't have the industrial capacity to build them.

But voters read the war news and trusted their President. Willkie got 22 million votes, Roosevelt got 27 million votes, and a bigger job than he had ever faced before.

1941

He started the year with a famous speech to Congress, defining what the Allies were fighting for: the Four Freedoms—freedom of speech and religion, freedom from want and fear. He wanted America to be "the great arsenal of democracy." In March, Congress signed his Lend-Lease Act, which allowed the president to lend or lease war material to countries whose defense was necessary for American security. Seven billion in military credits were made available to Britain; China, Brazil, and other countries also received arms. After Hitler broke his non-aggression pact and invaded the Soviet Union, that country, too, became eligible for Lend-Lease weapons.

German and Italian troops were fighting in North Africa; Germany took over Greece and Yugoslavia. The United States occupied Greenland and Iceland, and American ships were ordered to sink German U-boats on sight. In August, FDR left Washington for a fishing trip and did, in fact, fish off the shore of Cape Cod for a day. But the purpose of his trip was a secret meeting with Winston Churchill on the battleship Augusta. This was the historic Atlantic Conference, at which the two men wrote the Atlantic Charter, a document that certainly echoed many of Wilson's Fourteen Points in its statement of principles, and was designed to gain support for the Allied war effort.

But in spite of the fact that most Americans now knew that a war could not be far off, there was still a vocal isolationist faction in Congress, and thousands of mothers and fathers opposed the draft, Lend-Lease, the Atlantic Charter, any involvement. They continued to hope and pray that their sons would be spared the kind of combat that many fathers had experienced in Europe less than twenty-five years before.

Their hopes were shattered on Sunday morning, December 7, when they learned that Japan had attacked the navy base at Pearl Harbor, on the Hawaiian island of Oahu. Three battleships and sixteen other ships were sunk or badly damaged, two hundred planes destroyed, 3,000 people killed including more than 2300 servicemen. There were simultaneous attacks on the Philippines, Wake, Guam, and Midway Island. Stunned Americans spread maps on the dining room table and tried to locate these places, names they didn't know but would soon, and painfully, learn.

Through the evening Cabinet members and Congressional leaders crowded into the President's study. He reported all that he had been able to learn about the attack, and the horrifying losses suffered by the Pacific command. It was no time to ask the questions on everyone's mind, to try to fix blame for the country's unpreparedness. All factional differences were set aside in the shared pain and outrage of the moment.

At noon on the following day, Franklin Roosevelt addressed both houses of

Congress. December 7, 1941, he said, was "a day which will live in infamy"— and he called for a declaration of war on Japan. The Congress immediately approved, with only one dissenting vote. The sixty-year-old pacifist Jeanette Rankin, first elected as a representative from Montana in 1916, had opposed American entry into World War I, and she would not cast a war vote now. On December 11, Germany and Italy declared war on the United States; the president asked for and got unanimous Congressional recognition of the state of war existing between the United States and the Fascist powers.

1942

In less than a month after Pearl Harbor, the Japanese had taken the British port of Hong Kong and Wake Island, an American possession in the middle of the North Pacific. The Japanese landed 43,000 troops in the Philippines, and by January 3, General Douglas MacArthur was leading a retreat down the Bataan peninsula to the fortress of Corregidor. His American and Filipino troops held out there until April. MacArthur was ordered to fly to safety in Australia.

If average Americans had long thought of Japan as a country of cherry blossoms and cheap trinketry, they were now learning some hard lessons, for little Japan had a grand plan—the Greater East Asia Co-Prosperity Sphere. It had invaded China in 1894, taken Formosa (now Taiwan) in 1895, and Korea in 1909. After World War I, it got German island holdings. In 1933 Japan occupied all of Manchuria. Now it intended to drive western colonialists out of Asia and build an empire that included French Indo-China, Malaya, Burma, and the Netherlands East Indies. In that extended territory, Europeans had huge investments, and military installations to protect their commercial interests. The Europeans had to be annihilated, the American fleet destroyed; swift Japanese success would force a negotiated peace that left

Japan in control of Asian land and sea from the Aleutian Islands to within easy reach of Australia. That was the grand plan, and the assault was well underway.

West Coast Americans responded to Japanese aggression with panic. Momentarily they expected Japanese bombing, and they were convinced that neighbors of Japanese ancestry might be enemy agents. In February, after the President signed Executive Order 9066, the army began to arrest every Japanese-American on the West Coast. Without any warrants or hearings, 110,000 men, women, and children—more than half of them American citizens—were rounded up. They lost their homes, their businesses, their farms, their possessions, and were moved to internment camps in interior states, where they existed in various degrees of misery for the next three years. The astonishing response of many of their young men was enlistment in the United States Army. No unit in American military history won as many decorations as the 442nd Infantry, the Japanese-Americans who fought in the Italian campaign and were with the troops that liberated concentration camp survivors after the war.

Homefront morale was lifted in April, when Major General James Doolittle led sixteen army B-25 bombers from the United States carrier *Hornet* to bomb Tokyo and other Japanese cities. But of more military importance were the naval battles of the Coral Sea in April and Midway Island in June. Because of the Doolittle raid and losses suffered in the Coral Sea, the commanding Japanese admiral decided to send overwhelming strength against the American fleet and take Midway Island, at the end of the Hawaiian chain. But the Americans had broken the Japanese codes, and Admiral Chester Nimitz was able to catch the force of 185 Japanese ships by surprise, inflicting huge losses.

These victories were offset by the fall of Corregidor and the surrender of General

Jonathan Wainwright, with 10,000 American and 45,000 Filipino troops. Then began the March of Death, as the prisoners were goaded along the 120-mile road to Japanese prison camps. Without food, clean water, or rest, many dropped in their tracks. During their first two months of confinement, 30,000 captives died of starvation or brutal treatment.

Meanwhile, German armies held all of Europe; the only scrap left for the Italians was the conquest of Albania. German and Italian armies were also gathering in North Africa. But Hitler was intent on victory in Russia, and pushed his forces across its vast plains to begin an August offensive against Stalingrad, opening with a three-month siege of that city. Premier Josef Stalin pleaded with British and American commanders to open a second front in Europe and relieve his exhausted fighting men. But Winston Churchill remembered the nightmare of trench warfare in World War I and refused. Although General George Marshall, Chief of Staff, and General Dwight Eisenhower, Chief of the War Plans Division, favored a European invasion and had already made preliminary plans for a cross-Channel operation, Roosevelt wavered. Winston Churchill was with him in Washington when they learned that 25,000 British soldiers in Libya were taken prisoner by the Germans after their defeat at Tobruk. Over the objections of Marshall and Eisenhower, an invasion of North Africa was agreed upon.

American forces landed in French Morocco in November and began to fight their way east along the Mediterranean coast. At the same time, Marines were engaged in desperate combat on the Pacific island of Guadalcanal. Their August landing was the first American counter-offensive in the Pacific Theater, and a turning point in the war with Japan. It would take six months of bloody combat to secure that one small island, a foretaste of what it would cost to win the stepping-stone islands leading to an invasion of Japan.

But in the city of Chicago, under the football stands of Stagg Field at the University of Chicago, occurred an event that would forever change the nature of warfare. On December 2, directed by physicists Arthur Compton and Enrico Fermi, scientists secretly produced the first nuclear chain reaction. It was three years since President Roosevelt had received the letter from Albert Einstein warning him of German attempts to develop a bomb based on the fission of uranium atoms. British scientists, too, were experimenting with atomic bombs. Roosevelt first hesitated to fund such research, but after the fall of France, army engineer General Leslie Groves was put in charge of the Manhattan Project. In Chicago, the feasibility of the bomb had been dramatically demonstrated.

What concerned the American public was the announcement of rationing and price control. Now every citizen got a ration book full of stamps, every stamp worth forty-eight "points" each month, good for purchases of rationed goods—everything from sugar to shoes. The price of such items was controlled (though a black market on which you could buy almost anything soon developed) and Americans got used to the system. Hardest to bear was the rationing of tires and gas. Gas rationing was mainly an effort to save tires, because rubber was one of the commodities for which the United States had no domestic source, and Japan had cut off the Asian supply on which the western world depended.

1943

The siege of Stalingrad turned into a German defeat. The surrender came in February, when the starving and freezing German armies were surrounded, their casualties having reached 300,000 men. Hitler ordered a withdrawal of all his remaining forces from Russia.

He had more success in North Africa, managing to beat the Americans in Tunisia before they could link up with British troops in a joint offensive. After three months of desert warfare, all German and Italian armies collapsed, and the Allies were able to begin the invasion of Italy. It opened in July with an assault on the Island of Sicily. There, as in North Africa, the Fascist powers suffered staggering losses.

The President had created a Fair Employment Practices Commission (FEPC). It was supposed to prevent racial discrimination in hiring and job placement; defense contractors were specifically barred from such practices. In fact, not much was done to enforce those orders. Though there was a desperate need for both skilled and unskilled labor, blacks rarely found employment except at the bottom end of the skill and pay scale. In Mobile, Alabama, white welders refused to work next to black welders in shipyards. The FEPC approved assignment to separate shipways.

Segregation persisted throughout the country. One of the most blatant expressions of racism occurred in the blood bank system administered by the American Red Cross. Dr. Charles Drew was the black doctor who developed the blood bank idea. He was in charge of wartime donations and knew how stupid it was to separate blood from black and white donors. When he tried to put an end to the practice, he was fired. But racist examples could be cited from every aspect of American life, from schools and factories to the armed forces. Black anger erupted into riots in Detroit and Harlem. In Detroit, federal troops were finally called to put down the violence that left twenty-five blacks and nine whites dead, with a thousand injured.

Congress had been slow to enact legislation needed for the president's wartime economic program, which included rationing, the sale of war bonds, wage and price controls, and heavier taxation. But little by little, the measures were implemented. Coffee drinkers were limited to one cup a day for everybody over fifteen. Celebrities took to the road to promote bond sales. Over loud union objections, wage controls were imposed. On July 1, the pay-as-you-go income tax went into effect, and taxes were withheld from wage and salary checks.

After planes had dropped millions of leaflets on Italian cities, calling for Italian surrender, they began to drop bombs on Rome. Benito Mussolini, the strutting little dictator who had ruled Italy for twenty years, was deposed. In his vain effort to equal Hitler's military success, he had joined with Germany in the 1936 war in Spain. In the same year he had taken Ethiopia, but now he was finished, and imprisoned until the Germans rescued him two months later. The new Italian prime minister signed an armistice with the Allies, soon followed by full surrender. In October, Italy declared war on Germany.

The Marines continued the island-by-island campaign in the Pacific. In the Gilbert Islands, they fought the costly battle of Tarawa; under heavy Japanese fire, hundreds of Marines died in the water as they waded onto the beaches. In four days of fighting, 4,500 Japanese were killed before they got orders to evacuate. When the Marines occupied the island, they found only twenty Japanese alive. But the Americans had lost 3,000 men.

For the first time, Franklin Roosevelt, Winston Churchill, and Josef Stalin met together, in the Iranian city of Teheran. The December conference was preceded by a meeting in Cairo with the Chinese president, General Chiang Kai-chek, and his sharp, determined wife. Although China could not offer much help in the war against Japan, Roosevelt used all his diplomatic charm to assure the Chiangs of their importance to the Allied cause. Then he flew on to Teheran and the truly crucial talks, plans for a cross-Channel invasion of Europe.

Stalin was not interested in the Italian fighting. American and British troops were meeting fierce resistance from Hitler's best armies as they pushed up the peninsula toward Rome. But Stalin didn't care about Rome, and he would not listen to any of Churchill's ideas about other possibilities, strategies that would delay an invasion through France. Operation Overlord was the code name for that plan. Stalin promised that Russia would join the war against Japan as soon as Germany fell, but Overlord had to begin on May first. In the last hours of their conference, it was decided to give General Dwight Eisenhower the supreme command.

1944

Just after midnight on June 6, the biggest invasion force in history hit the beaches of Normandy. It was D-Day for Operation Overlord, committed to the final defeat of Adolph Hitler. Six thousand six hundred men died on the first day. Carrying almost seventy pounds of equipment, many men drowned when they jumped out of landing craft; others were hit by German fire as they crossed the beach to scramble up the bluffs and into the hedgerows that bordered French fields and orchards. The tangled spring greenery offered plenty of cover for enemy guns, but the sheer size of the invading force, the immense quantity of ships, planes, land vehicles, supplies, and fighting men that America could supply, overwhelmed the German defenders. Within weeks there were a million Allied troops moving across France toward Germany.

The United States celebrated D-Day with firecrackers and church bells, an outpouring of nervous excitement, patriotic racket, speeches, and prayer. At the end of the month, President Roosevelt signed a G.I. Bill of Rights that passed both houses of Congress without a dissenting vote. Service men and women who survived this war would get a tangible expression of national gratitude in the form of home and business loans and, most important, money for college tuition and expenses. It was legislation that transformed a generation; it offered a future that none of their parents had been able to imagine.

There was no question about Roosevelt's candidacy in 1944. Though at sixty-two he showed physical signs of stress—he had high blood pressure and heart problems—he let the Democratic party know that he was available. It was a great relief to party leaders, since they had never seriously considered anybody else to head the ticket. Of course, many objected to the idea of a fourth term, but nobody could match Roosevelt's abilities as a wartime administrator, his personal relationship with Churchill, his more recent contacts with Stalin and Chiang, or his close working association with military commanders. He was the acknowledged leader of the Free World. As the convention approached, he seemed to have little interest in his running mate. He proposed some possibilities, but in the end, he let the party dump Henry Wallace and name Harry Truman, a senator Roosevelt scarcely knew.

Though liberal Republicans still supported Wendell Willkie, the traditional conservative wing of the party backed Thomas E. Dewey, governor of New York. He had made his reputation as the crime-busting district attorney of that state, a dapper, vigorous man who ran a hard race for the White House. But the country stuck with the old wisdom about not changing horses in the middle of the stream, and Roosevelt beat Dewey by more than 3.5 million votes.

Rome had fallen and American troops in Italy continued to push north toward southern France. In the Pacific, American forces fought at Saipan, Guam, and Tinian in the Mariana Islands, and finally General Douglas MacArthur was able to return to the Philippines—American troops landed on Leyte in October. The navy withstood Japanese suicide plane attacks which destroyed hundreds of ships; 10,000 American lives were lost, but the battle ended in a major naval defeat for Japan.

At the end of the year there was a last terrible fight in Europe. Hitler had gambled on a surprise attack in Belgium's Ardennes Forest, pushing Allied troops back and demanding surrender. The Battle of the Bulge lasted two weeks until the arrival of General George Patton's tanks ended the German offensive. It cost 19,000 American lives and 48,000 wounded. The Germans lost 120,000 men, killed, wounded or missing, and huge quantities of irreplaceable equipment. The Allies now began the final drive, to cross the Rhine River and take Berlin.

1945

While the outcome of the battle was still undecided, all black units in Europe got an unprecedented call to action. In the army, blacks served in black divisions, mainly as truck drivers, construction workers, and ditchdiggers. Now they were offered a chance to fight side-by-side with white infantrymen. And because they wanted combat adventure, or because they were determined to prove their fighting ability and their courage, 4,000 blacks immediately volunteered. They would be sent "without regard to color or race" to the units "where assistance is most needed." Their platoons would be all black, but the companies and battalions would live together, sleep together, use the same toilets—and fight and die together. So they fought superbly and helped win the Battle of the Bulge. But when the battle was over, black soldiers were sent back to the segregated divisions from which they had been called. They were used to broken promises.

In February, Roosevelt, Churchill, and Stalin met again, in the Crimean city of Yalta. Like Woodrow Wilson at the end of the first World War, Roosevelt was eager to talk about the proposed organization to guarantee peace and stability in the post-war world. But first they agreed that surrender terms for Germany must be unconditional, and the country would be divided into four zones for occupation by the forces of Britain, Russia, France, and the

United States. To get a Russian commitment in the war against Japan, Roosevelt was forced to make many trade-offs and concessions to Stalin. If Russia entered the Japanese fighting, tens of thousands of American live might be saved. At last it was decided that an April meeting in San Francisco would create the United Nations.

It was a terrible strain on a president with weakening health. Roosevelt got as much agreement on UN issues as circumstances permitted, and won Stalin's pledge of engagement in the Far East within three months after the end of the European conflict. He returned to America exhausted but optimistic. Reporting on his trip to the Congress, he allowed himself to be pushed to the podium in his wheelchair, for the first time letting legislators, the press, and the public see him as he was. Throughout his public life, he had always forced himself to stand on such occasions, supported by heavy steel braces on his withered legs. Now he jokingly asked for Congressional indulgence while he sat and spoke to them of the prospects ahead.

American troops in the Philippines recaptured Manila, and the Pacific war moved on. Iwo Jima is an eight-square-mile island, but it took 25,000 American casualties to win it. The first day of the Iwo Jima invasion was more costly than the Normandy invasion on D-Day. The next battle was even bloodier, the worst in the whole Pacific campaign; there were 48,000 casualties in three months before Okinawa could be secured.

In Europe, terrible bombing raids methodically destroyed German cities. American troops crossed the Rhine, then halted at the Elbe, fifty miles from Berlin, waiting for Russian forces advancing from the east.

Franklin Roosevelt did not live to see victory in Europe. He dealt with all the matters that waited for his attention after his return from the Yalta Conference, and then went to Warm Springs, Georgia. Many times in the years that followed his crippling attack of polio, he had gone to bathe in the healing waters of that famous old health resort. He hoped to swim and relax, with a minimum of official business. In his familiar cottage, arrangements had been made for an artist to paint his portrait, and a card table was set up so he could sign papers—there were always papers to sign—while she worked at her easel nearby. He chatted with her and his visitors, in easy good spirits that spring morning, until he suddenly slumped in his chair and said, "I have a terrible pain in the back of my head." He had suffered a massive cerebral hemorrhage and lost consciousness before a doctor could arrive.

Roosevelt died the next day, in his bed, in the early hours of April 12, 1945. In Washington, Eleanor Roosevelt got the news that her husband had passed away, and struggled to maintain her composure while she cabled her four sons, all in military service, and placed a call to Vice President Truman. Her daughter helped her pack for the trip to Warm Springs.

Harry Truman

Harry Truman had been performing his usual role as presiding officer during the morning meeting of the Senate, and after adjournment he joined the legislators who usually met for drinks and informal talk in a lower room of the Capitol. There he got the call summoning him to the White House, but no other information. He was taken to the private family sitting room where Eleanor Roosevelt waited. "Harry," she said, "the President is dead."

By six o'clock, the news had been released and spread around the world. Truman called his wife and their daughter, Margaret. By seven, they had arrived, and members of the administration were assembled in the Cabinet Room; somebody found a Bible. A few reporters and photographers were admitted. Then Harry Truman raised his hand as Chief Justice Harlan Stone administered the oath of office. Later the new President said he felt like the moon, the stars, and all the planets had fallen on him. And events were to prove him just about right.

Harry Truman had been Vice-President for about three months. Except for Cabinet meetings, he had met with Roosevelt only twice, never on matters of importance. He was never taken into the President's confidence. Now he attended Roosevelt's burial at the family estate in Hyde Park, New York, and the next day spoke to Congress. Everybody in Congress, and the country, wished him well, but only a few of his oldest friends thought he was up to the job. He was a farm boy from Lamar, Missouri, who never held a good job before he entered the army and went to France as a first lieutenant in World War I. He came to the Senate from the politics of Kansas City, at best a dubious connection.

The American generals now winning World War II in Europe—Eisenhower, Bradley, and Patton—were dismayed by the loss of their Commander-in-Chief. Truman had no experience in foreign affairs, knew none of the players. The Russians were wartime allies, but nobody could predict their stubborn attitudes and demands when the fighting was over.

Truman never had any administrative responsibility above the county level, but he did have a legislative record of considerable interest. In 1941, in his second term as a senator, he had proposed a committee to investigate how war procurements were awarded. It was a frantic time of military build-up in the United States. The first peacetime draft in history had become law, and new federal agencies were created to deal with the complexities of equipping and supplying the rapidly expanding military establishment. Top corporation executives, the "dollar-a-year" men, were brought to Washington to manage the task. Truman saw almost limitless opportunities for waste and extravagance, if not downright corruption, in the rush to prepare

America for the war.

The Senate Special Committee to Investigate the National Defense Program, later always called the Truman Committee, began with a hard look at the construction of camps where draftees were housed. Military men resented the intrusion of senatorial busybodies, but the committee soon proved what Truman suspected: building contractors were making fantastic profits. Within a few months, committee oversight and recommendations saved the government millions of dollars. Then it began investigating military production industries. Those companies were no more receptive to committee inquiries than the army and navy had been. Top union officials were often bristling with resentment. But Senator Truman was tough, and he was fair. He didn't take any sass from anybody, and moved committee business along at a brisk pace.

That was the first thing that reporters and White House staff discovered about President Truman: he moved fast. Now he had to, because there was so much to know, so much to read, so much to be explained in briefings by Cabinet members and top aides, so much to learn.

On his eleventh day in office, he met with Vyascheslev Molotov, the Russian foreign minister. In their blunt talk, Truman learned a truth of which Churchill and State Department people had warned him. The Russians had no intention of fulfilling the promises implied in the Yalta agreements; they intended to impose their communist rule on all the territory they occupied in eastern Europe, and whatever else they could grab.

The following day, Truman met with the Secretary of War, Henry Stimson, and learned for the first time about the atomic bomb project. It was the most closely guarded secret in American government. They were alone while the president read the papers Stimson had brought, and he was certainly astounded by the report. The United States—

and only the United States—had a weapon that could immediately end the war; enough atomic bombs could destroy civilization, possibly end human existence on much of the planet. They were joined by General Leslie Groves, the man who was directing the Army Corps of Engineers in the development and production of this terrifying weapon. Groves brought another twenty-five page report, with more details of the Manhattan Project, as it was called. Truman had many questions. The bomb would be ready for testing in three months. It was up to Harry Truman to decide: would he sign an order putting an end to the $20 billion dollar experiment, as leading scientists hoped he would do? Or would he tell Groves to go ahead, as Franklin Roosevelt certainly intended? Henry Stimson suggested a special select committee to advise the president. Truman authorized such a committee, and for the moment the Manhattan Project would proceed on schedule.

On the same day, the United Nations Conference was opening in San Francisco. Truman could not attend, but he spoke to the delegates over the radio, urging them to get on with building an organization that might prevent, or make less likely, the horror of global war.

Two days later, American and Russian troops met at the Elbe River. The soldiers embraced, for they were all combat veterans and shared a profound understanding of what war means. The next day, Benito Mussolini, who had ruled Italy for twenty-three years, was caught by Italian partisans and killed, his carcass hung by the heels and surrounded by jeering mobs. On April 10, the end came to Adolph Hitler. He had retreated to his bombproof bunker under the Chancellery, amid the ruins of Berlin. He was joined by faithful Nazi henchmen and his longtime female companion. In the last hours of his thousand-year Reich, he married her and then they swallowed poison suicide pills and died.

The bodies were never found.

As the Army moved into German-occupied territory, troops saw for the first time the concentration camps about which reports had reached America for several years. The fact that Jews were being rounded up and a process of systematic extermination had begun did not find much response in American government or media. Roosevelt left it to the State Department, where bureaucrats gave it little or no priority. Now American G.I.s liberated the camps, meeting and touching the half-dead survivors of Hitler's "ethnic cleansing." The soldiers vomited, cried, the press took pictures. America began to understand what was meant by The Holocaust.

The first meeting for purposes of organizing the United Nations convened in San Francisco at the end of April, and adjourned at the end of June. In those two months, much was accomplished. Forty-six nations sent representatives; four more joined before it ended. Almost 10,000 people were involved in one way or another: members of the six international organizations in attendance; various consultants and advisors; translators and secretaries who prepared records of the proceedings each day, in five languages; reporters and newsreel cameramen; and the huge staff that saw to arrangements.

(Germany surrendered on May 7, gloriously celebrated in America as V-E Day.)

Delegates quickly got down to the business of writing a charter. The purpose of the organization was to prevent war, the use of force in the settlement of international disputes. The member nations would try to guarantee their own security by guaranteeing security for all. They would join together to oppose any aggressor nation.

Even in this first meeting, there were serious arguments and issues, not many settled but most compromised or put off for further discussion. They could at least create a forum for such discussion. They would have a

General Assembly in which each nation, large or small, rich or poor, had one vote. They would have a Security Council with five permanent members—the "big four" plus France (later it was expanded by the addition of rotating members). The UN would have an armed force to call on when needed; but as yet no nation had committed any part of its own forces to UN command. The UN would establish agencies to assist nations that had been devastated by battles and bombing as well as to cope with problems of poverty, disease, illiteracy, and the abuse of human rights everywhere. By October, fifty-one nations had ratified the charter. The League of Nations had failed: now the UN must succeed.

Nobody believed that more ardently than Harry Truman. Almost as soon as the UN meeting adjourned, he left for a meeting with Churchill and Stalin in the German city of Potsdam, outside Berlin. He traveled with a huge entourage of military and diplomatic people, and by the evening of July 16 they were finally settled in the large house provided for the American party. He had a chance to meet Churchill and Stalin before the conference would begin the next evening. Truman was asked to chair the meeting. The seventy-year-old Churchill was characteristically long-winded and indirect. Both Stalin and Truman were characteristically direct, coming right to the point. Truman read from the list of matters he wanted to discuss, making it clear that he was dissatisfied with the way agreements made at the Yalta conference had been ignored. Stalin produced his own list. They circled each other in wary discussion for a couple of hours, deciding nothing except that the second meeting would begin an hour earlier, at Truman's request.

But while he waited the next day, the Secretary of War, Henry Simpson, brought him a coded cable. The first atomic bomb had been successfully tested. It had been put together in a lab at Los Alamos, New Mexico, by a team of scientists working under the direction of physicist J. Robert Oppenheimer. It was exploded at Alamogordo, New Mexico, with results that were at once satisfying and terrifying to Oppenheimer and everyone else who observed it. The sound carried fifty miles and was heard by people with no idea of what caused it. The flash could be seen for 250 miles.

At lunch he showed the message to Winston Churchill, and they debated whether or not to tell Premier Stalin. In the end, Truman waited a week before he almost casually mentioned that America had a promising new weapon in the works. Stalin showed little interest, asked no questions, but he knew more about the new bomb than he revealed. The very widespread system of Soviet spies and informants had already provided him with information, and Russian scientists were already working on their own atomic weapons.

Four days after the first cable, Stimson received the full test report from General Groves. America had spent $2 billion and bought the most devastating weapon that anyone could conceive. Truman had wanted the Russians to join in an invasion of Japan, calculating that it would save the lives of hundreds of thousands of American soldiers; Stalin had agreed to send troops on August 15. Now Truman knew that he didn't need Russian help. The atomic bomb could end the war; there need be no invasion. He only had to decide whether or not America would use the bomb, and if so, when and where.

In fact, he had already decided the first part of the question. So while very serious discussions went on during the evening sessions of the Potsdam Conference, Harry Truman and Henry Stimson, joined by other State Department and military advisors, held private morning meetings, to read cables from Washington and settle the details. More bombs would be available in August. Furthermore, although some military men thought Japan was already defeated (Dwight Eisenhower thought so; but he was in Europe), military intelligence argued, convincingly, that the Japanese would never surrender.

The draft of a warning declaration was sent from Washington. It promised the "prompt and utter destruction" of Japan unless its armed forces immediately surrendered, unconditionally. If ignored, America would use the atomic bomb.

While the warning proposal was being considered, a political bomb was dropped on Winston Churchill. He had led the people of Britain through the long, dark night of the war, a symbol of their courage and tenacity. Now Britain had held a general election, his party had lost, and a new prime minister would arrive to take Churchill's chair for the rest of the Potsdam Conference. When the warning to Japan was issued as the Potsdam Declaration, it was in the names of President Truman, Generalissimo Chiang Kai-chek, and prime minister Clement Atlee. The prime minister of Japan ignored it. Planes dropped millions of copies on Japanese cities, to no effect. Winston Churchill shook hands and said goodbye, taking his colleagues back to London.

Three days later, another cable from Washington urged President Truman to make his decision about using atomic bombs in Japan. He replied at once. Go ahead, he cabled, but not before August 1.

The evening meetings of the conference went on, and the tensions between Communist Russia and the democratic West were more evident. Truman wanted agreement on the future of Germany, now divided into four zones occupied by American, British, French, and Russian armies. Berlin was inside the Russian zone, but divided like the country into four zones of military administration. The conference was agreed on the demilitarization of Germany, and on trials for Nazi war criminals, to be conducted by an international military tribunal in the city of Nuremburg.

(Eventually, twenty-four Nazi leaders were tried; three were acquitted, nine given prison terms, twelve executed.) And the distribution of German reparations was agreed upon; the Russians would soon begin to dismantle factories and seize stockpiled materials for shipment to Russia, in partial repayment for the losses they had suffered.

But the Americans had wanted guarantees of free elections in the eastern countries Hitler had overrun. It was soon obvious that wherever Soviet armies were now in place, free elections were unlikely. The borders of postwar Poland took much discussion but were finally decided. Free elections for Poland remained vague. The future of Italy and other countries allied to Germany was put off. And, at the end, there was some talk about southeast Asia, mention of places like Korea, Vietnam— but they weren't of urgent concern. First the islands of Japan had to be subdued, demilitarized, and administered.

President Truman was on his way home, in mid-Atlantic, when he learned that an atomic bomb had been dropped on the Japanese city of Hiroshima on August 6. Nobody knew the extent of the damage, only that the drop was a complete success, and the president's message promised a "rain of ruin" on Japan unless there was immediate surrender. Everybody on the ship cheered, easily and fully able to share the relief felt by more than a million American servicemen in the Pacific Theater, and by their families. No one doubted that Harry Truman had made the right decision, the only decision possible.

A second bomb was dropped on Nagasaki on August 9. None of the scientists who worked on these bombs had been able to predict their effects in a real attack. The numbers began to come in, reporting that the damage had been much greater than expected. The first, a uranium bomb, had wiped out 60 percent of Hiroshima; between 80,000 and 100,000 people died instantly, and probably more than

50,000 died in the next weeks and months from terrible burns and radiation poisoning. The plutonium bomb dropped on Nagasaki—two miles off target—killed 60,000 people. Eventually there would be photographs of the survivors: sick, scarred, horribly mutilated in body and soul. And these were the results of only two bombs on the mostly civilian population of two cities. What could many such bombs do in an atomic war?

Japan surrendered on August 14. All America rose up in jubilation, rang church bells, blew horns, marched, and danced to celebrate V-J Day. The long struggle that had destroyed so many lives, homes, factories and farms, whole nations, left America strong, the undisputed leader of the world. But in many minds there were dark thoughts about how the war was won. Were the atomic bombs necessary? Doubts were expressed then and persist to this day. After all, one night of firebombing in Tokyo had taken 80,000 lives. The military had intercepted Japanese messages and broken the code: They believed that beaten Japan wanted peace negotiations if they could keep the Emperor—which, in the end, they did. But the bombs were a demonstration of American power, a lesson to the Japanese, to the Russians, and to the world.

General Douglas MacArthur accepted the Japanese surrender in a ceremony aboard the USS Missouri on September 2, in Tokyo Bay. He would go on to head the occupation forces that disarmed the enemy and led to democratization and economic reconstruction. Most Japanese received the occupation with astonishing cheerfulness and cooperation. The reputation MacArthur had earned in battle continued to grow.

1946

The war had brought America boom times— low unemployment, high incomes for workers and farmers, an increase of almost $4.5 billion in corporate profits. But both wages and prices had been controlled during the war, and peacetime brought a season of strikes, by oil workers, lumber workers, and employees of General Motors. Phil Murray, head of the steel workers, led off the new year by demanding a substantial wage increase for his people. When the industry turned it down, 800,000 steel workers went on strike, closing a thousand mills. On April 1, John L. Lewis called out 400,000 coal miners.

Lewis had spent his whole life in the labor movement, rising from president of the mine workers to vice president of the AFL, and then head of the CIO. He had been a prominent Republican, but he joined the Democratic party in 1932 to work with Franklin Roosevelt during the early depression years, changing parties again to campaign for Republican Wendell Willkie in 1940. Harry Truman despised John L. Lewis for his arrogance. He had been a formidable opponent when the Truman Committee was investigating costs in defense procurement. He had a theatrical appearance, glaring fiercely from under bushy black eyebrows, speaking in the tones of a Biblical prophet. He led a miners strike in 1943, at the height of the war. Now he wanted a wage increase and other benefits, plus a miners' welfare fund to be created by a 5 cent royalty on every ton of coal.

This labor strife was a headache and a heartache for Harry Truman, who regarded himself as a friend of labor. The threat of a railroad strike on top of the crippling steel and coal strikes was almost the last straw. Under the Railway Labor Act, he could and did order a mediation period. Negotiators made progress, but two unions, with 280,000 members, held out. On the eve of the strike, he signed an order for the government to take over and run the railroads. The union leaders quickly agreed to another delay before railroad men walked out. But further negotiation produced no wage agreements, so Truman spoke to the country in a radio address that told the strikers to get back to work or he would call out the army to operate the country's railroads. He wanted to draft the strikers and order them to work. He was ready to announce that action when he appeared before Congress the next day. Many of his advisors, including the Attorney General, warned him that such a procedure was unconstitutional. But Truman grimly took the rostrum and began his speech. The strike threatened "all our industrial, agricultural, commercial, and social life." It had to be stopped. Then, in a dramatic moment, he was interrupted and handed a note. The strike had been settled, on the terms he proposed. The Congress exploded in deafening applause, but when he went on and asked for a bill to draft the strikers, he won in the House but was defeated in the Senate. Anyway, the trains were running, and a few days later, John L. Lewis signed a contract that gave the coal miners everything he had asked for—the wage increase, the five-day work week and the welfare fund.

And then there were the Russians. Winston Churchill came to America to deliver a speech at a small college in Fulton, Missouri. He used a memorable phrase that soon entered the country's vocabulary. "An iron curtain," he said, "had descended across the European Continent. Behind it lay all the capitals of the ancient states of Central and Eastern Europe. Warsaw, Berlin, Prague, Vienna, Budapest, Belgrade, Bucharest, and Sofia, all these famous cities and the populations around them lie in what I must call the Soviet sphere, and all are subject in one form or another, not only to Soviet influence, but to a very high and in many cases, increasing measure of control from Moscow—"

Almost lost in the news was the War Department announcement of ENIAC— the Electronic Numerical Integrator and Computer. It was designed by J.P. Eckert and J.W. Mauchly of the University of Pennsylvania to calculate ballistic trajectories. It weighed thirty tons, needed a room 30 x 50 feet, and used 18,000 vacuum tubes to compute problems which would previously have required years to solve on mechanical calculating devices. So the word "computer" entered the American vocabulary, and nobody would have guessed that fifty years later most school children would be able to operate a little computer that has become as familiar as a bicycle.

1947

Enthusiastically received was Truman's appointment of sixty-seven-year-old George C. Marshall to be Secretary of State. Marshall had given his country forty years of military service. At the pinnacle of that career, Roosevelt made him General of the Army, outranking all the five-star generals and admirals except Admiral Leahy. He resigned that commission to accept a diplomatic assignment in China, where his effort to reconcile Nationalist and Communist factions failed. It was an impossible mission; even Marshall's superb ability to break deadlocked confrontations could not deal with the political chaos in China.

He assumed the responsibilities of the Secretary of State in January, and immediately began to assist the president in formulating and administering what became known as the Truman Doctrine. The governments of Greece and Turkey were the next targets of Communist domination, opening the way for further Soviet success in the Middle East and Asia. In March, Truman addressed Congress and asked for $400 million in aid and military support for those countries. It was a shockingly large commitment, a clear indication that Harry Truman had decided to get tough with the Russians. America would not continue to debate the question while another dictator swallowed chunks of the map as Adolf Hitler had done. Churchill's Iron Curtain was a fact, imposed by the military realities at the end of the war. But the spread of Communism had to be stopped, by the United States, now. Backed by the authority of George Marshall and the legislative leadership of Senator Arthur Vandenberg, the President overrode Congressional objections and the bill was passed.

However, such a powerful warning about the Communist threat encouraged conservatives who wanted to uncover a threat at home. J. Edgar Hoover was eager to investigate suspects in the State Department and other government departments. The House Committee on Un-American Activities was ready to pounce on subversive elements wherever they could be discovered. To head off these zealots, Truman signed an Executive Order creating a Federal Employees Loyalty and Security Program; everybody on the federal payroll would be checked—more than three million people in the next four years. It was an expensive search. No subversive plots were uncovered, and only a couple of hundred people were fired, though indications of their disloyalty did not warrant any arrests or indictments.

George Marshall returned from Europe to underscore the real danger in Europe: the ruin, poverty, and despair that prevailed in western Europe gave Communism a perfect environment in which to flourish. It was easy to convert people to revolutionary doctrine when their present conditions of life were so brutal, and the future so bleak. On June 5, Marshall gave a speech at the Harvard commencement exercises. He called for a program to revive the European economy, asking Europeans to design a program which could be agreed to by "a number, if not all, European nations." In other words, he invited the Russians to join in recovery efforts. The Russians refused, but sixteen countries agreed to the terms of a plan and gratefully received $13 billion in loans between 1948 and 1951. Many people have argued that the Marshall Plan was intended to rebuild Europe and create a market for American products as well as opportunities for American investment—which it certainly did. But it was unquestionably a program of impressive statesmanship on the part of George Marshall and Harry Truman, and of generosity on the part of the American people.

A Republican Congress decided to restrain the power of unions by passing a bill co-sponsored by Senator Robert Taft of Ohio and Representative Fred Hartley, Jr., of New Jersey. It made the closed shop—the practice of hiring only union members—illegal; it required unions to register and file financial reports with the Department of Labor, and permitted states to pass right-to-work laws; it called for an eighty-day cooling off period during which unions and employers could negotiate the issues and avoid a strike in any industry that affected the country's safety or health. President Truman vetoed the bill, which brought labor voters back into the Democratic ranks; but Congress passed the Taft-Hartley Act over his veto.

It may be hard for today's baseball fans to remember that the major leagues were completely segregated in 1947. That was not always the case. Some blacks played on major league teams until the color line hardened, after Reconstruction. Then black teams emerged, toured, and show-cased the abilities of black athletes before enthusiastic (and unsegregated) fans. Jack Roosevelt Robinson became the first black in major league history when he signed with the Brooklyn Dodgers. He stayed with the club during his ten-year career, in spite of furious letters, bean-balls, and death threats, which cooled off as he demonstrated his exceptional abilities and took the Dodgers into six World Series. Jackie won the Rookie of the Year award in the same season that he broke baseball's color line; two years later he won the Most Valuable Player award. He retired in 1949 and became the first black man in baseball's Hall of Fame in 1962.

Satchel Paige was forty-two before he got his chance to pitch in the majors; Josh

Gibson never made it. But both men are now in the Hall of Fame, and so is Branch Rickey, the tough Brooklyn manager who changed the history of sports in America.

1948

The nation of Israel declared its independence in May. To give a history of Israel would require a volume, but perhaps the involvement of the United States can be described in a few sentences. The League of Nations had given Britain a mandate over the territory known as Palestine, at the east end of the Mediterranean Sea, after the first World War. It was uneasily shared by Arabs and half a million Jews, both of whom attacked British troops. When it became a UN issue after World War II, America endorsed the partition of Palestine into Jewish and Arab states joined in an economic union. In 1942, the UN voted for partition, which made Jews happy, but Arabs walked out. In 1946, America recommended that Britain permit 100,000 Jews to enter Palestine; these were homeless people, victims of Nazi persecution, still in camps but not welcome in any European country or in the United States. In 1948, after much UN debate, the American ambassador to the UN abandoned the idea of partition in favor of a UN "trusteeship" over Palestine.

President Truman learned of this action by reading the newspapers, and he was furious. Eleanor Roosevelt resigned her seat as a UN delegate. Truman called a meeting to reformulate American policy, but the opinion of his advisors was divided. However, after the Jews announced the independence of a new country, to be called Israel, it took just eleven minutes for the United States to grant the government de facto recognition. It was an area at the northern end of Palestine, about the size of New Jersey, and its continued existence amid enemy Arab neighbors was far from assured. But though arms shipments to Israel were still embargoed, the American commitment to the new country would remain constant.

Harry Truman's ratings in the popularity polls had gone up and down, but he was certainly the underdog in the 1948 elections. A Republican victory was predicted even before the campaigns began. When the President was invited to receive an honorary degree and deliver the commencement address at the University of California at Berkeley, he seized the opportunity for a cross-country rail trip, billed as non-political. There were plenty of reporters and cameramen aboard his train and it drew good crowds. He spoke from the back platform at small "whistle-stops," and to large audiences in major cities, whaling away at Congress, for more than 9,500 miles and enjoying every minute of it.

The Republican convention met in June in Philadelphia. It took only three ballots to nominate Governor Thomas Dewey of New York to head the ticket, and he chose California Governor Earl Warren as his running mate. Both were vigorous and attractive young men; they seemed to be an unbeatable team.

In the same week, Russia began a blockade of the Allied zones in Berlin, preventing any supplies from coming in by truck or rail. It lasted almost a year, while the Allies imposed a counter-blockade and airlifted (with mostly American planes) more than two million tons of food and fuel into the city. It was a costly, difficult, and dangerous mission to feed and to bolster the morale of Berliners until the Russians were ready to give up. Harry Truman did not intend to give up, because these were early days in the Cold War, and he was not going to lose it.

In contrast to the orderly Republican proceedings, the July Democratic convention was a rambunctious affair. In the first place, many Democrats remembered that Tom Dewey had nearly beaten Franklin Roosevelt four years earlier; he would almost certainly defeat Harry Truman. Roosevelt's sons promoted General Dwight Eisenhower as the party's nominee, soon joined by long-time New Dealers, labor leaders, Southern Democrats and big city party bosses. Even the left-of-center followers of Henry Wallace wanted Eisenhower. Not until the general definitely took himself out of consideration did the boom cool off.

The next fight was about civil rights. Mayor Hubert Humphrey of Minneapolis made a powerful speech, urging a platform plank that listed all the abuses and indignities to which black citizens were subjected, conditions that must be changed, and the Democratic party had to be the party of change. The plank he offered was based on Truman's own civil rights program, but Truman didn't like it. He foresaw a walkout by Southern delegates, and he was right. When the Humphrey plank was—surprisingly—adopted by the convention, Southern delegations left the floor. Two days later, they assembled in Birmingham, Alabama, to form a states' rights party, the Dixiecrats, and chose Governor Strom Thurmond of South Carolina as their presidential candidate.

This was the first convention covered by TV. Viewers at home could watch all the battling before Harry Truman was finally nominated, with Senator Alben Barkley of Kentucky for the Vice-Presidency. They saw the President arrive to make a fiery acceptance speech. He ended with the announcement that he was calling Congress back into session immediately, asking them to pass all the bills he had presented—not only civil rights legislation but bills for farm support and an increased minimum wage, the whole liberal agenda they had blocked for so many months.

Another convention took place in Philadelphia at the end of the month, bigger than either the Republican or Democratic meetings. The Progressive Citizens of America met to nominate Henry Wallace and Glen Taylor (the "Singing Cowboy" from Idaho) as their candidates. Although their platform was almost identical to the platform of the Communist party (still tiny but in the running), 30,000 people applauded Wallace's speech.

Truman threw himself into the campaign with inexhaustible energy. By refusing to pass the legislation Truman asked for, Congress gave him a political stick to whack them with, and he used it. But it would be a close call; the *Chicago Tribune* tried to scoop the press by publishing an early edition with the bold headline: DEWEY WINS! Truman grinned broadly when he held that paper up before cheering Democrats on the day after the election. He had won with more than 24 million popular votes; Dewey got something less than 22 million. Henry Wallace received about 1.2 million; about the same number were cast for Strom Thurmond, and the Dixiecrats carried four states. So Harry Truman would go back to the White House as a President elected in his own right.

Another breaking story stunned the nation in December. Alger Hiss had been a promising young New Dealer, who went on to a fourteen-year career in the State Department. Now he was president of the Carnegie Endowment for International Peace, a slender, impeccably groomed, Harvard-educated and well-spoken man—and he was accused of spying for the Soviets.

His accuser was the rather overweight and rumpled editor of Time magazine, admittedly a former member of the Communist party. Whittaker Chambers told the House Committee on Un-American Activities that Hiss, a fellow party member, had given him secret papers in the 1930s, information to be passed on to the Russians. When Chambers repeated the charges on television, Hiss sued him for libel. But Chambers assured Representative Richard Nixon that he could produce evidence and led Nixon to his farm, where microfilmed documents were found in a hollowed out pumpkin. Because the statute of limitations had run out, the government could not indict Hiss for spying. Instead he was tried for perjury; the first trial ended in a hung jury. Another trial began, and the case dragged on for months.

1949

In April, the Chinese Communist army, a million men, took the southern provinces and the long Chinese civil war was over. The Nationalist Kuomintang, led by Generalissimo Chiang Kai-chek and Madam Chiang, fled across the narrow Formosa Strait to the island of Taiwan, taking their families, their fortunes, shiploads of Chinese art treasures, and almost anything else that was valuable and portable. As George Marshall and General Douglas MacArthur had predicted, the Communist victory was cruel and complete.

Chiang Kai-chek did not recognize the Communist government established on the mainland; he insisted that the two million Nationalists on Taiwan constituted the Republic of China, and set up a legislature representing the mainland provinces—a government temporarily operating from Taiwan but still the only true and legitimate rulers of their native land. They still occupied China's seat on the UN Security Council, which so infuriated the Russian representative that he walked out and did not return for many months. Mao Tsetung called his Communist country the People's Republic of China (his name, after Pinyin renomination, is now spelled Mao Zedong). The two implacable enemies would continue to glare at each other, and occasionally fire upon each other across the strait, for almost half a century. Though Chiang's administration was far from democratic, Taiwan made tremendous progress. With American help, it would become one of the world's strongest economies.

But in 1949 the Communist takeover of China was seen as a terrible blow to American power and prestige. Loud Republican critics charged that an America weakened by inept

Democratic leadership had "lost" China. And when it was revealed that Russia had successfully tested an atomic bomb, the chorus grew louder. Even when Russia abandoned the Berlin blockade, Republican opponents of the Truman administration were not appeased. For reasons of health, George Marshall retired as Secretary of State and was replaced by Dean Acheson. It would have been hard to follow Marshall in the best of times, but now Acheson found himself in the middle of a political tornado. In October, President Truman held a press conference to announce the development of a super-weapon, a hydrogen bomb, which would re-establish national supremacy in the arms race.

1950

The second trial of Alger Hiss ended in January; he was convicted and sentenced to five years in prison. Reporters asked Dean Acheson what he thought of the sentence. He gave an unequivocal answer: "I do not intend to turn my back on Alger Hiss."

Republican leaders jumped on that statement for what became their campaign theme: a Communist conspiracy permeated the entire Truman administration. The clamor intensified when it was learned that Klaus Fuchs, a former Los Alamos scientist, had confessed to spying for the Soviet Union. Within months the FBI uncovered a whole network of men and women. Harry Gold was a Philadelphia chemist whose friend, David Greenglass, had been stationed at Los Alamos. Greenglass had a sister, Ethel, married to Julius Rosenberg, and the Rosenbergs received from Greenglass crude drawings of an atomic weapon, which they passed along. In July the Rosenbergs, alleged Communists, were arrested, along with a former official at the Russian consulate. The chief witness against them was David Greenglass; they were convicted and became the first American citizens ever sentenced to death for espionage. There were appeals to the Supreme Court and to the

White House, and worldwide outrage because many believed that the Rosenbergs were the victims of anti-Semitism and anti-Communist hysteria.

But long before the Rosenberg case reached its conclusion, Senator Joe McCarthy took the offensive. He was from Wisconsin, forty-one years old, and voted the worst member of the Senate in a poll of Congressional reporters. He drank heavily, and his career was going nowhere until he grasped at the issue of Communist conspiracy. In February he made a speech claiming that he had the names of 205 known Communists working in the State Department. Though the numbers changed, he repeated the speech until he got the attention of the media. When he harangued the Senate, his attacks on the President were vicious and unsupported. Finally the Senate Democrats insisted that McCarthy's charges must be investigated. In six weeks, he could not name even one Communist, but he wallowed in the attention and continued to drop dark hints, suggest vague connections, and churn the waters of suspicion with considerable success. Harry Truman defended himself and his administration as best he could, staying cool and maintaining his dignity.

At the end of World War II, the occupation of Korea ended as Japan handed it over to Russian troops in the north and an American army in the south, divided by a border at the thirty-eighth parallel. When they failed to reunite the country by negotiation, the UN called for elections, but Russia refused to permit UN-supervised voting on the reunification issue in the area it controlled. Both armies had recently withdrawn, leaving the People's Republic of Korea in the north and the Republic of Korea in the south, still separated by the same line. On June 25, 90,000 North Korean troops, armed by Russia, swarmed across that line in a surprise attack on the weak and unprepared South.

President Truman called his advisors

together to decide on an American response, and their decision was immediate. The UN had already passed a resolution calling for a cease fire and withdrawal by the North, which the North ignored. Americans agreed that there had to be prompt action. General MacArthur, already commanding a huge force in occupied Japan, would proceed to supply the South Koreans with arms and war material as quickly as possible; the Seventh Fleet would be sent from the Philippines; the Air Force was put on alert. The UN passed a second resolution calling for the commitment of ground troops, and fifteen countries joined the United States in creating the first UN army, with Douglas MacArthur in command. But North Korea had already captured the South Korean capital, the city of Seoul. Only the arrival of American aircraft prevented their offensive from taking the whole peninsula.

Though the American forces were poorly equipped and not in good shape for combat, softened by months of occupation duty, they were able to hold a defensive line around Pusan until General MacArthur could mount a daring thrust behind the North Korean armies, an amphibious assault on the port city of Inchon. The North Koreans retreated back across the border, and UN troops recaptured Seoul. The war might have ended then, with the UN mission accomplished, but Syngman Rhee, the president of South Korea, was determined to punish the North and reunite a country which he would then rule. General MacArthur agreed with this plan, and it was supported by the top brass in Washington. But any action that might bring Communist China into the war must be avoided.

So the UN armies, mainly American and South Korean, invaded North Korea, paying no attention to angry Chinese threats, or the million Chinese troops mobilized on the Yalu River, the border between Korea and Manchuria. In October President Truman met with General MacArthur on Wake Island. He wanted to be sure that MacArthur understood his orders and would not overstep the instructions he had received from Washington. Truman left the meeting feeling confident that MacArthur had been restrained from recklessly aggressive strategies. MacArthur had already been given far more men than Truman intended to send to the Korean fighting, and the President had asked Congress for huge increases in military appropriations. The draft had been stepped up, and concerned parents were swamping the White House with letters begging the President to stop the war, to use the atomic bomb if he had to. But the United States was now deeply involved; in addition to the expanding operations in Korea, America was sending aid to the French, who were trying to regain their colonies in Indochina. The policy had changed from simply containing Communism to one of defeating Communism in a military confrontation.

United Nations troops moved north, capturing Pyongyang, the capital of North Korea, and moving on toward the Yalu River. MacArthur had assured Truman that the Chinese were no threat on the ground, though if they were joined by Soviet planes from Siberia, the situation might be drastically different. Truman did not second-guess the general.

On November 1, the President escaped an assassination attempt by two Puerto Rican nationalists; one of his residential guards was killed, another wounded, before help arrived. The next day brought bad news from Korea. The Chinese had indeed attacked from Manchuria, and within the week were arriving in staggering numbers. With the Eighth Army in retreat, MacArthur called for reinforcements; the United Nations forces were split and being driven out of the north. Harry Truman declared a national emergency and ordered the army to be built up to 3.5 million men. MacArthur demanded an atomic attack on Red China, while the Communists relentlessly advanced to retake Seoul.

The General seemed to be at war with the Commander-in-Chief, critical of all the President's decisions. It was winter in Korea, and UN troops were suffering terrible losses. But the Eighth Army was now under the command of General Matthew Ridgway. Morale and performance improved, and the army began to move north again. MacArthur was willing to take the credit for the renewed offensive. He did not, however, agree with the President's desire to explore cease-fire possibilities. Truman wanted to communicate with China and suggest peace talks. The Pentagon and the State Department prepared a draft of such a statement and sent it to the governments of the other nations which had troops in the UN army and to General MacArthur. Rather than approve the Washington statement, the General released his own proclamation which, in effect, threatened China with attack unless it immediately accepted his terms, capitulated, and got out of Korea. It was an act of total arrogance and insubordination, completely undercutting any American peace initiative. But he had the support of Republican Congressional leaders and other MacArthur admirers, of whom there were many, in and out of government.

Harry Truman took a month to think it over. He gave the Joint Chiefs of Staff and diplomatic people plenty of time to weigh the military and political consequences of the decision he now faced. Should Douglas MacArthur be removed from command of the UN forces? He listened to all their advice and was finally satisfied, deciding to ignore the political firestorm he was about to ignite and assert a fundamental principle: The President of the United States, the civilian Commander-in-Chief of the American military, had to be respected and obeyed. On April 11 his press secretary handed his decision out to the waiting reporters and the papers rushed to print the headlines: TRUMAN FIRES MACARTHUR.

The public reaction was overwhelming and on Capitol Hill there was an uproar and talk of impeachment. Across the country, state and local lawmakers agreed, furious editorials praised the gallant general and damned the President, citizens deluged the White House with thousands of violent letters and telegrams; when Truman threw out the first baseball to open the season in Washington, the fans jeered and booed; Joe McCarthy and others who charged treason in the White House had a field day. But the president had thoughtful defenders who realized that a Constitutional issue was at stake; he told his staff that the furor would die down in a month or so.

General MacArthur had received the letter telling him that he was relieved of his command at his Tokyo headquarters, and there he got an invitation to address Congress and state his side of the matter. He returned to the United States, for the first time in fourteen years, and was greeted at the San Francisco airport by a mob of ten thousand wildly excited admirers. Thousands waited for his midnight arrival in Washington. And when at last he appeared before the Congress, he got a tumultuous ovation.

All over America, people were glued to their radio or television sets as he began to speak, and they were rewarded with an hour of the highest drama. A record audience was spellbound as he evoked every emotion that a great orator could kindle. He brilliantly defended his assertion that the Korean War must be carried to the mainland Chinese, though he did not mention his willingness to use atomic bombs in a larger war. He was continuously interrupted by deafening applause. He stated and restated his conviction that to limit the war could only encourage Communist aggression everywhere; a policy of containment was a policy of indecision and appeasement. His emotional conclusion brought the house down, and none of his listeners has ever forgotten it. He quoted an army song: "Old soldiers never die. They just fade away." His audience was hushed. "And like the old soldier of the ballad, I now close my military career and fade away—an old soldier who tried to do his duty...Good-bye." All over America, people wept.

The following day, New York gave him a ticker-tape parade that attracted 7.5 million onlookers, most cheering, some not. Six weeks later, a Senate committee began hearings into the MacArthur dismissal. Again he defended his opinions, though in response to questions he was not quite so persuasive. And he was refuted by unimpeachable military authorities: by George Marshall, who had returned to the Cabinet to serve as Secretary of Defense; by General Omar Bradley; by the Joint Chiefs of Staff, who respectfully disagreed with MacArthur in every detail. If it was a choice between limited war, the war President Truman had chosen to fight, and the possibility of a world-wide war with atomic weapons, there could be no question. Above all, military men could not defy the principal of civilian control. Even the senators who had applauded the General most loudly could not argue that point.

MacArthur's popularity began to diminish; he started to fade away. Peace talks opened in Korea with a clear American objective—to return the North and the South to their pre-war territorial limits, on either side of the thirty-eighth parallel. A cease-fire took effect in July.

It should not be forgotten that during all these weeks, Harry Truman and his administration had to conduct the daily work of governing the country. For example, in September a peace treaty with Japan was finally concluded, formally ending the second World War. A year earlier a general strike of all railroads had begun, and Truman ordered the army to take over operations; the strike was still going on. Senator Estes Kefauver was conducting an investigation of organized crime in America. And there were other events to report: Julius and Ethel Rosenberg were executed; the H-bomb was in production; and Senator Joe McCarthy, who refused to fade away, continued to make even wilder allegations concerning Communists in the State Department and the military.

1952

A year earlier, the Twenty-second Amendment to the Constitution was ratified. It stated that "No person shall be elected to the office of president more than twice—" There would be no more Franklin Roosevelts as long as that amendment continued in force. Harry Truman had served almost two full terms, but he had been elected only once, so the amendment didn't apply to him. Many people hoped he would run again. Those who didn't were gratified and relieved when he announced, at the end of March, that he would not be a candidate. The person most relieved was his wife, Bess. Immediately the speculations, rumors, and coalition-building began. The name of General Dwight Eisenhower was often mentioned. Harry Truman talked to Illinois Governor Adlai Stevenson.

But the President didn't have much time for politics because of the steel strike. The railroads were being returned to the owners. Now it was steel. The union contract with the steel companies had expired in December. A strike ensued when the companies refused to accept the union's demand for a 35 cents an hour pay increase. The dispute was referred to the Wage Stabilization Board, and it recommended a 26 cents wage increase, which the companies would not accept unless they could add twelve dollars a ton to the price of steel. Truman thought that a price increase of $4.50 a ton was plenty, since steel industry profits were already high. He worried about the effects of a loss in steel production on supplies for the army in Korea.

So on April 8 he spoke to the country from the White House, announcing that the army would take over the steel plants. The secretary of commerce would operate the plants until a satisfactory strike settlement could be reached. He was immediately denounced as a dictator in the press and in Congress. The steel makers sued to get their property back, and eventually the case reached the Supreme Court. There Harry Truman lost. The Court ruled that his action was unconstitutional. So the strike went on into the summer, the longest work stoppage in the history of the industry. At the end of July, the president called Phil Murray, head of the union, and Benjamin Fairless, president of United States Steel, to his office, and told them to end it. And they did, on almost the terms the Wage Stabilization board had recommended months earlier. But by that time the Republican convention had already met, and public attention was focused on the candidate it had chosen.

General Eisenhower became the President of Columbia University in 1948, but he had been made a five-star general for life, and arranged a leave of absence from Columbia to take command at the Supreme Headquarters of the Allied Powers in Europe. He was responsible for creating a military force that could confront any Communist aggression in western Europe, an army for the North Atlantic Treaty Organization. That did not prevent both political parties from sounding him out as a possible presidential candidate. The editor of a New Hampshire newspaper had published a clear call to the General. Eisenhower replied with an equally clear refusal: "It is my conviction that the necessary and wise subordination of the military to civil power will be best sustained...when lifelong professional soldiers...abstain from seeking high political office. Politics is a profession; a serious, complicated, and in its true sense, a noble one. My decision to remove myself completely from the political scene is definite and positive."

Nevertheless, in 1952 his name was entered in several Republican primaries, which he easily won, and the July Republican convention nominated him on the first ballot. For Vice-President, the delegates chose Senator Richard Nixon of California, whose main qualification was his solid record as an anti-Communist. As a member of the House, his service on the Un-American Activities Committee and his persistence in the Hiss-Chambers case brought him, for better or worse, a national reputation. He was not Eisenhower's first choice for the office, but he satisfied the right wing of the party.

The Democrats met at the end of the month and nominated Adlai Stevenson, who had moved between government office and private law practice since the first days of the New Deal. He had worked for the Agricultural Adjustment Administration, the Navy Department, and the State Department, participating in the organization of the United Nations. As the governor of Illinois, he proved to be an effective reform administrator with a unique gift for communicating with voters. He did not want to run against General Eisenhower (any sensible politician could calculate his chances) but accepted the Democratic nomination and quickly won the admiration of liberal voters as a man of conscience and lively wit.

Eisenhower brought military expertise to charges of Democratic incompetence in handling the Korean conflict. He pledged that if elected, he would go to Korea, where peace talks had been stalled for weeks and bloody fighting continued. But it was Richard Nixon who supplied the campaign drama with his "Checkers" Speech. There had been questions about a secret "slush fund" provided by his rich Republican backers. Democrats built these rumors into such an issue that Nixon considered resigning from the ticket. Instead, he made an emotional TV speech about himself and his family. They were just plain folks. His wife didn't own a mink coat; she wore a respectable Republican cloth coat. And yes, a Texas fan had sent them a cocker spaniel, which his daughters named Checkers. They loved it, and he wasn't going to give it back. Nixon was endearingly defiant.

This speech was the high point of public debate in an election year. It spoke to voters who were tired of reading and thinking about Hiroshima and Nagasaki, the Holocaust, the Berlin airlift, Korea, the tensions and tumult of the outside world. Millions of men were going to college on the G.I. bill; millions of families were moving into new homes— most of their parents had never owned a house, but developer William Levitt showed how affordable housing could be mass produced in new suburbs, his Levittowns. These Americans filled their new homes with kids in an astonishing "baby boom," and read Dr. Benjamin Spock's book to learn about parenting. They worked hard, and they relaxed with television, the miraculous new family entertainment—not yet a purveyor of sex and violence, but informative and amusing.

In November General Dwight Eisenhower won a landslide victory when voters went to the polls in record numbers. In December he left for Korea. The Trumans were already back in Missouri, enjoying real life.

Dwight Eisenhower

1953

That war had already reached a stalemate, and both sides were ready for truce talks. In July an armistice was reached and the war ended where it began, at the thirty-eighth parallel. After the deaths of 54,000 Americans and two million Koreans, nothing was settled. American troops remained in the south and American aid continued to the Republic of Korea, but its government was unstable. In the north, the People's Republic of Korea was under Communist control, developing its nationalized industry and abundant natural resources.

Since the great era of European colonization in the nineteenth century, much of southeast Asia had belonged to the French who conquered Vietnam in 1858. It was occupied by Japanese troops in 1940; soon independence movements began under the leadership of the communist Ho Chi Minh. He proclaimed an independent republic during World War II. In 1946, the French attempted to regain control of their colonies, and that war had been going on for seven years. The United States had already given France $60 million in aid, and by now was paying most of the costs of the struggle, an expenditure justified as part of the effort to contain Communism. Now President Eisenhower announced more aid for the desperate French.

But overall, the country was well pleased with the performance of the new administration. The country was prosperous, employment was high; taxes were maintained at a level necessary to balance the budget; federal policies encouraged business and checked inflation.

The President's biggest domestic headache was Wisconsin Senator Joe McCarthy, who had built himself a power base that even Eisenhower hesitated to attack. Americans had watched Communist gains in Europe and Asia, and many were prepared to believe that their own country was menaced from without and within. As chairman of the Committee on Government Operations, the senator continued his "investigations" of loyalty and security risks in government departments and agencies. Eisenhower insisted that security issues were a matter for the executive branch, but McCarthy recklessly pushed on, damaging reputations, wrecking careers and infecting the body politic with his own cynical and increasingly malicious cascade of accusations.

In April he began two months of tele-vised hearings on alleged Communist influ-ence in the army, accusing the Secretary of the Army of covering up espionage and harboring security risks (the army had promoted a den-tist with Communist ties). But the army had been Dwight Eisenhower's life; he encouraged his Secretary to fight back and demonstrated his own contempt for the Wisconsin dema-gogue's tactics.

Two men finally used television to show America the kind of vicious menace McCarthy had become. One was Joseph Welsh, the older, soft-spoken, well-mannered lawyer hired to represent the Army. He showed the senator up as a bully and a boor. The other was Edward R. Murrow, a CBS reporter known to the country through his wartime coverage from London during the Blitz. Now he used his feature program to present highlights (or depths) from McCarthy's career—the bluster, the ravings, the lies.

The previously intimidated Senate nerved itself up and condemned the Senator for conduct "contrary to senatorial traditions." By a vote of sixty-seven to twenty-two he was censured, and Joe McCarthy's season of power was over. But the damage done the country was not easily repaired. Sensible security pol-icy was twisted into something like national paranoia and an inability to think clearly about Communism for years to come.

The biggest achievement of Eisenhower's first term was the end of racial segregation in America's public schools. In 1896, the Supreme Court had handed down an historic verdict in the case of *Plessy v. Ferguson*, establishing the "separate but equal" doctrine which prevailed in America for half a century. White America knew exactly what it meant by "separate" accommodations, and the ruling was rigidly enforced in the south: separate dining rooms and lunch counters, drinking fountains and lavatories, barber shops and polling places, prisons and public schools. Total segregation broke down in northern cities, but every effort was made to keep blacks confined to certain residential areas and shopping facilities. To illustrate the ultimate absurdities of segregation: In the mid-1920s, jazz recordings featuring both black and white musicians were banned.

The concept of "equal" was somehow overlooked, and nowhere were the results more observable than in the schools. In 1951, the father of an eight-year-old girl in Topeka, Kansas, decided to challenge the system. When his daughter was refused admission to an all-white neighborhood school, the Reverend Oliver Brown sued the school board. The National Association for the Advancement of Colored People had been fighting school segregation since the 1930s. When a black student was barred from the University of Missouri Law School, lawyers argued that Missouri could continue segregation only if it provided a separate law school for blacks. A Supreme Court decision in a Texas Law School case won admission for all academically qualified students, and an Oklahoma case decided that students admitted to graduate schools could not be segregated after admission. These cases were argued by Thurgood Marshall, who had assumed leadership of the NAACP strategy for legal justice.

Eisenhower made an important appointment when he chose Earl Warren to be chief justice. Nothing in his California record suggested any liberal leanings; as the state's Attorney General, he had accomplished the removal of all Japanese-Americans from the West Coast during World War II. But Warren takes his place beside Chief Justices John Marshall and Charles Evans Hughes as one of the most important men to preside over the court in a time of crucial decisions.

Earlier Courts had been sharply divided on the issue of school segregation; was it enough for districts to improve the "tangible assets" of black schools, to keep them separate but make them more nearly equal? In some districts this had been done. But Chief Justice Warren brought the Court together for a unanimous verdict in *Brown v. Board of Education of Topeka*, ruling that segregated schools were "inherently unequal" because segregation itself implied intangible inequalities. It told black children and their parents that black kids were not sufficiently equal to sit in a classroom with white classmates. It denied them equal protection under the law. Later the Court provided implementation guidelines requiring the courts to supervise desegregation "with all deliberate speed." The Reverend Brown had won his case, and black students willing to run a gauntlet of hostile whites began to integrate public schools, often guarded by police.

1955

The United States, while paying the mounting costs of the French war in Vietnam (as much as 80 percent), had avoided military intervention until the French suffered a disastrous loss at Dien Ben Phu in 1954. France was finished as a colonial power in southeast Asia. An international conference arranged a cease-fire and a north-south division of the country until elections could be held and a new government established, but neither the United States nor South Vietnam would participate. Fearing that Communists might win the elections and continue their advance into adjacent countries, Eisenhower urged and supported formation of a democratic regime in the south, and poured $100 million into the effort to prop up President Dien—dubious choice of leader to build democracy in a culture where the local elite didn't understand the whole idea. Including aid to Cambodia and Laos, the aid bill soon reached $200 million.

In Montgomery, Alabama, forty-three-year-old Rosa Parks was a seamstress and a civil rights activist. She was going home after work and some Christmas shopping, riding a segregated bus. Blacks customarily

317

sat in the back of the bus, but she was tired and took the first empty seat. When the driver told her to get up and give a white man her seat, she refused and was arrested.

Mrs. Parks attended a church served by young pastor Dr. Martin Luther King. He came from a family of ministers and organizers. A precocious student, he entered Morehouse, a black college in Atlanta, when he was fifteen, and then went to Crozer Theological Seminary in Chester, Pennsylvania, one of six blacks in a class of one hundred; he was elected senior class president and its outstanding student. After some work at the University of Pennsylvania, he received his Ph.D. in theology from Boston College, and returned to his father's church in Atlanta. But he was soon called to the pulpit of the Dexter Avenue Baptist Church in Montgomery, the Cradle of the Confederacy. In college he had been deeply impressed by the writings of Henry David Thoreau and Mahatma Gandhi. He hoped to shape the civil rights movement on a foundation of their principles, on non-violence and civil disobedience.

1956

Thus began the boycott of city buses in Montgomery: a peaceful refusal by black citizens to ride a segregated bus. For more than a year they walked—to their jobs and home again, to schools, shops, and churches. The boycott was directed by the new Montgomery Improvement Association, with Dr. King as its first president. In January he was arrested on a flimsy speeding charge; four days later his parsonage was bombed. An all-white grand jury indicted leaders of the boycott, including Martin Luther King. The Ku Klux Klan marched again. Rosa Parks was fired (she later found work at the Hampton Institute in Virginia). The boycott lasted for 385 days. It resulted in a Supreme Court case, and a decision that overturned bus segregation laws. During the next Christmas shopping season, black and white citizens rode buses without a color line.

Eisenhower took little part in the growing civil rights movement. His energies were focused on foreign affairs, on the possibility of a thaw in the Cold War after the death of Stalin; perhaps a new relationship could be forged with Stalin's successor, Nikita Khrushchev. The President had ended the Korean conflict and refused to send American forces to Vietnam. He launched his "atoms for peace" plan, a way to use new discoveries in atomic science for the good of the world. When leaders of the United States, Great Britain, France, and the Soviet Union met in Geneva in 1955, he wanted to talk about international control of atomic weapons and open-sky inspection of military installations. But a heart attack in 1955 and abdominal surgery in 1956 interrupted his work for significant disarmament. When he recovered, he let the Republicans know he would accept a second nomination for the presidency. With somewhat less enthusiasm, the party also renominated Richard Nixon.

The Democrats renominated Adlai Stevenson, and chose Senator Estes Kefauver of Tennessee for the vice presidential place. He had made a reputation during Senate investigations of organized crime, and now campaigned wearing a Davy Crockett coonskin hat, a case of politics imitating a popular television show about that Tennessee hero.

But war flared up across the ocean. Egypt had seized the Suez Canal. To regain control of that vital military and trade link, France and Great Britain immediately attacked. Anti-communist revolts broke out in Poland and Hungary. Israel invaded Egypt to defend itself against frequent border violence. So America wanted a general in the White House, and Eisenhower won an even greater number of states than he had carried four years earlier. His personal popularity didn't help Republican Congressional candidates. There would be a Democratic majority in both the

House and the Senate when he returned to office.

1957 In April, Congress passed the first civil rights legislation since the time of Reconstruction. Although a hundred southern Congressmen had expressed massive resistance to desegregation rulings by the Supreme Court, a Civil Rights Commission would now protect black voters. Seven states continued to fight school integration. In Arkansas, Governor Orval Faubus called out National Guardsmen to prevent nine black students from entering the all-white Central High School. A federal court ordered removal of the Guard and the students bravely entered, but were so threatened by mobs that local authorities insisted they leave for their own safety.

President Eisenhower had to uphold the courts. He sent eleven hundred paratroopers to Little Rock and put the state Guard under his personal orders as President. Though one child was too terrified to return, eight others finished the school year. They suffered months of harassment, but the paratroopers prevented rioting and physical abuse. Congress could pass civil rights laws, and Martin Luther King could preach non-violence to 50,000 blacks in their first Prayer Pilgrimage to Washington, but the struggle for equal treatment would be long and painful in mid-century America.

In October the Soviet Union launched the first earth-circling satellite, their "little traveler," Sputnik. It was about the size of a basketball, weighed 185 pounds, and sailed through space at 18,000 miles an hour, only 550 miles over our heads. In November they launched Sputnik II, an 1,100 vehicle big enough for a passenger, the space-dog Laika, who was hooked to monitoring equipment to test whether satellite conditions could sustain life. Laika returned to earth no worse for the adventure. And in December, the rocket that was supposed to propel America's first satellite into orbit blew up on its launching pad at Cape Canaveral, Florida.

Americans, who assumed that their country was the foremost scientific and technological power in the history of the world, were stunned. The Soviet achievement was disastrous proof that they had not only caught up, but surpassed us; power had shifted. While American kids had been watching the Mouseketeers, their kids had been learning advanced math and sophisticated engineering.

1958

The nation breathed easier in January, when we successfully launched our satellite, Explorer I. But it was clear that something had to be done about American education. The schools are always an easy target for national frustration, so now projects for school reform were developed. It would be expensive, and so would the public and private experimental programs essential to winning what was now called the "space race." Congress created the National Aeronautics and Space Administration (NASA) to coordinate American research and development.

Evidence of Communist aggression could be observed in Asia, when mainland Chinese attacked the small islands of Quemoy and Matsu, off the shore of Taiwan. That big island was held by the United States-backed Chinese who had escaped from the mainland after the communist takeover in 1949. The danger of American involvement was imminent until the mainlanders cooled down. On the other side of the world, Eisenhower sent Marines into Lebanon at the request of that government, which was threatened by pro-Egyptian leftists opposed to Lebanon's elected President. The Russians were again talking tough in Berlin.

A civil war raged in Cuba, where Fidel Castro was about to overthrow the corrupt regime of President Batista. Castro was not yet a declared Communist, and America no longer had formal control of Cuba, but the United

States still dominated the country's economy. Not only the United Fruit Company and the American sugar industry, but American mining and oil interests and even the Mafia were major players.

Indeed, the whole Caribbean and Central American region seemed to be a hotbed of revolution and violence. For many years the United States tolerated, and even supported, dictators who protected American investment and kept order in those countries (we did not inquire too deeply into their methods). Now every popular uprising was labeled a Communist plot by the Central Intelligence Agency. Some were.

1959

After the death of John Foster Dulles, his Secretary of State, the President took personal charge of foreign policy. A European editor had called Dulles the "conscience and straitjacket of the free world." Certainly the Secretary—and his brother, Allen Dulles, who headed the CIA—had taken a dim and largely negative view of foreign affairs. There was only one true faith, and the rest of the world had to be converted, had to accept American dogma or be cast into outer darkness.

Now Eisenhower took a look at issues from the world's point of view. He saw that we were (of course) envied for our wealth and resented for our power, but actively disliked and resisted when we tried to impose our purpose and policies on other governments. The President had seen the hottest of hot wars, and hated "its brutality, its futility, its stupidity." He saw no reason to prolong the futility and stupidity of the Cold War. He flew to Europe to confer with British, French, and German leaders. He invited Soviet Premier Khrushchev to make an unprecedented tour of the United States. The Premier accepted, and during September he visited Washington D.C., New York City (where he addressed a general session of the United Nations), Los Angeles (including Hollywood, where he watched the filming of *Can-Can* and saw an "indecent" dance, but admired Shirley MacLaine), San Francisco, Pittsburgh, and Coon Rapids, Iowa (where he discussed hybrid corn with mega-farmer Roswell Garst).

The last thing the President needed was major economic unrest at home, a steel strike like the walk-out that had confronted Harry Truman. At that time, the Supreme Court had ruled the government takeover unconstitutional; this time the Eisenhower administration waited more than four months before getting an injunction that made workers return to the job while arbitration proceeded. In the end, many strike issues were still unsettled, but work in the steel industry resumed.

The strike further weakened public sympathy for organized labor. The 1955 merger of the American Federation of Labor and the Congress of Industrial Organizations had brought together the country's two largest union groups which, as the AFL-CIO, had an estimated membership of fifteen million. The president was former AFL head George Meany; the vice president was Walter Reuther, former head of the CIO. Both were veterans of the labor movement, and both had major responsibilities during the World War II effort to increase American production of essential military requirements.

While George Meany reflected the traditional AFL philosophy of confining union energies to union issues—the improvement of wages and working conditions, the right to collective bargaining, and so on—Walter Reuther had a larger view of labor's role in society, in the civil rights movement, and international organizations. Both groups had fought to rid organized labor of pervasive Communist influence; both became more conservative as they got bigger and older. But there were many problems within the union bureaucracy, and after investigation, Congress passed the Labor Management Reporting and

Disclosure Act, designed to eliminate corruption and the influence of organized crime in unions by requiring financial reports that revealed how union dues were spent.

Alaska and Hawaii were admitted as the forty-ninth and fiftieth states.

As another election year began, black activists tried a new strategy. Four students from the North Carolina Agricultural and Technical College in Greensboro sat down at a lunch counter where blacks had previously been denied service. Ordered to leave, they refused, enduring insults and blows in the first of many sit-ins to end lunch-room segregation. During the next year, more than 70,000 students, black and white, joined sit-ins throughout the south. To encourage local action, they organized the Student Non-Violent Coordinating Committee (SNCC) and stepped up their efforts to change laws and attitudes at the community, rather than the national, level.

The national political parties, in an election year when both would be seeking Southern votes, could not afford to take a strong position on black rights. At the summer political conventions, both parties nominated young men, but the difference in their backgrounds and style could not have been more marked.

Richard Nixon, the GOP choice, was a poor boy from Quaker antecedents. He got a degree from Whittier College in California, and his law degree from Duke University. He served as a Navy lieutenant J.G. in the Pacific Theater of World War II, and saved the money he won in poker games. After the war, California sent him to the House of Representatives and then to the Senate, where he worked hard and won the admiration of right-wing Republicans for his tough anti-communism. Eisenhower did not seek Nixon for the vice-presidency—an office that has often been the obscure grave of political men— but he gave Nixon ample opportunity to use his drive and talents. He was included in Cabinet meetings and discussions of the National Security Council; he chaired important committees and commissions like that on Price Stability, which ended the steel strike. When illness incapacitated the President in 1956, 1957, and 1958, Nixon capably ran the executive branch. He made a hit in a 1959 appearance at the American Exhibition in Moscow, in his well-covered "Kitchen Debate" with Nikita Khrushchev.

He had a devoted wife, Pat, and two attractive daughters. But he wasn't, well, likable. There was always a shadow on Richard Nixon, on his heavy jowls (which cartoonists and television cameras exaggerated) and on his political nature. Enemies called him "Tricky Dick" from accusations of shady tactics in earlier campaigns. But his many admirers and Republican backers managed his nomination, and he would run a hard race.

Jack Kennedy was four years younger than Nixon, rich, privileged, and Catholic. A Harvard graduate, he assisted his father when Joseph Kennedy served as American ambassador to Great Britain. After his time at the London Embassy, Jack wrote "While England Slept," an analysis of the British response to the rise of Fascism. Like Nixon, he served in the navy in World War II, commanded a navy PT boat, earned a Purple Heart and the navy and marine corps medals. While he recovered from back surgery, he wrote *Profiles in Courage* and won the Pulitzer Prize for History (though many questioned his authorship). He won a Massachusetts seat in the House, and then in the Senate. Then he won the Democratic nomination for President.

His wife was the glamorous Jackie; he had a pretty little daughter and a son, the adorable toddler John-John. Even more importantly, he had his father's limitless resources. Joe Kennedy was a Boston Irish millionaire, determined that his sons would reach the heights of American power and prominence.

When his oldest boy died during the war, Jack was moved to the head of the line. Now his father's money, his mother's charm, the energy of his brothers and sisters, and his own likability would carry him through a galloping campaign.

Meanwhile, President Eisenhower hoped for opportunities to advance United States-Soviet relations during a trip to the Soviet Union. But on May 1, an American spy plane was shot down over Russia. According to their indictment, the plane had penetrated Soviet territory to a distance of more than 1,300 miles, flying at an altitude of 65,600 feet, on a route that lay over "large industrial centers and important defense objectives" of the Soviet Union. It was brought down ("with the very first shot") by a rocket; the pilot bailed out and was captured. The wreckage proved that the plane was specially designed and equipped for aerial reconnaissance; investigators found film, a tape that recorded signals from Soviet radar stations, and much other evidence of its mission. And they had the pilot, Francis Gary Powers, who flew for "a special American intelligence unit based in Turkey and known under the code name of Detachment 10-10."

The State Department admitted that the United States had such planes in the area, but claimed that they were engaged in weather research, took air samples, etc., and Powers had strayed off course because of a failure in oxygen supply; the pilot had lost consciousness, and the plane, on automatic pilot, had accidentally crossed the Soviet border. This denial stood up for a week, until Khrushchev cited more facts about the "premeditated, perfidious, and gangsterlike" violation, and the State Department had to admit that it was indeed a spy flight, ordered by President Eisenhower in accordance with the National Security Act.

On May 15, Vice President Nixon made a television speech not only admitting but justifying America's policy of such espionage, its right to spy. Powers was recruited from the Air Force by the CIA, paid $2,500 a month; he described Detachment 10-10 as "a kind of combination civilian and military service." After an elaborate trial, he was imprisoned by the Soviets for two years. They released him in exchange for one of their own spies who had been caught in the United States. Of course, this episode led Premier Khrushchev to cancel any plans for a summit meeting with President Eisenhower. The calculated policies of the Dulles brothers had led only to a renewal and intensification of the cold war.

The media loved Jack Kennedy. He was informed and articulate when interviewers wanted to be serious; he was funny when reporters wanted jokes. He was forthright with voters about his religion. He had Texas Senator Lyndon Johnson (himself a top contender for the presidential nomination) as a running mate; Johnson delivered Texas and the south. So Kennedy won a very close election.

1961

John F. Kennedy

On January 17, retiring President Eisenhower made his farewell address to the nation. His radio and television audiences were not surprised when he chose to talk about the Cold War, the global dangers America faced. Our ideological enemies, he said, were "ruthless" and "insidious," and the danger would be of "indefinite duration."

But few listeners expected him to speak so soberly about another threat. After all, Dwight Eisenhower had spent a lifetime in military service and reached the highest rank that career could offer. He led the country to victory in America's total war against Facist tyranny. Now that experience led him to warn his fellow citizens of a new danger: the "conjunction of an immense military establishment and a large arms industry" whose "total influence—economic, political even spiritual— felt in every city, every state house, every office of the federal government." He added a new phrase to our public vocabulary when he described that partnership as "the military-industrial complex."

This was Eisenhower's last speech, the most important of his presidency, and probably one of the most important speeches ever delivered by any President. He was emphatic. "The potential for the disastrous rise of misplaced power exists and will persist," he said, and "the military-industrial complex should never be allowed to endanger our liberties or democratic processes. We should take nothing for granted."

The speech was well-received, and he left office with the respect and affection of the country. But how many people fully understood Eisenhower's concern, or would remember his warning? The power of the military-industrial complex continued to grow, with increasing influence on American policy and an ever-tighter grip on the national purse.

1961

Following a gala inaugural, the handsome young Kennedys easily assumed their new roles. The White House sparkled as a cultural center. Artists, writers, musicians, distinguished Americans from many fields gathered there and gave the country a glimpse of how life was lived by people who not only respected but appeared to enjoy the fine arts. The administration, too, attracted exceptional intellectual and political talent, though there was some muttering when Kennedy appointed his brother, Robert, as attorney general. Because the Democratic victory had been so narrow, they did not control the House of Representatives, but the President pushed ahead with a legislative program that explored The New Frontier.

In his first hundred days, he created the Peace Corps. "Ask not what your country can do for you," he said in his inaugural address, "ask what you can do for your country." Thousands of young men and women responded, volunteering to serve overseas as teachers, medical personnel, farm technicians, and to promote world peace; it was an impressive demonstration of American idealism and generosity. It was directed by the president's brother-in-law, Sergeant Shriver. But it should be acknowledged that, as time went on, many draft age men joined the Peace Corps because the Vietnamese war was in the headlines.

Thus far, American involvement had been limited to sending aid and providing military training for the South Vietnamese army. More than 3,000 American personnel were stationed there. Now Kennedy's advisors recommended sending 8,000 troops. But in his first eight months, the new president was dealing with crises in every part of the world—in Angola, South Korea, the Dominican Republic, Tunisia, Brazil, the Congo—and many of these were Communist inspired, but by no means all. America and its European allies often had trouble seeing the difference between Communist-led uprisings and the growing determination of former colonies and underdeveloped nations to be free of foreign rule and capitalist exploitation. There was no question about the August confrontation in Berlin, when the Soviets closed off their zone with a twenty-eight-mile wall of concrete and barbed wire, mine fields, checkpoints—every obstacle to anyone who sought escape from East Berlin.

Close to home, the United States had broken relations with Cuba. Fidel Castro was a ruthless dictator, now an avowed Communist, who had begun to nationalize American companies and threatened the American installations at Guantanamo Bay. (The U.S. had leased that site for a naval base in 1903, after American occupation troops left Cuba following the Spanish-American war.) Castro got his military muscle from the Soviets, and as the regime became more repressive many anti-Castro Cubans left the island, creating a vocal community of militant anti-Communist agitators in Florida.

Allen Dulles saw the Cuban exiles as potential recruits for a Cuban invasion. They would certainly inspire a revolt and overthrow the dictatorship. He proposed his deceptively simple plan to President Kennedy. He was organizing La Brigada, a fighting force of highly trained men, provided with the best American weapons and equipment. He might enlist Mafia help in a plot to assassinate Castro by a variety of illegal devices. Dulles had worked on this scheme for months. Eisenhower had serious reservations, but Nixon was enthusiastic and other Cold War "experts" guaranteed its success if the new President approved it. Reluctantly, Kennedy did.

Almost everything that Dulles told the President was wrong, if not an outright falsehood. La Brigada consisted of about 1,400 men, most ill-equipped, poorly trained, and ignorant about details of their assignment—though dozens of Miami journalists seemed to know about it. Certainly it was no secret after an airstrike by old U.S. planes, which the Central Intelligence Agency had flown to Cuba from various Latin American countries, and which didn't make a dent in Castro's air force.

In April, leaky boats carried La Brigada into the Bay of Pigs, where they were battered by uncharted reefs and strafed by Cuban planes. Kennedy was suddenly scared off by the possibility of a Soviet response to further American involvement. He refused to give the doomed invaders more support. The men who reached shore were not welcomed by jubilant anti-Castro dissidents. Contrary to CIA reports, most Cubans supported their president. Yes, he could be harsh, and was certainly long- winded, but they approved his programs for education and housing. Yes, he seized land from American corporate owners, but he distributed it to landless peasants. The prosperity he promised had not yet arrived, but they were ready to fight and die for Fidel.

Many members of the brigade perished, more were captured and stayed in prison until they were ransomed by $53 million in American food and military supplies. It was a humiliating fiasco for the United States.

And the nation was further humiliated when Yuri Gagarin, a Russian astronaut, became the first human in space, circling the planet in a one-orbit mission. A month later the United States navy sent Commander Alan Shepard, Jr., up in the first American suborbital space flight.

1962

Lieutenant Colonel John Glenn, Jr., was the first American to orbit the earth. His Mercury rocket capsule made three trips around the planet, while fascinated American television viewers got a look at the world, the Big Blue Marble they shared, however uneasily, with almost three billion other human beings.

America appeared to be holding its own in space, but our side was losing in Vietnam. An American Assistance Command was formed and based in Saigon; American advisors soon numbered almost 12,000, and they had orders to fire if fired upon. Aid had reached almost a billion dollars without solving the economic, military, or political problems of the incompetent and corrupt South Vietnamese government. Communists expanded their operations into Laos; President Kennedy sent 5,000 Marines and fifty jet aircraft to resist further incursions.

And he sent 3,000 troops to Oxford, Mississippi, where James Meredith had attempted to register as the first black student at the University. The town erupted with vicious anger. Under army control, the rioting was quelled, but Kennedy did not follow the advice of the Civil Rights Commission, which urged that he cut off all federal funds to the state. Such an action would have sparked a firestorm in the halls of Congress and throughout the state.

The U2 affair did not mean the end

of American spy flights. Another U2 now revealed the presence of Soviet nuclear missiles in Cuba. Kennedy's ambassador to the UN exhibited pictures of the camouflaged sites from which an attack on the United States could be launched. The President demanded that the missiles be removed and the launching sites dismantled. He ordered a naval blockade of Cuba to prevent any further Soviet shipment of military aid and insisted that all offensive weapons on the island be eliminated. Castro blustered; Premier Khrushchev toughed it out. For thirteen days America and the Soviet Union were on the brink of war. It was the most frightening confrontation since the end of World War II, and the world held its breath until Moscow announced that it accepted Kennedy's terms. The missiles were crated up and returned to Russia, but Khrushchev was slow to recall the 23,000 Soviet troops stationed in Cuba.

Kennedy realized that the next such face-down might have a different outcome. His British allies urged him to negotiate with the Russians, to work for a treaty that would relieve some of the global anxiety about nuclear war. Khrushchev, too, had learned some lessons. The U.S. now had many more missile-equipped long-range bombers, more intercontinental ballistic missiles, more submarine-based missiles, than he could command or afford to build. He finally agreed to negotiations on all outstanding disputes. Kennedy's first objective was a treaty banning further above-ground testing of nuclear weapons. Underground tests would go on, but after thirteen years of above-ground tests by both sides in the Cold War, radioactive poisons were accumulating in the atmosphere. This was a sufficiently urgent reason to reach a limited test-ban agreement. Even this small step toward international sanity took months of talks, setbacks, nit-picking, and argument, but in July a treaty was signed.

Meanwhile, civil rights violence flared up in cities large and small, north and south. Birmingham, Alabama, was one of the worst. Black protests and petitions, boycotts, sit-ins, and almost daily demonstrations were met with stubborn resistance. Police Commissioner "Bull" Connor did not hesitate to use all the force available to him—his cops had fierce dogs, tear gas, armored vehicles, and powerful firehoses, and they made mass arrests. More than 3,000 blacks, including Dr. Martin Luther King, were jailed. Other black leaders wanted the President to send troops, as he had done in Mississippi, but Kennedy sought legal remedies, meeting with the mayor and local businessmen.

As the Alabama conflict worsened, Kennedy ordered troops to military bases near Birmingham; Governor George Wallace announced that he would "stand in the doorway" of any schoolhouse the government tried to integrate. Troops were already boarding helicopters at Fort Benning when Wallace capitulated. He made a theatrical appearance before the State University at Tuscaloosa (Alabama was still the only state left with a segregated University), but after three hours, two black students registered without interference.

Dr. King was now under continual surveillance by the FBI because director J. Edgar Hoover was convinced that any civil rights leader must be part of a communist conspiracy. They bugged his phone, opened his mail, threatened his life, harassed him in every way, but he kept working and praying. Almost a quarter of a million people, black and white, joined his civil rights march to Washington. He spoke to them in front of the Lincoln Memorial, in words that cannot be forgotten by Americans of any color: —"in spite of the difficulties and frustrations of the moment, I still have a dream. I dream that one day this nation will rise up and live out the true meaning of its creed: 'We hold these truths to be self-evident;

that all men are created equal...' I have a dream—"

Less than three weeks later, a bomb exploded in a black Birmingham church. Four young girls, attending their Sunday School class in the basement, were killed.

On November 22, President Kennedy was shot dead in Dallas, Texas.

He had gone to Texas for political reasons. With an election year coming up, he needed to build a national consensus on civil rights policy and on new approaches to a stable relationship with the Soviet Union. On the previous day, he spoke in Houston about an America that was "both powerful and peaceful...prosperous and just." He delivered the same message in Fort Worth. Friends and advisors warned him that Dallas would be unfriendly and told him to avoid it. In fact, he had been greeted by enthusiastic crowds. As he rode through town in a limousine with Jackie, and the Governor and Mrs. Connally, curbside onlookers cheered their motorcade.

As they passed the Texas School Book Depository, shots were fired. The President and the Governor were hit. Both men were rushed to a hospital, where Connally's wounds were treated, but John Kennedy died. His body was removed to Air Force One for the somber flight back to Washington. On the plane, Lyndon Johnson was sworn in as President, Jackie in her blood-stained pink travel suit beside him.

Lyndon B. Johnson

Within hours the alleged assassin murdered a Dallas policeman and then was taken into custody. There seemed to be no doubt about his guilt. Lee Harvey Oswald was a twenty-four-year old loner, a misfit and self-taught Marxist who had been discharged from the Marines and immediately left for the Soviet Union. there he was given a factory job (but closely watched) and married a Russian wife. After some months, he brought her back to the States. In New Orleans he worked for something called the "Fair Play for Cuba Committee" and made a trip to the Cuban embassy in Mexico City before he drifted to Dallas and got work in the Book Depository. He was a competent marksman and bought a high-powered rifle with a telescopic sight.

But the police had little time to investigate the character, background, or motives of Lee Harvey Oswald. Two days later they were transferring him to a safer jail when Jack Ruby, owner of a sleazy Dallas nightclub, pushed through the surrounding crowd and killed him. This shooting was covered by television news cameras. The grieving nation was stunned again.

Even as John Kennedy's body lay in state in Washington, a hundred questions were being asked. Had there been shots from the "grassy knoll" the motorcade passed? Both bystanders and members of the Kennedy party were sure they heard shots from behind a fence on the knoll (or were they echoes?). Was Oswald the fall-guy for a larger plot, and if so, who were the plotters? Anti-Castro Cubans? Russians? Mafia? CIA? As rumors multiplied, President Johnson appointed a commission headed by Chief Justice Earl Warren to conduct a thorough inquiry. After ten months, their report concluded that Oswald acted alone. Jack Ruby continued to insist that he shot Oswald to spare Mrs. Kennedy the pain of appearing as a witness if the assassin had been brought to trial in Dallas. Ruby was under a death sentence, but already dying. Nevertheless, dozens of theories were advanced, and books written about the Dallas killings. Many Americans still believe that such a tragic event must have a more complicated explanation.

1964

Lyndon Johnson was only four years older than John Kennedy, but he seemed to come from another generation. He certainly came from a different world, the hill country of Texas. He was not a poor boy, the family had enough money to send him to South West Texas State Teacher's College, but that was a long way from Harvard. Politics was his whole life. He taught school in Houston for only a short while before he served as a Congressional aide in Washington. He then went back to Texas as state director of the National Youth Administration, a New Deal agency. He was elected to the House of Representatives and given a leave of absence for naval duty during World War II. Johnson's record in the House was not excessively liberal; he voted against an anti-lynching law, the abolition of poll taxes, and a Fair Employment Practice Commission. After six terms he moved on to the Senate, serving as both minority and then as majority leaders.

He wanted to be President and was sure he could be nominated by the Democratic convention in 1960. He had been a much more impressive senator than that kid from Boston; the boy was a flash-in-the-pan. It came as a shock when Jack Kennedy was named; Johnson pragmatically accepted the second spot on the ticket.

But after the assassination, he kept most of the Kennedy team around him, and he accepted the Kennedy agenda. He achieved passage of most of Kennedy's legislation, and more. Kennedy's Economic Opportunity Act became the core of Johnson's "war on poverty," Perhaps he was remembering his earlier political idol, Franklin Roosevelt. He had gone to Congress in 1937, at the start of Roosevelt's second term. He had grown up in the Depression years, among poor people, and though he was now a rich rancher, he was serious about ending poverty and building The Great Society. Medicare, Medicaid, a Civil Rights Act, a Voting Rights Act, a higher minimum wage and increased Social Security, a National Endowment for the Arts and Humanities, aid for education and mass transit. even the beautification of American highways (the personal cause of his wife, Lady

Bird)—all these took shape under Johnson's adroit Congressional management. During the Kennedy years, America had experienced the strongest economic expansion in the country's modern history. Johnson was determined to bring the people who had been left out to the bountiful national dinner table.

But there was a war in Vietnam. In August, North Vietnamese boats reportedly shelled two United States destroyers in the Gulf of Tonkin off the North Vietnam coast. The President asked for and got a Congressional resolution, authorizing "all necessary measures" against any North Vietnamese attack on the growing American force in South Vietnam; which meant that Johnson could escalate hostilities without an actual declaration of war. Immediately, U.S. planes began bombing the North.

In the same month, the bodies of three civil rights workers, missing since the beginning of the year, were found buried in Mississippi. They had come with the Student Non-Violent Coordinating Committee (SNCC) and others to join a voter registration drive during Mississippi Summer—a period during which the Justice Department recorded more than 1,400 demonstrations. Many students suffered physical attacks, but these men had been arrested, beaten, and shot. For the murders of James Cheney, a young black, and Michael Schwerner and James Goodman, two white volunteers, twenty-one white men, most members of the Ku Klux Klan, were charged. Seven, including the sheriff and deputy sheriff involved, were convicted and jailed. The work went on; a million new black voters were registered.

But half the black population still lived with segregation and poverty, and Dr. King's sermons about turning the other cheek didn't get results fast enough for men like Malcolm X. Congress passed more civil rights laws, but a new militancy was growing among black leaders. Summer passed, but the climate of confrontation did not cool down.

Lyndon Johnson and Senator Hubert Humphrey, a liberal Minnesotan, were nominated by the Democratic convention, and easily won the election. Arizona Senator Barry Goldwater was Johnson's ultra-conservative Republican opponent, opposed to social programs like the war on poverty, in favor of a winning war in Vietnam—more bombs. He suffered a decisive defeat.

1965

Vietnam was certainly not Johnson's only international concern. He had problems in Latin America, where Panama had broken off relations with the United States in a dispute over American rights to the canal. Rioting stopped when negotiations for a new treaty were begun. And there was trouble in the Caribbean; after the first free elections in thirty-eight years, the President of the Dominican republic was overthrown and civil war broke out. Johnson sent 14,000 marines to support the rebels against the elected government, which was said to include some communist elements. And Johnson's European allies were beginning to question the wisdom of American policy in southeast Asia.

That policy was based on the prevailing "domino theory"—the idea that if you toppled one piece in a row of standing dominoes, all the rest would fall: A loss in Vietnam would mean the loss of Thailand, Laos, and Cambodia, probably communist success in the Philippines and Pakistan, and then.... John Kennedy bought into that theory, and so did President Johnson, so he ordered continuous bombing of North Vietnam, and sent 200,000 more American troops. Their commanding general assured the president that we were inflicting such damage that the North Vietnamese, the Viet Cong, could not last much longer. It was their will to fight against ours; they would soon collapse.

With such assurances Johnson returned to building The Great Society. In

August the Watts area of Los Angeles, a depressed black ghetto, erupted in the worst urban violence since World War I. It started with the drunk-driving arrest of a twenty-one-year-old man and connected incidents of rough handling by police officers. Six days of rioting, police fighting, and brutality followed; stores were looted and firebombed until two hundred businesses were destroyed. Twenty thousand National Guard troops arrived. Thirty-four people, mostly black, were killed, more than a thousand were injured, and 4,000 arrested. Damages were estimated at $200 million.

The mostly white members of Students for a Democratic Society (SDS) had tried to organize poor people for what they called "the new insurgency," a leftist political effort which would transfer power from government to communities and individuals. It made little headway among the poor (for its sixty-three-page platform was not easy to read or comprehend) but had great success with college students when it turned to anti-war demonstrations. The first, in Washington, drew 15,000 people; the next, in November, brought twice as many.

1966

There were now 385,000 American soldiers in Vietnam, 33,000 in Thailand, 60,000 off shore. The United States was firing into Cambodia. The CIA was beginning to round up Communist sympathizers in South Vietnam, allegedly members of a Communist underground; prison camps were built to hold the growing number of those arrested. But the North Vietnamese were distributing land to peasants.

President Johnson suspended the bombing of North Vietnam and offered a peace plan that would be, at least, a basis for negotiation. It was rejected. Ho Chi Minh, the seemingly frail but indomitable Northern leader, intended to dictate peace terms. So the American bombing was resumed and increased. But it was not easy to pinpoint targets. Except for cities and nearby installations like oil fields, much of the country was jungle, with small villages and clusters of huts hidden by dense foliage. The Americans began to spray chemicals like Agent Orange to kill that cover and expose the peasant enemy to American bombers. Johnson held talks with his allies in the war—Australia, New Zealand, the Philippines, South Korea, Thailand, and South Vietnam—and they joined the call for North Vietnamese withdrawal. When there was no response, American strategists suggested that bombing be directed at the system of locks and dams that created rice paddies on which the population depended for food. By flooding the rice, a million people might be starved to death, and North Vietnam forced to capitulate. There was no response.

At the mid-term elections, Edward Brooke, the liberal Republican State's Attorney of Massachusetts was elected to the Senate. He was the first black man to serve in that Chamber for eighty-five years, since Reconstruction.

1967

It was now clear to Washington that bombing North Vietnam was not winning the war. Casualties since the arrival of the first advisers sent by President Kennedy amounted to 6,664 dead, almost 40,000 wounded, and more troops were arriving every month. The war was having a disastrous effect on the American economy, and protest mounted throughout the country. Young men were refusing to show up for the draft, mailing their draft cards back to Washington. On college campuses, students demonstrated; faculty members and college presidents joined them. Nuns and priests, mothers and fathers, athletes and Hollywood stars, Peace Corps volunteers, concerned clergy, concerned lawyers, converged on the Capitol to plead with their legislators. The majority leader of the house went to the President and told him that the war was wrong and hopeless.

But Lyndon Baines Johnson and Robert McNamara, his Secretary of Defense, did not intend to lose in Vietnam. Under the windows of the White House, people chanted "Hey, hey, LBJ—how many kids did you kill today?" He sent more troops. By the end of the year, there were 475,000 soldiers, sailors, marines, and members of the air force serving—and among them, too, protest increased. It must have been relaxing and reassuring for Johnson to have a friendly meeting with Soviet Premier Kosygin in New Jersey, where they promised each other that no crisis would cause a war between them.

Thurgood Marshall was a distinguished liberal lawyer who had spent his career fighting for civil rights. He argued landmark cases before the Supreme Court before he became its first black member. In Gary, Indiana, and Cleveland, Ohio, the first black mayors of big cities were elected. But among the despairing urban poor, the rioting went on, killing twenty-six people and injuring more than a thousand in Newark, leaving forty dead and 5,000 homeless in Detroit. Rioters were put down by National Guardsmen and paratroopers, but on the home front, too, a war went on.

1968

The new year began with even worse news. The USS *Pueblo*, with a crew of eighty-three men, was captured in the Sea of Japan by communist North Koreans. In South Vietnam, the communists launched a Tet offensive. As the start of their lunar New Year, Tet had been observed with a holiday cease-fire since the war began. This time the enemy commanders took American commanders by surprise with an attack on hundreds of towns and cities, even invading the American embassy grounds in Saigon. There were thousands of casualties among the invaders, the South Vietnamese, and the American forces before the attack was turned back. Finally peace talks began in Paris, and bombing was halted in North Vietnam.

And it was an election year. Eugene McCarthy of Minnesota had served as a member of the House since 1948, and was elected to the Senate ten years later. He was a handsome, bookish man, not the typical politician except that he wanted to be President. He had supported Adlai Stevenson against John Kennedy and Lyndon Johnson, and now he entered the March Democratic primary in New Hampshire, winning a surprising 42 percent of the vote as an anti-war candidate. Three weeks later, an exhausted President told the nation: "I shall not seek, nor will I accept, the nomination of my party..." The race for the White House was on.

Robert Kennedy, John Kennedy's younger brother and attorney general, immediately declared himself a candidate. He, too, ran on an anti-war platform. Vice-President Hubert Humphrey, now a moderate with a lifelong liberal background, declared his candidacy and endorsed the administration's Vietnam policy.

On April 4, in Memphis, Tennessee, Martin Luther King was assassinated. He had opposed the war in Vietnam and won the Nobel Peace Prize, but his main objective was to organize non-violent resistance to racial injustice. Early in the year, he had begun a "poor people's campaign" to address the economic problems which new civil rights laws could not solve. He had gone to Memphis to help settle a strike by sanitation workers. Standing on the balcony of his motel, he was shot by an escaped white convict, James Earl Ray. The killer was almost immediately arrested, pleaded guilty, and was sentenced to ninety-nine years in prison.

Robert Kennedy conducted an exciting campaign in California, climaxed by victory in that state's Democratic primary. He joined a celebration party at the Hotel Ambassador in Los Angeles, where he was surrounded by campaign workers and well-wishers. As he was leaving, he was shot by a Palestinian immigrant, Sirhan Sirhan. This assassin, too, was arrested and convicted.

But two assassinations in two months left the country reeling and contributed to the anger and frustration expressed when the Democratic convention met in Chicago. Longtime mayor and political boss Richard Daley was privately opposed to the war, and had urged Johnson to withdraw American troops. But he was furious when his city and his Democratic convention were assaulted by protesters. Many were the long-haired "flower children" who preached peace and love, rejected their parents in favor of communal lifestyles, didn't eat meat but tried every available new drug, writhed to nasty new music, and generally represented everything the sixty-six-year-old mayor despised. Most belonged to one of the organized factions within the anti-war movement, Students for a Democratic Society, led by Tom Hayden, or the Youth International Party led by Abbie Hoffman, the Mobilization Against the War, or another.

Ten thousand protesters jammed parks and streets, chanting and jeering, throwing stink bombs. When police arrived, there were bloody fights as demonstrators pelted the cops with rocks and the police tore into the crowd with clubs and tear gas. Inside the hall were many young people who had cut their hair and taken a bath and now passed out McCarthy literature, the contingent that was "Clean for Gene," but politics prevailed over protest. Hubert Humphrey was nominated on the first ballot, and badly shaken regular party members went home to see if they could salvage an election. Hayden, Hoffman, and others who had rioted in the streets were arrested and tried (the Chicago Seven); two were convicted, the convictions later overturned.

By contrast, the Republican party convention was a model of order. There were delegates for the segregationist governor of Alabama, George Wallace, and for Air Force

Richard Nixon

1969

General Curtis LeMay, who favored using nuclear bombs in Vietnam, but in the end the Republicans nominated Richard M. Nixon. He had lost to Kennedy in 1960, and lost an election for Governor of California in 1962. After that loss he was momentarily discouraged, sourly promising reporters, "You won't have Nixon to kick around anymore." But he survived with all his old energy and determination undiminished. His credentials as a fervent anti-Communist were beyond question, and now he said he had a "secret plan" to end the war. It was a very close race, but Nixon won.

His policy for the war was Vietnamization; he would strengthen the government in Saigon, supply them, and tell them to win their own civil war. Peace talks in Paris were expanded to include South Vietnam and the Viet Cong. There were now 543,000 American troops engaged in the fighting. Nixon insisted that the North Vietnamese leave simultaneously with Americans, and to demonstrate his good faith he recalled 25,000 men. But he was secretly expanding the war by sending American bombers into Cambodia to destroy Communist bases.

When Martin Luther King's widow, Coretta Scott King, led the first national War Moratorium march to Washington, the President responded with a speech claiming that the "silent majority" of Americans supported his policy. Perhaps they did, but a second Moratorium demonstration a month later brought another quarter of a million marchers to the Capital, and ten bills were offered in Congress for a faster end to American involvement.

The country was thrilled in July, when astronauts Neil Armstrong, Air Force Colonel Edwin Aldrin Jr., and Lieutenant Colonel Michael Collins reached the moon. It was the eleventh mission in the Apollo project, which had been tragically marred in 1967 when a fire aboard their spacecraft killed astronauts Virgil

Grissom, Edward White, and Roger Chaffee. This time the three-day flight went perfectly. Collins took the controls of Columbia, the command module, while Armstrong and Aldrin entered the lunar landing vehicle Eagle and descended. Armstrong was first down the ladder, saying, "That's one small step for a man, one giant leap for mankind." Millions watched on television while they bounced along in the moon's low gravity, taking pictures, collecting forty-eight pounds of rock and soil samples, conducting experiments with solar winds and metal welding, a seismic experiment, and other studies. After twenty-one and a half hours, they rejoined the Columbia and returned safely to earth.

The country was sickened in November. In a 1968 atrocity, American soldiers had massacred almost five hundred civilians in the South Vietnam village of My Lai. The bodies of old women and children were found among those that had been herded into a ditch and then methodically shot by troops under the command of Lieutenant William Calley. When the mass grave was discovered, Calley was tried, convicted, and given a life sentence. But the sentence was shortened to three years, and President Nixon ordered Calley to serve that time under house arrest, rather than in prison. Later he was paroled. Well, shrugged other servicemen, it wasn't the first such incident in the ugly war.

1970

The conservation movement had grown during the time of Teddy Roosevelt, and taken many directions in later years—the national park system, the reclamation of lands destroyed by floods and erosion, and the control of timbering to preserve our forests. The 1960s added a vast program to save America's unspoiled wilderness. Then, in 1962, marine biologist Rachel Carson published "Silent Spring." Her concern was the effect of chemicals, pesticides like DDT, which destroyed unwanted bugs and saved farmer's crops, but had unforeseen consequences. Thirty years of scientific observation convinced her that birds ate poisoned bugs and died; that fish were poisoned when such non-selective and long-lasting chemicals built up in rivers and streams; that even humbler creatures which converted rotting vegetable matter into rich soil were being lost. That was Rachel Carson's lesson: human beings were threatening the fragile chain on which all life depended and endangering their own existence as well.

In 1970, as if they welcomed a cause other than the war, millions of Americans marched in Earth Day demonstrations. With pictures from space, the astronauts had shown us our planet, the big blue marble that was ours to save or destroy. The word "ecology" was added to the national vocabulary. "Environmentalism," as a political and personal cause, was born.

The bombing in Cambodia was followed up with an invasion by American and South Vietnamese troops. President Nixon announced on television that 150,000 more draftees would be needed by the Army, and huge protests erupted on college campuses across the country. When students at Kent State University in Ohio rallied and set fire to the ROTC building, the governor called out the National Guard. The young people were unarmed, but somebody heard a shot, and Guardsmen opened fire, killing four students and wounding nine. Reports and news photos from Kent State enraged the public.

The draft announcement fed black anger, because they saw a link between poverty, the draft, and battle deaths in Vietnam. Most men in the armed forces were volunteers, but the draft supplied most of the infantry. Riflemen were the soldiers who died, and the draft took them from the lower brackets of the working class, black and white. Combat in Vietnam revived a saying heard in earlier American wars—it was a rich man's war and a poor man's fight. During a student protest at Jackson State University, an all-black school in Mississippi, police fired into a dormitory; two students were killed, nine wounded. Blacks interpreted the little publicity given this incident as more evidence that whites were indifferent to killing, if the victims were black.

1971 The war expanded into Laos, as South Vietnamese forces invaded that country with air and artillery support by United States forces. At the end of the year, Americans claimed that North Vietnam had violated previous agreements that brought a bombing halt. For five days, U.S. bombers subjected the north to massive attack. But troops were being brought home. More than three-quarters of the 1969 strength had been withdrawn.

And it must not be supposed that the President had done nothing but fight the Vietnamese war during his first term. He had done much at home, funding President Johnson's anti-poverty programs, reducing the inflation rate, and working for an increase in Social Security payments. He created an Environmental Protection Agency. Many historians rate Richard Nixon as one of the best qualified and most competent presidents ever elected. But he was a nervous, striving man, cynical about others who had achieved easy success while he had had to work and struggle to get ahead. In 1960 he had lost to Jack Kennedy in a close election; he believed (and there was evidence to support his belief) that Kennedy money and a vote count by crooked Democratic political bosses explained that defeat. He had won a very narrow victory over Hubert Humphrey in 1968 to reach the White House. Now he wanted a huge win, an overwhelming popular mandate, so he could push his domestic legislative program through Congress while bringing American forces home from Vietnam.

A Twenty-sixth Amendment to the Constitution was approved by Congress, lowering the voting age from twenty-one to eighteen. Agreeing that citizens old enough to fight were certainly old enough to vote, the states gave the necessary ratification in a month.

The Pentagon is headquarters for the Department of Defense, an enormous building in Arlington, Virginia, just across the Potomac River from Washington, D.C. Among its thousands of employees was Daniel Ellsberg, a researcher who helped compile the two-million-word "History of the U.S. Decision-making Process in Vietnam." This document was "classified"—that is, top secret, to be read only by authorized people. But Ellsberg, who had formerly supported the war effort, was now deeply disillusioned. He leaked the document to the *New York Times*, and with publication of the Pentagon Papers, the country learned how it had been deceived for almost thirty years. At first Nixon was delighted, because this damning record of executive deceit was largely a Democratic record. But as the *Times*, and later the *Washington Post* and other papers began running excerpts, he tried to get a court order preventing publication.

The United States Supreme Court upheld the First Amendment to the Constitution, protecting freedom of the press and forbidding prior restraint. The order was voided, and the American people could read about their betrayal. Daniel Ellsberg was indicted for theft, espionage, and conspiracy, but the charges were eventually dropped. The *Times* won a Pulitzer Prize. And the printing of the Pentagon Papers helped set in motion a whole series of events which would come to be known as Watergate, and cost Richard Nixon his presidency.

1972   Meanwhile he could announce the withdrawal of another 750,000 troops and progress in peace talks with the North Vietnamese. The Paris negotiations (in which the government of South Vietnam refused to take part) produced

348

an eight-point plan. It included the release of all American prisoners in return for complete American withdrawal. But the talks broke down when the North launched the biggest attack in four years, across the demilitarized zone and deep into South Vietnam. The United States resumed bombing the North, and the U.S. Navy began mining Northern ports.

In February Nixon traveled to Beijing, beginning an eight-day trip that would open a new relationship with the People's Republic of China. He had been pursuing a policy of détente, a relaxation of the strained relations with the Soviet Union, and he wanted to assure Chairman Mao and Premier Zhou Enlai that China was not threatened. Though they were both Communist countries, China had feared the Russians for centuries; with this unprecedented "Journey for Peace," Nixon soothed Chinese anxieties. The visit ended with toasts to the "normalization" of their interests. He followed this initiative with a May trip to Moscow, the first time an American President had gone to the Soviet Union. A week of discussion with Soviet leaders produced an historic agreement on strategic weapons. Personal diplomacy was adding to Nixon's stature as a world leader.

The headquarters of the Democratic National Committee were located in the elegant Watergate complex of offices, apartments, restaurants and hotel overlooking the Potomac River. There, in mid-June, a security guard caught five clumsy burglars in the act of breaking into the DNC suite. The big brains behind this imbecilic crime were outside, protecting the burglars by their vigilance; they, too, were arrested. Four of the burglars were Cubans, veterans of the Bay of Pigs fiasco; the fifth was a former FBI and CIA man, supposedly a technical expert on bugging and other exciting spy stuff. The two sentries in the corridors also had FBI and CIA connections—one of them had been a major field operations man during the Bay of Pigs episode.

After the seven were fingerprinted, questioned, and identified, they proved to be employees of the Committee to Re-Elect the President (CRP or, as it came to be called, CREEP), and on the White House payroll. In the aftermath of the Pentagon Papers, Richard Nixon suspected that inside information about his administration was being leaked to his political opponents. A special "Plumbers Unit" was set up to stop leaks (a little White House humor), and the Watergate burglary was approved because DNC files could yield the names of informers. The "plumbers" might learn something about Democratic campaign strategy, or dig up dirt about Democratic leaders. While they were at it, they could plant bugs in the office phones. Now they were caught, and it was an embarrassment. But since bugging unfriendly phones and other political dirty tricks were not unknown in prior administrations and campaigns, Watergate was almost forgotten as the election year heated up. The Republican convention renominated Richard Nixon and Spiro Agnew. There were rumors about the fantastic amounts of money being raised by CREEP in a year when they couldn't lose.

The Democrats nominated an anti-war candidate, Senator George McGovern of South Dakota. He named Sergeant Shriver, head of the Peace Corps and John Kennedy's brother-in-law, as his running mate. Alabama Governor George Wallace was running as a third party candidate, but had to drop out of the race when he was shot and critically wounded during a campaign appearance in a Maryland shopping center. His assailant was twenty-one-year-old Arthur Bremer, who also wounded two other people in the shooting. He was tried, convicted, and received a sentence of sixty-three years.

The Democrats were badly beaten in the November election. George McGovern carried only the state of Massachusetts.

In December the wife of one of the

Watergate masterminds died in a Chicago plane crash. She was found to be carrying $10,000 in cash, all in $100 bills, and presumably it was hush money—but for whom?

In January Paris negotiations ended the American involvement in Vietnam. The Peace Agreement called for withdrawal of all United States forces, the return of U.S. prisoners of war, and a cease fire. The civil war went on as long as a separate government could pretend to hold the South, but American troops began to come home.

When Betty Friedan published *The Feminine Mystique* in 1963, it struck a chord in even the happiest housewife. In 1966 she became the first president of the National Organization of Women (NOW), which attracted thousands of women from those who made up more than 40 percent of the country's workforce. NOW tried to get a Constitutional Equal Rights Amendment (ERA) to ban discrimination against working women because of their sex (an idea that women had discussed since the 1920s). Congress adopted it in 1972, and sent it to the states for ratification, but it failed.

Nevertheless, equal job opportunities and equal pay remained as central objectives of the feminist movement. Another was a woman's right to control her own body. Abortion was strongly opposed by the Catholic Church, some other religious denominations, and many conservative Americans. Forty-six states still banned the operation, condemning many desperate women to painful and often fatal back-alley procedures to terminate a pregnancy. *Roe v. Wade* was the 1973 Supreme Court case in which the Justices overturned those laws, seven-two. The states could not prevent abortion during the first three months of pregnancy, and could regulate but not prohibit abortion in the second trimester.

These were also times of increased militancy among Native Americans. Indians were now American citizens, and tribes dealt with the states and with Washington on a government-to-government basis. But twenty years earlier, Congress had voted for termination of federal support for the tribes, and in many ways the 1950s had seen major reversals of government Indian policy. This sparked organized protest in the 1960s and early 1970s.

There were "fish-ins" in Washington State to protest government restrictions on Indian fishing rights. Water rights for tribes living in the arid west became a bitter issue as many tribes chose to fight through the courts for a larger share of scarce water resources. In 1969, several hundred Indians seized Alcatraz Island, site of the abandoned federal prison in San Francisco Bay. They held it for nineteen months and briefly focused media attention on Indian anger. In the 1972 Trail of Broken Treaties incident, Indians took over the Bureau of Indian Affairs headquarters in Washington.

Wounded Knee, South Dakota, was remembered by Indians for the massacre of men, women, and children by the United States seventh Cavalry Division in 1890—the last "battle" between U.S. military forces and Indians, provoked by white fear of the growing Ghost Dance religion among the Sioux and white greed for the rumored gold in the Black Hills. In February, 1973, nearly three hundred Oglala Sioux returned to Wounded Knee and demanded the restoration of Indian rights and land.

Poverty programs of the Kennedy and Johnson administrations had brought some economic development to the reservations, and Johnson inaugurated re-emphasis on Indian self-determination. More gains were made under Richard Nixon, who returned sacred lands taken from New Mexico's Taos Pueblo in 1906. The Alaska Native Claims Settlement Act gave Indians, Aleuts and Inuits 40 million acres of land along with mineral rights and compensation for past losses. The 1972 Indian Education Act established major new education programs. But Indians remained the poorest ethnic group in the country. The Supreme Court upheld Indian rights to half the harvestable fish in the state of Washington, but discouraged hopes for more water rights in the west. Though some tribes had income from minerals or timber, the natural resources that had sustained traditional tribal economies were gone. For too many Indian families, reservation life was one of unemployment, disease, and grinding poverty.

In October Egypt and Syria launched a three-week war on Israel, which recovered some previously lost territory and restored Arab self respect. President Nixon, a strong supporter of the state of Israel, anxiously watched the early fighting, and as Israeli war supplies appeared to be running low, he wanted to re-supply the threatened country. His national security advisor restrained him, warning of a Russian entry into the conflict, and a Russian-American confrontation. Fortunately, Egypt's President Sadat decided for withdrawal. Israel won the war with only minimal American airlifted help.

Meanwhile, the Watergate burglars had been tried and convicted. The case might have been closed, but by now there was too much talk about the "plumbers," and about huge contributions to the Nixon campaign fund. The Senate created a Select Committee on Presidential Campaign Activities, chaired by courtly Senator Sam Ervin of North Carolina. Televised hearings made it clear that CREEP had been up to some very fishy business. There had been other break-in attempts before the Watergate event, including a ransacking of the office of Daniel Ellsberg's psychiatrist.

One of the Watergate burglars wrote a letter to his judge, admitting that they had been pressured by the administration to keep quiet. Nixon's former Attorney General, who was now running CREEP, was named, as were more and more of Nixon's top aides. He tried to distance himself from even his closest associates; got resignations from his Chief-of-Staff, his adviser on domestic affairs, his legal adviser. The acting director of the FBI resigned, after revealing that he had been told to destroy Watergate evidence. When a witness before the Senate committee told of tape recording equipment in the Oval Office and other rooms of the White House, and secretly taped conversations there, Senator Ervin demanded that the tapes be made available to the committee. The President refused, claiming "executive privilege."

And he had other problems. Vice President Spiro Agnew had just pleaded "no contest" in a case that had nothing to do with Watergate. He was facing tax-evasion charges dating back to his time as governor of Maryland.) After Agnew resigned, Nixon had to name a Vice-President, and he appointed Gerald Ford of Michigan, the House Minority Leader.

But the secret tapes were the issue, a clear confrontation between the executive and legislative branches of government. In May, Nixon was forced to appoint a special prosecutor, and a federal grand jury subpoenaed the tapes. The President refused again, offering a "synopsis" of their contents. Archibold Cox, the special prosecutor insisted. The president ordered his Attorney General to fire the special prosecutor. Instead, both the Attorney General and his deputy resigned; the man next in line at the Justice Department had to do the firing. This "Saturday Night Massacre" created an uproar in Congress as members were flooded with mail from furious citizens. (And all this went on while Richard Nixon was trying to make decisions during the Egyptian-Israeli war; when American troops were being alerted to a possible face-off with the Soviet Union.)

Months earlier a member of the House had introduced a resolution calling for the President's impeachment. At that time the House had refused to vote, but now New

York Representative Peter Rodino announced that the House Judiciary Committee would investigate impeachment charges, and he put out a book of historical documents on the process for House study.

Finally Nixon turned over some of his tapes to the Senate Committee, but one had a mysterious eighteen and a half minutes of silence, which his secretary called an accidental erasure while she was typing a transcript. New charges and more confessions were in the news every day. Officials from top American corporations pleaded guilty to the illegal Nixon campaign contributions extracted by the campaign treasurer, the former Secretary of Commerce. It was learned that the Secretary of State had his own secret wiretaps on government officials and journalists. That material had disappeared from FBI files, but later turned up in a White House safe. Over the next months, twenty-one top White House staff members and lesser members of the administration team were indicted and convicted—former Cabinet members, the new Attorney General and several legal aides, consultants, and, of course, the Watergate "plumbers;" also some corporate executives. Charges ranged from refusal to answer questions on the witness stand, lying to the Senate committee or the grand jury; violations of the federal Corrupt Practices Act, or of civil rights; forgery; obstruction of justice; giving or taking illegal campaign contributions; plain and fancy skullduggery. Fines and prison sentences were handed out, but not many served their full time.

1974

Meanwhile the embattled President himself was investigated by another congressional committee, and agreed to pay $400,000 in back taxes; later there were more complicated tax questions. He made a trip to Egypt in July, just before the grand jury named him a co-conspirator in the Watergate mess. Still he continued to withhold tapes and subpoenaed documents, saying he would provide a 1,200 page transcript instead. Not until the Supreme Court issued an order did he finally comply.

The tapes proved what most people had come to believe—that Nixon had not only known about the Watergate break-in and other illegal activity that went on before and after his re-election, but that most of it was instigated by his orders.

Gerald Ford

The House Judiciary Committee had already approved two articles of impeachment, and later added another. Without any debate, the House of Representatives accepted the Judiciary Committee report and its recommendation of impeachment. President Nixon did not wait for the humiliation of an impeachment trial. On August 9, he resigned and departed for California, waving to friends and the weeping White House staff from the door of the helicopter, giving the V-sign, with his exhausted wife and expressionless daughters behind him. Gerald Ford was sworn in as President, and he named New York Governor Nelson Rockefeller as Vice-President. In September President Ford granted Nixon a "full, free, and absolute pardon" for all offenses he "has committed or may have committed or taken part in while president."

1975

There continued to be news about Watergate convictions and sentencing, but the country turned off the television coverage and shook itself awake, as if from a long nightmare.

And the nightmare in Vietnam ended in April as helicopters evacuated the last American civilians. Desperate South Vietnamese civilians clawed and trampled each other, begging to be taken aboard before the Viet Cong arrived in Saigon. There was no room for them, but two weeks later Congress voted $405 million for aid, and planes were provided to fly more than a hundred thousand refugees to America. It had been the nation's longest war; it killed more than a million

Vietnamese; it cost 58,000 American lives; the tonnage of bombs dropped on North Vietnam was more than the United States dropped in World War II. But after a generation of fighting, the Communist takeover was complete. Revolutionary peasants had beaten us in South Vietnam, and in Cambodia and Laos.

An embarrassing postscript to U.S. involvement in Southeast Asia was the Mayaguez incident. It was an American merchant ship, seized by Cambodia at an island in the Gulf of Siam, the crew of nineteen taken to the mainland and detained for two and a half days. Nobody was hurt; the prisoners were well treated. After they were released and headed for the U.S. Navy in a fishing boat, President Ford ordered a Marine attack on the island, and American planes bombed a mainland airbase. Forty-one Americans died; the number of Cambodians killed by bombing and strafing was unreported. But President Ford, his Secretary of State, the Secretary of Defense, and all but a few members of Congress glowed with pride. This country might have lost in Vietnam, but it could not be trifled with. It could unleash its deadly force on any enemy, whenever necessary. And even when completely unnecessary, costly, dumb, and wrong.

Watergate had tarnished the image of the Federal Bureau of Investigation and the Central Intelligence Agency. The Senate set up the Church Committee to investigate the CIA, which had gone far beyond its military intelligence assignment. The agency had information about 300,000 citizens and about organizations involved in anti-war and black protest; many of those groups had been infiltrated by CIA agents. It had connections with teachers at more than a hundred colleges and universities, pushing CIA propaganda in the classroom; it subsidized books read by thousands of students and other Americans. It was implicated in several unsuccessful assassination attempts on foreign leaders. It tried to "destabilize" elected governments in Latin

America and Africa.

A House committee held hearings on the FBI. Director J. Edgar Hoover had begun his career during the Red Scare of 1920; in the 1930s his G-men fought organized crime, the Sicilian Mafia that had seized a business opportunity during Prohibition, as well as home-grown criminal talent like John Dillinger and "Machine Gun" Kelly; in the 1940s, G-men broke up Nazi spy rings; in 1961, Attorney General Robert Kennedy urged Hoover to investigate the criminal activities of organizations like the Ku Klux Klan; but Hoover was less interested in crime than in his first enthusiasm—the pursuit of suspected subversives and social deviants. He collected dossiers on thousands of citizens, including some very prominent people. The FBI penetrated left-wing groups and conducted many illegal covert operations, forgeries, burglaries, possibly even a murder plot. Powerful political leaders who shared Hoover's anti-Red obsessions (and feared his dossiers) protected him. Hoover gave them useful information; they let him build his own power base and operate almost independently, outside the law.

Both Congressional committees worked with the agencies they were investigating. If the CIA wanted facts omitted, they were left out of the Senate committee report. The House committee kept its report secret; publication was suppressed. So, in the end, the public learned very little about either agency, and had no way to judge if they were useful or destructive in matters of national security or crime control.

1976

July brought the 200th anniversary of American independence, an occasion for great celebration. There were parades and festivities across the country. Most spectacular was New York's "Operation Sail," when tall sailing ships from around the world arrived in the harbor to delight the city multitudes, while six million watched on television.

Something was certainly needed to raise national morale, because at the same time that the country was enduring Watergate, there had been an economic recession. The number of people counted as "poor" had risen 10 percent; unemployment rates had gone up; inflation continued to rise. After the Egypt-Israel war, the Organization of Arab Petroleum Exporting Countries (OPEC) embargoed oil shipments to countries that had sided with Israel. The United States, with about 6 percent of the world's population, used more than a third of the world's oil, and immediately felt the result of the embargo. At the gas pump, drivers got a rude shock when the price was increased almost twenty cents a gallon. To conserve oil, a national speed limit of fifty-five miles per hour was established. Many Americans suspected that oil companies—among the richest corporations in the nation—were using the embargo to get even richer. As tea had been dumped into Boston harbor two hundred years earlier, boxes labeled "Gulf Oil" and "Exxon" bobbed in the water now.

Political scandal and economic woes led to a Republican defeat in the November election. President Ford could not justify the pardon he had given Richard Nixon, nor offer a quick answer to the recession. He lost to a Washington outsider, former Georgia Governor Jimmy Carter, who ran with Senator Walter Mondale of Minnesota. Carter was a graduate of the U.S. Naval Academy, and had worked on the navy's nuclear reactor project. During his single term as governor he accomplished reorganization of state government and took a strong stand on civil rights. The turnout at the polls was larger than in 1972, but Carter's margin of victory was narrow.

Jimmy Carter

1977

Though he had never strongly opposed the war in Vietnam, Carter quickly pardoned most of the ten thousand draft evaders. That was about his last gesture toward the "peaceniks."

Though he had told the Democratic platform committee that military expenditures could be reduced by "five to seven percent annually," his first budget called for a ten billion dollar increase in defense spending. That meant that social programs could not be funded, even though unemployment stayed high and inflation continued to rise. Still the poor got poorer. He appointed Patricia Harris, a black woman, to his Cabinet, and Andrew Young, a civil rights activist, to be ambassador to the United Nations. But almost 30 percent of young black people were out of work. A new Cabinet office was the Department of Energy, created in response to the oil crisis. It developed new conservation programs and coordinated energy policy, looking for alternative energy sources. However, there was no easy fix—the appetite of a gas-guzzling society was not easily appeased.

1978

In February, Carter talked to the country about energy conservation. Drive your car less, and slower; turn down the thermostat. He was right, of course, but the message didn't have much effect on the American people. A second speech had to do with the energy legislation he would send to Congress. It arrived in five volumes, each as big as a telephone book. It was enormously complex because the problem was complex. Members of Congress were lobbied hard by automobile and oil companies. The bill they passed was far from what the President wanted.

In April the Senate voted to approve President Carter's renegotiation of the Panama Canal treaty. America had created the Republic of Panama in a 1903 revolution, in return for a treaty that gave us the Canal Zone "in perpetuity," forever. It was Teddy Roosevelt's greatest achievement because it gave the United States much faster and cheaper transport from the Pacific Ocean to the Atlantic, for commercial and naval purposes, as well as several military bases. It saved American shippers more than a billion dollars a year; the government collected over a million in toll charges, and we paid Panama about 1.5 percent of that amount for "rent." No wonder that the Panamanians, seventy-five years later, felt that they had been ripped off. Anti-American demonstrations, and the fact that the Canal had lost much of its importance to the U.S. Navy (big ships couldn't use it) led to the new Carter treaties. One agreed that Panama would take over the Canal in 1999, and the Neutrality Treaty guaranteed Panamanian neutrality after the year 2000.

The President had more success when he met at Camp David with Egyptian President Anwar Sadat and Israeli Prime Minister Menachem Begin, attempting to broker a peace agreement between two long-standing enemies. It was a tense week, requiring all the President's intelligence, patience, and determination. It was also a dangerous week, because there was always a chance that assassins might penetrate the tight security and kill one or all of the negotiators. When a treaty was finally reached, the whole world breathed easier, for it was truly an historic shift in Middle East relations and brought the hope that this global flashpoint could be damped down. It won the Nobel Peace Prize for Begin and Sadat.

1979

One result of the oil crisis was a tremendously increased interest in the development of nuclear power as an alternative energy source. After American atomic bombs ended World War II, the government established the Atomic Energy Commission to regulate the production and use of atomic power for peaceful as well as military purposes. A 1974 reorganization ended the work of the Commission and separated its functions into the Energy Research and Development Administration and the Nuclear Regulatory Commission, which set safety standards and issued licenses. Many projects were undertaken and facilities built, mainly by big oil companies.

In March an accident occurred at the nuclear electric-power generating facility at Three-Mile Island near Harrisburg, Pennsylvania. One of the reactors went into a partial meltdown of its core and released radioactive gases into the air. When the accident was finally reported, state and local officials tried to give the public warnings and advice, but citizens were terrified; eventually 100,000 people were evacuated from the area. Despite reassurance by the Nuclear Regulatory Commission, anti-nuclear demonstrations were held across the country; the New York protest brought out more than 200,000 demonstrators. The TVA stopped construction on three nuclear plants, and other new projects were halted. Later in the year, OPEC announced another huge increase in the price of oil. Inflation reached 18 percent.

No industry was hit harder by oil prices than the automobile industry. Not only the direct costs of driving went up for public transportation, trucking, and private citizens, but the costs of car manufacturers and their suppliers. Petroleum was an essential material in the production of chemicals used in thousands of parts and processes. In the third quarter of 1979 Chrysler reported an operating loss of more than $460 million, and went to the government for a loan guarantee of $1.5 billion to save the company from bankruptcy. In a shaky economy, the jobs of half a million Chrysler employees and their dealers were at stake. After heated debate, Congress approved the loan guarantees, and Chrysler was saved.

During the Eisenhower administration, the CIA helped install the Shah of Iran in power, a military dictator who ruled for almost twenty-five years. The Shah, of course, was grateful to his American friends and American government, including Jimmy Carter's administration. He maintained order, and a tightly controlled political climate was good for American big business. But the people of Iran, whipped up by a fundamentalist Islamic leader, revolted against the dictatorship. Student militants took to the streets of Teheran, assaulted the American embassy, and seized ninety people, of whom sixty-three were Americans. Nineteen of those taken were released in a few weeks; the rest were held hostage for almost a year. President Carter first tried negotiations for a hostage release, then froze Iranian assets in the United States. But the turbulent internal politics of Iran worked against all his efforts.

Finally he attempted a helicopter rescue mission which failed miserably. Some of the aircraft malfunctioned, eight Americans died and five were wounded, none of the prisoners were rescued. The doomed effort also doomed Carter's political future.

1980

He had not been able to deal with the country's economic problems and could not control inflation. He responded to a Soviet invasion of Afghanistan by placing an embargo on United States shipments of grain and high technology to the Soviet Union (which did not bother most Americans) and by asking the U.S. Olympic Committee not to participate in the Moscow summer games (which angered millions who anticipated the international sports competition). And the hostages were still held in Iran. It was clear that he faced defeat in the upcoming elections.

The country was distracted by the tremendous eruption of Mount St. Helens, an 8,400 foot volcano in Washington State. The first blast was estimated to be five hundred times as powerful as the atomic bomb dropped on Hiroshima; it was followed by two more within a month, costing sixty lives and almost $3 billion in damages. The surrounding forest land, destroyed by lava flows and volcanic ash, would take generations to recover.

The election was a Republican explosion. President Kennedy's youngest brother, Ted, ran against Jimmy Carter for the

Democratic nomination. He was a liberal favorite, but still stained by a tragic and scandalous episode in his private life. He campaigned in ten primaries before he with drew. The Democratic party renominated Carter and Mondale.

Representative John Anderson, a liberal Republican from Illinois, wanted the GOP nomination, and George Bush from Massachusetts and Texas fought hard for the top spot on the ballot, but the convention favorite was former movie star and Governor of California Ronald Reagan. Bush had to settle for the vice presidential nomination; Anderson formed a third party and ran as an independent.

Ronald Reagan

1981

Ronald Reagan won a landslide victory. It was certainly impressive in terms of the electoral vote—he won forty-four of the fifty states. Jimmy Carter got 41 percent of the count, and the independent John Anderson got something over 6.5 percent. Reagan's win carried the Senate with him, and gained many new Republican seats in the House.

Mysteriously, moments after Reagan's inauguration, the hostages held in Iran were released and were flown home to appropriate rejoicing. In return, the United States returned $8 billion in frozen Iranian assets.

In March, after finishing a speech in Washington, President Reagan was the target of an assassination attempt. Shot in the chest, he narrowly escaped death, but he endured his hospitalization with gallantry and good humor. When he was fully recovered, he went to work on the program he had promised during the campaign. Reagan had been a New Deal Democrat; he voted four times for Franklin Roosevelt. But now the New Deal was over.

In his first year he accomplished the biggest increase in defense spending in American history, replacing outdated military hardware to regain at least parity with the Soviet Union, though leaving land-based missiles vulnerable to Soviet superiority. The president proposed to balance the budget with huge cutbacks in domestic programs. His eight hundred page legislative package called for reductions in Social Security and Medicare payments; college education benefits and student loans were cut; unemployment compensation was reduced from thirty-nine to twenty-six weeks; food stamp recipients got less or were struck off the roles entirely.

This was coupled with the biggest tax cuts in history. Administration spokesman explained their thinking as "supply-side" theory, a trickle-down policy which, by benefiting the rich, would eventually help the middle class and the poor. When he had run against Ronald Reagan in Republican primary campaigns a year earlier, George Bush had called this "voodoo" economics. Even earlier, Republican Progressives had called it "feeding the sparrows by feeding the horses." But Congress accepted it, despite a recession, interest increases, and growing unemployment.

Ronald Reagan was a small-town boy who had reached the top in Hollywood. He knew how to package himself and his programs. He was a handsome man with a genuinely warm and engaging grin; the media loved his relaxed style and quotable quips. The superb work of White House staff, and the president's affability, managed Congress and held an effective coalition together. His wife, Nancy, had also enjoyed a Hollywood career; now they had the brightest spotlights and the loudest applause of their lives. It was the ultimate stardom.

1982

On the whole, the record of the feminist movement was mixed. A ten-year campaign for ratification of the Equal Rights Amendment had attracted a larger and more diverse membership to the National Organization of Women. By 1982 it had reached 210,000, ranging from the more conservative members with a legislative focus to the fiercest liberationists, who challenged the basic assumptions of American life. For the "women's libbers," the struggle went beyond equal pay to issues of gender attitude and sexual harassment, class, violence within relationships, health care, and much more. The law had given them the right to vote, but birth control pills had given them another kind of freedom, which they intended to exercise.

In this year, the ERA campaign failed. The movement ran into a backlash from the political and religious right, and the weakening of the economy distracted women from liberation theory. Yes, the number of women elected to public office (particularly in state and local government) had risen rapidly. A bright spot was the 1981 appointment of Sandra Day O'Connor as an Associate Justice of the Supreme Court. She proved to be a centrist judge who generally agreed with restrictions on abortion, but refused to overturn *Roe v. Wade*. The number of women in professional careers had dramatically increased 20 percent of the students in medical, law, and business schools were women, compared to 5 percent twenty years earlier; many colleges had created programs in women's studies.

But the recession that began in 1979, after the OPEC oil crisis, had gotten steadily worse, and the promised benefits of Reaganomics were slow to trickle down. Unemployment continued to rise all year, reaching 10.8 percent of the labor force in December, a forty-two year high. A quarter of the country's children were now living in poverty. Without the national purchasing power that jobs provided, businesses failed, factories closed, and bankruptcies multiplied. Housing starts dropped drastically; farmers, as usual, took a beating.

Then suddenly the oil shortage ended. New oil discoveries in non-OPEC countries— Great Britain, Norway, Mexico—broke the

Middle East hold on international business, and America began to recover.

1983 Lebanon was a Middle Eastern country that had been in a more or less constant state of uproar for many years. Various factions were aided by outside support and troops, notably Palestinians, Syrians, and Israelis. United States Marines intervened in 1958. A 1975-1976 civil war killed 60,000 people and did billions of dollars in damage. Terrorism became a way of life.

In 1983 a bomb exploded in the American embassy, killing fifty people. Later in the year, 240 American servicemen and fifty-five French soldiers died in Muslim suicide attacks. In the following year, there was more civil war, and terrorists took seventeen American hostages at the Beirut airport. Kidnappings went on throughout the Reagan presidency, and many victims were held for ten years or more. During that time nobody knew if they were alive or dead and, if alive, where they were held. One was the CIA head of station, and he was of special concern to the administration because of the likelihood of torture and what he could be forced to reveal. (He did, in fact, die under torture, but it was years before our government learned his fate.) Remembering Jimmy Carter's failure in Iran, President Reagan refused to negotiate or make any deal that could encourage more kidnappings.

While Marines were dying in Lebanon, Marines and army rangers landed in Grenada, a 120-square-mile island (a little bigger than the State of Delaware) in the Caribbean. The invasion, called Urgent Fury, was undertaken because a revolutionary coup overthrew the government and killed the prime minister. There were Cuban troops on the island, thinly disguised as "workers," but possibly training terrorists. There was some risk to American students attending an island medical school. Although a *New York Times* report said that there was no evidence that the students couldn't leave if they wanted to, and none of them was harmed, President Reagan claimed that the Marines got there "just in time." Within a few days, all Americans were evacuated and the Communist revolution was finished. Unfortunately, Reagan had forgotten to inform British Prime Minister Margaret Thatcher about Operation Urgent Fury, although Grenada was a part of the British Commonwealth. She was really furious. American troops left the island in December, after Congress invoked the War Powers Act.

The American space program continued to grow. There had been successful shuttle launches in 1981-1982, demonstrating the potential usefulness of a reusable space vehicle. The Challenger was launched in 1983, and Sally Ride became the first woman in space as a crew member on its second flight. The third crew included Guion Bluford as the first black astronaut.

1984

There would be fourteen shuttle launches in 1984-1985, because President Reagan supported developments in space science. He was particularly intrigued by the "Star Wars" project, the Strategic Defense Initiative (SDI). The American people were told that American space technology could create a system that intercepted enemy missiles in mid-flight, a "shield" in space to render any missile attack harmless. It was certainly a scenario right out of a television drama, but it didn't work. Billions were spent, but the first tests of the technology were ambiguous, and it hasn't worked yet.

Money was also poured into conventional weapons. The CIA constantly submitted information about Soviet military spending. Though in 1984 it was admitted that much CIA data was exaggerated and misleading, "Defense" spending in Reagan's first term was increased by $181 billion. Federal spending far outran income.

The administration was determined to live down the American humiliation in Vietnam. It turned its attention to Nicaragua, where a "Sandinista" revolution had deposed a corrupt regime and started programs of land reform and other help to the peasant population. The sorry history of Nicaragua included many instances of American intervention. Marine occupations in the early part of the twentieth century ended with Franklin Roosevelt's Good Neighbor policy. Now the CIA organized a counter-revolution, to overthrow what was seen to be a Communist success. Contra-Sandinista forces were armed and trained in Florida, and then operated from bases in Costa Rica and Honduras. After the CIA admitted putting mines in Nicaraguan waters, Congress passed a resolution making it illegal for the United States to support "directly or indirectly, military or paramilitary operations in Nicaragua." But the administration found ways to get money and weapons to the Contras, which would lead to an enormous and very complicated scandal.

Meanwhile, the President visited China for the first time and held discussions with Chinese leaders, maintaining his high visibility and popularity with voters in an election year. There was no question of his Republican renomination.

The Democrats turned to Walter Mondale, Jimmy Carter's vice president and former Senator from Minnesota. The surprise nomination was that of Geraldine Ferraro, a Representative from New York, to be his running mate. She thus became the first woman to run for the second highest office in the country. She was a liberal and a Catholic, supported ERA and a pro-choice position on abortion. But 56 percent of women voters preferred Ronald Reagan and vice presidential candidate George Bush. This election was the greatest Republican victory in history. Ronald Reagan carried forty-nine states.

Reagan's new term began with resumption of U.S.-Soviet talks on nuclear arms reduction, while he continued his efforts to get Congressional approval for increased funding to support a counter-revolution in Nicaragua. A Marine Lieutenant-Colonel named Oliver North was already working on a scheme to bypass the Congress. It involved procuring Contra aid from other governments. Both Saudi Arabia and Israel agreed to supply covert arms; the hostile government of Iran got United States weapons after it promised to use its considerable influence with Muslim terrorists to obtain the release of kidnapped Americans. Money from arms sales to Iran could be used for Nicaragua's Contras.

Though the secretaries of state and defense opposed such shady deals, the president decided to go ahead. He was joined by Robert MacFarlane, the national security advisor, and also by Admiral John M. Poindexter. Lieutenant-Colonel North was MacFarlane's deputy, a Vietnam veteran who still smarted from that defeat. He was grimly resolved to be a winner in Nicaragua. With the help of military men and the CIA, he would put together his own cloak-and-dagger connections and subvert Congressional restraints; he hoped to give the president two public triumphs— return of American hostages from Lebanon and return of the Contras to power in Nicaragua. But all of this complicated plot remained a closely-kept secret for more than a year.

At the same time, the President pursued the diplomatic high road at a summit conference in Geneva, Switzerland, where U.S. and Soviet leaders met for the first time in six years. For two days he held private talks with General Secretary Mikhail Gorbachev, for whom the costs of the Cold War had become an unbearable burden.

Colonel North continued to implement his plans for secret weapons sales to Iran. The first shipment of anti-tank missiles arrived; the second failed; he went to work on a third delivery. And the President continued to praise the Contra "freedom fighters." Politically disinterested observers—men and women, missionaries and medical workers—called the Contras racketeers and thugs whose savage tactics would disgrace any cause.

1986

On January 20, Martin Luther King Day was observed as a national holiday for the first time, but the President declined to take a strong stand against blatant American racism. Foreign governments agreed on economic sanctions against South Africa, designed to end the white supremacist policy of apartheid, which cruelly oppressed the majority black population, but when Congress voted to join the international effort, President Reagan vetoed the bill, arguing that it would hurt blacks more than it could help them. Congress overrode his veto.

The country had other concerns. A terrible shock came in January, when the ninth Challenger space shuttle exploded moments after liftoff, killing all the crew. The tragedy was laid directly at the door of NASA, which had ignored safety problems.

And then, one day before the mid-term Congressional elections, the country learned about the sale of United States weapons to the anti-American government of Iran; Robert MacFarlane and Oliver North had traveled to Iran as part of the undertaking. Newspapers printed the first reports of the scandal; within weeks the rest of the story began to unravel. The proceeds of this Iranian deal had paid for arms to the Contras. As the North scheme was exposed, top American officials lied about the whole affair. The Secretary of State and the assistant secretary lied. At his November press conference, the President lied. When the press refuted their stories, Reagan appointed a commission to investigate.

1987

The President's commission reported that the

President was confused and uninformed about Iran-Contra, and rebuked him for failing to control the National Security Council. But this did not satisfy the Congress; both Houses insisted on their own investigations. So the public was once again entertained by weeks of televised hearings. Oliver North was given immunity to testify, and the hearings made him a star. The handsome and candid young officer freely admitted details of his activities. The crimes—and they were crimes—were committed by the National Security Advisor, or by the head of the CIA. William Casey, head of the CIA, died before he could be called. William MacFarlane attempted suicide but survived. North stuck to his simple defense: he was trying to help the Contras in Nicaragua overthrow the communist Sandinistas, a goal so important that (as his secretary testified) "Sometimes you have to go above the written law."

President Reagan and Vice-President Bush came out of the mess with no more than a few bruises. A House resolution for the President's impeachment was suppressed. Others were indicted, including Oliver North, who stood trial for perjury. He was found guilty on three counts and sentenced to prison, but a sympathetic judge suspended the sentence and said that North had been made a fall guy. He walked away a hero to many citizens. Later he ran for the Senate, and lost. But others would keep trying to nail the Contragate villains—six years later the Secretary of Defense was indicted for lying to Congress—and some of the shine on the Reagan administration was tarnished. The basic questions raised by the scandal were never answered. The administration had wanted to pursue a foreign policy prohibited by Congress—and got away with it.

In December President Reagan and Mikhail Gorbachev reached an historic agreement to dismantle missiles with a range of 300 to 3,400 miles. They agreed to meet again in 1988, when President Reagan would be seventy-nine years old and in the last year of his presidency.

What was American policy in international affairs? The Cold War was ending; the Soviet Union, whose nuclear capabilities had terrified us for so long, was coming apart at the seams. But Presidents continued to use the fear of Communism to justify huge expenditures for defense, and sleazy operations like the illegal Contra support in Nicaragua. Reagan would admit only that his policy had "gone astray," and while White House staffers continued to point fingers at each other, neither Congress nor the press demanded a clear statement of what the policy had been.

1988

The new Immigration Reform and Control Act, passed in 1986, took effect. In May the Immigration and Naturalization Service offered amnesty to illegal aliens living in the United States, an opportunity to obtain the precious "Green Card" which gave foreigners the right to work. The Act was designed to penalize the employers of undocumented aliens, though penalties were light and not uniformly enforced. Almost a million and a half immigrants met the amnesty deadline. Nationwide, more than 70 percent were Mexican, and more than half of the applicants lived in California.

The new law was the latest Congressional effort to "control" immigration and "reform" policy. One of the earliest laws was the Chinese Exclusion Act of 1882. Chinese labor had been imported to build western railroads and to meet labor shortages during the Gold Rush, but when western white men began to worry about the growing Asian population, legislation slammed the door on Chinese immigrants. A gentlemen's agreement with Japan in 1907 ended the admission of Japanese laborers.

Ellis Island, in New York harbor, was the chief immigration station for newcomers from Europe. Nearby an inscription by poet Emma Lazarus spoke for the Statue of Liberty: "—Give me your tired, your poor...the wretched refuse...the homeless..." But the poet did not speak for legislators who began to devise quota systems. The intent of nationality-based quotas was to maintain the ethnic mix of the Old

Immigrants, the English-speaking Protestants, the Germans, and others from northern and western Europe. Even the Catholic Irish, feared and despised by Nativist "Know-Nothings" in the 1850s, were seen as preferable to the thousands of Italians, Poles, Russian Jews, Greeks, and assorted Slavs who flooded in from eastern and southern European countries. In 1924, the National Origins Act limited the annual number of immigrants to 154,000, plus the wives and minor children of immigrants who had become citizens. The base year for calculating national quotas was 1890. Future admissions of each nationality would be limited to 2 percent of its number in the 1890 U.S. population. That is, the number of Italians living in the United States in 1890 was determined, and 2 percent of that number would be admitted from Italy thereafter, and so on.

Of course, entry was much easier for Mexicans and people from Central America who traveled through Mexico to El Norte. The United States already had a large population of Mexican ancestry—since we had seized a third of that country in the Mexican War. During the 1920s nearly half a million Mexicans crossed the border. No passports were required; they could enter at any border town, or simply wade across the shallow Rio Grande. Driven north by poverty and civil war, as much as a tenth of Mexico's population migrated to the cotton fields of Texas, and the beet fields, orchards, and vineyards of California. They were needed, for southwest agriculture offered plenty of stoop labor jobs that no "Anglo" would accept. The Spanish-speaking population also grew with Puerto Ricans—American citizens—who established themselves in New York City; Cubans—admitted as refugees from Castro's rule—became a major presence in south Florida.

The deportation of illegal immigrants from any country was a continual headache, and a costly procedure. The Chinese Exclusion Act was allowed to expire in 1920, and by 1965, quotas based on nationalities were discontinued. New annual immigration limits were set. The country went on tinkering with immigration law, and it was a great subject for demagoguery, but no satisfactory answers could be found.

George Bush

The Republican convention nominated Vice President Bush by acclamation, after a challenge by Kansas Senator Bob Dole failed to gather much steam. Bush was exceptionally well-qualified. Son of a Connecticut Senator, George Bush served in World War II as a naval pilot, and was graduated from Yale University. After two terms in the House of Representative she was appointed United

States ambassador to the United Nations, and followed that service with a year in Beijing as head of the U.S. Liaison Office. During the Ford administration, he was director of the CIA. He sought the Republican nomination as President in 1980 but lost to Ronald Reagan, who immediately chose him to be Vice-President. With this experience, particularly in foreign affairs, the sixty-four-year-old Bush was seen as a strong successor to Reagan. For his running mate, he named personable young Senator Dan Quayle from Indiana.

The Democrats had to choose among several contenders for the top spot on the ballot: Michael Dukakis, governor of Massachusetts; the noted black civil rights leader, Jesse Jackson; Texas Senator Lloyd Bentsen; and Senator Gary Hart of Colorado, who dropped out of the race after some embarrassing exposure of his love life. The convention chose Dukakis, with Bentsen for Vice-President.

It was an easy win for George Bush because the economy was finally expanding, growing at a faster rate than at any time in four years. Unemployment was at a fourteen year low. Bush campaigned in the aura of Reagan popularity, but in his own style, calming American nerves, asking for a "kinder, gentler" nation.

1989   Since 1933, when many banks were forced to close, all banks that belonged to the Federal Reserve system had been required to insure their deposits; this protected depositors from the losses they suffered at the start of the Depression. But during the 1980s, many of the country's savings and loan institutions began to go under, due to mismanagement and sometimes to outright fraud, against which no insurance could guarantee protection. Now Congress had to pass a bill to save the industry. It provided $166 billion to shut down or merge failed S&Ls, and the total cost to taxpayers over the next thirty years would probably reach $500 billion. Six Senators came under fire for receiving improper gifts from beneficiaries of the bail-out.

President Bush nominated Army General Colin Powell as chairman of the Joint Chiefs of Staff, the first black man to hold the highest post in the American military. Black candidates for elected office also made notable gains. Douglas Wilder became the first black governor since reconstruction when he was elected in Virginia; David Dinkins became the first black mayor of New York City.

The United States invaded Panama in December, with 26,000 troops. The dictator of that country was General Manuel Noriega, a corrupt and brutal tyrant who had been indicted by two U.S. grand juries on drug charges. Noriega was long tolerated by the United States because he was useful to the CIA. Panama had been a base for Contra operations in Nicaragua; Noriega had cooperated and consulted with Oliver North, and was protected by George Bush when Bush was head of the CIA. With North's plotting at an end and Noriega's drug activities more blatant, he was an embarrassing nuisance. He seized power in the spring, invalidating a democratic election. In December the U.S. overthrew his regime and restored the elected government. Noriega took refuge in the Vatican diplomatic mission, but finally surrendered.

1990 The President signed a bill to raise the minimum wage from $3.35 to $4.25 an hour by 1991; it permitted a $3.35 training wage for young people sixteen to nineteen years of age in their first three months on a job. In another economic measure, he proposed to reduce the huge federal budget deficit by almost $500 billion over five years. Though "No New Taxes" had been the centerpiece of his '80 campaign, he signed a bill raising the top income tax rate and phasing out exemptions for the rich; it also increased the tax rate on gas, cigarettes, and liquor, and imposed a luxury tax on some items like planes, boats, cars, furs, and jewelry.

Despite these efforts, the economic picture grew more dismal. In the fourth quarter of the year, gross domestic product (the sum total of all the goods and services produced in the country) plunged, while the deficit inherited from Ronald Reagan continued to climb, reaching almost $259 billion dollars. Unemployment was rising, as were consumer prices. The pesident might tax yachts, but the basic maldistribution of wealth in America remained. Violent crime, and drug related crime, increased sharply.

1991

American forces won a short war in Iraq. It was not, at the outset, a war that any American favored. Most people probably confused Iraq with Iran, but those with a grasp of Middle Eastern geography and politics probably knew that Iraq had invaded and attempted to annex Kuwait, its small, oil-rich neighbor. The United Nations had voted sanctions against Iraq, which seemed to be having some effect. But Saddam Hussein, the dictator of Iraq, now appeared to be threatening Saudi Arabia, and a victory there would give him control of the region's oil supply. The UN set a January deadline for Iraqi withdrawal. When Hussein ignored the order, President Bush asked Congress for authority to send troops.

Since protection of Saudi Arabia was the ostensible reason for the war, it was called Operation Desert Shield. On January 17 the United States air force and navy aircraft, supported by gunnery and cruise missiles from warships in the Persian Gulf, began an air attack to crush strategic targets in Iraq and to cripple Saddam's ground forces. Then, brilliantly led by General H. Norman Schwartzkopf, U.S. infantry, armored, airborne, and marine divisions, augmented by Saudi Arabian forces and North Atlantic Treaty Organization (NATO) divisions from France and Britain, surrounded and cut off enemy troops in five days.

Modern weaponry played a major role in the brief war. Particularly fascinating were the so-called "smart bombs," laser-guided missiles that could hit military targets with perfect precision and leave the civilian population untouched. At least that's what Pentagon officials told the public, and that's what the media told the television audience. In fact, this surgical procedure was less effective than reported; the air force had to bring in B-52s with conventional bombs, which had little concern for dead civilians but got the job done. Two hundred Americans died in Operation Desert Shield. Pentagon estimates of Iraqi combat death was about 100,000—Hussein's soldiers were mercilessly bombed as they fled from Allied attack. The Iraqi civilian dead were uncounted, though the number is thought to include 40,000 children under the age of five.

Hussein was reviled in the United States media as a conscienceless monster, but he was not pursued into his own country. The United Nations Security Council demanded tough reparations, including destruction of all Iraqi chemical and biological weapons, but otherwise he remained in power. The war was a demonstration of American military prowess, meant to impress OPEC countries and guarantee an unlimited supply of Arab oil for the U.S. There was a short surge of popularity for President Bush (he said, "The specter of Vietnam has been buried deep in the desert sands of the Arabian peninsula"). General Schwarzkopf and Chief of Staff Colin Powell emerged as heroes.

Justice Thurgood Marshall, the first black to serve on the Supreme Court, announced his retirement. The president nominated and the Senate narrowly approved another black Justice as conservative as Marshall was liberal, to succeed him on the bench. Clarence Thomas survived testimony by a young black woman law professor, who accused him of sexual harassment. The hearings were another television funfest. Thomas was confirmed by a fifty-two-forty-eight vote.

As unemployment continued to climb, President Bush signed a bill to extend benefits to unemployed workers, from six to twenty weeks. On the other hand, the stock market boom continued, the Gross National Product rose, and Bush said, "The recession appears to have ended." But mixed economic signals worried voters. Major retail chains and airlines filed bankruptcy. The Big Three auto manufacturers announced huge losses, as did IBM. By mid-year, the unemployment level was higher than at any time since the spring of 1984. Congress voted to extend benefits further for long-term unemployed workers during a recession. A proposed Constitutional Amendment to require a balanced budget was introduced in Congress and defeated.

The most frightening news of the year came from Los Angeles, where four policemen were accused of beating a black man, Rodney King, within an inch of his life. A jury that included four blacks acquitted the police. (They were convicted in a later trial on federal charges.) When television showed video tapes of the beating, massive riots, looting, and arson broke out in Los Angeles and other major cities. The Los Angeles death toll was fifty-two people. Six hundred buildings were torched, and damages ran to $1 billion. An uneasy calm was not restored until army, marine, and national guard units moved into the battle area. But Rodney King was not forgotten, and increasing racial violence would be America's most serious problem for the rest of the decade. Much of the violence was perpetrated by blacks against other blacks, by gangs in crowded housing projects where unemployment, poverty, and drugs increased the tension and misery, and guns were too easily available. The struggle for racial justice was increasingly complicated by the psychosociology of black youths with no hope of a better future.

President Bush and Vice-President Quayle ran

Bill Clinton

379

for re-election. Bill Clinton, Governor of Arkansas, headed the Democratic ticket, with Senator Al Gore of Tennessee. Multi-millionaire Ross Perot was an on-again, off-again independent candidate who attracted a large following, and debated with Clinton and Bush in a widely-viewed television event. On November 3, he got 19 percent of the vote. Clinton won by a respectable margin, and Democrats retained both houses of Congress. Women, black, and Hispanic candidates captured 102 House seats, and Carol Moseley-Braun, a black woman was elected to the Senate.

EPILOGUE

In 1992, while most of the country prepared to celebrate the quincentennial of the arrival of Christopher Columbus, many native Americans decided to protest. Not only in North America, but throughout the hemisphere and the Caribbean Islands, indigenous people agreed that they had nothing to celebrate. Conquest of their ancestors by Europeans had brought disease, dispossession, enslavement, and murder. Their civilizations had been destroyed, their history obliterated.

The protest included books like this one, which began with Columbus, and totally ignored the obvious fact that there was a lot of American history before Columbus got here, Well, the author of this book is too ignorant to be able to include pre-Columbian people and events in this short account, but the protest has been heard by better writers, and by research scholars, and future educators will have to teach as much pre-Columbian history as can be recovered. It is not simply a question of "political correctness," but a commitment to tell the truth.

This book could only give a couple of pages to the Spanish 16th century of exploration and territorial acquisition, and a very brief summation of the next hundred years—how a handful of ill-prepared colonists landed in what is now Virginia, and starved but somehow hung on. From that unpromising beginning grew the United States of America, which in 1992 was the world's reigning super-power.

It is history unlike that of any other country. The early explorers and first settlers found a huge country with tremendous natural resources, thinly settled by many tribes who spoke many languages and could mount no effective resistance to the invaders. They were followed by wave after wave of smart, strong, and desperately determined immigrants. Never before had there been such a movement of people from all over the world, in such numbers, toward a new continent. New technologies and tools made it possible to develop the country with astonishing efficiency and productivity. Americans freed themselves from the restraints of colonialism and invented a new kind of government. They began to move out into the world with confidence. The United States was a rich country, able to afford unbeatable armies.

It was truly a land of hope and glory—and luck: Americans were lucky in their place and their time; beneficiaries of European genius, the Enlightenment and the Industrial Revolution; lucky in the leadership that emerged at critical moments.

That's exactly the kind of self-congratulatory history to which native Americans objected in 1992 because it omits the cruelties and crimes that darken the record—the thievery that stole this country from the American Indians, and penned them up on scraps of the continent for which the new claimants had no profitable plans, deprived of all the rights in which the nation took such pride. Much was written in our schoolbooks about the horrors of slavery but not enough about the treatment of black men and women in the years that followed emancipation of the slaves. It was bad enough to treat human beings as mere chattels, owned by other human beings like a mule or a hog or a hoe. Maybe it was worse to subjugate blacks through systematic intimidation and degradation, intended to convince the black man that he had even less value than a mule or a hog, no claim to respect, no place in the white man's world and to deny black children an education and an opportunity to achieve respect, find an equal place.

And let us not forget the crimes against nature itself, as blind greed devastated our hills and forests, poisoning the land and the water and the very air.

But, you may say, these were the crimes of our youth. And that's wrong because you can look around and see the same crimes committed every day. All right. We've heard the charges and we confess. From now on we'll go straight, be personally responsible and caring, get involved in the community, take political action.

Well, perhaps. In any case, this is a book that celebrates America, with all its scars and warts. We have much to celebrate, and a wonderful future to anticipate, if we keep our promises to each other. This great country can be made better and greater, if we love it.

Acknowledgment of Sources

Allan, Frederick Lewis. *Since Yesterday.* New York: Bantam Books, 1940.

Applebone, Peter. *Dixie Rising.* Random House, 1996.

American Heritage. *(selected readings)* December 1954 until March 1986. New York: American Heritage.

Axelrod, Dr. Alan. *Chronicle of the Indian Wars.* New York: Prentice Hall General Reference, 1993.

Axelrod, Dr. Alan, and Charles, Phillips. *What Every American Should Know about American History.* Holbrook, Massachusetts: Adams, 1992.

Ayres, William, ed. *Picturing History.* New York: Rizzoli, 1993.

Ballantine, Better, and Ballantine, Ian, ed. *The Native Americans.* Atlanta: Turner, 1993.

Barabba, Vincent P. *Bicentennial Edition, Historical Statistics of the U.S.—Colonial Times to 1970.* Washington, D.C.: U.S. Department of Commerce.

Beard, Charles A. *The Republic.* New York: The Viking Press, 1943.

Beardsley, Tom. *Willimantic Women: Their Lives & Labors.* Willimantic, Connecticut: Windham Textile & History Museum: 1990.

Bellamy, Francis Rufus. *The Private Life of George Washington.* New York: Crowell, 1951.

Berman, Harold J. *The Trial of the U2.* Chicago: Translation, World Publishers, 1960.

Bill, Alfred Hoyt. *Valley Forge: Making of An Army.* New York: Harper & Brothers, 1952.

Botking, B.A. *A Civil War Treasury of Tales, Legends and Folklore.* New York: Random House, 1960.

Bowen, Catherine Drinker. *John Adams and The American Revolution.* Boston: Little, Brown, 1950.

Bowen, Catherine Drinker. *Miracle at Philadelphia.* Boston: Little, Brown, 1966.

Brodie, Fawn M. *Thomas Jefferson an Intimate History.* New York: Norton, 1974.

Brogan, D.W. *The American Character.* New York: Random House, 1956.

Buckley, Monica, ed. *Illinois Women—75 Years of the Right to Vote.* Chicago: Sun-Times, 1996.

Burns, James MacGregor. *Roosevelt: The Soldier of Freedom.* New York: Harcourt Brace Jovanovich, 1970.

Burstein, Andrew. *The Inner Jefferson-Portrait of a Grieving Optimist.* Charlottesville: University Press of Virginia, 1995.

Butterfield, Roger. *American Past.* New York: Simon & Schuster, 1947.

Catton, Bruce. *Glory Road.* New York: Doubleday, 1952.

Catton, Bruce. *Never Call Retreat.* New York: Doubleday, 1965.

Chester, Lewis and Godfrey, Hodgson. *An American Melodrama.* New York: Viking Press, 1969.

Churchill, Winston S. *The New World.* New York: Dodd, Mead, 1962.

Churchill, Winston S. *The Age of Revolution.* New York: Mead, 1957.

Churchill, Winston S. *The Great Democracies.* New York: Mead, 1958.

Coates, Robert M. *The Outlaw Years.* New York: Macaulay, 1930.

Commager, Henry Steele. *The Blue and the Gray*. New York: Bobbs-Merrill, 1950.

Commager, Henry Steele, and Richard B. Morris,*The Spirit of 'Seventy-Six*. New York: Harper & Row, 1958.

Cooke, Alistair *Alistair Cooke's America*. New York: Knopf, 1973.

Coulter, E. Merton. *The Confederate States of America 1861-1865*. Louisiana: Louisiana State Univ. Press, 1959.

Crouse, Anna Erskine, and Crouse, Russell. *Alexander Hamilton & Aaron Burr*. New York: Random House, 1958.

Davidson, Marshall B. *Life in America. Vol. 2*. Boston: Houghton Mifflin, 1951.

Davis, Kenneth C. *Don't Know Much About History*. New York: Crown, 1990.

Debs, Eugene V. *Walls & Bars*. Chicago: Kerr, 1973.

DeVoto, Bernard. *The Course of Empire*. Boston: Houghton Mifflin, 1952.

Doren, Carl Van. *Benjamin Franklin's Autobiographical Writings*. New York: Viking Press, 1945.

Douglas, William O. *An Almanac of Liberty.* New York: Doubleday, 1954.

Edey, Maitland A., ed. *Time Capsule 1933.* New York: *Time,* 1967.

Elson, John. *History, the Sequel. Time, 7* November 1994

The Encyclopedia Britannica. *(selected readings)* Wm. Benton, Pub., 1963.

Fadiman, Clifton. *The American Treasury 1455-1955.* New York: Harper & Brothers, 1955.

Fawcett, Edmund and Tony Thomas. *The American Condition.* New York: Harper & Row, 1968.

Filippeli, Ronald, ed. *Labor Conflict in the U.S.* New York: Garland, 1990.

Flexner, Doris. *The Optimist's Guide to History.* New York: Avon Books, 1995.

Foner, Eric, ed. *The Reader's Companion to American History.* Boston: Houghton Mifflin, 1991.

Frank, Gerold. *An American Death.* New York: Doubleday, 1972.

Furnas, J.C. *The Americans.* New York: G.P. Putnam's Sons, 1969.

Galbraith, John Kenneth. *How to Get Out of Vietnam.* New York: Signet Books, 1967.

Galbraith, John Kenneth. *The New Industrial State.* Boston: Houghton Mifflin, 1967.

Gannett, Lewis. *Dreamers of the American Dream.* New York: Doubleday, 1957.

Goodwin, Doris Kearns. *No Ordinary Time.* New York: Simon & Schuster, 1994.

Grant, Gerald and Riesman, David. *The Perpetual Dream.* Chicago: Univ. of Chicago Press, 1978.

Groner, Alex. *American Business & Industry.* New York: American Heritage, 1972.

Halberstam, David. *The Best & the Brightest.* Connecticut: Fawcett, 1972.

Halberstam, David. *The Powers that Be.* New York: Dell, 1979.

Hancock, Lyn Nell. *Red, White—And Blue. Newsweek,* 7 November 1994.

Handlin, Oscar. *Race & Nationality in American Life.* New York: Doubleday, 1957.

Henry, Robert Selph. *Reunion and Reaction.* Boston: Little, Brown, 1951.

Hoffman, Abbie. *Woodstock Nation.* New York: Vintage Books, 1969.

Hofstadter, Richard. *The Paranoid Style in American Politics & Other Essays.* New York: Vintage Books, 1967.

Hoopes, Townsend. *The Devil & John Foster Dulles.* Boston: Little, Brown, 1973.

Hunt, Draper. *Dearest Father.* Unity, Maine: North Country Press, 1992.

Isaac, Rhys. *The Transformation of Virginia.* North Carolina: Norton, 1982.

Jackle, John A. *The American Small Town.* Hamden, Connecticut: Archon Book, 1982.

Jacobs, Jane. *The Death & Life of Great American Cities.* New York: Vintage Books, 1992.

James, D. Clayton. *The Years of MacArthur: Triumph & Disaster 1945-1964.* Boston: Houghton Mifflin, 1985.

Jensen, Oliver and Kerr, Joan Paterson and Belsky, Murray. *The American Album*. New York: Simon & Schuster, 1968.

Johnson, Paul. *The Birth of the Modern*. New York: Harper Collins, 1991.

Kelly, Alfred H. and Winfred A. Harrison. *The American Constitution Its Origin and Development, Vol. 1 and 2*. New York: Norton.

Kennan, George F. *Memoirs-1925-1950*. Boston: Little, Brown, 1967.

Leech, Margaret. *Reveille in Washington 1860-1865*. New York: Harper & Brothers, 1941.

Lewis, David Levering. *W.E.B. DuBois*. New York: Holt, 1993.

Lewis, Meriwether. *The Lewis and Clark Expedition, Vol. 1, 2, 3*. New York: Lippincott, 1961.

Lilienthal, David E. *The TVA Years 1939-1945*. New York: Harper & Row, 1964.

Lilienthal, David E. *The Atomic Energy Years 1945-1950*. New York: Harper & Row, 1964.

Lilienthal David E. *Venturesome Years*. New York: Harper & Row, 1964.

Lorant, Stefan. *The Presidency.* New York: MacMillan, 1951.

MacDonald, Dwight. *Politics Past.* New York: Viking Press, 1957.

Maxwell, James A., ed. *America's Fascinating Indian Heritage.* New York: The Reader's Digest Association, 1978.

McCullough, David. *Truman.* New York: Simon & Schuster, 1992.

Montross, Lynn. *Rag, Tag and Bobtail.* New York: Harper & Brothers, 1952.

Morgenthau, Hans J. *The Purpose of American Politics.* New York: Vintage Books, 1964.

Morris, Edmund. *The Rise of Theodore Roosevelt.* New York: Coward, McCann & Geoghegan, 1979.

Moynihan, Danial Patrick. *Pandemonium.* Oxford, New York: Oxford Univ. Press, 1993.

Nagel, Paul C. *Descent From Glory.* New York: Oxford Univ. Press, 1983.

Navasky, Victor S. *Naming Names.* New York: Penguin Books, 1980.

Nettels, Curtis P. *The Roots of American Civilization*. New York: Meredith, 1963.

Newman, Eric P. *The Early Paper Money of America*. Racine, Wisconsin: Whitman Publishing, 1967.

O'Neill, Thomas P., Jr. *Man of the House*. New York: St. Martin's Press, 1987.

Parrington, Vernon Louis. *Main Currents in American Thought*. New York: Harcourt, Brace, 1930.

Peattie, Donald Culross. *An Almanac of Liberty*. New York: Doubleday, 1954.

Peirce, Neal R. and Jerry Hagstrom. *The Book of America, Inside 50 States Today*. New York: Norton, 1983.

Plowden, David. *Lincoln & His America 1809-1865*. New York: Viking Press, 1970.

Pringle, Henry F. *Theodore Roosevelt*. New York: Harcourt, Brace, & World, 1956.

Reeves, Richard. *American Journey*. New York: Simon & Schuster.

Rossiter, Clinton. *1787 The Grand Convention*. New York: MacMillan, 1966.

Russell, Francis. *The Shadow of Blooming Grove.* New York: McGraw-Hill, 1968.

Sandburg, Carl. *Abraham Lincoln-The Prairie Years & The War Years.* New York: Harcourt, Brace & World, 1954.

Schachner, Nathan. *Thomas Jefferson.* New York: Appleton, Century, Crofts, 1951.

Schachner, Nathan. *The Founding Fathers.*New York: G.P. Putnam's Sons, 1954.

Schlesinger, Arthur M. Jr. *The Coming of the New Deal.* Boston: Houghton Mifflin, 1958.

Schlesinger, Arthur M., Jr. *The Crisis of the Old Order.* Boston: Houghton Mifflin, 1957.

Shapley, Deborah. *Promise and Power.* Boston: Little, Brown, 1993.

Sheehan, Neil, ed. *The Pentagon Papers.* New York: Bantam Books, 1971.

Sobel, Robert, and David B. Sicilia. *The Entrepreneurs, an American Adventure.* Boston: Houghton Mifflin, 1986.

Sorensen, Theodore C. *Kennedy.* New York: Harper & Row, 1965.

Stafford, Jean. *A Mother in History.* New York: Farrar Straus & Giroux, 1965.

Stein, Susan R. *The Worlds of Thomas Jefferson.* New York: Harry N. Abrams, 1993.

Stewart, George R. *Pickett's Charge.* Boston: The Riverside Press, 1959.

Takaki, Ronald. *A Different Mirror.* Boston: Little, Brown, 1993.

Tocqueville, Alexis de. *Democracy In America.* New York: AlfredA.Knopf, 1963.

Waldman, Carl. *Who Was Who in Native American History.* New York. Facts on File, 1990.

Ward, Christopher. *The War of the Revolution.* New York: The MacMillan Co., 1952.

White, Theodore H. *The Making of the President 1968.* New York: Atheneum, 1969.

Wills, Garry. *Inventing America.* Garden City, New York: Doubleday, 1978.

Wills, Garry. *The Kennedy Imprisonment.* New York: Gulf & Western, 1981.

Wilson, Edmund. *The Fifties.* New York: Farrar Straus & Giroux, 1986.

Wilson, George F. *Behold Virginia: The Fifth Crown.* New York: Harcourt, Brace, 1951.

Wood, Gordon S. *Radicalism of the American Revolution.* New York: Knopf, 1992.

The 1994 World Almanac and Book of Facts, ed; Robert Famighetti, Funk and Wagnalls.

Woodward, C. Vann. *Mary Chestnut's Civil War.* NewHaven: Yale Univ. Press, 1981.

Wyden, Peter. *Bay of Pigs.* New York: Simon & Schuster, 1979.

Yanket, Ted, and Pam Cornelison. *The Great American History Fact-Finder.* Boston: Houghton Mifflin, 1993.

Zinn, Howard. *A People's History of the United States 1942-Present.* New York: Harper Collins, 1995.